Contributions to Economics

More information about this series at http://www.springer.com/series/1262

Daniel Oto-Peralías • Diego Romero-Ávila

Legal Traditions, Legal Reforms and Economic Performance

Theory and Evidence

Springer

Daniel Oto-Peralías
School of Management
University of St Andrews
St Andrews, United Kingdom

Diego Romero-Ávila
Department of Economics, Quantitative Methods and Economic History
Pablo de Olavide University
Seville, Spain

ISSN 1431-1933 ISSN 2197-7178 (electronic)
Contributions to Economics
ISBN 978-3-319-67040-9 ISBN 978-3-319-67041-6 (eBook)
DOI 10.1007/978-3-319-67041-6

Library of Congress Control Number: 2017952375

Printed on acid-free paper

This Springer imprint is published by Springer Nature
The registered company is Springer International Publishing AG
The registered company address is: Gewerbestrasse 11, 6330 Cham, Switzerland

Acknowledgements

Diego Romero-Ávila would like to dedicate this book to the memory of his father, Pedro José Romero de Ávila Aguilar, for encouragement and support throughout his career. This book is based on the study "Legal Reforms and Economic Performance: Revisiting the Evidence" prepared as a background paper for the World Development Report 2017 "Governance and the Law." The authors are particularly indebted to Jesús Crespo-Cuaresma, Luis-Felipe Lopez-Calva, Joaquín Maudos, Siddharth Sharma, and Carlos Usabiaga for valuable comments and suggestions. We also thank seminar participants at Pablo de Olavide University, St. Andrews University, Vienna University of Economics and Business, and the World Bank for valuable comments and suggestions. The authors acknowledge financial support from the Spanish Ministry of Economics and Competitiveness (grant ECO2012-35430) and from the World Bank.

Abstract

This book investigates whether legal reforms intended to create a market-friendly regulatory business environment have a positive impact on economic and financial outcomes. After conducting a critical review of the *legal origins* literature, we first analyze the evolution of legal rules and regulations during the last decade (2006–2014). For that purpose, we use legal/regulatory indicators from the *Doing Business Project* (2015). Our findings indicate that countries have actively reformed their legal systems during this period, particularly French civil law countries. A process of convergence in the evolution of legal rules and regulations is observed: countries starting in 2006 in a lower position have improved more than countries with better initial scores. Therefore, for those indicators that exhibit convergence between the civil law tradition and the British common law, the legacy of legal origins did not prevent cross-legal tradition differences from narrowing down over the past decade. This would contradict the Legal Origins Theory that predicts the persistence over time of the differences in legal and regulatory standards across legal traditions. Also, French civil law countries have reformed their legal systems to a larger extent than common law countries and, consequently, have improved more in the majority of the *Doing Business* indicators used. Second, we estimate fixed-effects panel regressions to analyze the relationship between changes in legal rules and regulations and changes in the real economy. Our findings point to a lack of systematic effects of legal rules and regulations on economic and financial outcomes. This evidence holds when the difference and system GMM estimators are used to control for the endogeneity of the regressors. This result stands in contrast to the widespread belief that reforms aiming to strengthen investor and creditor rights (and other market-friendly policies) systematically lead to better economic and financial outcomes. It seems that improvements in these legal rules are not sufficient conditions for that. Finally, we conduct an exploratory analysis of the determinants of the effectiveness of legal reforms and the gap between legal rules and the reality on the ground. Concerning the determinants of the effectiveness of legal reforms, although the importance of each factor depends on the specific rule and outcome variable, institutional quality and mineral abundance have a positive impact on legal reform effectiveness. As regards the determinants of the gap between law on the books and the reality on the ground, the evidence supports the fact that common law countries are systematically associated with a larger gap in both creditor rights and investor protection with respect to financial depth and entrepreneurship. Institutional quality is found to reduce the gap between creditor rights and investor protection relative to performance in terms of financial depth and entrepreneurship.

Contents

Chapter 1
Introduction

Abstract This chapter introduces the main purpose of this book, which consists of using data on legal rules and regulatory outcomes from the Doing Business Project over the period 2006–2014 in order to establish whether the variation in legal rules has affected financial and economic developmental outcomes, as suggested by the law and finance view. This chapter then advances the main results of the empirical analysis: (i) the existence of catching-up of the French civil law to the average legal and regulatory standards of the British common law, (ii) lack of a clear-cut effect of legal rules and regulatory indicators on financial and economic performance, and (iii) the existence of a gap between legal rules and the reality on the ground.

Nowadays it is widely accepted both in the academic and law-making spheres that legal reforms aiming to create market-friendly regulatory environments are crucial for economic growth. Indeed, some political leaders set as goals for their mandates to improve their countries' ranking in *Doing Business* (i.e., the World Bank's classification of the ease of doing business across countries).[1] For instance, Indian Prime Minister Narendra Modi and Russian President Vladimir Putin explicitly targeted improving in the *Doing Business* ranking as one of their objectives for their administrations (Belsley 2015). The Abe Administration in Japan also aims to improve Japan's rank, in this case to one of the top three among OECD countries (Haidar and Hoshi 2015).

The view that law matters, that is, that legal reforms can make a difference in improving countries' economic performance, is to a large extent the legacy of the *law and finance literature*, also known as *Legal Origins Theory* (La Porta et al. 1998, 2008, 2013). According to this theory, countries whose legal systems provide a stronger protection to investor and creditor rights (typically common law countries) have more developed financial markets and more dynamic market economies. The conclusion reached by many scholars and politicians is that legal reforms aiming to improve the protection of investor and creditor rights should lead to financial development and, consequently, economic growth.

However, the evidence suggesting that legal reforms can improve countries' economic performance is mainly based on cross-section regression analysis. This

[1]All the information about the Doing Business Project is available at http://www.doingbusiness.org/

D. Oto-Peralías, D. Romero-Ávila, *Legal Traditions, Legal Reforms and Economic Performance*, Contributions to Economics, DOI 10.1007/978-3-319-67041-6_1

type of analysis does not specifically study whether changes in legal rules are associated with improvements in economic activity. There may be many confounding factors behind these findings. What would be really informative is to analyze whether changes in legal rules are associated with improvements in financial and economic outcomes by keeping constant all potential confounding factors (such as culture, political institutions, etc.), which are largely fixed at the country level. This is one of the goals of our analysis.

The purpose of this book is to use data on legal rules and regulatory outcomes from the Doing Business Project over the period 2006–2014 in order to establish whether the variation in legal rules has affected financial and economic developmental outcomes, as suggested by the law and finance view. In doing so, we first try to determine whether there has been legal change within legal traditions by testing for mean differences between 2014 and 2006 scores for each of the legal and regulatory indicators studied. The evidence appears to indicate that there has been legal change, particularly in French civil law countries. This legal tradition has experienced an improvement in the following areas: law on the books as measured by the indices of strength of creditor rights and investor protection, depth of credit information, and in the regulatory burden associated with starting a business, registering a property, obtaining construction permits, paying taxes and trading across borders.

Second, we try to establish whether there is a legal origin effect on legal rules and regulatory outcomes both at the beginning and end of the period, and whether the relative position of legal traditions changed after the reform. The evidence indicates that in many areas such as creditor rights and investor protection, efficiency of debt enforcement, and in the regulatory burden linked to obtaining construction permits, paying taxes and trading across borders, the statistically significant differences relative to the British common law have diminished between 2006 and 2014; and in the case of starting a business these differences have vanished. This supports the existence of catching-up of the French civil law to the average legal and regulatory standards of the British common law.

Third, bearing in mind the large number of legal reforms implemented over the period 2006–2014, particularly in French civil law countries, we attempt to establish whether variations in legal rules and regulatory outcomes have been associated with an improvement in financial and economic developmental outcomes. By estimating panel specifications using a fixed effects estimator with data averaged over 3-year periods, the evidence does not support the existence of a clear-cut effect of legal rules and regulatory indicators on financial and economic performance. This finding appears to accord with the view of those that question the widespread tendency in the lawmaking sphere over the past decade to imitate tools related to the common law (the pretended winning origin). If the common law does not systematically lead to better legal rules and institutions than the French civil law (as the recent critical literature suggests),[2] it is far from clear that adopting common-law tools will improve the efficiency of the legal system and the performance of the economy.

[2]The critical literature review in Chap. 2 provides many references of studies that fail to find statistically significant differences in outcomes between the French civil law and the British common law for a wide variety of legal and regulatory indicators.

The lack of a consistent effect of legal reforms on financial and economic outcomes does not mean that legal reforms are always ineffective. This simply reflects that on average we do not find a significant effect, but there are countries in which legal reforms have been successful. The final part of the monograph tries to address the question of what factors contribute to the effectiveness of legal reforms. The results of our exploratory analysis suggest that institutional quality and mineral resource abundance are important factors. In addition, we study the related question of the determinants of the gap between legal rules and the reality on the ground, which is a consequence on the lack of efficacy of legal rules. Institutions also appear to be important in reducing the gap, and common law countries exhibit larger gaps than other legal traditions. The latter finding is congruent with the results by Oto-Peralías and Romero-Ávila (2014b), who differentiate within the British common law tradition between settler colonies and indirectly ruled colonies. In the settler colonies of North America and Australasia, the common law was well implanted by European practitioners and worked optimally. In these sparsely populated places at the time of colonization, property rights and private contracts were enforced, which fostered the development of the legal system. However, in large parts of its empire, Britain conducted a colonial policy known as "indirect rule" which did not intend to effectively introduce its legal system, especially in territories politically organized or extensively occupied by native population, like Sub-Saharan Africa (Zweigert and Kötz 1998). Instead, local rules were left almost intact and traditional chiefs concentrated all political and judicial powers, which resulted in the control of economic resources by elites, with little incentive to protect property rights and enforce contracts, thus rendering underdeveloped legal systems.

The remaining of the book is organized as follows. Chapter 2 provides a critical review of the literature dealing with the Legal Origins hypothesis. Chapter 3 describes the data on legal rules and regulations employed in the empirical analyses. Chapter 4 provides a brief description of the main studies dealing with the effect of legal rules and business regulations on economic and financial outcomes, both from a macro and micro perspective. Chapter 5 conducts an analysis of legal change as well as several exercises of convergence in legal and regulatory standards among legal traditions. Chapter 6 estimates panel data specifications to shed some light on the impact of variations in legal rules and regulatory indicators on financial and economic performance over the period 2006–2014. Chapter 7 presents a large battery of sensitivity analysis using alternative datasets and estimators. Chapter 8 conducts an exploratory analysis of the determinants of the effectiveness of legal reforms and the gap between law on the books and the reality on the ground. Finally, Chap. 9 draws some policy implications and concludes.

Chapter 2
Revisiting the Legal Origins Hypothesis: A Brief Review of the Literature

Abstract This chapter describes the foundations of the Legal Origins Theory, some of which are questioned by, among others, Rajan and Zingales (J Financ Econ 69: 5–50, 2003), Klerman et al. (J Legal Anal 3:379–409, 2011), Spamann (Rev Financ Stud 23:467–486, 2010a, J Inst Theor Econ 166:149–165, 2010b) and Oto-Peralías and Romero-Ávila (J Law Econ 57(3):561–628, 2014a, J Money Credit Bank 46(1):43–77, 2014b). Given the important policy implications of these criticisms in the lawmaking sphere—as the common law may not systematically lead to better legal rules and outcomes—, it is crucial to conduct a critical revision of the state of the literature about the Legal Origins Theory as well as to assess the impact of the new evidence from the point of view of legal reforms. Hence, the rest of the chapter categorizes all the criticisms to the Legal Origins Theory into three main blocks. A first set of criticisms builds on colonialism and the associated distribution of legal traditions, another set of criticisms is based on political economy arguments, and a third set is based on the quality and reliability of early indicators of legal rules and outcomes.

2.1 The Legal Origins View

One of the most influential explanations of why some countries have well-functioning legal and financial systems and others do not is undoubtedly the Legal Origins Theory (La Porta et al. 1998, 2008, 2013). It is generally accepted that countries belonging to each legal tradition received "specific laws and codes and the more general styles or ideologies of the legal system" in the transplantation process from the origin countries (mainly England and France) and, despite further legal evolution at the national level, "the basic transplanted elements have remained and persisted" (La Porta et al. 2008, p. 288). Most importantly, it has been implicitly assumed that the implantation process was homogeneous within legal traditions. This explains why countries are simply grouped into four legal traditions (the British common law and the French, German and Scandinavian civil law) and why many legal features and outcomes are associated with these legal families abstractly, that is, without differentiating countries within them.

The high persistence of the influence of legal origins over time is explained on the basis of what the transplantation process involved. More specifically,

D. Oto-Peralías, D. Romero-Ávila, *Legal Traditions, Legal Reforms and Economic Performance*, Contributions to Economics, DOI 10.1007/978-3-319-67041-6_2

"transplantation involves not just specific legal rules (many of which actually change later), but also legal institutions (of which judicial independence might be the most important), human capital of the participants in the legal system, and crucially the strategy of the law for dealing with new problems. Successive generations of judges, lawyers, and politicians all learn the same broad ideas of how the law and the state should work. The legal system supplies the fundamental tools for addressing social concerns, and it is that system, as defined by Zweigert and Kötz, with its codes, distinctive institutions, modes of thought and even ideologies, that is very slow to change" (La Porta et al. 2013, p. 456). It is when these features of the legal system are sufficiently similar that one can categorize national legal systems into major families of law (Zweigert and Kötz 1998; La Porta et al. 2008; and references therein).

According to La Porta et al. (2008, p. 289), the civil law tradition "originates in Roman law, uses statutes and comprehensive codes as primary means of ordering legal material, and relies heavily on legal scholars to ascertain and formulate rules (Merryman 1969). Dispute resolution tends to be inquisitorial rather than adversarial". The French civil law tradition is associated with the French Revolution and Napoleon's codes, which were written in the early nineteenth century and were introduced by Napoleon's armies into their conquered European territories. In the colonial era, the civil law tradition was exported to France's colonial dominions. Napoleonic influence was also substantial in Portugal and Spain, whose colonial dominions in Latin America adopted the French civil code by imitation after gaining independence.

The German legal tradition is also based on Roman law, though the German Commercial Code of 1897 was issued after Bismark unified Germany. Even though the law is codified under a code as in the French civil law, it shares with the common law the use of judicial interpretation and jurisprudence. The Scandinavian legal tradition derives to a much lesser extent from Roman law than the French and German legal families, and according to prominent legal scholars like Zweigert and Kötz (1998), it should be categorized separately.

The civil law tradition sharply contrasts with the common law tradition. The latter is based on case law and judicial precedents formed by appellate judges through legal dispute resolution, which is adversarial. Judicial independence acts as a guarantee that the executive will strongly protect private property rights versus the interest of the State. The British common law was exported to the settler colonies of North-America and Australasia, the plantation colonies of the Caribbean, the strategically trade-oriented colonies of Hong Kong and Singapore, India and the extractive colonies of sub-Saharan Africa, among others. Figure 2.1 provides a world map with the distribution of the different legal families around the world.

According to the Legal Origins Theory, common law countries are associated with stronger investor and creditor rights,[1] lower legal formalism, more efficiency

[1]This implies that investors, both minority shareholders and creditors, are protected by law from expropriation by firms' majority shareholders and the management.

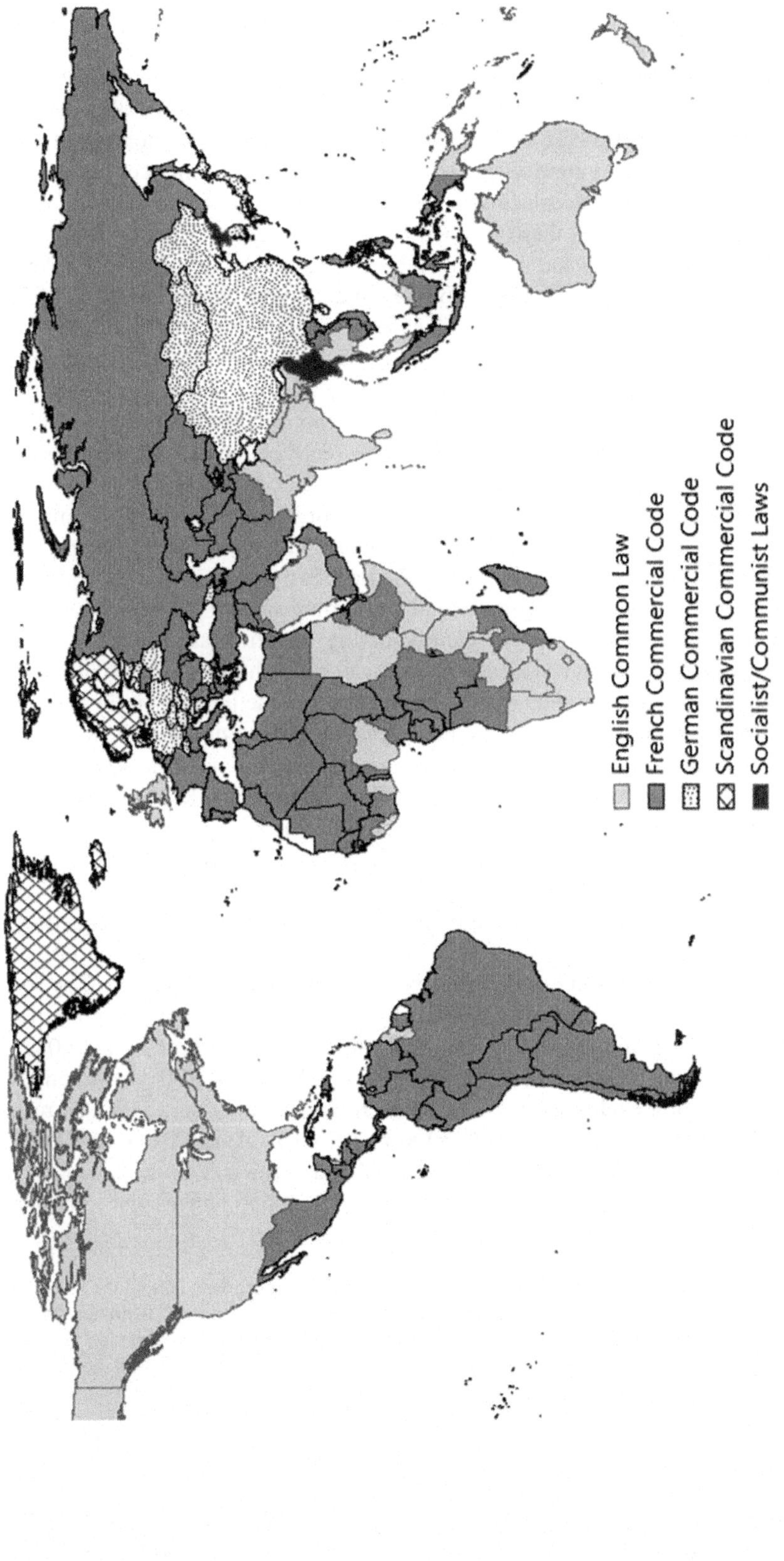

Fig. 2.1 The distribution of legal traditions around the world. Note: Own elaboration based on data from La Porta et al. (2008)

of contract and debt enforcement, and higher judicial independence than civil law countries. It has also been found that governments in common law countries intervene and regulate to a lesser extent the economy. In addition, common law countries seek solutions to problems in market-oriented contract-based private arrangements. In the words of La Porta et al. (2008, p. 286), "common law stands for the strategy of social control that seeks to support private market outcomes, whereas civil law seeks to replace such outcomes with state-desired allocations". The consequence of all of these results is that, supposedly, common law legal systems lead to better legal and financial outcomes than civil law systems (La Porta et al. 2008, 2013). Michaels (2009, p. 769) remarks that the "ingenious idea" of La Porta et al. (1997, 1998) to solve the endogeneity problem between legal rules and economic performance was "to look at settings in which law was not co-original with society but instead was imposed as an external factor", which they found "in the context of colonization, where law was [...] imposed externally by the colonizing power, with a random distribution of different legal systems depending on which European country colonized parts of the non-European world".

Two mechanisms might explain the superior performance of the British common law: the "political" and the "adaptability" channels, with the former implying that legal traditions differ in the weight assigned to private property versus the rights of the State, while the second focusing on judicial formalism and the ability for each tradition to evolve. The historical victory of the coalition among the English Parliament, bourgeoisie and judges against royalists in the English civil wars in the seventeenth century promoted the protection of private property rights. Moreover, the case-law principle, based on the judicial precedent, provided Britain with a legal system that could easily adapt its law to changing circumstances (Beck and Levine 2005). In contrast, in the French Revolution the principle of separation of powers relegated judges to a secondary role of mechanical application of the law, while the state's powers were strengthened.[2] The evidence provided by Beck et al. (2003) mainly supports the "adaptability channel".

The pretended superiority of the common law has had important consequences. Policy makers imitate legal tools related to the common law (the winning origin) instead of improving existing institutions typical of the civil law tradition (Roe and Siegel 2009). Indeed, it has been observed certain catching up of civil law countries in terms of legal features typical of common law systems (Armour et al. 2009a). However, a growing number of scholars have recently criticized the assumptions and findings of the Legal Origins Theory (e.g., Rajan and Zingales 2003; Klerman et al. 2011; Spamann 2010a, b; Oto-Peralías and Romero-Ávila 2014a, b). Therefore, given the important policy implications of this criticism in the lawmaking sphere—as the common law may not systematically lead to better legal rules and

[2]However, as pointed out by Merryman (1996), soon after the French Revolution, the situation would be relaxed and French courts would be granted the power to interpret laws. However, "when the French exported their system [to their colonies] they did not include the information [saying] that it really does not work that way" (p. 116), thus hindering the development of the judicial system in many developing countries.

outcomes—, it is crucial to conduct a critical revision of the state of the literature about the Legal Origins Theory as well as to assess the impact of the new evidence from the point of view of legal reforms. Hence, in the rest of the chapter we categorize all the criticisms to the Legal Origins Theory into three main blocks. A first set of criticisms builds on colonialism and the associated distribution of legal traditions, another set of criticisms is based on political economy arguments, and a third set is based on the quality and reliability of early indicators of legal rules and outcomes.

2.2 Arguments Based on Colonialism and the Distribution of Legal Traditions Around the World

One of the key criticisms of the Legal Origins Theory is the "Transplant Hypothesis" proposed by Berkowitz et al. (2003a, b) who argue that the manner in which legal systems are obtained is more important than the specific countries' legal traditions to explain the quality of legal systems. Thus, they overcome the failure of the Legal Origins Theory to differentiate between the origin countries of legal families from those receiving their law via legal transplantation, which is tantamount to saying that the only thing that mattered was the transmission of a particular code, but not the process of transplantation. They differentiate among origin countries, receptive transplants and unreceptive transplants, with the first two categories being related to higher legal effectiveness. According to these authors, law is effective provided a demand for law exists so that the law on the books is used in practice and legal intermediaries developing the law show responsiveness to this demand. Whether legal transplants are receptive or not depends on the adaptation of the imported law to local conditions and on the population's familiarity with law principles. Their evidence supports the fact that countries in which the law was not adapted to local conditions or the population of the recipient country was not familiar with the law exhibit a lower level of legal effectiveness and economic development.

To the extent that legal origins are exogenous and more or less fixed at the point of its transplantation, and hence shape legal rules protecting investors—as predicted by the Legal Origins Theory—, this may be incompatible with the responsiveness of legal practitioners to change the law due to markets demand. Indeed, as argued by Roe and Siegel (2009, p. 784), one of the pillars of the Legal Origins Theory is that basic law has been imposed from the outside, while we know that "too much law was voluntarily imported or consciously rejected". In addition, referring to Dam's (2006a) work, Roe and Siegel (2009) point out that the colonization argument is not sufficiently strong because most of the recipient countries (including most common and civil law countries in Africa and many in Latin America) may not have been receptive.

A related criticism to the Legal Origins Theory has to do with the distribution of legal traditions around the world (Oto-Peralías and Romero-Ávila 2014a, b). In that work, we focused on the key point of the distribution of legal tradition from origin countries (colonial powers) to recipient countries (colonies) in the historical process of European colonization.[3]

The Legal Origins Theory implicitly assumes that: (i) All colonial powers exported their legal system in a homogeneous way, which explains why countries are simply grouped into four legal traditions (the British common law, and German, Scandinavian and French civil law).[4] (ii) The basic features of the legal tradition were transplanted to the recipient country. (iii) It is thus not necessary to differentiate countries within legal traditions. We questioned assumptions 1 and 3 by arguing that: (i) Colonial powers had different strategies when implanting their legal systems in the colonies because they exhibited different responses to the initial conditions (endowments) existing in colonized territories. (ii) The way legal systems were implanted matters for legal/economic outcomes. We find that the relative legal rules and outcomes of the British common law versus the French civil law are associated with the colonial strategies followed by mother countries when implanting their legal systems in their colonial dominions.

As regards the distribution of the British common law, the transplantation of the common law was inversely related to the recipient country's level of population density at the time of colonization. This was due to the nature of British colonial policy, which did not want to interfere with preexisting native law and rules of indigenous societies. In sparsely populated territories with a temperate climate the common law was extensively transferred by European practitioners, and fitted well with the colonial society. This made it possible to develop a legal system in the recipient country that is comparable in many respects to the British. This occurred in North-American and Australasian colonies. In contrast, in those places with a large indigenous population and unfavorable disease conditions, the legal and institutional transfer was very superficial and could even have negative consequences.[5]

Concerning the distribution of the French civil law, France imposed its civil law rigidly across its empire, leading frequently to conflicts with existing laws. This

[3]Colonialism was a historic event of extraordinary importance. In 1914, the territory occupied by European powers and their new and former colonies extended over approximately 85% of the global surface. This meant an enormous influence of Europe around the world, leading to the implantation of different legal systems (Oto-Peralías and Romero-Ávila 2016).

[4]Daniels et al. (2011) agree on this point by arguing that one of the assumptions underlying the claim about the superior performance of the British common law is that transplanted institutions were imposed uniformly across territories; an assumption they clearly question.

[5]This is because the widespread use of indirect rule in these colonies (particularly in sub-Saharan Africa and some parts of Asia) led to the empowerment of local elites who, unlike precolonial times, were no longer subject to traditional checks by the native population and could mold customary law in their own benefit, thereby leading to abuses of power and imperfect protection of property rights (Mamdani 1996; Lange 2004).

legal colonial policy was coherent with the nature and character of the French empire, which was more centralized than the British and ruled with a very different ideology, namely, the consideration of the colonial empire as an intrinsic part of the Republic and the ideal of assimilation (Fieldhouse 1966; Kumar 2006). Since this colonial policy was largely independent of the particular circumstances of the colonized territories, the distribution of the French civil law across colonial dominions was more uniform than in the British case. In addition, former Spanish colonies deserve separate treatment since they share a common Castilian law legacy and a different adoption of the Civil Code by imitation. Arguably, former Spanish colonies experienced a better assimilation of the civil law (during almost 300 years) and, therefore, one expects better legal outcomes for this group compared to French colonies.

Our results from this previous work (i.e., Oto-Peralías and Romero-Ávila 2014a, b) indicates that the common law does not generally lead to superior legal rules and outcomes or to a higher level of credit and stock markets development than the French civil law when precolonial population density and/or potential European settler mortality are high. Our results further indicate that the superior performance of the common law is largely driven by countries where Britain extensively implanted its legal tradition (i.e., the Neo-Europes). Hence, the statement by La Porta et al. (2008, p. 326) that "legal rules and regulations differ systematically across countries, [which] are accounted for to a significant extent by legal origins. [T]he basic historical divergence in the styles of legal traditions explains well why legal rules differ" can be qualified since to explain "why legal rules differ" one must consider both the contents or styles of legal traditions and the way they were distributed by the origin countries.

Daniels et al. (2011) emphasize the high degree of variability in jurisdictional arrangements and legal institutions in the British Empire, which were responsive to the initial conditions encountered by colonizers, including the pre-existing indigenous legal order. Outside of the settler colonies, territories under British control did not experience a complete transplantation of the common law and a subsequent displacement of native rules. In practice, the implantation process of the British law in each colony led to a unique corpus of law that differed from that in other colonies. According to these authors, whether a colony developed a long-run stable commitment to legality and high legal effectiveness depended to some extent on two features of colonial administration and legal transplantation: (i) the degree of representation in legislative institutions afforded to the indigenous population, and (ii) the degree of integration of indigenous and British common law courts and animated values, with higher integration fostering the development of a localized common law jurisprudence.

As a matter of fact, in Nigeria, where indirect rule was extensively exercised, there existed two parallel courts: colonial courts applicable only to matters involving Europeans and native courts that—under indigenous customs and rules—dealt with all disputes between non-Europeans, who under certain conditions could also appeal to the British court. This dual court system implied that the common law hardly applied to the great majority of the indigenous population. In addition, since native chiefs were granted extensive executive powers by the British, and, unlike precolonial times, were no longer subject to check and balances by the native population, they undermined the historical legitimacy of the native court system as well as the effectiveness of their customary law. Unlike indirectly ruled areas in Africa, India was administered as a "direct/indirect rule hybrid" and managed to gradually adapt the colonial legal system to the needs of the Indian population, which resulted in the creation of "a court hierarchy and a body of law that was both effective and accepted by the native population" (Daniels et al. 2011, p. 135).

Klerman et al. (2011) explain the observed cross-country differences in economic growth between common and civil law countries on the basis of non-legal colonial factors, which they measure through colonial identity dummies. By exploiting the imperfect overlap between colonial and legal origin, they discard that the channel given by the structure of the legal system is important because the growth estimates for juries, case law and Supreme Court tenure are in general neither individually nor jointly statistically significant. These results lead them to wonder whether legal origins are really meaningful.

2.3 Arguments Based on Political Economy

A second body of criticisms is related to political factors and twentieth century historical events that have influenced the approach by which countries regulate the financial system and the economy. A major contribution in this regard is the Great Reversal hypothesis of Rajan and Zingales (2003). They show that in 1913, French civil law countries had a higher level of financial development—as measured by the average stock market capitalization to GDP ratio—than common law countries. However, when they compute this ratio for the same sample of countries in 1999, it is found to be much larger in common law countries (130%) than in French civil law countries (74%). The lack of persistent outcomes in financial development that should be present according to the Legal Origins Theory leads Rajan and Zingales (2003) to reject it. To explain the great reversal in financial development they employ a political economy argument. Accordingly, this reversal in financial development levels appears congruent with the incumbent industrial and financial elites in civil law countries preventing start-up competitors from having open access to new finance. This enabled the former to get rid of potential competition that could erode the incumbents' industrial position. All this would translate into financial repression, whereas in common law countries financial liberalization would prosper.

Roe (2006) provides an alternative political economy based explanation of the patterns observed in securities markets development and divergent ownership structures in the world's richer nations over the course of the twentieth century. According to Roe (2006), those countries suffering greater destruction in World War II were civil law countries. This weakened the capacity of influence in the polity of capital oriented interests whose main asset (capital) was largely destroyed during the war. In contrast, labor was the dominant force in postwar continental Europe as they could influence the polity via voting. This led to a marked left-right political conflict, which gave rise to laws and regulations in favor of the workforce and against capital. Hence, those nations in which leftish actors dominated the political scene, promulgated strong employment protection laws, but had weaker financial markets (Roe and Siegel 2009).

In a similar spirit to Rajan and Zingales (2003) thesis, the following papers also question the pretended fixed and path-dependent link of legal origins with the levels of protection of creditors and minority shareholders as well as of financial development. For instance, Musacchio (2008) documents that even though today Brazil affords creditors a low level of protection, it provided them with strong rights before 1945. Such a big variation in creditor rights does not square with the Legal Origins Theory, but it can be explained by political economy. He conjectures that the fact that in civil law countries lawmaking is highly centralized makes it more susceptible to capture by interest groups. He also finds a high degree of variation over time in bond market size and court enforcement of debt contracts. The reason for the decline of Brazil's bond market after World War I must be sought in changes in international capital markets and macroeconomic instability rather than in legal origin. With a focus on a wider sample of 20 countries, Musacchio (2007) provides evidence of relative convergence in corporate governance practices concerning the extent of creditor protection included in the bankruptcy laws and the weak level of shareholder rights across common and French civil law countries circa 1900. Thus, if one observes today wide cross-country variation in the development of financial markets, it must be due to events of the twentieth century rather than to persistent differences caused by legal traditions.

As argued by Roe (2007), legal origin institutions such as the jury system that should have been transferred by Britain to its colonies are trumped easily by modern political economy forces. The reason was that the implementation of the British colonial policy—whose main political goal was to run a vast empire—conflicted with the implantation of the jury in its colonial dominions, which previously undermined legal effectiveness as a means of colonial control in Ireland and the North American colonies (Young 1988).

Focusing on an early form of shareholder company in ancient Rome, the *societas publicanorum*, Malmendier (2009) is able to gather evidence that this institution flourished and could access broad financing in a legally underdeveloped but politically supportive environment during the Roman Republic, whereas it practically disappeared during the Roman Empire in which Roman law grew highly sophisticated but the political environment became much less supportive. This suggests that provided the "law as practice" was flexible enough to adapt to the economic needs posed by the prevalent political interests, the development of the legal system was little important for economic development and entrepreneurship.

Acemoglu and Johnson (2005) examine the relative importance of legal institutions related to the protection of contractual rights versus political institutions related to the protection of property rights in explaining economic and financial development. They use an instrumental variables approach that exploits exogenous variation in both types of institutions on the basis of colonial history. The evidence favors strong first-stage relationships between property rights institutions and the determinants of European colonization strategy (measured through settler mortality and precolonial population density) and between contracting institutions and the identity of the colonizer. Their evidence is supportive of the dominant role of political institutions not only by raising investment and long-run economic growth, but also by increasing financial development in terms of credit to the private sector and stock market capitalization. In contrast, better contracting institutions only appear to affect the form of financial intermediation by raising stock market capitalization. According to Acemoglu and Johnson (2005, p. 949), "[a] possible explanation for this pattern is that individuals often find ways of altering the terms of their formal and informal contracts to avoid the adverse effects of weak contracting institutions but find it harder to mitigate the risk of expropriation in this way." In addition, as pointed out by Malmendier (2009), the ultimate superiority of political versus legal institutions can be explained by the fact that a poor legal environment can be counteracted with private arrangements and reputational effects, whereas weak political institutions that protect against property expropriation from the elites or the state cannot.

2.4 Arguments Based on Measurement and Recoding of Legal Data

In this block we find several studies which, by virtue of recoding or using more recent or alternative legal data, find no systematic differences between common and civil law countries in many areas of the legal sphere. For instance, Spamann (2010b) challenges the common view still supporting the existence of clear differences in the area of civil procedure involving judicial adjudication and enforcement of private claims between common and civil law countries. Unlike Djankov et al. (2003) who used data from the World Bank's first Doing Business report and found that civil law countries exhibited on average more complex and formalistic procedures (that were also longer and costlier), Spamann (2010b) used the corrected and expanded data (from the same source) on complexity, formalism, duration and cost of procedure in courts of first instance for a sample of up to 181 countries over the period 2003–2008. The evidence with the updated and arguably highest-quality data does not indicate the existence of any statistically significant difference between common law and civil law countries.

As argued by Spamann (2010b, p. 163), "if the historical common-civil-law division does not manifest itself economically meaningfully in the area where it originates, it is unlikely to explain differences in much more remote areas". Therefore, it is hardly surprising that when Spamann (2010a) corrects the *anti-director rights* index originally used by La Porta et al. (1998) for 33 of the

46 countries initially investigated, the corrected index no longer renders a higher level of shareholder protection in common law than in civil law countries.[6]

Jackson and Roe (2009) construct resource-based measures of public enforcement and finds no evidence of the pretended superiority of private enforcement mechanisms (more prevalent in common law countries) in propelling securities market development. Indeed, they show that public enforcement is overall as important as disclosure in explaining the development of financial markets around the world and more important than private liability rules. This contrasts with the studies by La Porta et al. (2006) and Djankov et al. (2008b) that provided clear-cut evidence that private enforcement of investor protection via both disclosure and private liability rules leads to greater securities market development, whereas public enforcement does not.[7]

Using time-series data for three parent systems, Britain, France and Germany, and the United States and India over the period 1970–2005, Armour et al. (2009a) cast doubts on the empirical validity of the Legal Origins Theory since there have been great changes in their index of shareholder rights over the past three decades, with a high degree of convergence between legal traditions in recent years due to a substantial rise in shareholder protection in civil law countries.[8] Contrary to the Legal Origins Theory, they find no significant differences between common law and civil law countries in the case of creditor protection. However, the evidence for workers protecting laws appears more consistent with the Legal Origins Theory, with a higher degree of labor protection in civil law countries. In sum, Armour et al. (2009a) document diverging patterns in legal rules across legal traditions until the late 1980s, whereas convergence has set in over the period 1990–2005, particularly in the case of shareholder protection rights. They explain these patterns on the basis of institutional complementarities at the national level, which implies that legal systems (the regulatory style and the substantive content of legal rules) are

---

[6]In contrast to La Porta et al. (1998) who mainly used secondary sources such as Price Waterhouse's Doing Business reports for various years, Spamann (2010a) constructed the revised index on the basis of raw legal data directly derived from primary sources analyzed with the help of local lawyers.

[7]La Porta et al. (2006) employed a public enforcement index which captures the regulators' formal authority based on several dimensions measuring their power reach, and Djankov et al. (2008b) used an index aggregating several dimensions concerning whether particular suspect corporate transactions can lead to a fine or jail sentences for the approving body or the principal wrongdoer. In contrast, Jackson and Roe (2009) developed several measures of the intensity of public enforcement of securities market regulation based on information on the regulators' budgetary resources and staffing rules.

[8]This is an important advancement relative to the majority of La Porta and associates' initial legal indices that only offered a cross-sectional view of the law at one moment in time, mostly in the second half of the 1990s. This had the limitation that it provided only a static description of the law as it stood at that point, without taking into account the evolution of legal rules caused by either external transnational convergence trends to best-practice standards or the influence of internal economic and political factors. However, the Doing Business Project is also making progress along similar lines to Armour et al. (2009a) by publishing the scores in many legal and regulatory indicators on a yearly basis for a much wider sample of countries.

endogenous to the economic and political environments in which they are placed. In addition, recent transnational trends of standardization of company law, insolvency law and labor market regulations lead to convergence of law and regulations across different legal traditions.[9]

With a focus on the construction of a new shareholder protection index for 20 countries over the period 1995–2005, Siems (2008) finds evidence that most countries have improved their shareholder protection records in the last years, with a general converging trend in the past decade.[10] Within this general trend, the three origin countries have constantly improved their investor protection index, while in the case of the transplant countries, it depends on whether they continue to take developments in the origin countries into account and thus improve their laws, as well as whether they take advantage of common values and a common legal language, facts that more usually take place in common law countries.[11] Likewise, Katelouzou and Siems (2015) find a pattern of global convergence in shareholder protection standards among 30 countries over the period 1990–2013. The convergence is toward best-practice regulatory standards set by the Doing Business, irrespective of countries' legal tradition or level of economic development.

Using Siems' (2008) dataset, Armour et al. (2009b) find evidence that common law countries protected shareholder interests to a larger extent than civil law countries in the period 1995–2005. Nonetheless, there is a more rapid growth in shareholder protection standards in civil law relative to common law countries. This has led to a clear catching-up in shareholder protection in the past decade, which a legal origin effect has not prevented from occurring. In addition, contrary to the law and finance view, they fail to find any evidence supporting the existence of a statistically significant positive impact of these legal changes on three proxies for stock market development (stock market capitalization as a percentage of GDP, the value of stock trading as a percentage of GDP, and the stock market turnover ratio).

Finally, Gahan et al. (2014) apply leximetric techniques to account for the changes in the level of worker and shareholder protection in six countries between 1970 and 2005. An increase in both the protection of workers and shareholders is documented for France, Germany, India, the UK, and the US, while in the case of Australia only the shareholder protection index increased over the 35-year period. Statistical analysis rejects the hypothesis that stronger shareholder protection comes at the expense of workers' formal protection. Aytekin et al. (2013) compare

---

[9]This idea is not new since Reimann (2001), Husa (2004) and Armour et al. (2009c) have argued that over the past two decades legal systems are becoming global in nature, which makes the idea of strictly differentiating between common and civil law "an anachronism".

[10]Lele and Siems (2007) constructed a new shareholder protection index for five countries (Britain, France, Germany, India and the United States) over a lengthier period (1970–2005) on the basis of a much longer number of variables (60) relative to Siems (2008) who only considered 10.

[11]This does not imply that some common law countries like Pakistan, due to weak legal adaptability, record relatively low levels of shareholder protection.

the development of corporate governance practices in two countries with different legal origins and levels of economic development: Turkey versus Canada. They document that a clear improvement has taken place in many aspects of modern corporate governance in Turkey, thus closing the gap in corporate governance practices with respect to a high-income country like Canada. However, not much progress is observed in the development of efficient boards.[12]

2.5 Recapitulation

Despite the aforementioned criticisms,[13] the prominence of the Legal Origins Theory has had significant implications in the law-making process. Arguably, it has deeply influenced our understanding of how to improve legal systems in order to foster financial development and promote economic activity. The pretended superiority of the common law in many areas of the legal system advocated by the extant legal-origins literature has had important consequences. Policymakers in the lawmaking sphere imitate tools related to the common law (the winning origin) by adopting, for instance, private micro-institutions of investor protection instead of improving existing institutions of public enforcement of securities laws (Roe and Siegel 2009). If the common law does not systematically lead to better legal rules and institutions than the French civil law—as stressed in many of the criticisms to the Legal Origins Theory—, then it is not clear that adopting common-law tools will improve the performance and efficiency of the legal system and therefore, legal reforms in this direction may not have the desired positive impact on the economy.

[12]Segal (2007) focuses on the differences in the rights of secured creditors during reorganization between two British common law countries: the UK versus the US. The comparison is made on the basis of the following dimensions: automatic stay, enforcement rights of secured creditors, the "after-acquired" property clause in bankruptcy proceedings, debtor's power to dispose of the collateral that is free of secured creditors' interest, costs involved in the proceedings, and the cram-down of security interests in bankruptcy proceedings. The comparative analysis shows the superiority of the English approach in terms of stronger rights protection of secured creditors in reorganization procedures. Notwithstanding, legal evolution has brought the British and US approaches closer to each other. LoPucki and Triantis (1994) make a comparison of the judicial reorganization systems of the US and Canada. Even though these systems were expected to work differently, there has been functional convergence due to the similarity of both countries in targeting court-supervised reorganization and in their economic system based on a market economy.

[13]See the box containing a summary of the criticisms to the Legal Origins Theory at the end of this chapter.

Box: Criticisms to the Legal Origins Theory
In this Box we present the most relevant criticisms to the Legal Origins Theory, which we divide into three main blocks. A first set of criticisms builds on colonialism and the associated distribution of legal traditions, a second set of criticisms is based on political economy arguments, and a third set is based on the quality and reliability of early indicators of legal rules and outcomes.

Arguments Based on Colonialism and the Distribution of Legal Traditions Around the World

One of the key criticisms of the Legal Origins Theory is the "Transplant Hypothesis" proposed by Berkowitz et al. (2003a, b) who argue that the manner in which legal systems are obtained is more important than the specific countries' legal traditions to explain the quality of legal systems. They differentiate among origin countries, receptive transplants and unreceptive transplants, with the first two categories being related to higher legal effectiveness. Whether legal transplants are receptive or not depends on the adaptation of the imported law to local conditions and on the population's familiarity with law principles. Their evidence supports the fact that countries in which the law was not adapted to local conditions or the population was not familiar with the law exhibit a lower level of legal effectiveness and economic development.

A related criticism to the Legal Origins Theory has to do with the distribution of legal traditions around the world (Oto-Peralías and Romero-Ávila, 2014a, b). In that work, Oto-Peralías and Romero-Ávila (2014a, b) focus on the key point of the distribution of legal tradition from origin countries (colonial powers) to recipient countries (colonies) in the historical process of European colonization. They argued that: (i) Colonial powers had different strategies when implanting their legal systems in the colonies because they exhibited different responses to the initial conditions (endowments) existing in colonized territories. (ii) The way legal systems were implanted matters for legal/economic outcomes. As regards the distribution of the British common law, the transplantation of the common law was inversely related to the recipient country's level of population density at the time of colonization. This was due to the nature of British colonial policy, which did not want to interfere with preexisting native law and rules of indigenous societies. In contrast, France imposed its civil law rigidly across its empire, leading frequently to conflicts with existing laws. Their results indicate that the common law does not generally lead to superior legal rules and outcomes or to a higher level of credit and stock markets development than the French civil law when precolonial population density and/or potential European settler mortality are high. According to these findings, the superior

(continued)

performance of the common law is largely driven by countries where Britain extensively implanted its legal tradition.

Daniels et al. (2011) emphasize the high degree of variability in jurisdictional arrangements and legal institutions in the British Empire, which were responsive to the initial conditions encountered by colonizers, including the pre-existing indigenous legal order. Whether a colony developed a long-run stable commitment to legality and high legal effectiveness depended to some extent on two features of colonial administration and legal transplantation: (i) the degree of representation in legislative institutions afforded to the indigenous population, and (ii) the degree of integration of indigenous and British common law courts and animated values. In practice, the implantation process of the British law in each colony led to a unique corpus of law that differed from that in other colonies.

Klerman et al. (2011) explain the observed cross-country differences in economic growth between common and civil law countries on the basis of non-legal colonial factors, which they measure through colonial identity dummies. These results lead them to wonder whether legal origins are really meaningful.

Arguments based on Political Economy

A political economy based criticism is related to the Great Reversal hypothesis of Rajan and Zingales (2003). They show that in 1913, French civil law countries had a higher level of financial development—as measured by the average stock market capitalization to GDP ratio—than common law countries, occurring the opposite in 1999. This reversal in financial development levels appears congruent with the incumbent industrial and financial elites in civil law countries preventing start-up competitors from having open access to new finance, thus getting rid of potential competition that could erode the incumbents' industrial position. In contrast, in common law countries financial liberalization would prosper.

Roe (2006) provides an alternative political economy explanation of the patterns observed in securities markets development and divergent ownership structures in the world's richer nations over the course of the twentieth century. The greater destruction in World War II in civil law countries weakened the capacity of political influence of capital oriented interests whose main asset (capital) was largely destroyed during the war. In contrast, labor was the dominant force in postwar continental Europe as workers could influence the polity via voting. This led to a marked left-right political conflict, which gave rise to laws and regulations in favor of the workforce and against capital.

In a similar spirit to Rajan and Zingales (2003) thesis, other papers also question the pretended fixed and path-dependent link of legal origins with the levels of protection of creditors and minority shareholders and of financial

(continued)

development. These include Musacchio (2008) for the case of the development of bond markets in twentieth century Brazil, and Malmendier (2009) for the case of an early form of shareholder company in ancient Rome, the *societas publicanorum*.

Arguments based on Measurement and Recoding of Legal Data

In this block we find several studies which, by virtue of recoding or using more recent or alternative legal data, find no systematic differences between common and civil law countries in many areas of the legal sphere. For instance, Spamann (2010b) challenges the common view still supporting the existence of clear differences in the area of civil procedure involving judicial adjudication and enforcement of private claims between common and civil law countries. Likewise, Spamann corrects the *anti-director* rights index originally used by La Porta et al. (1998) for 33 of the 46 countries initially investigated. The corrected index no longer renders a higher level of shareholder protection in common law than in civil law countries.

By constructing resource-based measures of public enforcement, Jackson and Roe (2009) find no evidence of the pretended superiority of private enforcement mechanisms (more prevalent in common law countries) in propelling securities market development. Rather, public enforcement is overall as important as disclosure in explaining the development of financial markets around the world and more important than private liability rules.

Using time-series data for three parent systems, Britain, France and Germany, and the United States and India over the period 1970–2005, Armour et al. (2009a) cast doubts on the empirical validity of the Legal Origins Theory since there have been great changes in their index of shareholder rights over the past three decades, with a high degree of convergence between legal traditions in recent years due to a substantial rise in shareholder protection in civil law countries. In addition, they find no significant differences between common and civil law countries in the case of creditor protection. Similar evidence is provided by Armour et al. (2009b) for a larger sample of 20 countries over the period 1995–2005. In both studies, the use of time-series legal data is an important advancement relative to the majority of La Porta and associates' initial legal indices that only offered a cross-sectional view of the law at one moment in time, mostly in the second half of the 1990s. This had the limitation that it provided only a static description of the law as it stood at that point, without taking into account the evolution of legal rules caused by either external transnational convergence trends to best-practice standards or the influence of internal economic and political factors. The World Bank's Doing Business initiative is also providing researchers with time-series data on a wide range of legal rules and outcomes for a much wider sample of countries than Armour et al. (2009b).

Chapter 3
Data Description

Abstract This chapter describes the legal/regulatory rules and outcomes, which are obtained from the *Doing Business* Project (2015). This dataset is built following the methodology developed in their papers by such prominent authors as Djankov, La Porta, Lopez-de-Silanes, Shleifer, Vishny and others. A very important advantage of using this source relative to the original papers' data is the much wider coverage of countries and the availability of time series for each indicator over a period covering the last 10 years. As regards the selection of indicators, we consider three important dimensions of legal rules/outcomes that have been previously investigated in the legal origins literature: (a) *creditor and investor rights and disclosure*, (b) *legal system efficiency*, and (c) *regulation. Doing Business* data are obtained from local experts on a specific legal/regulation area, which aim to measure what a standardized firm should expect if it complies with all official regulations and legal requirements in place on the respective area. This chapter also describes the main variables used to account for financial and economic development. Finally, it provides an account of the Doing Business reforms implemented since 2006 for each of the legal and regulatory indicators considered across the different legal families.

The rest of the monograph is devoted to the analysis of the evolution of legal rules and regulations during the last decade, and whether changes in legal indicators have had an effect on economic and financial outcomes. In this chapter we describe the data used in the empirical analysis.

3.1 Legal and Regulatory Indicators

Concerning the selection of legal/regulatory rules and outcomes, we rely on the *Doing Business* Project (2015) dataset for the legal and regulatory indicators. This dataset is built following the methodology developed in their papers by such prominent authors as Djankov, La Porta, Lopez-de-Silanes, Shleifer, Vishny and others. A very important advantage of using this source relative to the original papers' data is the much wider coverage of countries and the availability of time series for each indicator over a period covering the last 10 years. Additional

D. Oto-Peralías, D. Romero-Ávila, *Legal Traditions, Legal Reforms and Economic Performance*, Contributions to Economics, DOI 10.1007/978-3-319-67041-6_3

advantages of the *Doing Business* dataset entail the update of the dataset and enhanced coverage in terms of indicators, in addition to improvements in the methodology and the correction of coding errors and inconsistencies in the data.[1] *Doing Business* offers indicators on 11 different topics of business regulations: Protecting Minority Investors, Getting Credit, Enforcing Contracts, Resolving Insolvency, Starting a Business, Registering Property, Dealing with Construction Permits, Getting Electricity, Paying Taxes, Trading across Borders and Labor Market Regulation. The Doing Business project gathers quantitative data on the regulations faced by small and medium-size enterprises across 189 economies over time.[2] According to Belsley (2015, p. 106), "the main achievement of the Doing Business project has been to shed light and create a more informed debate on a range of differences in laws and regulations across countries in areas where little was known on a systematic basis before the project began".

As regards the selection of indicators, we consider three important dimensions of legal rules/outcomes that have been previously investigated in the legal origins literature: (a) *creditor and investor rights and disclosure*, (b) *legal system efficiency*, and (c) *regulation. Doing Business* data are obtained from local experts on a specific legal/regulation area, which aim to measure what a standardized firm should expect if it complies with all official regulations and legal requirements in place on the respective area.

Concerning the first dimension, we select the indicator "Strength of legal rights index", denoted by *creditor rights*, which measures the extent to which collateral and bankruptcy laws protect borrowers and lenders' rights. Another important indicator considered is "Strength of investor protection index" (*investor protection*), which assesses the strength of minority shareholder protection against directors' misuse of corporate assets for personal gain and self-dealing in related-party transactions. Both indicators range from 0 to 10, with higher scores implying better designed laws to expand access to credit as well as to protect investors. These two measures are clear examples of "law on the books" indicators. Figures 3.1 and 3.2 present a worldwide distribution of the scores in these two legal indicators. The third indicator is "Depth of credit information index" (*information sharing*) that, on a scale from 0 to 6, measures rules and practices affecting the scope, coverage and accessibility of credit information either through a public credit registry or a private credit bureau, with higher values reflecting more credit information availability. Figure 3.3 depicts the scores in the depth of credit information index around the world.

[1]For instance, the enforcing contract indicators measure the cost, time, and number of procedures required to resolve a commercial dispute between two firms so as to capture the efficiency of the commercial court system. As highlighted in World Bank's Doing Business Report 2016, this indicator has been extended to also include well-established good practices conducive to raise court system efficiency.

[2]Note that the Doing Business dataset was first published in 2003 with 5 (instead of 11) sets of indicators, initially covering only 133 economies.

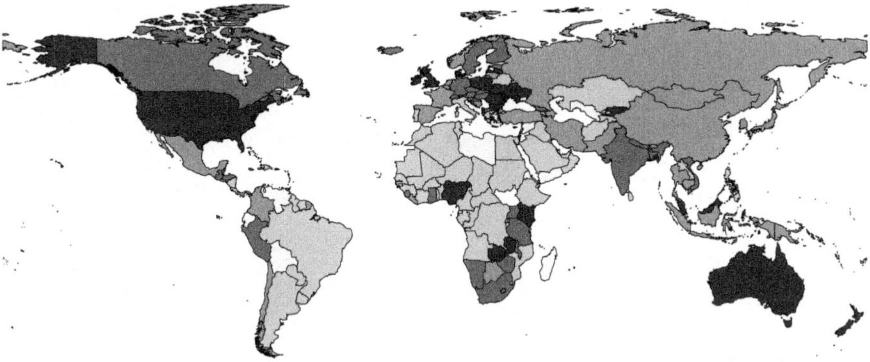

Fig. 3.1 Strength of creditor rights index. Notes: Average annual value in creditor rights during the period 2006–2014 (a *darker* color means a higher value). Countries with missing data on legal rules do not appear in the map

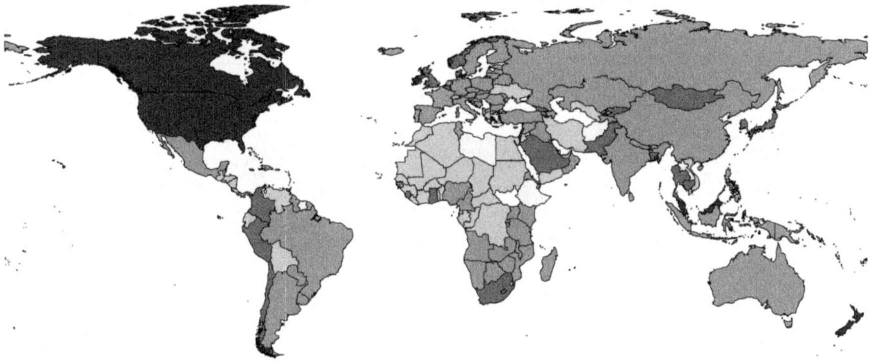

Fig. 3.2 Strength of investor protection index. Notes: Average annual value in investor protection index during the period 2006–2014 (a *darker* color means a higher value). Countries with missing data on legal rules do not appear in the map

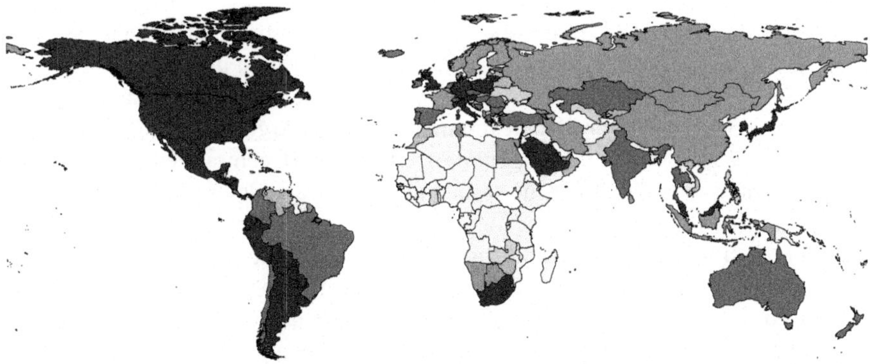

Fig. 3.3 Depth of credit information index. Notes: Average annual value in credit information index during the period 2006–2014 (a *darker* color means a higher value). Countries with missing data on legal rules do not appear in the map

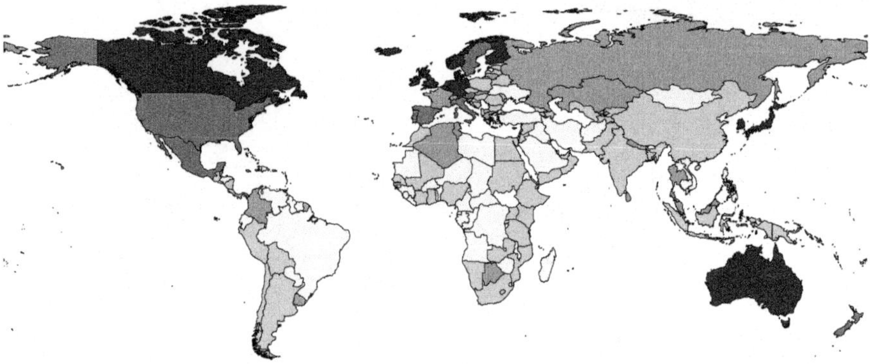

Fig. 3.4 Recovery rate (%). Notes: Average annual value in recovery rate during the period 2006–2014 (a *darker* color means a higher value). Countries with missing data on legal rules do not appear in the map

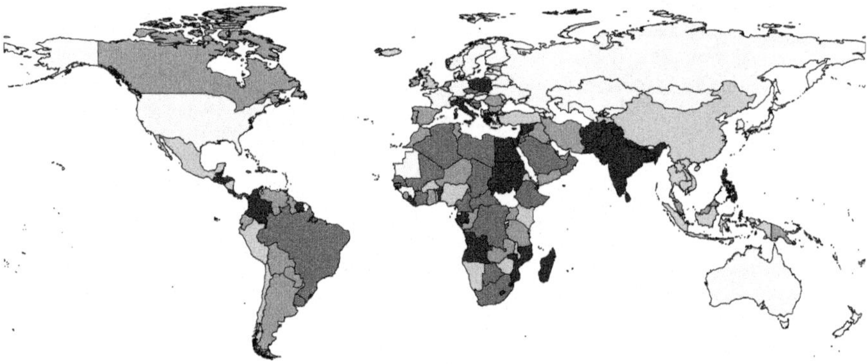

Fig. 3.5 Time to enforce a contract. Notes: Average annual value in time to enforce a contract (ln) during the period 2006–2014 (a *darker* color means a higher value). Countries with missing data on legal rules do not appear in the map

As regards the second dimension given by the measurement of legal system efficiency, we select two legal outcome indicators. In the first place, "time required to complete procedures" (*contract enforcement*) indicates the time in days required to resolve a commercial sale dispute through the courts. Arguably, this indicator can be considered as an objective measure of efficiency of contract enforcement by courts (Djankov et al. 2003). In the second place, the variable labelled as "recovery rate" measures the present value of debt recovered by creditors in insolvency proceedings, after deducting the official costs of the proceedings and the loss of value due to assets depreciation. This indicator constitutes a measure of efficiency of debt enforcement. Figures 3.4 and 3.5 provide a depiction of the worldwide distribution of the scores in the indicators of efficiency of contract and debt enforcement, respectively.

Concerning the third dimension of regulation, the regulatory indicators used are "number of days required to register a firm" (henceforth *starting a business*),

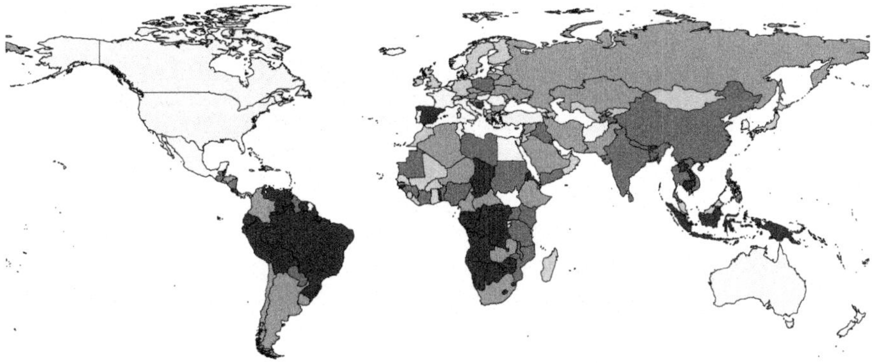

Fig. 3.6 Time to start a business. Notes: Average annual value in time to start a business (ln) during the period 2006–2014 (a *darker* color means a higher value). Countries with missing data on legal rules do not appear in the map

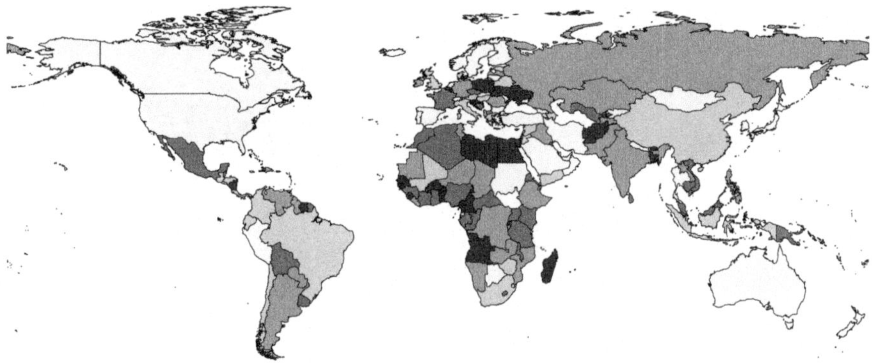

Fig. 3.7 Time to register a property. Notes: Average annual value in time to register a property (ln) during the period 2006–2014 (a darker color means a higher value). Countries with missing data on legal rules do not appear in the map

"number of days required to register a property" (hereafter *registering a property*), "number of days required to build a warehouse" (henceforth *dealing with construction permits*), "time it takes to prepare, file and pay (or withhold) the corporate income tax, value added or sales tax, and labor taxes, including payroll taxes and social contributions (in hours per year)" (hereafter *paying taxes*), "time for border compliance that includes time for obtaining, preparing and submitting documents during port or border handling, customs clearance and inspection procedures" (hereafter *time to export* and *time to import*, respectively).[3] Figures 3.6, 3.7, 3.8,

[3]Logarithmic transformation is applied to indicators measured in days in order to reduce the high variability in the data. In the absence of a comprehensive indicator that measures the different aspects of a dimension by aggregating other indicators (for example, creditor rights), we prefer indicators measuring the duration of procedures. The latter constitutes a fundamental feature of

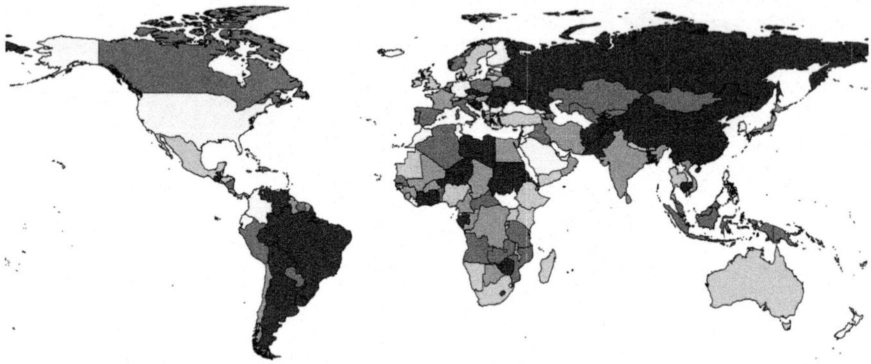

Fig. 3.8 Time to obtain construction permits. Notes: Average annual value in time to obtain construction permits (ln) during the period 2006–2014 (a *darker* color means a higher value). Countries with missing data on legal rules do not appear in the map

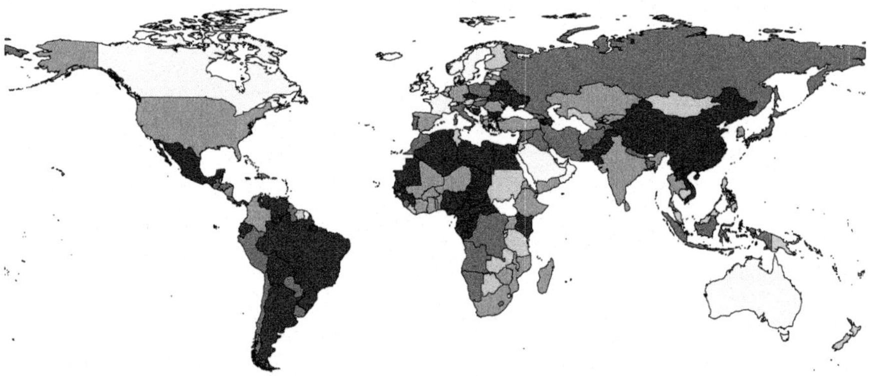

Fig. 3.9 Time required to pay taxes. Notes: Average annual value in time required to pay taxes (ln) during the period 2006–2014 (a *darker* color means a higher value). Countries with missing data on legal rules do not appear in the map

3.9, 3.10 and 3.11 present world maps with the cross-country distribution of the scores in each respective regulatory indicator.

Other variables employed are the legal origin dummies, which are obtained from La Porta et al. (1999, 2008), who identified the legal origin of the Company Law or Commercial Code in each country. In our sample we have 64 British common law countries, 100 French civil law countries, 20 German civil law countries and 5 Scandinavian civil law nations (see Fig. 2.1).

legal and judicial systems, which is reflected in the principle "justice delayed is justice denied". In this regard, Spamann (2010b) argues that measures of complexity, such as the number of steps, have an unclear meaning because they combine and uniformly weight disparate steps that differ greatly in importance and length.

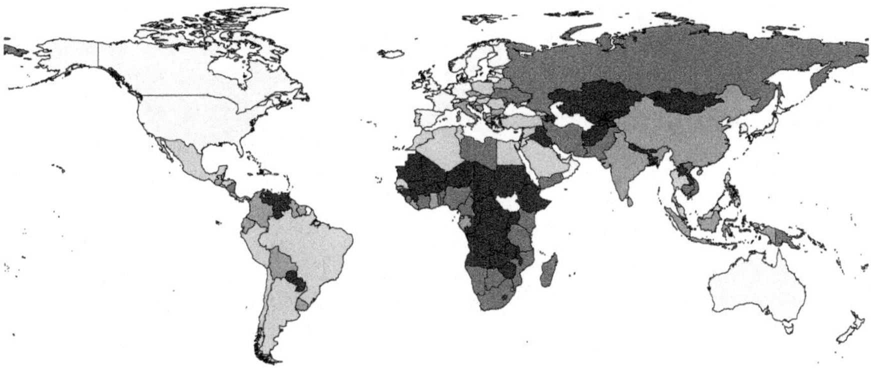

Fig. 3.10 Time to export. Notes: Average annual value in time required to export (ln) during the period 2006–2014 (a *darker* color means a higher value). Countries with missing data on legal rules do not appear in the map

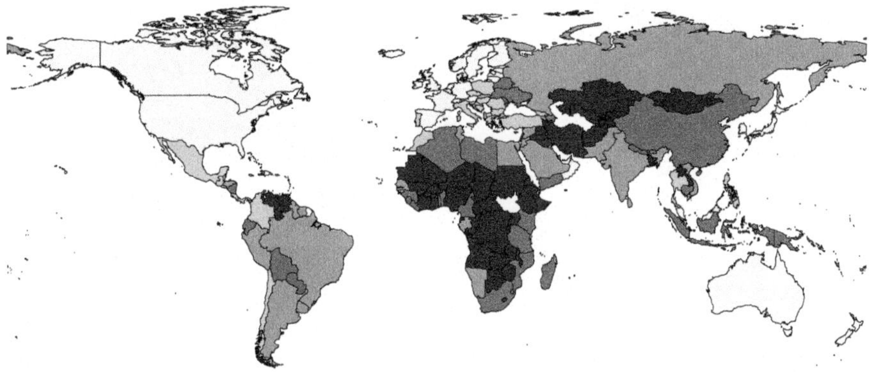

Fig. 3.11 Time to import. Notes: Average annual value in time required to import (ln) during the period 2006–2014 (a *darker* color means a higher value). Countries with missing data on legal rules do not appear in the map

3.2 Economic and Financial Outcomes

The dependent variables to be explained on the basis of the evolution of legal/regulatory rules and outcomes are several measures of financial development and economic development. Concerning the measurement of financial development, for stock markets we use the market capitalization of listed domestic companies as a percentage of GDP and the total value of stocks traded as a percentage of GDP, and for financial intermediaries we use domestic credit to the private sector by banks as a percentage of GDP (CREDIT1), domestic credit provided by the financial sector as a percentage of GDP (CREDIT2), and domestic credit to the private sector as a percentage of GDP (CREDIT3). The latter differs from CREDIT1 in that it incorporates also credit granted by non-bank financial institutions. Both CREDIT1 and

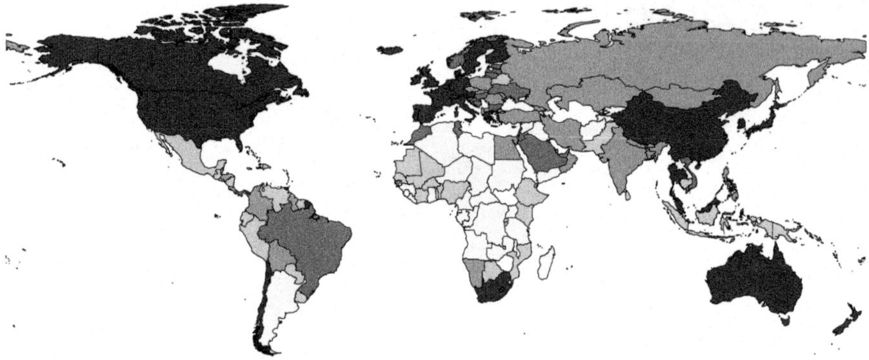

Fig. 3.12 Private credit by deposit money banks and other financial institutions to GDP. Notes: Average annual value in private credit to GDP during the period 2006–2014 (a *darker* color means a higher value). Countries with missing data on legal rules do not appear in the map

Fig. 3.13 Stock market capitalization to GDP (%). Notes: Average annual value in market capitalization (% of GDP) during the period 2006–2014 (a *darker* color means a higher value). Countries with missing data on legal rules do not appear in the map

CREDIT3 differ from CREDIT2 in that the latter not only considers credit granted to the private sector, but also to public enterprises and other entities. Therefore, of the three financial intermediary development variables, CREDIT3 constitutes the most complete measure. Figures 3.12 and 3.13 provide a world map with the distribution of scores in domestic credit to the private sector as a percentage of GDP and the market capitalization of listed domestic companies as a percentage of GDP.

As contemporary economic development outcomes, we employ the ratio of exports plus imports to GDP, net inflows of foreign direct investment (FDI) as a percentage of GDP, gross fixed capital formation in the private sector as a percentage of GDP, new business density as measured by new registrations per 1000 people aged between 15 and 64, the unemployment rate, and the Gini index as a proxy for income inequality.[4] Both financial and economic development outcomes are obtained from the World Development Indicators of the World Bank (2015b).[5] Table 3.1 presents the descriptive statistics and sources for all the variables used in the empirical analysis.[6]

3.3 Description of Doing Business Reforms Since 2006

Table 3.2 presents a description of the Doing Business reforms implemented since 2006 for each of the legal and regulatory indicators considered across the different legal families. The figures provided represent the number of Doing Business reforms since 2006 divided by the number of countries in each legal tradition. Concerning the civil law tradition, we provide the information for the three civil law groups as well as for a weighted average of the civil law groups, using as weights the number of countries in each group. The latter can be used to summarize the Doing Business reforms per civil law country since 2006. Finally, the last column shows the ratio of the weighted average number of reforms per country in civil law traditions to the average number of reforms per country in the common law group. A ratio greater than one implies that civil law countries have implemented more reforms, on average, than common law countries.

Starting with protecting minority investors, the data indicate that British common law countries have implemented on average a lower number of reforms per country (only 0.5) than French, German and Scandinavian civil law countries (with 1, 0.9 and 1.2 Doing Business reforms per country, respectively). Not surprisingly, the ratio of per country reforms in civil law traditions to the number of per country reforms in the common law is well above one (1.9). This indicates that the number of reforms per country in civil law countries almost double that of the common law.

As regards the scores of getting credit, French and German civil law countries exhibit a larger number of Doing Business reforms per country (2.1) than British common law countries (1.4). In the case of Scandinavian civil law countries, the

[4]In Chap. 6, we have also used GDP per capita growth as an economic outcome. However, we present the results for this outcome only in the specification (with both annual and 3-year averaged data) that does not include lagged GDP growth as an additional control variable. One reason for not presenting the results for GDP per capita growth in the specification that includes lagged GDP growth as a control variable is that the correlation of lagged GDP growth with the country fixed effects would bring the Nickell (1981) bias. Furthermore, we prefer not to report the results for this indicator because it may be endogenous to legal reforms. According to unreported results, improvements in legal rules are not generally associated with faster GDP per capita growth.

[5]This, along with other datasets such as the Global Financial Development Database, can be accessed via the World Bank Open Databases, through the Stata command *wbopendata*. More details are available at http://data.worldbank.org/developers/apps/wbopendata

[6]Table A.1 in the Appendix provides a detailed description of each variable as well as its sources. Table A.2 provides a list of the countries included in the sample under study.

Table 3.1 Data sources and descriptive statistics

Variable		Source	Obs	Mean	Std. Dev.	Min	Max
Legal rules/regulations							
Doing business							
Strength of creditor rights index	}	Doing Business Project	1573	5.47	2.40	0.00	10.00
Strength of investor protection index			1573	5.02	1.61	1.00	9.70
Depth of credit information index			1573	2.53	2.47	0.00	6.00
Recovery rate (%)			1573	34.06	24.43	0.00	92.80
Time to enforce a contract (Ln)			1573	6.32	0.45	4.79	7.45
Time to start a business (Ln)			1573	3.10	0.96	−0.69	6.55
Time to register a property (Ln)			1573	3.69	1.15	0.00	6.86
Time to obtain construction permits			1573	5.12	0.54	3.26	6.58
Time required to pay taxes (Ln)			1566	5.44	0.71	2.48	7.86
Time to export (Ln)			1573	2.99	0.59	1.79	4.62
Time to import (Ln)			1573	3.06	0.68	1.39	4.76
Others							
Creditor rights 1995–2005		Siems (2008)	275	0.57	0.15	0.20	0.80
Shareholder protection index 1995–2005		Armour et al. (2009a)	275	0.49	0.16	0.15	0.74
Creditor rights 1978–2002		Djankov et al. (2007)	2970	1.80	1.19	0.00	4.00
Formalism index—Eviction 1960–2000		Balas et al. (2009)	1640	3.68	0.95	1.35	5.83
Form. index—Check collection 1960–2000		Balas et al. (2009)	1640	3.47	1.08	1.04	5.49

Dependent variables						
Market capitalization of listed domestic companies (% of GDP)	World Bank Open Databases	751	66.44	119.99	0.93	1254.47
Stocks traded, total value (% of GDP)		662	39.21	84.98	0.00	954.43
Domestic credit to private sector by banks (% of GDP)		983	43.25	34.60	2.09	312.15
Domestic credit provided by financial sector (% of GDP)		983	56.60	53.47	−27.96	373.79
Domestic credit to private sector (% of GDP)		983	46.36	38.71	2.10	312.15
Foreign direct investment, net inflows (% of GDP)		1615	6.30	15.45	−58.98	466.56
Trade (% of GDP)		1533	94.87	54.47	19.12	455.28
Gross fixed capital formation, private sector (% of GDP)		746	16.62	7.01	0.00	53.13
New business density (new registrations per 1000 people ages 15–64)		869	3.32	4.59	0.00	25.00
Unemployment, total (% of total labor force) (modeled ILO estimate)		1503	8.39	5.91	0.10	37.60
GINI index (World Bank estimate)		511	37.73	9.02	23.72	64.79
GDP per capita growth (annual %)		1634	2.24	5.28	−62.21	104.66
Private credit by deposit money banks and other financial institutions to GDP (%)	The Global Financial Development Database	1291	54.22	50.17	0.01	313.85
Stock market capitalization to GDP (%)		715	56.84	64.21	0.34	570.16
Stock market total value traded to GDP (%)		713	38.46	75.49	0.00	723.59
Number of listed companies per 1,000,000 people		757	27.15	41.33	0.15	247.97

(continued)

Table 3.1 (continued)

Variable		Source	Obs	Mean	Std. Dev.	Min	Max
Others							
GDP per capita, PPP (constant 2011 international $)		World Bank Open Databases	1605	17855.68	20578.96	546.03	136135.50
Rule of law (Worldwide Governance Indicators)		Kaufmann et al. (2009)	1275	−0.05	0.99	−2.67	2.00
Government effectiveness (Worldwide Governance Indicators)		Kaufmann et al. (2009)	1275	−0.27	0.84	−2.25	2.26
Legal origins		La Porta et al. (2008)					
GDP growth (annual %)		World Bank Open Databases	1635	3.77	5.48	−62.08	104.49
Variables used in Chap. 8 **(and not described above)**							
Dependent variables							
Effectiveness of creditor rights reforms in financial depth (private credit over GDP) 2006–2013	}	Doing Business Project, The Global Financial Development Database, and World Bank Open Databases	49	6.10	8.18	−8.73	33.95
Effectiveness of creditor rights reforms in entrepreneurship (new business density)			29	0.04	0.88	−2.19	2.39
Effectiveness of investor protection reforms in financial depth (private credit over GDP) 2006–2013			48	16.37	38.93	−174.84	97.43
Effectiveness of investor protection reforms in entrepreneurship (new business density)			34	0.22	2.38	−7.52	7.01
Gap between creditor rights and financial depth (private credit over GDP) 2006			156	7.36	23.48	−71.99	55.03
Gap between creditor rights and entrepreneurship (new business density) 2006			110	18.18	29.39	−81.25	70.27
Gap between investor protection and financial depth (private credit over GDP) 2006			156	12.31	26.41	−70.00	56.02
Gap between investor protection and entrepreneurship (new business density) 2006			110	20.83	28.74	−70.00	72.35

Gap between creditor rights and contract enforcement 2006	Doing Business Project	168	−13.2913	20.84503	−68.6	42.73
Gap between creditor rights and debt recovery 2006		168	8.802381	21.47004	−36.98	62.1
Gap between investor protection and contract enforcement 2006		168	−8.00637	18.25747	−50.75	45.85
Gap between investor protection and debt recovery 2006		168	14.08726	23.7163	−51.87	63.33
Independent variables						
Control of corruption (Worldwide Governance Indicators) 2006	Kaufmann et al. (2009), from Teorell et al. (2011)	180	−0.04	1.00	−1.84	2.55
Rule of law (Worldwide Governance Indicators) 2006		182	−0.05	1.00	−2.83	1.50
Political stability		183	−0.08	0.99	−2.89	1.41
Catholics	La Porta et al. (1999), from Teorell et al. (2011) (Religion: Protestants, Catholics, Muslims and others as a percentage of population in 1985–1995)	181	31.95	35.91	0.00	99.10
Muslims		181	23.86	36.17	0.00	99.90
Protestants		179	13.52	21.52	0.00	97.80
Other religion		179	30.69	30.84	0.00	100.00
Ethnic fractionalization (not corresponding to a specific year)	Alesina et al. (2003), from Teorell et al. (2011)	180	0.44	0.26	0.00	0.93
Latitude	La Porta et al. (1999), from Teorell et al. (2011)	181	0.28	0.19	0.00	0.72
Mineral resources (Average of mineral rents over GDP during the period 1960–2000)	World Development Indicators	185	0.79	2.43	0.00	15.57

Notes: All descriptive estatistics correspond to the period 2006–2014, except otherwise stated

Table 3.2 Doing business reforms since DB2006 (divided by the number of countries in each group)

	English common law	French commercial code	German commercial code	Scandinavian commercial code	Weighted average civil law	**Ratio civil law/common law**
Protecting minority investors	0.5	1.0	0.9	1.2	1.0	**1.9**
Getting credit	1.4	2.1	2.1	0.8	2.0	**1.4**
Enforcing contracts	0.7	0.8	1.5	0.6	0.9	**1.4**
Resolving insolvency	0.5	0.8	2.2	0.8	1.0	**2.0**
Starting a business	1.9	3.2	3.4	2.6	3.2	**1.7**
Registering property	1.1	1.6	1.9	0.8	1.6	**1.4**
Dealing with construction permits	0.6	1.3	1.6	0.4	1.3	**2.2**
Paying taxes	1.5	2.3	3.4	2.6	2.5	**1.6**
Trading across borders	1.3	1.8	1.4	0.0	1.6	**1.3**
Total	**9.9**	**15.2**	**18.7**	**9.8**	**15.6**	**1.6**
Number of countries	*59*	*93*	*20*	*5*	*118*	

Note: The weighted average of the civil law groups is computed using as weights the number of countries in each group

number of reforms per country is only 0.8. The combination of these groups renders a weighted average number of reforms per country in civil law countries of 2. The ratio of reforms per country in civil law groups to reforms per country in the common law is 1.4. This supports the existence of a greater reform impetus in civil law countries, particularly those in the French and German legal families, probably as a result of imitating the legal tools of the winning origin (i.e., the British common law).

Concerning the efficiency of contract and debt enforcement, the British common law implements 0.7 and 0.5 reforms per country, whereas French civil law countries accomplish 0.8 reforms per country in these two legal enforcement categories. German civil law countries are the ones enacting more reforms per country (1.5 for contract enforcement in court and 2.2 for debt enforcement in insolvency proceedings). The respective figures for Scandinavian civil law countries are only 0.6 and 0.8, which indicates that this legal tradition already had relatively strong contract and debt enforcement at the start of the reform period. As with the protection of minority investors and creditors, the ratio of per country reforms in the civil law to the common law equals 1.4 and 2 for enforcing contracts and resolving insolvency, respectively. This further indicates that civil law countries are reforming to improve not only their law on the books, but also their law in action so as to enhance the reality on the ground.

Concerning starting-a-business reforms, there has been a widespread tendency for countries all over the world to reform. As a matter of fact, British common law countries have implemented 1.9 Doing Business reforms per country, while this figure is greater for the three civil law groups (3.2, 3.4 and 2.6 per country reforms, respectively). The ratio of per country reforms in the civil law to those in the common law is again greater than one (1.7), thus supporting larger reform efforts made by civil law countries relative to British common law nations.

As regards registering property, the number of per country reforms in the French and German civil law groups (1.6 and 1.9) is clearly greater than those in British common law countries (1.1). As with the previous legal and regulatory indicators, the ratio of per country reforms in the civil law to those in the common law is greater than one (1.4), thus supporting the greater steps taken by French and German civil law countries to reduce the regulatory burden associated with registering property.

As far as dealing with construction permits is concerned, the number of reforms per country in French and German civil law countries (1.3 and 1.6) more than doubles that in British common law countries (0.6), with a ratio of per country reforms in civil law countries relative to the common law of 2.2. This again backs up the greater reform effort made by French and German civil law countries aimed at easing the process of obtaining construction permits.

Concerning the regulatory burden associated with paying taxes, the number of per country reforms across the three civil law groups (2.3, 3.4 and 2.6) is well above that in common law countries (1.5). Not surprisingly, the ratio of per country reforms in the civil law relative to the common law is 1.6, which supports the fact that civil law countries have implemented on average more business reforms aimed at easing the process of paying taxes than common law countries over the past decade.

Finally, concerning reforms affecting trading across borders, the number of per country reforms in French and German civil law countries (1.8 and 1.4) is slightly above the number of per country reforms in common law countries (1.3). The ratio of per country reforms in the civil law relative to the common law is 1.3, which further reflects that French and German civil law countries enacted more Doing Business reforms aimed at facilitating trade across borders than British common law countries.

Taken as a whole, this preliminary evidence shows that civil law countries, particularly those with French and German legal traditions, have implemented on average more reforms than British common law countries. This appears to be the case across all the Doing Business indicators under scrutiny, which involve law on the books, law in action, and regulatory indicators measuring the ease of doing business in such key areas as starting a business, registering property, dealing with construction permits, paying taxes and trading across borders.

Chapter 4
Literature Review on the Effect of the Ease of Doing Business on Economic and Financial Outcomes

Abstract This chapter provides a brief review of the main studies analyzing the effect of the legal rules and regulatory indicators—used in our empirical analysis—on economic and financial outcomes, both from a macroeconomic (country-level) and microeconomic (firm-level or industry-level) perspectives. The studies are framed within the following legal and regulatory areas: research on (i) protecting minority investors, (ii) getting credit, (iii) enforcing contracts, (iv) resolving insolvency, (v) starting a business, (vi) registering property, (vii) dealing with construction permits, (viii) paying taxes, and (ix) trading across borders. The pioneering study in each area is presented first, which is followed by other studies within that area.

Before presenting the results of the empirical analysis, this chapter provides a brief review of the main studies analyzing the effect of the legal rules and regulatory indicators—used in our empirical analysis—on economic and financial outcomes, both from a macroeconomic (country-level) and microeconomic (firm-level or industry-level) perspectives. The studies will be framed within the following legal and regulatory areas: research on (i) protecting minority investors, (ii) getting credit, (iii) enforcing contracts, (iv) resolving insolvency, (v) starting a business, (vi) registering property, (vii) dealing with construction permits, (viii) paying taxes, and (ix) trading across borders. The pioneering study in each area will be presented first, which will be followed by other studies within that area.

4.1 Research on Protecting Minority Investors

Djankov et al. (2008a) deal with the important issue of the protection of minority shareholders against self-dealing transactions (also known as tunneling) conducted by corporate insiders (managers and/or controlling shareholders) with the aim of expropriating minority investors. For that purpose, they construct an *anti-self-dealing* index to capture the legal protection of minority shareholders against expropriation practices by those controlling a corporation. In doing so, they use a questionnaire distributed to attorneys from Lex Mundi law firms with questions about how a country's legal system regulates a stylized transaction between two

D. Oto-Peralías, D. Romero-Ávila, *Legal Traditions, Legal Reforms and Economic Performance*, Contributions to Economics, DOI 10.1007/978-3-319-67041-6_4

companies controlled by the same person, who can be enriched improperly. The index is computed for 72 countries as of 2003 and focuses on mechanisms of private enforcement regulating the above transaction—such as information disclosure, approval by disinterested shareholders and litigation. According to the authors, the *anti-self-dealing* index appears to exhibit some of the same properties as the *antidirector-rights* index developed by La Porta et al. (1997, 1998) and the securities-law based shareholder protection indices of La Porta et al. (2006). As with other indices, the *anti-self-dealing* index is considerably higher in common law versus civil law countries, thereby predicting a variety of cross-country stock market outcomes.

La Porta et al. (2002) develop a model of the effects of legal protection of minority shareholders and of cash-flow ownership by a majority shareholder on the valuation of firms. Using a sample of 539 large firms from 27 developed countries, they find that those countries with better protection of minority shareholders and those firms with higher cash-flow ownership by the controlling shareholder exhibit a higher valuation of firms.[1]

Enikopolov et al. (2014) find evidence that country-level and firm-level governance institutions are complements with respect to their effect on firm valuation in crisis times. More specifically, they find that the fall in companies' value during the financial crisis of 2007–2009 showed more sensitiveness to firm-level transparency standards in economies with strong investor protection. This is consistent with the fact that, during a crisis, attracting outside resources to finance investment opportunities declines not only in countries with low investor protection, but also in those with strong protection. As a result, in that scenario the relative importance of firm-level governance rises.

Using a large sample of 78,000 firm-year observations from 40 countries over the period 1990–2007, Claessens et al. (2014) find that a strong protection of shareholder rights reduces financial frictions, particularly in those firms exhibiting large external financial dependence relative to their capital endowment. In contrast, creditor rights protection does not normally influence financial frictions. As a result, cross-country differences in firm-level investment can be accounted for to a much larger extent by financial frictions associated with shareholder rights than to debt-related financial frictions such as limited liability or collateral constraints. In addition, Kose et al. (2008) test whether better investor protection leads corporations to engage in riskier but value-enhancing investments. The evidence gathered for a cross-country panel and a U.S. panel points to a positive link of corporate risk-taking and firm growth rates with the quality of investor protection.

[1]Sevcik (2012) develops a political economy model with capital accumulation and occupational choice to analyze the joint dynamics of investor protection and economic development. An economy with less investor protection is associated with higher costs of external financing for entrepreneurs, which exclude poorer agents from becoming entrepreneurs. This in turn increases the profits of the remaining entrepreneurs. Agents' net worth and the expected return from entrepreneurship account for investor protection policy preferences.

Franks et al. (2012) analyze the factors responsible for the evolution of family firms. In financially developed countries, and in those with strong investor protection and active markets for corporate control, family firms evolve into widely held companies as they age. In contrast, in financially underdeveloped countries and in those with weak investor protection and inactive markets for corporate control, family control is highly persistent over time. In addition, family control is more prevalent in industries with low investment opportunities and low merger and acquisition activity only in countries with high investor protection.

Using panel data on corporate ownership in 34 countries over the period 1995–2006, Foley and Greenwood (2010) find that, after listing, firms in strong investor protection countries are more likely to experience a reduction in the concentration of ownership. This occurs in response to growth opportunities and is related to new issuance of shares, which dilutes blockholders as a result. Using a large longitudinal dataset of Italian listed firms, Cuomo et al. (2013) find that strengthening of investor rights protection is related to a lower use of control enhancing mechanisms and a lower separation of control and cash flow rights, whereas this link is less apparent under a more dispersed ownership.

Doidge et al. (2007) investigate whether a country's degree of protection of minority investors and levels of financial and economic development affect firms' assessment of costs and benefits in implementing measures to improve their own governance and transparency. The evidence indicates that country-specific characteristics explain a higher proportion of the variance in governance ratings (between 39% and 73%) relative to observable firms characteristics that account for between 4% and 22% of the variance, with the latter being close to zero in less developed economies.

4.2 Research on Getting Credit and Information Disclosure

Djankov et al. (2007) construct cross-country data of credit rules and institutions for creditor protection such as legal creditor rights and private and public credit registries in 129 countries over a 25-year period. The evidence supports the existence of a legal origin effect in credit market institutions, with a clear superiority of British common law countries relative to French civil law countries. This contradicts the view that legal systems are converging to the best-practice one, irrespective of a country's legal tradition. In addition, the degree of creditor rights protection and the presence of private credit registries are higher in more developed countries. Greater creditor protection via both creditor rights and credit registries is conducive to a higher ratio of private credit to GDP. An analysis of reforms also confirms that credit markets become more developed as a result of the strengthening of creditor rights and the introduction of credit registries. Legal protection of creditor rights plays a more important role in raising credit in richer countries, whereas credit registries do so in poorer countries. Public credit registries, which are prevalent in French civil law countries, appear to foster credit market development in developing countries. This suggests a key role for public administrations in facilitating credit information sharing. Safavian and Sharma (2007) find evidence that creditor rights protection is beneficial to the development of debt markets only if the country has a well-functioning court system.

Li et al. (2012) investigate the role of liquidity in improving corporate governance, information disclosure and in turn firm valuation for a sample of Russian firms. The evidence indicates that high liquidity enhances corporate governance, which in turn raises firm valuation. The effect found is sizable since a 10% reduction in the proportion of zero return days is associated with a 0.34% rise in transparency and information disclosure, which in turn increases firm valuation by 9.6%.

Berglöf and Pajuste (2005) argue for the need to disclose who owns and controls a firm and the specific governance arrangements in place. However, the evidence provided for a sample of 370 companies listed on stock exchanges in Central and Eastern Europe points to the widespread tendency for firms not to disclose even the most basic elements of corporate governance arrangements, despite existing regulation and surveillance mechanisms. Financial performance is found to strongly correlate with the ease with which information is available to the public. Their evidence also indicates that larger firms and firms with lower leverage, higher market-to-book ratios and more concentrated ownership exhibit higher information disclosure.

Using a laboratory experiment, Brown and Zehnder (2007) find that information sharing raises repayment rates of borrowers, who anticipate that a good credit record facilitates their access to credit. They find that the incentive effect of credit reporting is important when lending is dominated by one-shot transactions, whereas the incentive effect of credit information sharing becomes negligible when there is repeated interaction between borrowers and lenders. This occurs due to the disciplining mechanism of bilateral banking relationships. However, even in this scenario of repeated interactions, credit information sharing can enhance credit market outcomes by weakening lenders' ability to extract rents from relationships.

Using a difference-in-difference design on the effect of credit reporting and identification systems on financial intermediation in 172 countries over the period 2000–2008, Giannetti and Jentzsch (2013) show that the introduction of compulsory identification systems raises financial intermediation (as measured by bank credit to deposits and net interest margins) and financial access (as measured through private credit to GDP). This appears particularly the case in countries in which a credit reporting system is also in place.

In line with the predictions of Padilla and Pagano (1997, 2000) and Pagano and Jappelli (1993), the model by Doblas-Madrid and Minetti (2013) shows that improved access to information through credit information sharing substantially reduces contract defaults for a rich contract-level dataset from a U.S. credit bureau. This is particularly the case when firms are informationally opaque. In addition, improved access to credit information does not reduce the use of guarantees, thus failing to result in a weakening of lending standards. Beck et al. (2014) investigate the impact of credit information sharing and branch penetration on the extent of tax evasion. Their evidence points to lower tax evasion of firms in countries with better information sharing and higher branch penetration. This effect intensifies in firms of small size, firms in industries more dependent on external financing, firms in industries and countries with more growth opportunities and those located in smaller cities and towns.

Using the exogenous variation in the access to finance due to the introduction of credit bureaus, Ayyagari et al. (2016) find evidence that a rise in the access to finance leads to more job creation, particularly among micro, small and medium enterprises for a sample of 50,000 firms across 70 developing countries. Demirgüç-Kunt et al. (2016) investigate the effect of the ability to access long-term debt on firm-level growth volatility. The results indicate that firms operating in industries more dependent on long-term debt financing relative to short-term finance exhibit a lower degree of volatility, particularly in more financially developed countries due to the lowered risk of refinancing. This risk can be mitigated in the case of short-term financing in the presence of legal institutions facilitating the availability of credit information and contract enforcement.

Martinez Peria and Singh (2014) examine the effect of introducing systems of credit information sharing (credit bureaus and credit registry reforms) on firms' access to finance for a sample of over 75,000 firms in 63 countries between 2002 and 2013. Only credit bureau reforms are found to exert a statistically significant impact on firms' access to finance, thus raising financing and the share of working capital financed by banks, reducing interest rates and lengthening maturity. The circumstances under which these effects are more pronounced are: (i) the greater the coverage and accessibility of the credit bureau, (ii) the weaker the degree of contract enforcement in a country, and (iii) the smaller, less experienced and more opaque the firms. Using cross-country data between 1975 and 2006, Bueyuekkarabacak and Valev (2012) find that credit information sharing in the form of both public registries and private bureaus reduces the likelihood of banking crisis, particularly in low-income countries. In addition, credit information sharing counteracts the adverse effect of rapid credit growth on banking crisis.

There are also some studies investigating the effect of creditor rights. von Lilienfeld-Toal et al. (2012) challenge the common view that stronger legal enforcement of lender rights raises access to credit for all borrowers by expanding the set of incentive compatible loan contracts. By relaxing the common assumption of infinite elasticity in the supply of credit, the authors show that stronger legal enforcement of lender rights renders general equilibrium effects leading to a reduction in the access to credit for small borrowers and an increase in credit access for wealthy borrowers. They validate empirically this adverse distributive effect for a firm-level dataset that encompasses a judicial reform in India that raised banks' ability to recover bad loans.

Houston et al. (2010) investigate the relationship between stronger creditor rights and the extent of risk-taking for a sample of almost 2400 banks in 69 countries. Their evidence points to the existence of a positive link between stronger creditor rights and greater bank risk taking, which results in a higher likelihood of financial crisis. However, stronger creditor rights are conducive to higher economic growth. Concerning the effect of credit information sharing, it appears to be beneficial by raising bank profitability and economic growth as well as reducing bank risk and the likelihood of financial crisis.

Finally, Qian and Strahan (2007) examine the impact of legal differences in creditor rights on the ownership and terms of bank loans. Their evidence shows that strong creditor rights are conducive to a higher concentration in loans ownership, longer maturities and lower interest rates. Remarkably, they find that foreign banks appear to be particularly sensitive to changes in creditor rights protection, with their ownership falling relative to domestic banks as the legal protection of creditors declines.

4.3 Research on Contract Enforcement

As emphasized in the Doing Business Report 2016 (World Bank 2016), an efficient court-based system of contract enforcement based on the respect for the rule of law and effective property rights protection is key to economic and social progress. An efficient judicial system is a requirement for entrepreneurs to recognize the rights and responsibilities articulated in new legal rules and regulations, helping close the gap between law on the books and law in practice.[2] An efficient courts system is conducive to higher credit markets development and economic development (Dam 2006b), greater small firms' growth (Islam 2003), higher foreign direct investment and technological innovation (Esposito et al. 2014), greater firms' investment (Sereno et al. 2001; Herrero and Henderson 2001), and larger and more efficient firms (World Bank 2004b).

Djankov et al. (2003) construct a measure of the quality of courts in terms of efficiency of contract enforcement using the exact procedures used by litigants and courts in two particular cases: the eviction of a tenant for nonpayment and the collection of a check returned for nonpayment. Data assembled with the help of Lex Mundi member law firms in 109 countries are used to construct an index of procedural formalism of dispute resolution for each country. More specifically, the authors obtain information on the exact legal procedures necessary for dispute resolution in court and the exact articles of the law. The responses are then used to build measures of formalism, defined as "the extent to which regulation causes dispute resolution to deviate from the neighbor model" (Djankov et al. 2003, p. 456). Several interesting findings arise from their data construction and analysis. They find support for the Legal Origins Theory since judicial formalism is systematically greater in civil law countries, particularly those with legal transplantation

[2]More details on Sherwood et al. (1994), Dakolias (1999), Dam (2006b), Rosales-López (2008), Ball and Kesan (2010), and Esposito et al. (2014).

from the French legal tradition, than in common law countries. Besides, legal traditions alone account for about 40% of the variation in procedural formalism across 109 countries. In addition, there is more formalism in judicial adjudication in poorer than richer countries. Higher formalism is found to be associated with several pervasive features of the judicial system, which include a lengthier process of dispute resolution, low enforceability of contracts, and higher corruption, among others. There is also consistent evidence of a link between procedural formalism and a lower score in survey measures of the quality of the legal system. The latter usually occurs in less developed countries. According to the authors, courts inefficiency and high procedural formalism and the associated difficulty to deliver justice stem from the transplantation of legal systems, which can partly account for the quality of contemporary courts.

Balas et al. (2009) extend the measure of the quality of contract enforcement given by the formalism of civil procedure—introduced by Djankov et al. (2003) for 109 countries as of 2000—by computing it for every year since 1950. The results show that the existing large differences in procedural formalism between common and civil law countries in 1950 widened by 2000. This evidence contradicts the hypothesis of the convergence of national legal systems. This in turn supports the empirical validity of the Legal Origins Theory, which conceives legal origins as having a long-term influence on legal indicators.

Bae and Goyal (2009) investigate whether cross-country differences in legal protection in terms of creditor rights and contract enforcement influence the size, maturity, and interest rate spread on loans to borrowers in 48 nations. Stronger creditor rights appear to reduce interest rate spreads, but they do not affect loan size and maturity. In contrast, poor enforceability of contracts not only reduces the size of loans, but also shortens loan maturities and increases loan spreads. In addition, contract enforceability is far more important than creditor rights in explaining the structuring and pricing of loans.

Esposito et al. (2014) focus on the inefficiency of the Italian judicial system that has inhibited investment and growth. More specifically, the enforcement of civil and commercial claims is poor due to the existence of excessive delays in judicial proceedings, which results in large bottlenecks of pending cases. The authors suggest implementing the following measures: reviewing court fees, enhancing the functioning of the new mandatory mediation scheme, reforming the system of appeal and strengthening court management.

Nunn (2007) investigates whether a country's score in contract enforcement can be an important source of comparative advantage. Combining data on the proportion of a good's intermediate inputs requiring relationship-specific investments with data on trade flows and contract enforcement, Nunn shows that countries with a high degree of contract enforcement exhibit a pattern of specialization based on the production of goods for which relationship-specific investments are most important. As a result, the pattern of comparative advantage is explained to a larger extent by contract enforcement than by the classical combination of skilled labor and physical capital.

Using Indian manufacturing data that match state-by-state firm-level data with state-by-state judicial quality data, Chakraborty (2016) provides consistent evidence that courts quality raises firms' performance both in terms of exporting and domestic sales. Lower-bound estimates indicate that raising judicial quality by 10% leads to a 1–2% rise in a firm's sales. Axworthy (1976) emphasizes the fact that efficient contract enforcement leading to a fast and less costly resolution of disputes is particularly important for small and medium-size firms, since they usually lack the necessary resources to stay operating during long, costly litigation processes.

Focusing on a sample of 38 European countries, Ippoliti et al. (2014) show that highly efficient judicial systems that resolve incoming cases quickly also exhibit high legal reliability and confidence in contract enforceability. García-Posada and Mora-Sanguinetti (2015) exploit province-level variation in court efficiency in Spain to investigate the effect of judicial efficiency on firms' size and entry rates. Moving from the least efficient provincial court to the most efficient one increases firm size by 0.6–2.8% and firm entry rates by 8.8–9.5%. Dougherty (2014) investigates the link between legal reform, contract enforcement and firm size in terms of output, employment and fixed assets across the Mexican states. Shifting from the Mexican state with the worst judicial quality to the one with the highest judicial quality doubles the average firm size in that state, thereby bringing firm productivity gains conducive to a rise in state output by up to 8%. Similar evidence is provided by Giacomelli and Menon (2013) for the case of the variation in municipal courts efficiency in Italy. In fact, moving from the most efficient municipal court to the least efficient one leads to a 23% fall in average firm size in the affected municipality.

4.4 Research on Resolving Insolvency

Djankov et al. (2008b) study debt enforcement with respect to a hypothetically insolvent hotel with the help of insolvency practitioners in 88 countries. The hotel can be considered a midsize firm with a given number of employees, capital and ownership structure, a certain firm's value as a going concern and a lower value if the hotel is sold piecemeal. These characteristics are set to be identical across countries, with the only difference being the fact that the economic values are normalized by the country's per capita income. Insolvency practitioners are then asked to provide the detailed steps on how debt enforcement in his or her country must proceed. This provides the authors with information about which debt enforcement procedure is used in each country (foreclosure by senior creditor involving or not a court, liquidation and reorganization). This allows them to estimate the time and cost of the debt enforcement procedure, and whether the hotel will be held together or sold piecemeal. All this information is used to compute an indicator of the efficiency of debt enforcement in each of the 88 countries studied.

Their calculated worldwide averages of time, cost and efficiency of debt enforcement indicate that debt enforcement is, on average, slow, costly and inefficient. In fact, only 36% of the countries manage to keep the hotel as a going concern, which is considered the efficient outcome. A worldwide average of 48% of the hotel's value is lost in all the steps involved in the insolvency proceedings. The authors document higher debt enforcement efficiency in richer countries and in British common law countries, with richer countries showing a comparative advantage at more complex insolvency procedures. Moreover, debt enforcement efficiency is found to be a strong predictor of debt market development.

Dakolias (1999) conducts a comparative analysis of the performance of the judicial administration in 11 countries considering the following dimensions: number of cases filed per year and number of cases disposed per year, ratio of cases disposed to cases filed (clearance rate), number of cases pending at the end of the year, ratio of pending and filed cases to resolved cases (congestion rate), average case duration and number of judges per 100,000 inhabitants. Even though the judicial administration in most countries was capable of meeting the demand for justice in a specific time period, eventually deficiencies became apparent and the need for judicial reforms arose. The author suggests introducing alternative dispute resolution mechanisms based on mediation, raising the number of judges at least transitorily, and fostering judicial productivity by introducing information and telecommunications technologies.[3]

Araujo et al. (2012) examine the effects of the Brazilian reform introducing a new bankruptcy law in 2005 with the aim of strengthening creditor rights and raising the efficiency of the bankruptcy system within a poorly developed credit market. Focusing on a sample of Brazilian and non-Brazilian firms, the authors find that the bankruptcy reform led to a rise in long-term debt, thereby reducing the cost of debt. In contrast, no statistically significant impact is found on loan's ownership structure. Focusing on the comparative analysis of seven key bankruptcy dimensions in a large sample of 50 countries, Azar (2008) documents that the replacement of the management of a firm undergoing reorganization, though costly, leads to a stronger protection for creditors. In addition, he recommends to sell a debtor's assets in liquidation promptly, using efficient, flexible and transparent arrangements. He also finds that creditors' recovery rates are lower in the absence of stay of individual proceedings in bankruptcy. In reorganization procedures, courts should guarantee the transparency of the process and provide a forum where to negotiate a viable reorganization plan in which creditors should take an important part.

Calvino et al. (2016) investigate the effect of national legal policies such as those related to debt and contract enforcement on the growth dynamics of start-ups. They also try to differentiate between the impact on entrants and incumbents within the same country, industry and time period. The evidence points to the greater exposure of new entrants to the policy environment than incumbents. Start-ups in industries

[3]Cabral et al. (2012) argue for the potential benefits that introducing the use of technology by courts and legal aid organizations can bring to U.S. low-income litigants in their access to justice.

with high volatility and growth dispersion are more affected by national policies than start-ups in other industries. In addition, a dynamic environment for start-ups requires the existence of timely bankruptcy procedures that ensure high debt enforcement efficiency as well as strong contract enforcement.

Dewaelheyns and Van Hulle (2008) examine the effect of the Belgian 1997 bankruptcy code reform on firms' bankruptcy rates, finding evidence of a fall in small and micro firms' bankruptcy rates. Controlling for some macro factors such as inflation, consumers confidence and real GDP growth, the beneficial effect of the introduction of the new bankruptcy code appears only significant in the manufacturing and trade industries. Among all the measures incorporated into the new code, those that limit domino bankruptcy effects are thought to have played a key role in reducing bankruptcy rates.

Using a sample of Hungarian firms, Franks and Loranth (2014) find strong evidence that most of the bankrupt firms remain as going concerns in spite of incurring in large operating losses and generating low recovery rates for pre-bankruptcy creditors. This outcome is explained on the basis of the allocation of rights between secured and unsecured creditors and the compensation scheme of the agent in charge of managing the bankruptcy process.

Favara et al. (2012) find evidence that a more favorable debt renegotiation to shareholders lowers firms' equity risk. Countries with bankruptcy laws favoring debt renegotiations versus liquidations, and firms in which bargaining power is more concentrated in the hands of shareholders relative to debt holders, are both conducive to lower equity beta and return volatility. They also find that in the limit, when renegotiation of debt contracts is not feasible, equity risk does not hinge on shareholders incentives to default strategically.

Using a difference-in-difference strategy applied to project loan data, Visaria (2009) assesses the impact of the 1993 Indian reform consisting of the staggered introduction of debt recovery tribunals across states with the aim of speeding up the achievement of debt recovery rates above a certain threshold. The evidence strongly backs up the existence of a statistically significant reduction in the cost of credit due to the introduction of debt recovery tribunals by lowering both the delinquency for the average loan and the interest rates charged on larger loans.

In contrast, Paik (2013) finds no statistically significant effect of the introduction of the Bankruptcy Reform Act of 2005 on entrepreneurship, proxied by self-employment. According to Paik, this is likely to be explained by the fact that potential entrepreneurs opted for limited liability as a means to offset the reduced wealth protection imposed by the new bankruptcy law. Focusing on transition economies over the period 1992–1998, Pistor et al. (2000) find no significant impact of reforms in corporate and bankruptcy laws on financial development. However, financial institutions tend to flourish when their legal institutions of contract enforcement gain efficiency. This supports the view that it is more important to provide an efficient enforcement of contracts than introducing new poorly-enforced legal rules.

4.5 Research on Starting a Business

Djankov et al. (2002) construct new data on the entry regulation of start-up firms in 85 countries with the aim of investigating whether long delays at government agencies concerning entry regulation give incentives for third parties to get involved in the process of company formation, thereby giving rise to big opportunities for rent extraction and corruption. In contrast to public interest theories that support the view that long administrative delays result from due diligence by the government agencies in coping with the bureaucratic steps required until entry is granted, there is strong evidence for the public choice view that entry regulation can be used for rent extraction by politicians and bureaucrats. In fact, greater corruption and a larger informal sector result from a more burdensome regulatory environment affecting the start-up process, which fails to provide better quality of public or private goods. In addition, more democratic countries and those establishing more constraints on the executive are found to present lighter regulation of entry.[4]

Djankov et al. (2006) use objective indicators of business regulations (including starting a business, hiring and firing, registering property, getting credit, protecting investors, enforcing contracts, and debt recovery after closing a business) in 135 countries to show that economies with better business regulations exhibit higher economic growth. The growth effect of moving from the worst quartile of business regulations to the best equals a 2.3%-point rise.

Using panel data on the number of new registrations in 92 countries, Klapper and Love (2010) examine whether the ease of registering a business and the magnitude of registration reforms influence registrations of new firms. The evidence indicates that small reforms implying less than a 40% reduction in costs, time and number of procedures required to start a business do not exert a significant influence on new firm registration, whereas big reforms do have a positive impact on new firm creation. The evidence also supports that policy success in the creation of new firms requires the implementation of larger, broader reforms in those economies with weak business environments.[5]

Employing harmonized firm-level data for 16 industrialized and emerging countries, Aghion et al. (2007) show that financial development in the form of private credit and stock market capitalization affects new firm entry and the post-entry expansion of successful new businesses, even after controlling for other potential entry barriers such as entry regulations and labor market regulations. The effect appears particularly important for the entry of small firms and in industries exhibiting higher external dependence, whereas it is negligible or even negative

[4]As pointed out by Djankov (2009), the inclusion of indicators of the regulation of entry in the Doing Business project has brought about a rise in the number of reforms implemented between 2003 and 2008. More specifically, a total of 193 reforms have been accomplished in 116 countries.

[5]Klapper and Love (2011) document the widespread sharp decline in new firm registration during the financial crisis in a sample of 93 countries, particularly in highly financially developed economies that were more severely hit by the financial crisis.

for the entry of large firms. Bertolini (2006) documents the potential benefits in terms of introducing online solutions for regulatory compliance that would reduce entry costs conducive to higher entrepreneurship and growth.

Using a field experiment conducted in Belo Horizonte, Brazil, de Andrade et al. (2016) test which government action is more effective in making informal firms registered. Firms were randomized to a control group or one of the following four treatment groups: the first group received information on how to register, the second group received this information in addition to zero registration costs and the use of an accountant for a year, the third was assigned an enforcement visit from a municipal inspector, and the fourth was assigned to neighbor a firm that was subject to an inspection visit to determine if enforcement has spillovers. The evidence fails to support the empirical relevance of information and free registration cost treatments, while a statistically significant but small rise in formalization is found to result from municipal inspections. All this indicates that informal firms will formalize only when they are forced to do so.

Focusing on a panel dataset containing more than 180 countries over a period of 10 years, Divanbeigi and Ramalho (2015) find strong evidence of a positive impact of business regulations on firm creation and per capita GDP growth. Among all business regulations, the authors stress the importance of sound entry and exit regulations as well as sound credit market regulations and court enforcement in driving growth. The authors find that shifting from the lowest quartile of improvement in business regulation to the highest quartile leads to a 0.8%-point rise in per capita GDP growth. With a focus on European firm-level data, Klapper et al. (2006) investigate the influence of market entry regulations on new limited-liability firms creation, entrants' average size and incumbent firms' growth. Costly regulations are found to inhibit the creation of new firms, particularly in naturally high-entry industries, thereby forcing new entrants to become larger and making incumbent firms grow more slowly. This evidence is robust to controlling for an information set that includes the availability of financing, labor market regulations and the protection of intellectual property.

Focusing on a sample of up to 43 countries between 2003 and 2004, Dreher and Gassebner (2013) find that more burdensome entry regulation (in the form of a larger number of procedures required to start a business and larger minimum capital requirements) inhibits markets' firm entry and entrepreneurship. Adding corruption to the specification, they show that corruption decreases the adverse effect of entry regulations on firm entry into markets in highly regulated countries. This appears to be consistent with the 'grease the wheels' hypothesis.

Employing a panel dataset containing 5 years and 44 countries, Chowdhury et al. (2015) examine the determinants of three types of entrepreneurship: new firm start-up, self-employment, and early stage entrepreneurial activity. Property rights protection, control of corruption and less burdensome entry regulations in the form of fewer procedures are positively associated with nascent/new firm start-up, while burdensome tax regulations reduce the start-up of new firms. This contrasts with the positive impact that the tax and regulatory burden exerts on self-employment.

Munemo (2014) investigates whether the degree of entry regulations required to start a new domestically owned firm in a host country affects the complementarity between foreign direct investment and domestic investment. In countries with a sufficiently high entry regulation cost, foreign direct investment is found to crowd out domestic investment. This usually occurs in low-income countries, for which there is a clear scope for reforming entry regulations as a way to foster the complementarity between foreign direct investment and domestic investment, bringing in turn higher economic growth. Klinger and Schuendeln (2011) use a regression discontinuity design to analyze the causal effect of engaging in a business training program held in Central America on the likelihood that an applicant to the workshop starts a business or expands an existing enterprise. Business training raises the probability of business entry or expansion, whereas financial constraints and gender heterogeneity reduce it.

Norbäck et al. (2014) use a lobbying model incorporating the conflict of interest between entrepreneurs and incumbents to study the effects of business entry costs for new entrepreneurs. They show that international market integration reduces entry costs, which makes foreign entrepreneurs less aggressive. In addition, it becomes more difficult to protect incumbents. These theoretical predictions are backed up by the empirical evidence obtained with Doing Business data showing a statistically significant negative correlation between international openness and entry barriers to new entrepreneurs.

Using a general equilibrium model approach, Herrendorf and Teixeira (2011) try to establish whether entry barriers can account for a large fraction of the income gap between developing countries and the United States. Taking the model to Penn World Table data in an attempt to match the main development facts, they show that large entry barriers are required to explain about half of the income gap between developing countries and the United States. Employing a benchmark model of time allocation, Fang and Rogerson (2011) investigate the effect of product market regulation on aggregate employment measured through total hours worked. The adverse effect on aggregate employment takes place via the size of income transfers associated with the regulations, with the labor supply elasticity being the key propagation mechanism.

Jerbashian and Kochanova (2016) employ industry-level data from 14 OECD economies to investigate the effects of several business regulations on investment in information and communications technologies. A rise in the strength of legal rights and a reduction in the cost of starting a business and registering property increase investment in information and telecommunications technologies, whereas the extent of director liability for self-dealing reduces it. In addition, the ability of shareholders to sue managers for misconduct raises software investments.

The evidence provided by Elgin and Oyvat (2013) and Williams (2014) shows that highly regulated economies with complex rules are associated with the prevalence of businesses remaining informal. Similar evidence is provided by the 2016 Doing Business Report, which shows that high firms' entry costs, particularly when there is third-party involvement, can increase firms' level of informality—as measured through the percentage of firms competing against the informal sector and the percentage of firms identifying informality as a major constraint to their business operations.

Lyons et al. (2014) challenge the view that World Bank's Doing Business reforms raise growth and formalization of micro enterprises. More specifically, they focus on a series of field studies dealing with the ease of street-vending in Tanzania in 2007 and 2011, finding no significant evidence supporting the rise in the growth and formalization of microfirms resulting from reforms affecting street-vending. Focusing on 39 countries, Stel et al. (2007) investigate the link between entry regulation and entrepreneurship. The evidence shows that the minimum capital required to start a business and labor market regulations reduce entrepreneurship rates. In sharp contrast to Djankov et al. (2002), key entry regulations such as the time, the cost, and the number of procedures required to start a business do not affect the formation of either nascent or young businesses.[6]

As previously argued, complex entry regulation and rules can discourage businesses from formalizing. The evidence summarized by Bruhn and McKenzie (2014) indicates that entry reforms aimed at making easier and cheaper for micro firms to become formal has resulted, at best, in a modest increase in the number of formal firms. In contrast, stronger enforcement of rules constitutes a better means of raising formality. Therefore, governments may have the fiscal incentive to make larger informal firms become formal, whereas it is not clear at all whether there is public benefit in making micro enterprises formalize.

4.6 Research on Registering a Property and Protecting Property Rights

Using sectoral value added data for a large sample of countries, Claessens and Laeven (2003) analyze the effect of a higher degree of property rights protection on firms' allocation of resources and growth. The evidence shows that stronger property rights are conducive to higher firm's growth through improved allocation of assets. The firms' growth effect from more secure property rights is comparable to that stemming from the greater access to financial resources as a result of higher financial development.[7]

---

[6]Using Bayesian Model Averaging methods to calculate the partial correlation between detailed policy measures and several institutional and regulatory indicators, Kraay and Tawara (2013) uncover a very important finding of high instability in the set of partial correlates of closely-related outcomes. This leads them to warn against the use of very specific cross-country policy measures to establish a reform agenda.

[7]Focusing on a panel of 129 countries between 1965 and 2008, Miletkov and Wintoki (2012) assess the effect of financial development on the quality of property rights institutions. The results suggest that there is a positive association between the development of financial and credit markets and property rights protection, particularly in emerging market economies.

Field (2007) uses both the differences across Peruvian regions induced by the timing of the program through which the Peruvian government issued property titles over 1.2 million urban households between 1996 and 2003 and the differences across target populations in level of pre-program ownership rights. The evidence points to a statistically significant positive impact of the titling reform on labor hours as well as a shift in labor supply from work at home to work in the outside market and a substitution of adult for child labor. Berkowitz et al. (2015) attempt to determine the importance of property rights by studying a property law enactment that granted creditors with more rights over the assets underlying their secured loans to private businesses, and at the same time private firms were afforded stronger protection against their assets' expropriation. The evidence strongly supports the positive impact of the property law enactment on firm value, particularly in firms with more tangible assets, lower internal cash flows, strong growth opportunities, and a lower level of political connection.

Focusing on a large sample of plots from an intensively titled rice-growing area of Madagascar, Jacoby and Minten (2007) compare land-specific investments, land productivity, and land values for titled and untitled plots cultivated by the same household. They attempt to examine whether formalizing land rights is conducive to agricultural investment and greater land market dynamism. In contrast to most existing literature, formal titling in Madagascar appears unrelated to plot-specific investment, land productivity and land values. This evidence suggests that there is little benefit in extending this system of formal titling in rural Madagascar.[8] Along similar lines, Durand-Lasserve and Selod (2007) find that formalizing residential property rights does not lead to greater credit market development among the poor in urban Latin America, who are reluctant to mortgage their prime asset.

Miceli and Kieyah (2003) propose a theoretical model of land title reform in which even if the adoption of the new system is Pareto efficient relative to the existing one, the voluntary adoption of the new system is not likely to succeed. This outcome is caused by a negative externality that prevents individual land owners from fully internalizing the benefits of the new system. This theoretical prediction is consistent with some historical efforts to establish land registration systems in the U.S. and England, thereby having some implications for the ongoing efforts in less developed economies to institute formal property rights systems for land as a policy instrument to foster investment and growth.

Using a panel dataset including the 16 main Indian states between 1958 and 1992, Besley and Burgess (2000) investigate the role of the large volume of land reforms implemented—as a way to improve the asset base of the poor—in reducing poverty. Overall, land reforms are found to significantly reduce poverty. With a focus on a survey of new firms in post-communist countries, Johnson et al. (2002)

[8]More generally, Deininger and Feder (2009) recommend a careful diagnosis of the policy, social and governance environment before implementing a program of formalization of land rights. If finally implemented, the performance of the land administration system should be controlled in terms of coverage, cost-benefits and service provision quality.

examine whether weak property rights or limited access to finance most tightly constrain private sector investment. They find clear-cut evidence that weak property rights protection discourages firms from reinvesting their profits and retained earnings, even in the presence of available bank loans.

Bose et al. (2012) find a U-shaped relationship between property rights protection and economic growth. This nonlinear effect of stronger protection of property rights is explained on the basis of the following two opposing effects. Stronger property rights raise capital formation and growth, but they also encourage bad borrowing practices. In financially developed economies, the latter negative effect appears to weaken.

4.7 Research on Dealing with Construction Permits

Using a general equilibrium model approach, Gete (2014) assesses the effect of the costs and time lags to obtain construction permits on the response of aggregate consumption, house prices and employment in construction to interest rate shocks. After documenting a large variation in the costs of obtaining construction permits among OECD countries exhibiting similar mortgage development levels, Gete estimates vector autoregressions to compare the effect of shocks across the sample of countries with varying degrees of costs of obtaining construction permits. The response to interest rate shocks is found to be much lower in countries with higher costs of obtaining construction permits.

Freund et al. (2014) investigate whether demanding bribes for particular government services cause delays in delivering those services. The evidence shows that it takes 1.5–1.8 times longer to obtain a construction permit and 1.5–1.6 times longer to get electrical connections when firms are faced with demands for bribes relative to those that are not. Similar evidence is found for the procedure of customs clearance. In addition, the evidence does not support that corruption favors a few firms or that corruption is less harmful when the regulatory environment is burdensome, thus rejecting the "grease the wheel" hypothesis.

Using six business regulation variables for a panel of 182 countries, Poel et al. (2014) examine the impact of administrative burdens on economic growth. Fixed effects regression estimates indicate that reducing administrative burdens concerning start-ups and paying taxes fosters economic growth rates. The effect is far from negligible since a 25% reduction in administrative burdens increases per capita GDP growth by 1.62% in a panel of 26 European countries.

Kenny (2007) documents that the construction sector is one facing high levels of corruption, which includes large bribe payments to gain or alter contracts, circumvent regulations, construct using low quality materials, devote low funds for maintenance, and build white elephant infrastructure projects with very low returns. In order to prevent this from happening, Kenny suggests that transparency, simplicity and enforcement of construction regulations, physical auditing and independent oversight of projects, along with a focus on the outcomes of poor construction, are more important than introducing a large number of poorly enforced regulations.

4.8 Research on Paying Taxes

Focusing on a cross-country survey of all taxes imposed on the same standardized mid-size domestic firm, Djankov et al. (2010a) compute effective corporate income tax rates in 85 countries as of 2004. Higher effective corporate income tax rates significantly reduce aggregate investment, foreign direct investment and entrepreneurial activity. There is also a statistically significant correlation with investment in manufacturing and the size of the shadow economy. The evidence indicates that a 10%-point rise in the first-year corporate tax rate lowers the aggregate investment income share by around 2% points and the official entry rate by 1.4% points.

Lawless (2013) investigates the effect of the complexity of the tax system in terms of fulfilling tax requirements on foreign direct investment. Higher tax system complexity can be time-consuming and imply a cost, while at the same time it can provide opportunities to lower the overall tax bill. Of these opposing effects, the former prevails when looking at foreign direct investment on a country pair, whereas no statistically significant effect is found for the level of foreign direct investment flows. The effect of a 10% reduction in tax complexity is non-negligible since it is comparable to a 1%-point decrease in effective corporate tax rates.

Using a macro-level panel dataset covering a large group of European countries, Baliamoune-Lutz and Garello (2014) investigate the impact of taxation and tax progressivity on nascent entrepreneurship as measured by new self-employment. Tax progressivity at higher-than-average incomes is found to significantly reduce new self-employment. Block (2016) provides empirical evidence on the negative effect of higher corporate income tax rates on business density and entrepreneurship entry rates. High tax code complexity reduces entrepreneurship entry rates, whereas tax rates progressivity increases them. Belitski et al. (2016) examine the impact of tax rates and their interaction with corruption on entrepreneurship entry rates for a panel dataset of 72 countries between 2005 and 2011. Tax rates and corruption are found to individually reduce entry rates, whereas the interaction term between tax rates and corruption appears to raise entry. This reflects the fact that corruption can to some extent offset the negative effect of high tax rates on entry.

Using a unique dataset containing estimates of bribe payments of Ugandan firms, Fisman and Svensson (2007) investigate the link of taxation and bribery payments on firm growth. Both taxes and corruption appear to retard growth. However, the adverse effect of corruption on firm growth is three times larger than that of taxation. Focusing on a large sample of European multinationals, Becker et al. (2012) investigate the relative importance of corporate taxation quality and quantity effects on foreign direct investment. The quantity effect is measured through the extent to which a country's equilibrium stock of foreign capital decreases as a result of higher corporate taxation. The quality effect arises if higher taxation reduces the contribution of investments to the corporate tax base and production's capital intensity. The quality effect concerning the impact on the corporate tax base accounts for up to 40% of the total effect. The quality effect as regards the increase in the labor intensity of production due to corporate taxation mitigates by almost 60% the adverse quantity effect.

Dharmapala and Hines (2009) analyze the determinants of the possibility that a country becomes a tax haven. Governance quality is found to be more important than low tax rates in the likelihood of a country becoming a tax haven. Evidence from U.S. firms shows that both countries' governance quality and low tax rates interact positively to attract foreign direct investment relative to countries that only offer low tax rates. Braunerhjelm and Eklund (2014) show that reducing the administrative burden of paying taxes (measured through time required to pay taxes and the number of tax payments per year) raises annual business entry rates by 3%, irrespective of the corporate tax rate.

4.9 Research on Trading Across Borders

Using data from 345 freight forwarders, port and customs officials operating in 126 countries, Djankov et al. (2010b) compute the average time required to transport a 20-foot container of an identical good from a factory in the country's largest city to a ship in the most accessible port. These data are used to estimate a difference gravity equation in order to establish the impact that time delays exert on relative exports of countries with similar geographic features and endowments, which are subject to the same tariffs in importing countries. The authors further condition on an information set that includes relative size, relative distance and relative income. As a way to deal with endogeneity in the relationship between time costs and volume of trade, the authors employ a sample of landlocked countries and exclude all domestic time costs by using as an input "the export time from the border and onto the ship in the neighboring country(ies)" (Djankov et al. 2010b, p. 167). According to Djankov et al. (2010b, p. 167), "it is unlikely that trade volumes affect export times in foreign countries, especially since landlocked countries are small and tend to provide only a fraction of the trade going through the foreign port". Moreover, the authors estimate a difference-in-difference equation that controls for exporter and industry fixed effects to show that each additional day of delaying a product prior to being shipped lowers trade by more than 1%. This effect is even larger for "time-sensitive goods", such as perishable agricultural goods.

Using data from the World Bank's World Business Environment Survey, LiPuma et al. (2013) test the hypothesis whether institutional quality matters for improving export performance of new and small firms to a much larger extent than for large firms. The evidence appears to provide broad support for this hypothesis. Employing cross-country data from 126 countries, Freund and Bolaky (2008) find evidence that business regulation, particularly the one affecting firms' entry is more important as a complement to trade liberalization than financial development, rule of law or human capital accumulation. Higher trade is found to raise the level of economic development in flexible economies, but it does not affect income levels in more rigid economies. This finding accords with the important role of new business entry in raising economic development levels according to the Schumpeterian view of creative destruction.

Exploiting a unique dataset covering all Uruguay's export transactions and the associated precise information on actual time needed for each transaction to go through customs, Volpe Martincus et al. (2015) investigate the effect of delays in clearing customs on firms' performance along several dimensions. The evidence shows the existence of an adverse effect of custom-related delays on firms' exports, with the effect being intensified in the case of sales to new buyers. Using data on trade facilitation in a sample of 118 developing countries,[9] Dennis and Shepherd (2011) assess the impact of trade facilitation on export diversification. A 10% reduction in international transport costs and domestic exporting costs raises export diversification by 4% and 3% respectively, with custom costs being a key factor in these findings. In addition, the influence of trade facilitation on export diversification is greater the lower the level of economic development.

Using panel data for 124 developed and developing countries between 2003 and 2004, Iwanow and Kirkpatrick (2009) examine the effect of trade facilitation reforms and other trade-related institutional constraints on the export performance of the manufacturing sector, paying particular attention to African economies. The evidence gathered shows the positive effect of trade facilitation on manufacturing export performance. However, results further indicate the need to also accomplish reforms to enhance regulatory quality and the quality of the basic transport and communications infrastructure.

Shepherd and Wilson (2009) document the existing variation in trade facilitation among members of the Association of Southeast Asian Nations. For instance, import and export costs exhibit significant variation across member countries, from very low to moderately high levels. Tariff and non-tariff barriers exhibit less variation, ranging from low to moderate levels. Infrastructure quality and competitiveness in the services sector also display substantial variation from fair to excellent. Estimating a standard gravity model, they show that improving transport infrastructure such as port facilities and raising investment in information and telecommunications technology are conducive to larger intra-regional trade flows in Southeast Asia.

Freund and Rocha (2011) focus on the effect of trade facilitation reforms implemented in Africa as an attempt to raise Africa's exports, whose share of global exports has halved over the past 30 years. The components of trade facilitation targeted by the reforms are transit times, documentation, ports and customs.

[9]Trade facilitation involves the reduction of transaction costs related to the enforcement, regulation and administration of trade policies (Iwanow and Kirkpatrick 2009).

Of these components, transit delays appear to matter the most. The evidence provided by the authors indicate that a 7% rise in exports results from a one-day fall in inland travel times, whereas delays in other areas exert a far lower influence on trade. They also document that transit times are primarily caused by institutional characteristics such as border delays, the quality of roads, fleet class and competition and security, rather than by geographical features.

Using highly disaggregated firm-level export data from Costa Rica between 2007 and 2013, Carballo et al. (2016) assess the impact of introducing information technologies as a way to facilitate the required procedures until exporting is authorized. More specifically, the authors focus on the gradual introduction of an electronic trade single window scheme across groups of products and ports, which is found to have raised both the number of exporting firms and firm's exports along the shipment extensive margin and the buyer extensive and intensive margins.

Fernandes et al. (2015) investigate the impact of trade facilitation on trade by studying the effect of the dramatic decline in the rate of physical inspections by Albanian customs rendering fewer inspection-related delays on imports' level and composition. When the probability of inspecting a shipment falls from 50% or more to under 50%, there is a 7% reduction in the number of days spent in Albanian customs as well as a 7% increase in import value. The changes in trade composition include rising average quantities and unit prices, a rise in the number of shipments, and the number of importing firms per product-country pair and the number of countries per firm-product pair.

Yakovlev and Zhuravskaya (2013) show for Russia that the simplification of licensing requirements for small firms in Russian regions with better public institutions leads to a 4.5%-point rise in annual firms' sales growth, whereas the reduction of state inspections per firm in the same regions increases annual sales growth by 12% points. Reforms introducing regulations favoring firms entry are more likely to succeed in regions with high government transparency, fiscal autonomy and population's level of education.

Levchenko (2007) investigates whether institutional differences concerning contract enforcement, property rights, shareholder protection, among others, exert an impact on trade flows. For that purpose, the author develops a model of international trade incorporating the modelling of institutional differences within the framework of incomplete contracts. The existence of cross-country institutional differences renders important changes to the law of comparative advantage. Not only poor countries may not benefit from trade, but also factor prices may not equalize as a result of trade. In addition, Levchenko tests the implications of the model using data on U.S. imports disaggregated by country and industry, finding clear-cut evidence that institutional differences constitute a source of trade flows.

Chapter 5
Legal Change Within Legal Traditions and Convergence

Abstract This chapter tries to determine whether there has been legal change within legal traditions by testing for mean differences between 2014 and 2006 scores for each of the legal and regulatory indicators studied. The evidence appears to indicate that there has been legal change, particularly in French civil law countries. This legal tradition has experienced an improvement in the following areas: law on the books as measured by the indices of strength of creditor rights and investor protection, depth of credit information, and in the regulatory burden associated with starting a business, registering a property, obtaining construction permits, paying taxes and trading across borders. Furthermore, it attempts to establish whether there is a legal origin effect on legal rules and regulatory outcomes both at the beginning and end of the period, and whether the relative position of legal traditions changed after the reform. The evidence indicates that in many areas such as creditor rights and investor protection, efficiency of debt enforcement, and in the regulatory burden linked to obtaining construction permits, paying taxes and trading across borders, the statistically significant differences relative to the British common law have diminished between 2006 and 2014; and in the case of starting a business these differences have vanished. This supports the existence of catching-up of the French civil law to the average legal and regulatory standards of the British common law.

Before trying to explain current economic and financial development outcomes on the basis of the legal and regulatory reforms implemented over the period 2006–2014, we next attempt to shed some light on the extent of legal change within each legal tradition as well as of convergence in legal and regulatory standards among legal traditions.

5.1 Has There Been Legal Change over the Period 2006–2014?

We begin with Fig. 5.1 that depicts the evolution of the legal/regulatory rules considered over the period 2006–2014. The evolution of the average scores associated with each indicator is plotted for each of the four legal traditions: the British

D. Oto-Peralías, D. Romero-Ávila, *Legal Traditions, Legal Reforms and Economic Performance*, Contributions to Economics, DOI 10.1007/978-3-319-67041-6_5

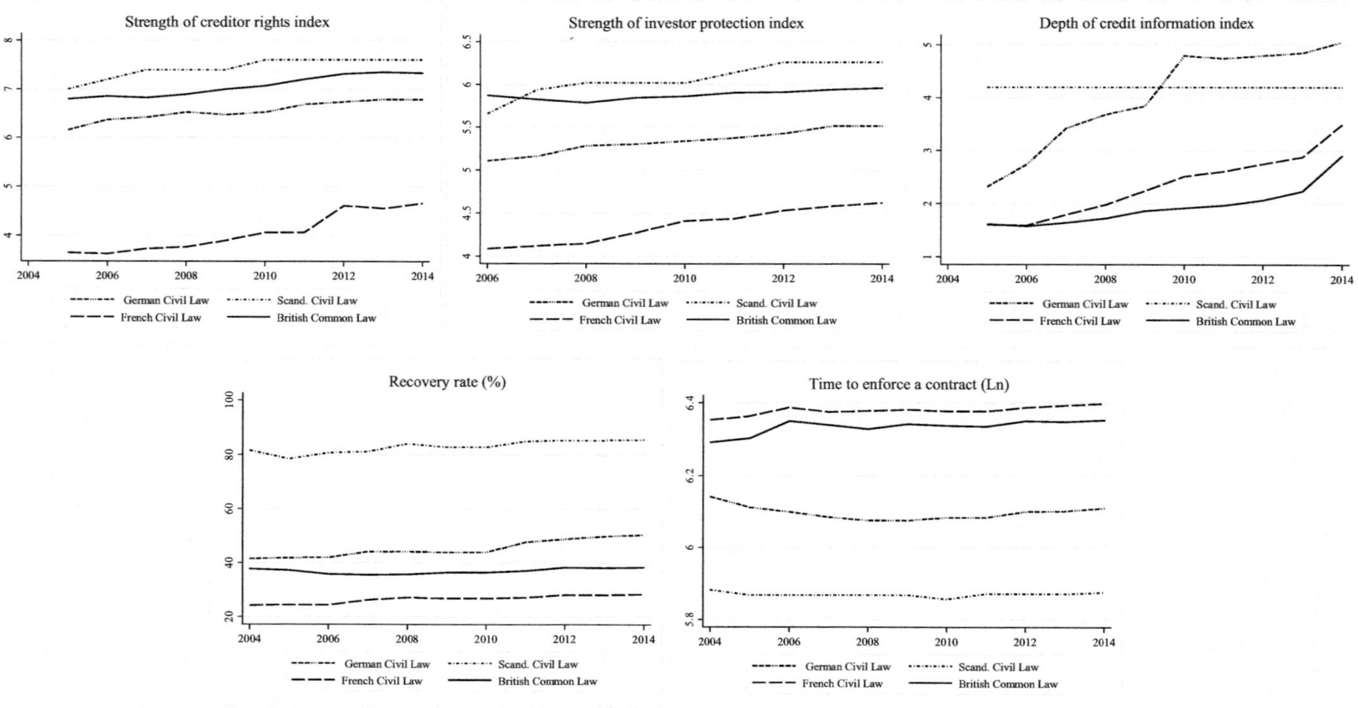

Fig. 5.1 Evolution of legal rules and regulatory indicators across legal traditions

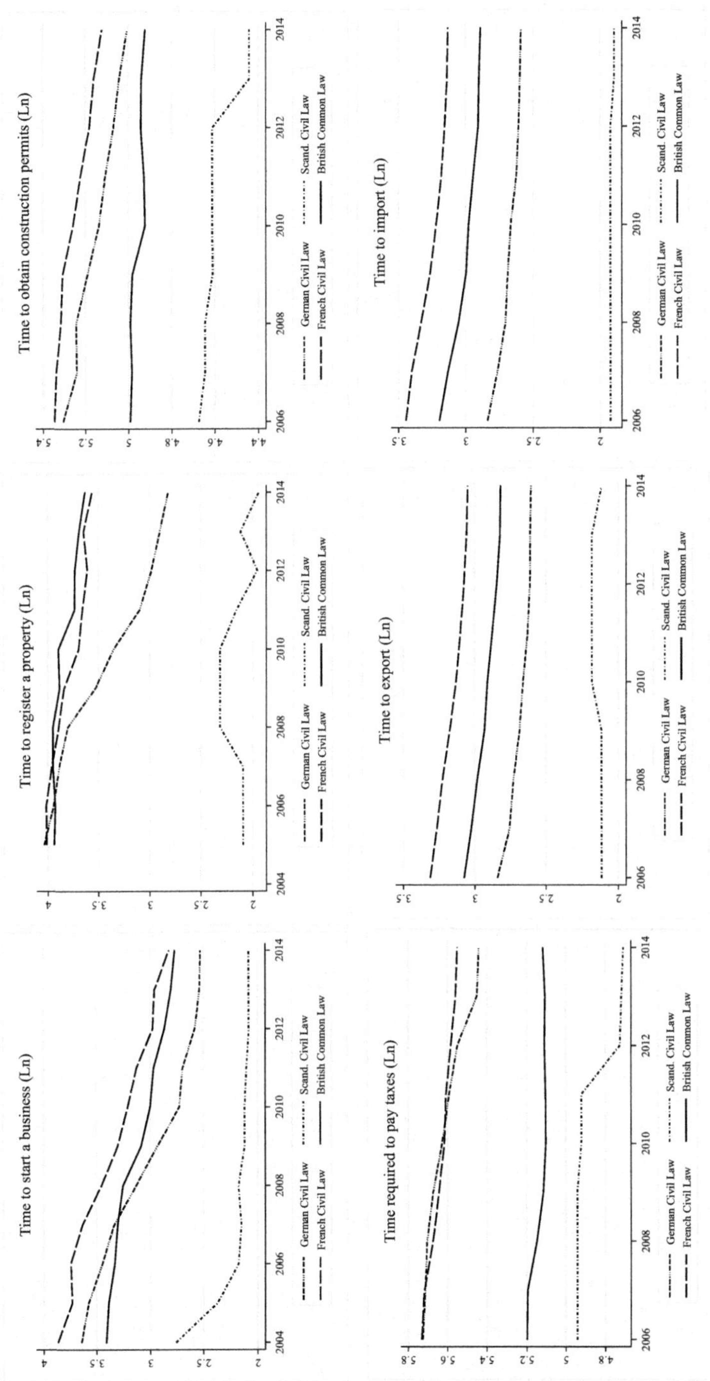

Fig. 5.1 (continued)

common law and the French, German and Scandinavian civil law. The first question we try to answer is whether there has been legal change within each legal tradition over the period under scrutiny. For that purpose, we conduct tests for mean differences between the 2006 and 2014 scores associated with each legal/regulatory indicator for each of the legal origins. The results of these tests appear in Table 5.1.

Table 5.1 Tests for mean differences between the 2006 and 2014 scores

		Mean values		Mean differences		
		2006	2014	Value	St. Error	P-value
English common law	Strength of creditor rights index	6.85	7.33	0.48	0.35	0.17
	Strength of investor protection index	5.87	5.96	0.09	0.30	0.78
	Depth of credit information index	1.57	2.90	1.33	0.43	0.00
	Recovery rate (%)	35.90	38.49	2.59	4.78	0.59
	Time to enforce a contract (Ln)	6.35	6.35	0.00	0.09	0.97
	Time to start a business (Ln)	3.33	2.77	−0.56	0.17	0.00
	Time to register a property (Ln)	3.93	3.63	−0.30	0.24	0.22
	Time to obtain construction permits (Ln)	4.99	4.92	−0.07	0.10	0.46
	Time required to pay taxes (Ln)	5.20	5.12	−0.08	0.13	0.53
	Time to export (Ln)	3.07	2.82	−0.26	0.10	0.01
	Time to import (Ln)	3.19	2.89	−0.31	0.13	0.02
French commercial code	Strength of creditor rights index	3.63	4.66	1.03	0.29	0.00
	Strength of investor protection index	4.08	4.62	0.54	0.21	0.01
	Depth of credit information index	1.59	3.49	1.91	0.33	0.00
	Recovery rate (%)	24.35	28.42	4.08	3.10	0.19
	Time to enforce a contract (Ln)	6.39	6.40	0.01	0.06	0.86
	Time to start a business (Ln)	3.75	2.82	−0.92	0.13	0.00
	Time to register a property (Ln)	4.02	3.56	−0.46	0.15	0.00
	Time to obtain construction permits (Ln)	5.35	5.12	−0.23	0.07	0.00
	Time required to pay taxes (Ln)	5.73	5.55	−0.18	0.10	0.06
	Time to export (Ln)	3.31	3.05	−0.27	0.08	0.00
	Time to import (Ln)	3.45	3.13	−0.32	0.09	0.00

(continued)

Table 5.1 (continued)

		Mean values		Mean differences		
		2006	2014	Value	St. Error	P-value
German commercial code	Strength of creditor rights index	6.37	6.79	0.42	0.62	0.50
	Strength of investor protection index	5.11	5.52	0.41	0.35	0.25
	Depth of credit information index	2.74	5.05	2.32	0.59	0.00
	Recovery rate (%)	42.03	50.54	8.51	7.19	0.24
	Time to enforce a contract (Ln)	6.10	6.11	0.01	0.14	0.93
	Time to start a business (Ln)	3.45	2.53	−0.92	0.22	0.00
	Time to register a property (Ln)	3.94	2.82	−1.12	0.39	0.01
	Time to obtain construction permits (Ln)	5.31	5.00	−0.30	0.19	0.11
	Time required to pay taxes (Ln)	5.73	5.44	−0.29	0.20	0.16
	Time to export (Ln)	2.84	2.61	−0.23	0.17	0.17
	Time to import (Ln)	2.84	2.59	−0.25	0.19	0.20
Scandinavian commercial code	Strength of creditor rights index	7.20	7.60	0.40	0.63	0.54
	Strength of investor protection index	5.66	6.26	0.60	0.45	0.22
	Depth of credit information index	4.20	4.20	0.00	0.28	1.00
	Recovery rate (%)	80.78	85.70	4.92	5.26	0.38
	Time to enforce a contract (Ln)	5.87	5.88	0.01	0.15	0.96
	Time to start a business (Ln)	2.18	2.08	−0.10	0.35	0.79
	Time to register a property (Ln)	2.09	1.94	−0.15	0.78	0.85
	Time to obtain construction permits (Ln)	4.67	4.44	−0.23	0.27	0.43
	Time required to pay taxes (Ln)	4.94	4.71	−0.23	0.21	0.31
	Time to export (Ln)	2.11	2.11	0.00	0.12	1.00
	Time to import (Ln)	1.92	1.90	−0.03	0.14	0.86

As can be observed, the French civil law tradition is the one that presents more statistically significant differences in the means of the 2006 and 2014 scores. More specifically, there are statistically significant differences at the 1% level for the strength of creditor rights index, depth of credit information index, and the following regulatory indicators: time to start a business, time to register a property, time to obtain construction permits, time to export and time to import. In addition, statistically significant differences at the 5% level are apparent in the strength of investor protection index, and at the 10% level in time required to pay taxes.

In the case of the indicators of creditor and investor rights and disclosure, there is a statistically significant rise in the degree of protection and information sharing. In a similar spirit, there has been a statistically significant fall in the value of the regulatory indicators, which indicates that in 2014 it takes less time to start a business, register a property, obtain construction permits, pay taxes or trade across borders than in 2006. The only two indicators for which there has not been a statistically significant change are those associated with the efficiency of contract enforcement by courts (time to enforce a contract) and the efficiency of debt enforcement (recovery rate). This appears to indicate that legal change has been a widespread phenomenon within the French civil law tradition, except for contract and debt enforcement that exhibit no significant differences between 2006 and 2014 values.

In the case of the German civil law tradition, there have been statistically significant differences between the 2006 and 2014 scores for only three indicators: a rise in the depth of credit information index and a fall in the number of days required to start a business and register a property. It is also interesting the fact that the Scandinavian civil law group has not exhibited statistically significant differences in their legal/regulatory indicators scores between the initial and final years, mainly due to the fact that their scores were already good in the initial year for most of the dimensions considered. In the case of the British common law tradition, there have been statistically significant improvements in four areas: the depth of credit information index, and the number of days required to start a business as well as to export and import.

Overall, there is evidence to support the claim that legal change has been more prevalent in French civil law countries, relative to other legal traditions. One of the reasons for this is that their scores in the initial year were worse than those in the other legal traditions, and another may be related to the fact that policymakers in the lawmaking sphere tend to imitate the legal and regulatory tools of the winning origin according to the extant literature (i.e., the British common law). The latter has the shortcoming that if the common law does not always lead to more advanced legal systems than other legal traditions, then it is far from certain that adopting common-law tools will improve the efficiency of the legal system and in turn the level of economic and financial development. Perhaps it is more recommended to deepen the reforms within the existing legal tradition (for instance by enhancing existing institutions of public enforcement of securities laws) rather than radically moving to private micro-institutions of investor protection (Roe and Siegel 2009).

5.2 Have Legal Reforms Reduced the Differences in Legal Rules/Regulations Across Legal Traditions?

To investigate whether French civil law countries had worse legal and regulatory rules and outcomes than the British common law both at the beginning and end of the period considered or whether the relative position changed after the reforms, Figure 5.2 plots the evolution of each legal and regulatory indicator distinguishing between British common law and civil law countries, and further differentiating on the basis of their level of development, i.e., less developed countries for those with GDP per capita below the median and developed countries for those with GDP per capita above the median.

As can be observed, law on the books as measured by the indices of strength of creditor rights and investor protection is higher in the British common law than in the civil law over the whole period for both developing and developed countries. In the case of the depth of credit information index, civil law countries score higher than the British common law group in both developing and developed countries. This appears in line with the findings in Oto-Peralías and Romero-Ávila (2014b), who showed that Spanish law legacy has much higher public registry coverage than the other legal traditions, whereas there are no significant differences in private registry coverage. However, former French colonies appear to exhibit significantly lower private registry coverage than the British, but no statistical differences exist in terms of public registry coverage. Therefore, the common perception that civil law colonies exhibit significantly better public registry coverage vis-a-vis common law colonies appears to be driven by the high coverage in former Spanish colonies.

Concerning the efficiency of debt enforcement, as measured by the recovery rate, the British common law group is more efficient than the French civil law, irrespective of the countries' level of development. In the case of the efficiency of contract enforcement, at the beginning of the period it was higher in the group of developed common law countries than in the group of developed civil law countries. However, there has been a clear process of convergence among the two, and by the end of the period the civil law group slightly surpasses the common law group. In less developed countries, time to enforce a contract is substantially lower in civil law countries. This is consistent with the evidence provided by Oto-Peralías and Romero-Ávila (2014b), which indicated that contract enforcement is not always superior in British common law countries relative to French civil law nations. That was particularly the case in those ex-colonies characterized by adverse endowments, that is, high precolonial population density and high potential settler mortality of European settlers.

As far as the regulatory outcomes are concerned, the time required to start a business in 2006 is lower in British common law than in civil law countries, irrespective of the countries' level of development. However, in 2007 the civil law group overtook the British common law group in developing countries, while for the group of developed countries the time required to start a business is always lower. In the case of the time required to register a property, initially the British

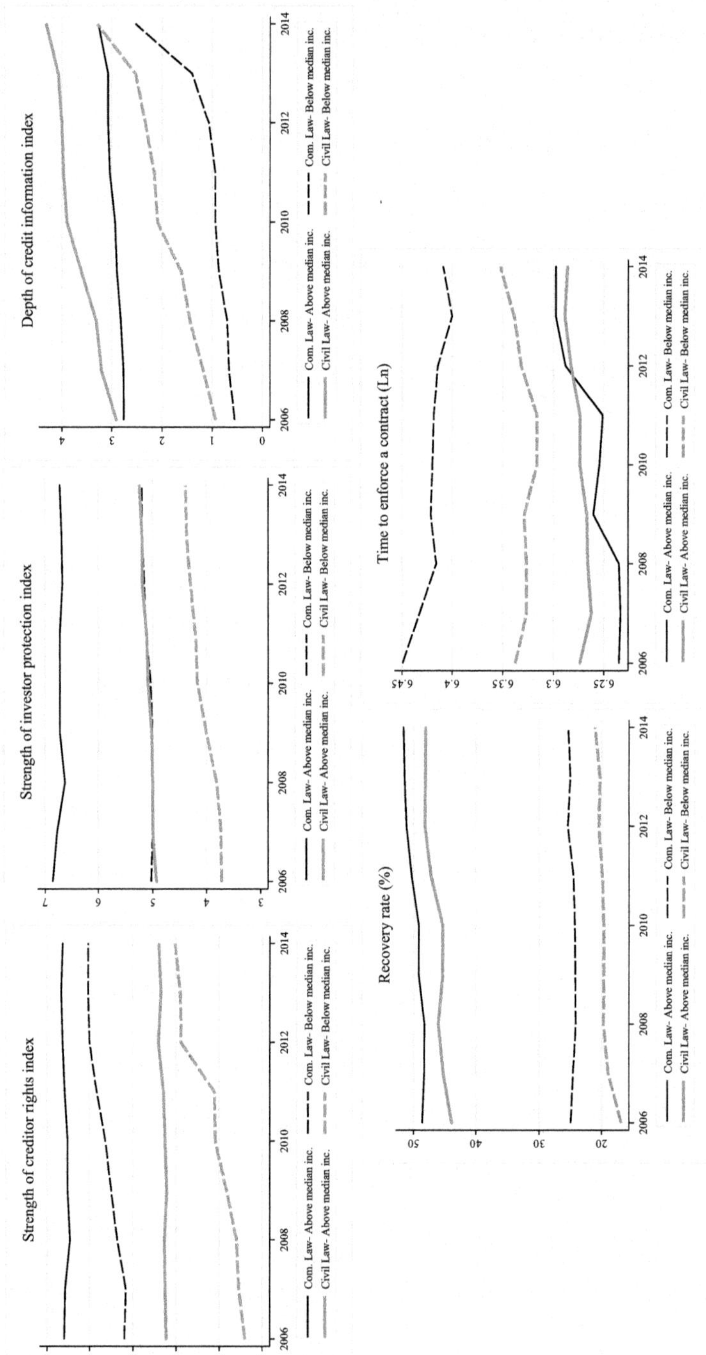

Fig. 5.2 Evolution of legal rules and regulatory indicators distinguishing between common and civil law and level of development

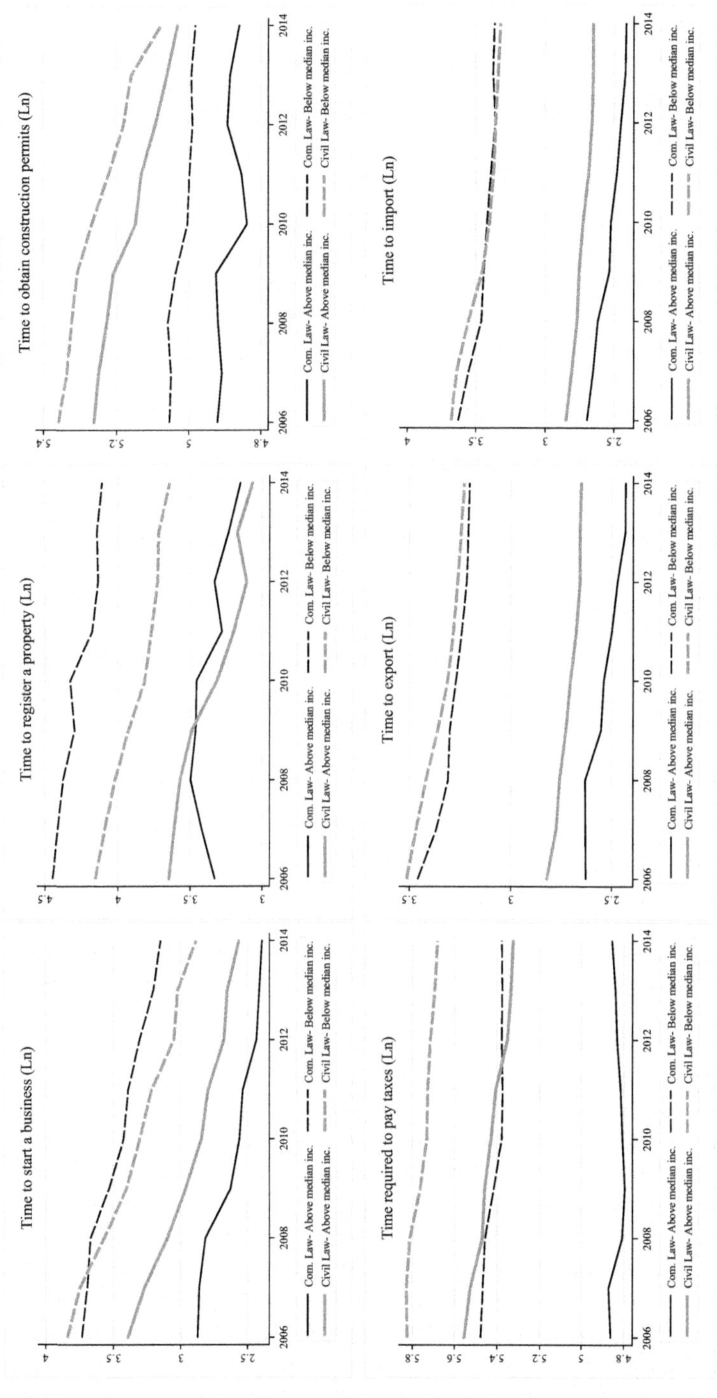

Fig. 5.2 (continued)

common law was superior to the civil law in the developed group, but that trend reversed since 2009. For less developed countries, the civil law group exhibits superiority over the British common law group during the whole period. Concerning the indicators of dealing with construction permits and paying taxes, the British common law group is always superior to the civil law group, irrespective of the countries' level of income. Finally, in the case of trading across borders in terms of both exporting and importing goods, the British common law is more efficient than the civil law in the group of developed countries, whereas there is no significant differences between the two in the developing countries' group over most of the years under scrutiny.

In order to deal more rigorously with whether legal reforms have led to a reduction in legal rules/regulations differences across legal traditions, panels A and B of Table 5.2 regress the respective values of the legal and regulatory indicators in 2006 and 2014 on the French, German and Scandinavian civil law dummies, taking the British common law as the omitted category. It is worth noting that the coefficients on the legal origin dummies represent mean differences with respect to the common law, which is the omitted legal family. Concerning the results for the initial year, the French civil law tradition has statistically significant negative differences at the 1% level in the strength of creditor rights and investor protection indices as well as in the recovery rate, relative to the British common law. As regards the regulatory indicators, the French civil law tradition is associated with a statistically significant higher time required to start a business, obtain construction permits and pay taxes (at the 1% level), and trade across borders in terms of both exporting and importing at the 5% level.

If we look at the coefficient on the French civil law dummy in 2014, there are still statistically significant differences with respect to the British common law in the indices of strength of creditor rights and investor protection, in the recovery rate and in the regulatory outcomes given by the time required to obtain construction permits, pay taxes and both export and import. It is worth highlighting the fact that the statistically significant differences have either diminished in these seven dimensions or vanished in the case of the time required to start a business between 2006 and 2014. The pattern observed in the evolution of the mean differences between the legal and regulatory scores of the French civil law versus the British common law is favorable to the existence of convergence trends conducive to the catching-up of the former to the latter.

In the case of the German civil law, in 2006 there are statistically significant differences in the strength of investor protection index, depth of credit information index, time required to enforce a contract, time required to obtain construction permits, pay taxes and import, relative to the British common law. It is interesting to point out that in the case of information sharing, contract enforcement and importing goods is the score of the German civil law superior to the British common law. When we look at the mean differences in 2014 between the German civil law and the British common law, it is worth noting that there are statistically significant improvements in several dimensions. As a matter of fact, the relative lower level of investor protection and the higher time required to obtain construction permits in 2006 are no longer apparent at the end of the period under analysis. In addition, the

Table 5.2 Differences in scores across legal traditions in 2006 and 2014

	Creditor rights	Investor protection	Credit information	Recovery rate	Contract enforc.	Starting a business	Registering a property	Construction permits	Paying taxes	Time to export	Time to import
	(1)	(2)	(3)	(4)	(5)	(6)	(7)	(8)	(9)	(10)	(11)
Panel A: Mean differences in 2006											
French commercial code	−3.219***	−1.79***	0.015	−11.549***	0.037	0.415***	0.088	0.356***	0.535***	0.239**	0.251**
	(0.324)	(0.268)	(0.39)	(4.153)	(0.081)	(0.144)	(0.212)	(0.08)	(0.124)	(0.097)	(0.113)
German commercial code	−0.483	−0.769**	1.163*	6.13	−0.251**	0.117	0.016	0.315**	0.53***	−0.232	−0.358**
	(0.519)	(0.322)	(0.636)	(6.273)	(0.122)	(0.166)	(0.367)	(0.138)	(0.193)	(0.148)	(0.168)
Scandinavian commercial code	0.348	−0.214	2.626***	44.884***	−0.482***	−1.154***	−1.834***	−0.32	−0.255	−0.959***	−1.27***
	(0.429)	(0.441)	(0.355)	(5.318)	(0.134)	(0.236)	(0.611)	(0.229)	(0.195)	(0.111)	(0.133)
Constant	6.852***	5.874***	1.574***	35.896***	6.35***	3.332***	3.928***	4.992***	5.198***	3.073***	3.195***
	(0.263)	(0.228)	(0.305)	(3.484)	(0.066)	(0.114)	(0.185)	(0.063)	(0.102)	(0.077)	(0.094)
R^2	0.43	0.26	0.06	0.19	0.07	0.13	0.07	0.14	0.13	0.17	0.2
Observations	168	168	168	168	168	168	168	168	167	168	168
Panel A: Mean differences in 2014											
French commercial code	−2.67***	−1.34***	0.595	−10.061**	0.045	0.055	−0.068	0.201**	0.434***	0.229**	0.241**
	(0.323)	(0.258)	(0.374)	(3.936)	(0.073)	(0.159)	(0.189)	(0.09)	(0.109)	(0.092)	(0.107)
German commercial code	−0.544	−0.444	2.153***	12.052**	−0.243**	−0.241	−0.808***	0.084	0.325**	−0.211*	−0.3**
	(0.472)	(0.327)	(0.338)	(5.818)	(0.105)	(0.223)	(0.271)	(0.153)	(0.141)	(0.125)	(0.147)
Scandinavian commercial code	0.267	0.3	1.3***	47.215***	−0.477***	−0.686**	−1.687***	−0.48***	−0.403***	−0.704***	−0.991***
	(0.518)	(0.25)	(0.349)	(4.167)	(0.091)	(0.265)	(0.43)	(0.135)	(0.124)	(0.105)	(0.121)
Constant	7.333***	5.96***	2.9***	38.485***	6.353***	2.769***	3.629***	4.921***	5.116***	2.818***	2.889***
	(0.236)	(0.204)	(0.298)	(3.296)	(0.059)	(0.123)	(0.157)	(0.07)	(0.084)	(0.069)	(0.084)
R^2	0.3	0.16	0.08	0.2	0.07	0.02	0.1	0.06	0.11	0.12	0.14
Observations	179	179	179	179	179	179	179	179	179	179	179

Notes: Robust standard errors are in parentheses

*, ** and *** denote statistical significance at the 10, 5 and 1% levels, respectively

positive difference in the index of depth of credit information has increased and the higher time required to pay taxes has fallen. Most importantly, by the end of the period considered, German civil law countries on average have improved in three dimensions (relative to the British common law) in which there were no statistically significant differences in 2006. These dimensions are the efficiency of debt enforcement as measured by the recovery rate, and the time required to register a property as well as to export. In the two dimensions of contract enforcement by courts and importing, the relative superiority of the German civil law has remained fairly unaltered. Therefore, as in the case of the French civil law group, German civil law countries have tended to converge to the legal and regulatory standards of the "winning origin", and in the case of the recovery rate, registering property and exporting, they have overtaken them.

In the case of the Scandinavian civil law tradition, its relative superiority between 2006 and 2014 either remained fairly unchanged as in the case of efficiency of debt enforcement (recovery rate), contract enforcement by courts and time required to register a property, or slightly fell as in the case of information sharing, time required to start a business and trade across borders for both exporting and importing goods. In addition, in the two areas of obtaining construction permits and paying taxes for which there were not statistically significant initial differences, the Scandinavian civil law tradition exhibits superiority at the end of the period relative to the British common law. Overall, there is not a consistent pattern of convergence (in this case from above) of the Scandinavian civil law group to the legal and regulatory standards of the British common law. This is because, even though there has been a slight reduction in the extent of relative superiority of the Scandinavian civil law tradition in some of the legal and regulatory dimensions, this legal tradition has become superior in two areas in which it was not at the beginning of the period.

Taken as a whole, we find evidence of a legal origin effect on the legal and regulatory rules in 2006 which, despite the presence of some catching-up of civil law countries to the average standards of common law countries, still persists in 2014 for many of the indicators studied. The next section tries to shed more light on the extent of convergence observed among the legal traditions in each legal and regulatory indicator during the period 2006–2014.

5.3 Has There Been Convergence in Legal and Regulatory Standards Among Legal Traditions over the Period 2006–2014?

Having determined whether there are differences in legal and regulatory indicators among the legal origins in the initial and final years of the time span examined, we shift the focus to investigate how these differences have behaved over the period 2006–2014. This allows us to establish whether there is evidence of convergence in legal and regulatory standards among legal traditions. For that purpose, Table 5.3

Table 5.3 Comparing legal changes between 2006 and 2014 across legal traditions

		Ratio 2014/2006 (Mean value)		Mean differences			Difference 2014–2006 (Mean value)		Mean differences		
		Civil law tradition (on the left)	Common law	Value	St. Error	P-value	Civil law tradition (on the left)	Common law	Value	St. Error	P-value
French commercial code	Creditor rights	1.407	1.105	0.302	0.112	0.01	1.144	0.481	0.663	0.261	0.01
	Investor protection	1.174	1.059	0.115	0.061	0.06	0.548	0.228	0.320	0.152	0.04
	Credit information	1.280	1.155	0.124	0.174	0.48	2.044	1.426	0.619	0.345	0.08
	Recovery rate	2.093	1.706	0.387	0.956	0.69	3.601	1.378	2.223	1.114	0.05
	Contract enforc.	1.004	0.997	0.007	0.005	0.16	0.020	−0.027	0.047	0.030	0.13
	Starting a business	0.753	0.833	−0.080	0.037	0.03	−0.945	−0.561	−0.384	0.133	0.00
	Registering a property	0.892	0.921	−0.029	0.028	0.30	−0.471	−0.369	−0.102	0.127	0.42
	Construction permits	0.960	0.978	−0.018	0.014	0.21	−0.227	−0.114	−0.113	0.073	0.12
	Paying taxes	0.979	0.994	−0.014	0.009	0.12	−0.135	−0.051	−0.084	0.053	0.12
	Time to export	0.927	0.930	−0.003	0.014	0.83	−0.242	−0.223	−0.020	0.046	0.67
	Time to import	0.917	0.922	−0.005	0.016	0.75	−0.288	−0.263	−0.025	0.056	0.66
German commercial code	Creditor rights	1.115	1.105	0.010	0.071	0.89	0.421	0.481	−0.060	0.314	0.85
	Investor protection	1.088	1.059	0.029	0.047	0.53	0.411	0.228	0.183	0.154	0.24

(continued)

Table 5.3 (continued)

		Ratio 2014/2006 (Mean value)		Mean differences			Difference 2014–2006 (Mean value)		Mean differences		
		Civil law tradition (on the left)	Common law	Value	St. Error	P-value	Civil law tradition (on the left)	Common law	Value	St. Error	P-value
	Credit information	1.115	1.155	–0.040	0.096	0.68	2.316	1.426	0.890	0.548	0.11
	Recovery rate	1.340	1.706	−0.366	1.059	0.73	8.511	1.378	7.133	1.793	0.00
	Contract enforc.	1.003	0.997	0.006	0.008	0.45	0.011	−0.027	0.039	0.052	0.46
	Starting a business	0.738	0.833	−0.094	0.061	0.13	−0.922	−0.561	−0.361	0.185	0.06
	Registering a property	0.747	0.921	−0.174	0.050	0.00	−1.123	−0.369	−0.754	0.222	0.00
	Construction permits	0.944	0.978	−0.034	0.016	0.04	−0.302	−0.114	−0.188	0.085	0.03
	Paying taxes	0.955	0.994	−0.039	0.012	0.00	−0.287	−0.051	−0.236	0.072	0.00
	Time to export	0.930	0.930	−0.001	0.023	0.98	−0.233	−0.223	−0.011	0.078	0.89
	Time to import	0.923	0.922	0.001	0.026	0.96	−0.247	−0.263	0.016	0.089	0.86
Scandinavian commercial code	Creditor rights	1.054	1.105	−0.051	0.119	0.67	0.400	0.481	−0.081	0.528	0.88
	Investor protection	1.131	1.059	0.072	0.084	0.40	0.600	0.228	0.372	0.258	0.15
	Credit information	1.000	1.155	−0.155	0.129	0.24	0.000	1.426	−1.426	0.874	0.11
	Recovery rate	1.071	1.706	−0.636	2.065	0.76	4.920	1.378	3.542	2.039	0.09

	Contract enforc.	1.003	0.997	0.007	0.016	0.68	0.008	−0.027	0.036	0.100	0.72
	Starting a business	0.950	0.833	0.117	0.103	0.26	−0.096	−0.561	0.465	0.293	0.12
	Registering a property	0.876	0.921	−0.045	0.085	0.60	−0.152	−0.369	0.216	0.350	0.54
	Construction permits	0.956	0.978	−0.022	0.027	0.41	−0.231	−0.114	−0.117	0.138	0.40
	Paying taxes	0.958	0.994	−0.035	0.022	0.12	−0.229	−0.051	−0.179	0.118	0.14
	Time to export	1.000	0.930	0.070	0.034	0.04	0.000	−0.223	0.223	0.107	0.04
	Time to import	0.987	0.922	0.065	0.043	0.14	−0.027	−0.263	0.236	0.141	0.10

reports the mean value of both the ratio of 2014 to 2006 scores and the difference between the 2014 and 2006 scores for each of the 11 legal and regulatory indicators studied. Both the ratio and the difference are calculated for each civil law group and the British common law. The respective ratios and differences are used to test for mean differences between each civil law group and the common law group. Since the initial scores of the legal and regulatory indicators are usually worse for the French civil law group relative to those of the British common law, if the ratio is significantly higher in the former with respect to the latter for the first four indicators, this would imply that civil law countries have improved with respect to the 2006 scores more than British common law countries, which is a sign of convergence. The same can be inferred if the ratio is significantly lower for the measure of contract enforcement and the regulatory measures given by the time required to start a business, register a property, obtain construction permits, pay taxes and trade across borders in terms of exporting and importing goods.

As regards the French civil law, with the exception of the contract enforcement indicator, the scores of the legal and regulatory indicators in 2014 have improved over those in 2006. This is reflected in the fact that the mean value of the ratio is well above one or the mean differences between 2014 and 2006 are positive for the indices of strength of creditor rights and investor protection, depth of information disclosure, and the recovery rate, whereas the ratio is below one and the differences are negative in the case of time to start a business, register a property, obtain construction permits, pay taxes and trade across borders. This confirms the fact that investor and creditor rights protection, information sharing and the efficiency of debt enforcement have increased, whereas the regulatory burden related to starting a business, registering a property, obtaining construction permits, paying taxes and trading across borders has been lowered in French civil law countries.

In the case of the British common law, the ratio is also greater than one and the difference between the 2014 and 2006 scores is positive for creditor and investor protection, information disclosure, and the recovery rate, while the ratio is below one and the difference between the 2014 and 2006 scores is negative for contract enforcement and the regulatory outcomes related to starting a business, registering a property, obtaining construction permits, paying taxes and trading across borders. Hence, the scores of all the legal and regulatory indicators have improved in this legal tradition, though in general to a much lower extent than the French civil law group. This is expected to be the case because the initial scores of the French civil law tradition were much worse than those of the British common law for most of the legal and regulatory indicators considered.

In an attempt to establish whether, overall, French civil law countries have converged or diverged over the period 2006–2014, Table 5.3 reports the tests for mean differences in both the 2014/2006 ratios and the differences between the 2014 and 2006 scores of the average French civil law country relative to the average British common law country. When we look at the differences in the 2014/2006 ratio, there are statistically significant differences in the two indicators of law on the books (indices of strength of creditor rights and investor protection), and time to start a business. In the case of the differences between the two legal traditions in their respective 2014–2006 differences, they are statistically significant in the same three indicators as above and two additional ones: depth of credit information index and the recovery rate. From this analysis, we can confirm the existence of convergence between the French civil law and the British common law in these important dimensions of the legal system. In the other areas, with the exception of time to enforce contracts, there is also an indication of convergence since mean differences have the expected sign for convergence (i.e., improvement in French civil law countries is greater, on average, than in common law countries).

Concerning the results for the German civil law tradition, the scores associated with the legal and regulatory rules and outcomes between 2006 and 2014 have improved in all legal and regulatory indicators (to a lower extent than in French civil law countries), with the exception of contract enforcement. When we look at the differences in the 2014/2006 ratios between the German civil law and the British common law, they are statistically significant only in three regulatory outcomes: time required to register a property, time required to obtain construction permits and time required to pay taxes. As regards the differences in the respective difference between the 2014 and 2006 scores of the German civil law and the British common law, they are statistically significant in the same three indicators as above and in another two: debt enforcement efficiency measured through recovery rate and starting a business. In the areas of investor protection and credit information disclosure, the mean differences, despite being statistically insignificant, exhibit the expected sign for convergence, as given by a higher improvement in the legal score in German civil law countries relative to the common law.

In the case of the Scandinavian civil law group, the ratio of the 2014–2006 scores is very close to one in most indicators, and the respective differences between the 2014 and 2006 scores are very small. This lower evidence of legal change for this legal tradition stems from the fact that it already scored very high at the beginning of the period, as argued above. When we look at the differences in the ratio for this legal tradition relative to the British common law, the evidence supports the existence of statistically significant differences in only one indicator: time required to export. Likewise, there are statistically significant differences in the difference recorded over the period 2006–2014 between the Scandinavian civil law and the British common law in time required to export and debt enforcement efficiency, as measured by the recovery rate.

Taken as a whole, for those indicators that exhibit convergence between the civil law tradition and the British common law, the legacy of legal origins did not prevent cross-legal tradition differences from narrowing down over the past decade. This would contradict the Legal Origins Theory that predicts the persistence over time of the differences in legal and regulatory standards across legal traditions.

5.4 More on Convergence: Robustness Checks

In this section we provide additional evidence on the extent of convergence in legal and regulatory standards across legal traditions. Firstly, Table 5.4 regresses the average annual rate of change in each of the legal and regulatory indicators over the period 2006–2014 on French, German and Scandinavian civil law dummies, taking the British common law as the omitted category. The results are presented in three panels: Panel A with no additional control, Panel B with the average growth rate of GDP as an additional control, and Panel C with the log of GDP per capita at the beginning of the period. If the coefficients on the civil law categories are statistically significant and positive for the indices of creditor rights, investor protection, information sharing and the recovery rate, or significantly negative for the other legal and regulatory outcomes, there would be indications that there is a higher number of legal and regulatory reforms in the good direction in civil law countries relative to the British common law. Such a result would support the presence of convergence to the average legal and regulatory standards of the common law group. Since the results are fairly robust across specifications, in the exposition we focus on those in Panel C for the specification that controls for log initial GDP per capita.

Concerning the French civil law group, there is evidence of higher reforms conducive to the strengthening of creditor rights and investor protection, as well as to lowering the regulatory burden associated with starting a business, obtaining construction permits and paying taxes, relative to the British common law. This appears to support the fact that policymakers in the lawmaking sphere tend to imitate legal instruments related to the common law, which according to the Legal Origins Theory is the winning origin. This strategy is risky since if the common law does not systematically lead to better legal rules and institutions than the French civil law, the adoption of common law tools does not ensure an improvement in legal system efficiency and in the performance of the real and financial economy.

Similar evidence of more reforms are found for the German civil law group in the strengthening of creditor rights and lowering the regulatory burden associated with registering a property, obtaining construction permits and paying taxes. As regards the Scandinavian civil law group, there is an improvement in the strength of creditor rights index, whereas the regulatory burden associated with starting a business and trading across borders in terms of exporting and importing have worsened relative to the British common law. The reason for this must be sought in the relatively high initial scores in the time to both export and import exhibited by Scandinavian civil law countries, which have converged from above to the standards of common law countries over the period 2006–2014.

Secondly, Table 5.5 presents similar regressions to those presented in Table 5.4, but replacing the dependent variable with the ratio of the 2014–2006 scores in the

Table 5.4 Convergence among legal traditions: average of the annual rate of change in legal rules/regulations (2006–2014)

	French civil law		German civil law		Scand law			
	Coeff.	SEs	Coeff.	SEs	Coeff.	SEs	R^2	Obs
Panel A: Without control variable								
Creditor rights	0.032***	(0.01)	−0.001	(0.008)	−0.006	(0.006)	0.058	178
Investor protection	0.011**	(0.005)	0.002	(0.005)	0.007	(0.01)	0.021	179
Credit information	0.03*	(0.017)	0.014	(0.024)	−0.028***	(0.01)	0.032	109
Recovery rate	0.012	(0.058)	−0.02	(0.055)	−0.05	(0.054)	0.003	159
Contract enforcement	0.001	(0.001)	0.001	(0.001)	0.001	(0.003)	0.011	179
Starting a business	−0.01*	(0.005)	−0.016	(0.01)	0.016***	(0.005)	0.041	179
Registering a property	−0.005	(0.004)	−0.036**	(0.017)	−0.002	(0.024)	0.072	178
Construction permits	−0.002	(0.002)	−0.005*	(0.002)	−0.003	(0.003)	0.02	179
Paying taxes	−0.003	(0.002)	−0.006***	(0.002)	−0.006	(0.005)	0.044	179
Time to export	0.00	(0.002)	−0.001	(0.004)	0.009***	(0.001)	0.02	179
Time to import	−0.001	(0.002)	−0.001	(0.004)	0.008***	(0.002)	0.014	179
Panel B: Control variable is average growth rate of GDP								
Creditor rights	0.031***	(0.009)	0.003	(0.008)	0.007	(0.01)	0.091	177
Investor protection	0.01**	(0.005)	0.003	(0.005)	0.011	(0.01)	0.033	178
Credit information	0.03*	(0.016)	0.025	(0.025)	0.005	(0.019)	0.127	109
Recovery rate	0.011	(0.056)	−0.019	(0.058)	−0.044	(0.064)	0.003	159
Contract enforcement	0.001	(0.001)	0.001	(0.001)	0.00	(0.003)	0.025	178
Starting a business	−0.01*	(0.005)	−0.016*	(0.01)	0.014**	(0.006)	0.046	178
Registering a property	−0.005	(0.005)	−0.036**	(0.018)	0.00	(0.024)	0.074	177
Construction permits	−0.002	(0.002)	−0.005**	(0.002)	−0.003	(0.003)	0.023	178
Paying taxes	−0.003	(0.002)	−0.006***	(0.002)	−0.005	(0.004)	0.047	178
Time to export	0.00	(0.002)	−0.001	(0.004)	0.007***	(0.002)	0.042	178
Time to import	−0.001	(0.002)	−0.001	(0.004)	0.007***	(0.002)	0.02	178

(continued)

Table 5.4 (continued)

	French civil law		German civil law		Scand law			
	Coeff.	SEs	Coeff.	SEs	Coeff.	SEs	R^2	Obs
Panel C: Control variable is Log of GDP per capita in 2006								
Creditor rights	0.029***	(0.009)	0.017**	(0.008)	0.03***	(0.01)	0.194	174
Investor protection	0.011**	(0.005)	0.004	(0.006)	0.011	(0.011)	0.028	175
Credit information	0.03	(0.02)	0.014	(0.024)	−0.025	(0.017)	0.034	108
Recovery rate	0.014	(0.058)	0.016	(0.038)	0.024	(0.024)	0.037	156
Contract enforcement	0.001	(0.001)	0.00	(0.001)	0.00	(0.003)	0.025	175
Starting a business	−0.011**	(0.006)	−0.016	(0.01)	0.015**	(0.007)	0.044	175
Registering a property	−0.005	(0.005)	−0.035*	(0.018)	−0.001	(0.024)	0.072	174
Construction permits	−0.003**	(0.001)	−0.005*	(0.003)	−0.003	(0.003)	0.035	175
Paying taxes	−0.003*	(0.002)	−0.006***	(0.002)	−0.006	(0.005)	0.044	175
Time to export	0.00	(0.002)	−0.001	(0.004)	0.008***	(0.002)	0.026	175
Time to import	−0.002	(0.002)	−0.001	(0.004)	0.007**	(0.003)	0.02	175

Notes: Regressions include a constant term, which is omitted for space considerations. Robust standard errors are in parentheses
*, ** and *** denote statistical significance at the 10, 5 and 1% levels, respectively

Table 5.5 Convergence among legal traditions: ratio 2014/2006 in legal rules/regulations

	French civil law		German civil law		Scand law			
	Coeff.	SEs	Coeff.	SEs	Coeff.	SEs	R^2	Obs
Panel A: Without control variable								
Creditor rights	0.302***	(0.093)	0.01	(0.072)	−0.051	(0.047)	0.059	166
Investor protection	0.115**	(0.051)	0.029	(0.045)	0.072	(0.086)	0.026	168
Credit information	0.124	(0.147)	−0.04	(0.086)	−0.155**	(0.065)	0.028	66
Recovery rate	0.387	(0.921)	−0.366	(0.677)	−0.636	(0.665)	0.004	148
Contract enforcement	0.007	(0.005)	0.006	(0.008)	0.007	(0.024)	0.012	168
Starting a business	−0.08**	(0.038)	−0.094	(0.06)	0.117***	(0.039)	0.05	168
Registering a property	−0.029	(0.027)	−0.174***	(0.064)	−0.045	(0.161)	0.074	166
Construction permits	−0.018	(0.012)	−0.034*	(0.018)	−0.022	(0.025)	0.019	168
Paying taxes	−0.014*	(0.009)	−0.039***	(0.014)	−0.035	(0.034)	0.049	167
Time to export	−0.003	(0.013)	−0.001	(0.027)	0.07***	(0.01)	0.021	168
Time to import	−0.005	(0.016)	0.001	(0.027)	0.065***	(0.017)	0.016	168
Panel B: Control variable is average growth rate of GDP								
Creditor rights	0.296***	(0.088)	0.053	(0.071)	0.092	(0.101)	0.1	165
Investor protection	0.112**	(0.05)	0.045	(0.046)	0.126	(0.09)	0.046	167
Credit information	0.132	(0.146)	0.001	(0.072)	−0.061	(0.06)	0.055	66
Recovery rate	0.389	(0.922)	−0.384	(0.728)	−0.689	(0.831)	0.004	148
Contract enforcement	0.007	(0.005)	0.005	(0.008)	0.002	(0.024)	0.027	167
Starting a business	−0.081**	(0.038)	−0.098	(0.062)	0.103**	(0.046)	0.055	167
Registering a property	−0.03	(0.028)	−0.172**	(0.066)	−0.039	(0.161)	0.075	165
Construction permits	−0.017	(0.013)	−0.036**	(0.018)	−0.027	(0.026)	0.022	167
Paying taxes	−0.014	(0.009)	−0.04***	(0.013)	−0.041	(0.035)	0.057	166
Time to export	−0.002	(0.013)	−0.004	(0.028)	0.058***	(0.013)	0.035	167
Time to import	−0.005	(0.016)	−0.001	(0.028)	0.059***	(0.02)	0.019	167

(continued)

Table 5.5 (continued)

	French civil law		German civil law		Scand law			
	Coeff.	SEs	Coeff.	SEs	Coeff.	SEs	R^2	Obs
Panel C: Control variable is Log of GDP per capita in 2006								
Creditor rights	0.27***	(0.086)	0.183**	(0.081)	0.286***	(0.106)	0.174	163
Investor protection	0.115**	(0.05)	0.052	(0.051)	0.115	(0.096)	0.034	165
Credit information	0.107	(0.139)	−0.026	(0.095)	−0.095	(0.095)	0.043	65
Recovery rate	0.42	(0.932)	−0.052	(0.461)	−0.033	(0.375)	0.01	146
Contract enforcement	0.007	(0.005)	0.003	(0.008)	0	(0.024)	0.029	165
Starting a business	−0.086**	(0.037)	−0.081	(0.067)	0.143**	(0.055)	0.059	165
Registering a property	−0.032	(0.028)	−0.164**	(0.07)	−0.026	(0.163)	0.078	163
Construction permits	−0.024**	(0.011)	−0.034*	(0.02)	−0.022	(0.028)	0.033	165
Paying taxes	−0.015*	(0.009)	−0.038***	(0.015)	−0.034	(0.035)	0.05	164
Time to export	−0.002	(0.014)	−0.004	(0.029)	0.063***	(0.016)	0.024	165
Time to import	−0.009	(0.016)	0.002	(0.03)	0.066***	(0.023)	0.019	165

Notes: Regressions include a constant term, which is omitted for space considerations. Robust standard errors are in parentheses
*, ** and *** denote statistical significance at the 10, 5 and 1% levels, respectively

respective legal and regulatory indicator. Panel A includes no additional controls, Panel B incorporates the average growth rate of GDP as an additional control, and Panel C adds the log of GDP per capita in 2006. If we again focus on the specification that controls for log initial GDP per capita, the evidence of higher reforms in civil law countries is apparent in fairly the same indicators as those pinpointed in Table 5.4.

Finally, we also conduct analyses of absolute and conditional β-convergence as well as σ-convergence. Table 5.6 presents the results from regressing the ratio of the 2014 to 2006 scores on the initial score for each of the eleven legal and regulatory indicators considered. Panel A corresponds to the absolute β-convergence specification that contains no additional control, whereas panels B and C represent the conditional β-convergence specification that introduces the average annual growth rate in GDP and the initial log-level of GDP per capita, respectively. The existence of a statistically significant negative coefficient on the initial score would support the hypothesis of β-convergence, which implies that those countries with a lower initial score would experience greater legal change, as given by a higher 2014/2006 ratio.

It is worth noting that in the case of absolute β-convergence, there is supportive evidence for this hypothesis for every single legal and regulatory indicator considered. The coefficient on the initial score is statistically significant at the 1% level for the indices of strength of creditor rights and investor protection, contract enforcement and the regulatory outcomes associated with registering a property, obtaining construction permits, paying taxes and trading across borders in terms of both exporting and importing goods. In addition, the absolute β-convergence effect is statistically significant at the 5% level for the depth of credit information index, and at the 10% level for the efficiency of debt enforcement (as measured by the recovery rate) and time required to start a business. The evidence shown in Panels B and C also broadly supports the hypothesis of conditional β-convergence. As a matter of fact, the coefficient on the initial score is statistically significant at conventional confidence levels for all the legal and regulatory indicators, except for starting a business in Panel B and the recovery rate in Panel C.

Concerning the extent of σ-convergence at the aggregate level, Figure 5.3 depicts the coefficient of variation of each legal and regulatory indicator over the period 2006–2014. The evidence clearly points to a reduction in the coefficient of variation in the case of the indices of strength of creditor rights, investor protection and depth of credit information, and the recovery rate over the whole period, whereas in the case of contract enforcement and time required to pay taxes the fall is observed since 2009 and 2008, respectively. For all these legal and regulatory indicators σ-convergence has taken place, which implies a fall in the disparities in legal and regulatory scores among all the legal traditions. In contrast, for the regulatory outcomes associated with starting a business, registering a property, obtaining construction

Table 5.6 Beta convergence across legal traditions

	Initial value (2006) of the legal/reg. indicator			
	Coeff.	SEs	R^2	Obs
Panel A: Without control variable				
Creditor rights	−0.104***	(0.028)	0.15	166
Investor protection	−0.067***	(0.024)	0.11	168
Credit information	−0.349**	(0.153)	0.42	66
Recovery rate	−0.048*	(0.024)	0.06	148
Contract enforcement	−0.023***	(0.006)	0.13	168
Starting a business	−0.036*	(0.021)	0.02	168
Registering a property	−0.044***	(0.014)	0.07	166
Construction permits	−0.046***	(0.016)	0.09	168
Paying taxes	−0.037***	(0.007)	0.26	167
Time to export	−0.028***	(0.011)	0.04	168
Time to import	−0.026***	(0.009)	0.04	168
Panel B: Control variable is average growth rate of GDP				
Creditor rights	−0.096***	(0.022)	0.17	165
Investor protection	−0.064***	(0.022)	0.11	167
Credit information	−0.344**	(0.153)	0.44	66
Recovery rate	−0.058*	(0.031)	0.07	148
Contract enforcement	−0.023***	(0.006)	0.15	167
Starting a business	−0.034	(0.022)	0.02	167
Registering a property	−0.045***	(0.014)	0.07	165
Construction permits	−0.046***	(0.017)	0.09	167
Paying taxes	−0.038***	(0.007)	0.26	166
Time to export	−0.024**	(0.012)	0.04	167
Time to import	−0.027***	(0.01)	0.04	167
Panel C: Control variable is Log of GDP per capita in 2006				
Creditor rights	−0.079***	(0.023)	0.21	163
Investor protection	−0.073***	(0.023)	0.11	165
Credit information	−0.351**	(0.154)	0.43	65
Recovery rate	−0.063	(0.041)	0.06	146
Contract enforcement	−0.023***	(0.006)	0.14	165
Starting a business	−0.046**	(0.022)	0.03	165
Registering a property	−0.059***	(0.016)	0.13	163
Construction permits	−0.04***	(0.013)	0.08	165
Paying taxes	−0.042***	(0.007)	0.30	164
Time to export	−0.045**	(0.02)	0.05	165
Time to import	−0.049***	(0.016)	0.06	165

Notes: The dependent variable is the ratio of the 2014 to 2006 scores for each of the respective legal and regulatory indicator. Regressions include a constant term, which is omitted for space considerations. Robust standard errors are in parentheses

*, ** and *** denote statistical significance at the 10, 5 and 1% levels, respectively

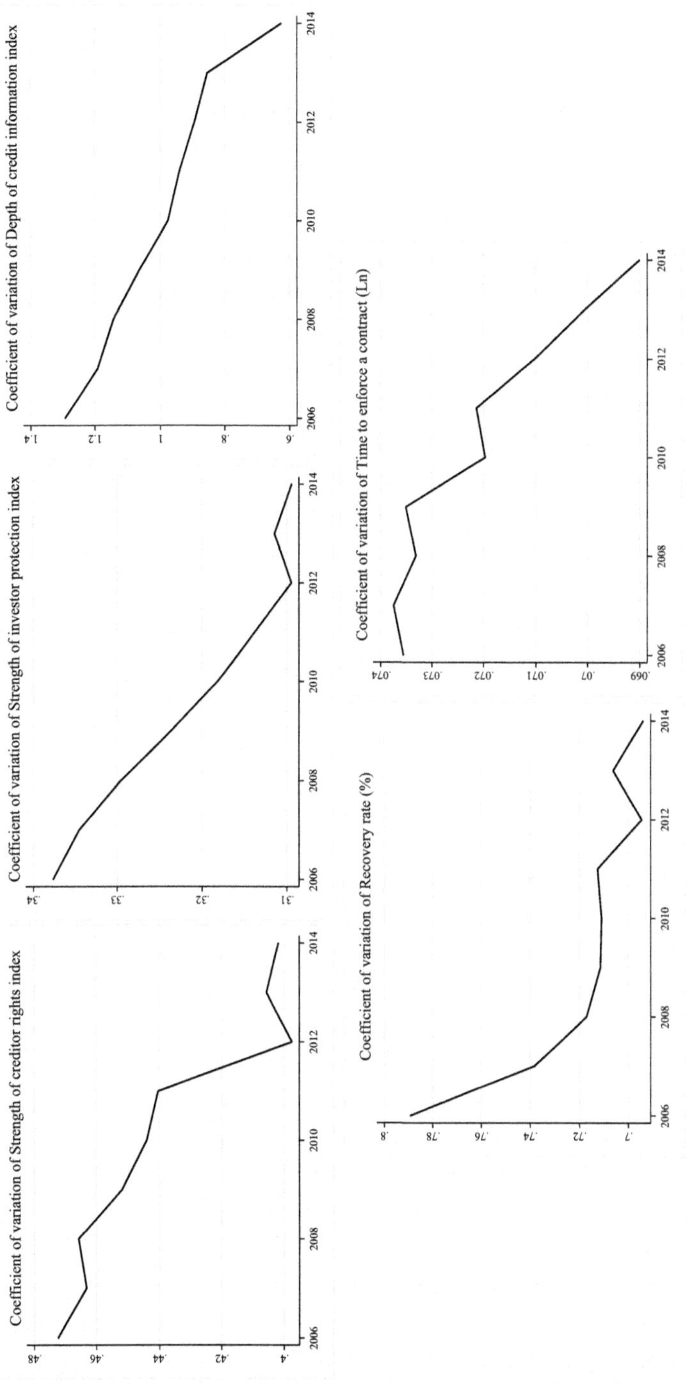

Fig. 5.3 Sigma convergence

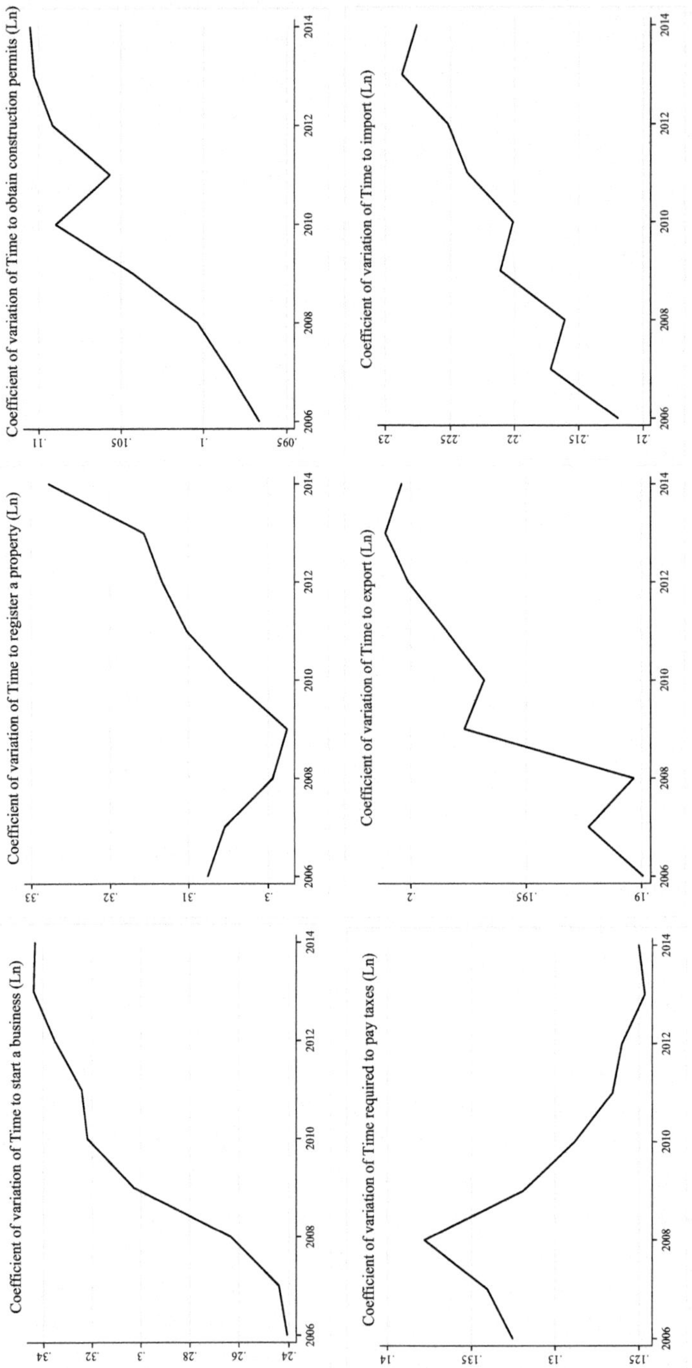

Fig. 5.3 (continued)

permits and trading across borders, the coefficient of variation has increased, and as a result, σ-convergence has not occurred at the aggregate level.

Overall, there appears to be widespread evidence of global convergence across legal traditions, particularly when one looks at the definition of β-convergence. This again indicates that the legal origins legacy has not prevented legal and regulatory standards from converging among legal traditions.

Chapter 6
Legal Rules Variation and Countries' Economic and Financial Performance

Abstract Considering the large number of legal reforms implemented over the period 2006–2014, particularly in French civil law countries, this chapter aims to establish whether variation in legal rules and regulatory outcomes have been associated with an improvement in financial and economic developmental outcomes. By estimating panel specifications using a fixed effects estimator with data averaged over 3-year periods, the evidence does not support the existence of a clear-cut effect of legal rules and regulatory indicators on financial and economic performance. This finding appears to accord with the view of those that question the widespread tendency in the lawmaking sphere over the past decade to imitate tools related to the common law (the pretended winning origin). If the common law does not systematically lead to better legal rules and institutions than the French civil law (as the recent critical literature suggests), it is far from clear that adopting common-law tools will improve the efficiency of the legal system and the performance of the economy.

Nowadays it is widely assumed that legal reforms can make a difference in economic development by creating a friendly regulatory environment for investors and entrepreneurs. This view that "law matters" is one of the legacies of the Legal Origins research agenda and is sponsored by the Doing Business Project (World Bank 2004a). This proposition is having great impact in the policy arena, as witnessed by the fact that the Doing Business Project counted 2500 legal reforms aimed at making it easier to do business since 2006 (World Bank 2015a). However, the supporting evidence for this proposition is largely based only on cross-section regressions. Some researchers are even challenging the view that legal reforms materialize into better economic performance (Armour et al. 2009b; Deakin et al. 2012). Therefore, it is crucial to systematically analyze the relationship between variation in legal rules and countries' economic and financial performance. Although it is hard to establish causal relationships using country-level data, a thorough panel analysis employing all the data at hand can help shed light on this issue. For this exercise, we benefit from the data collection effort conducted by the Doing Business Project, which has already compiled a panel data of legal and regulatory indicators covering more than 180 countries over a period of more than 10 years. Using econometric techniques based on the fixed effects estimator we aim to clarify: (1) whether improvements in legal indicators are associated with better

D. Oto-Peralías, D. Romero-Ávila, *Legal Traditions, Legal Reforms and Economic Performance*, Contributions to Economics, DOI 10.1007/978-3-319-67041-6_6

economic and financial outcomes; (2) which legal indicators are more strongly linked to variations in the economy; and (3) in which contexts or circumstances the effect takes place (for instance, whether the effect occurs in common law countries or in civil law countries, in developed or developing countries, in countries with strong or weak rule of law, etc.). Consequently, we now proceed to analyze these important questions.

6.1 The Effect of Legal Rules and Regulations on Economic and Financial Performance

We next report the results of estimations of the impact of legal rules and regulations over the period 2006–2014 on several proxies for financial and economic performance. Concerning the measurement of the evolution of legal rules and regulations, we employ the two law on the books measures given by the indices of strength of creditor rights and investor protection, the index of depth of credit information, two measures of law enforcement as given by the recovery rate and the time required to enforce a contract, as well as regulatory outcomes associated with the time required to start a business, register a property, obtain construction permits, pay taxes and trade across borders.

Given that we have time series data spanning only 9 years for the legal and regulatory indicators, we will make use of both annual and 3-year averaged data. The specification to be estimated is as follows:

$$Y_{i,t} = \beta \cdot legal\_rule_{i,t} + \delta \cdot X_{i,t} + \alpha_i + \theta_t + \varepsilon_{i,t}$$

where $Y_{i,t}$ denotes the respective financial or economic developmental outcome used, $legal\_rule_{i,t}$ stands for the respective legal rule or regulatory indicator employed, α_i and θ_t are sets of country and time specific effects and $X_{i,t}$ includes lagged GDP growth. Country fixed effects should control for countries' structural characteristics that do not vary over time, and time fixed effects account for common shocks that hit all countries in a specific period. Concerning the developmental outcomes, as measures of financial development we use stock market capitalization over GDP and stocks value traded over GDP to account for stock market size and stock market liquidity, respectively. As measures of financial intermediary development, we use domestic credit to private sector by banks, domestic credit provided by bank and nonbank financial institutions, and domestic credit to private sector provided by bank and non-bank financial institutions. The three credit measures are calculated as ratios over GDP. The other outcome variables are more associated with the real economy. They include the ratio of private gross fixed capital formation to GDP, new business density, the unemployment rate, the income Gini index, the ratio of exports plus imports to GDP, and the ratio of foreign direct investment to GDP.

Out of the eleven legal indicators, creditor rights, investor rights protection, credit information sharing, recovery rate and contract enforcement may be more directly related to the final outcomes associated with financial intermediary and stock market development than the other regulatory indicators, which may exhibit greater association with real economy final outcomes. For instance, trading across borders' regulations may be closely related to the ratio of exports and imports to GDP, and time required to start a business and get construction permits can affect the creation of start-ups (as measured by new business density) and the reduction of unemployment.

The use of the within estimator (also called Least Squares Dummy Variables—LSDV—estimator) enables us to determine whether legal rules and regulatory indicators have affected financial and economic developmental outcomes within countries. Standard errors are clustered by country to allow for the possibility of serial correlation of error terms, as recommended by Bertrand et al. (2004).

Since the existence of business cycle effects may bring higher pressure on countries so as to improve their legal and regulatory standards during a phase of economic upturn, our preferred specification will be the one that averages annual data over 3-year periods. This is tantamount to having only three time series observations per country. Between the specification with no additional control beyond the legal and regulatory outcomes included and the specification that incorporates lagged GDP growth as an additional control, we prefer the latter. Nonetheless, even though we focus in the exposition on the results from the 3-year averaged panel specification that incorporates lagged GDP growth, they are remarkably robust to using annual data and dropping lagged GDP growth. Panel data results using annual data as well as those for the specification with 3-year averaged data and no additional control are presented in Tables A.3–A.17 in the Appendix.

Table 6.1 presents the results using the LSDV estimator with data averaged over 3-year periods and lagged output growth as an additional control. It is worth noting that in very few cases are the coefficients statistically significant and with the right sign. Concerning the stock market development indicators, stronger creditor rights and investor protection, greater credit information disclosure and efficiency of debt enforcement as measured by the recovery rate are associated with a higher ratio of stocks value traded to GDP. In addition, greater time required to import goods also reduces the ratios of both listed and traded stocks to GDP. In the case of banking development, no single legal and regulatory indicator appears to explain the credit variables. Concerning the economic development outcomes, in very rare cases there is a statistically significant coefficient as well. Higher time to trade across borders appears to raise the unemployment rate, whereas a greater index of strength of creditor rights reduces income inequality, as measured by the Gini index. In the case of the law in action enforcement variables, there are no effects of any kind, except for the positive impact of the efficiency of debt enforcement on stocks value traded. Perhaps, the lack of an effect from the law enforcement variables is due to the fact that changes in these variables over time have been very small. The panel data analysis using annual data renders fairly similar results, though in this case we

Table 6.1 The effect of legal rules on financial and economic outcomes: LSDV model

	Creditor rights		Investor protection		Credit information		Recovery rate		Contract enforc.		Starting a business	
	Coeff/SE	Obs	Coeff/SE	Obs	Coeff/SE	Obs	Coeff/SE	Obs	Coeff/SE	Obs	Coeff/SE	Obs
	(1)		(2)		(3)		(4)		(5)		(6)	
Stock market capitalization	1.24	266	−0.908	266	−0.544	266	0.569	266	43.725	266	−6.165	266
	(2.752)		(5.32)		(2.113)		(0.482)		(53.998)		(5.621)	
Stocks traded	7.083**	243	10.905**	243	5.37**	243	1.337**	243	−55.403	243	−2.807	243
	(3.343)		(4.648)		(2.326)		(0.557)		(58.677)		(6.91)	
Domestic credit to private sector by banks	0.777	322	−0.197	322	0.802	322	0.073	322	−5.774	322	−2.012	322
	(0.831)		(1.18)		(0.941)		(0.152)		(13.712)		(1.749)	
Domestic credit provided by financial sector	0.382	322	−0.247	322	1.74	322	−0.006	322	−12.255	322	−2.06	322
	(1.045)		(1.662)		(1.099)		(0.253)		(16.371)		(2.107)	
Domestic credit to private sector	0.872	322	−0.178	322	0.768	322	0.077	322	−4.939	322	−2.189	322
	(0.777)		(1.295)		(0.95)		(0.152)		(13.643)		(1.794)	
Foreign direct investment	0.151	517	−0.19	517	−0.169	517	0.086	517	1.183	517	1.153	517
	(0.307)		(0.587)		(0.269)		(0.063)		(2.787)		(1.032)	
Trade	−0.641	498	0.227	498	−0.104	498	0.11	498	9.191	498	2.739	498
	(1.191)		(1.267)		(0.772)		(0.287)		(13.206)		(3.466)	
Private gross fixed capital formation	0.011	256	−0.563	256	−0.248	256	0.048	256	−6.34	256	−0.675	256
	(0.279)		(0.622)		(0.328)		(0.14)		(4.079)		(0.792)	
New business density	0.125	354	0.173	354	−0.068	354	0.016	354	−0.025	354	0.029	354
	(0.115)		(0.197)		(0.112)		(0.021)		(2.045)		(0.473)	
Unemployment rate	−0.102	481	−0.047	481	−0.167	481	−0.051	481	1.109	481	−0.017	481
	(0.08)		(0.264)		(0.142)		(0.047)		(2.631)		(0.264)	
Income GINI index	−0.541**	275	−0.13	275	−0.09	275	0.022	275	−1.697	275	−0.204	275
	(0.221)		(0.374)		(0.201)		(0.045)		(2.337)		(0.554)	

	Registering a property		Construction permits		Paying taxes		Time to export		Time to import	
	Coeff/SE	Obs	Coeff/SE	Obs	Coeff/SE	Obs	Coeff/SE	Obs	Coeff/SE	Obs
	(7)		(8)		(9)		(10)		(11)	
Stock market capitalization	2.423	266	−16.797	266	2.414	266	−31.734	266	−30.714*	266
	(3.959)		(21.02)		(11.462)		(25.907)		(18.147)	
Stocks traded	−5.794	243	11.107	243	−11.91	243	−35.785	243	−28.9*	243
	(4.929)		(19.266)		(13.65)		(31.368)		(17.273)	
Domestic credit to private sector by banks	0.312	322	−3.374	322	−0.641	320	−16.733	322	−8.695	322
	(2.048)		(3.535)		(3.948)		(14.087)		(6.875)	
Domestic credit provided by financial sector	0.145	322	−5.961	322	−8.501	320	−12.557	322	−4.102	322
	(1.962)		(3.69)		(5.153)		(15.076)		(8.011)	
Domestic credit to private sector	0.108	322	−3.61	322	−2.301	320	−17.61	322	−9.421	322
	(2.078)		(3.474)		(4.03)		(14.198)		(6.97)	
Foreign direct investment	1.123	517	−0.956	517	0.923	515	0.591	517	0.883	517
	(1.023)		(1.78)		(1.681)		(2.664)		(2.209)	
Trade	−0.723	498	4.931	498	−0.84	496	6.039	498	0.373	498
	(1.714)		(7.645)		(5.849)		(6.686)		(5.415)	
Private gross fixed capital formation	−0.609	256	−0.444	256	4.341**	256	2.326	256	2.728	256
	(0.927)		(1.858)		(1.78)		(2.803)		(2.232)	
New business density	−0.096	354	−0.921	354	0.882	352	−0.528	354	−0.528	354
	(0.232)		(0.688)		(0.707)		(1.749)		(1.132)	
Unemployment rate	−0.395	481	0.824	481	−0.421	479	2.393*	481	1.46*	481
	(0.411)		(0.802)		(0.739)		(1.235)		(0.804)	
Income GINI index	−0.044	275	1.097	275	−0.767	274	1.576	275	2.275	275
	(0.401)		(1.13)		(1.32)		(1.72)		(1.591)	

Notes: Panel specification with averaged annual data over 3-year periods (2006–2014). Clustered standard errors in parentheses. The regressions include the lag of GDP growth, country and period dummies, and a constant term. All these variables are omitted for space considerations

*, ** and *** denote statistical significance at the 10, 5 and 1% levels, respectively

are also able to uncover a negative impact of time required to enforce contracts on private physical investment and a marginally significant positive effect of information disclosure on domestic credit provided by bank and nonbank financial intermediaries. In addition, higher time required to obtain construction permits and pay taxes reduces the ratio of domestic credit provided by the financial sector to GDP. Time required to export also significantly reduces stock market capitalization and stocks value traded, while a lengthier process of importing both increases the unemployment rate and decreases domestic credit to the private sector. Detailed results for the panel with annual data are reported in Table A.4 in the Appendix.[1]

Overall, the broad picture that emerges from this analysis is one of no consistent pattern of a statistically significant effect of changes in legal and regulatory indicators on financial and economic development outcomes. This result stands in contrast to the widespread belief that reforms aiming to strengthen investor and creditor rights (and other market-friendly policies) lead to better economic and financial outcomes. At the very least, it seems that improvements in these legal rules are not sufficient conditions for that, which questions the empirical validity of the view that law matters for the real and financial economy. If we take this result seriously due to the lack of a consistent relationship between legal reforms and economic activity, it is not surprising that the literature has begun to question the success of a legal strategy based on adopting common law tools as a way to improve the efficiency of the legal system and in turn the performance of the real and financial economy.

6.2 Distinguishing the Circumstances Under Which the Effect Takes Place

Even though there is very limited evidence of an impact from legal and regulatory change on financial and economic developmental outcomes, we next try to determine in which contexts and circumstances the effect might take place. For that purpose, we distinguish in the specification between those countries with GDP per capita in 2004 below and above the median, those with rule of law below and above the median,[2] those with government effectiveness below and above the

[1]The fact that results remain unchanged irrespective of the inclusion or not of lagged GDP growth indicates that endogeneity issues may not be important for this result. Likewise, the robustness of the baseline finding to using either annual or 3-year averaged data further indicates that business-cycle effects inducing reverse causality may not be important either. Notwithstanding, below we explicitly deal with the issue of endogeneity by employing the difference and system GMM estimators, which render fairly similar results to those obtained from the application of the LSDV estimator.

[2]The rule of law index measures confidence in and compliance with the rules of society in 2000. The scale ranges from −2.5 to 2.5, where a higher value indicates better institutions. It comes from the Worldwide Governance Indicators (WGI) project [see Kaufmann et al. (2009), from Teorell et al. (2011)].

median,[3] and common law versus civil law countries. In other words, we estimate two coefficients for each legal rule/regulatory indicator to differentiate its effect by the level of development, rule of law, government effectiveness or legal tradition.

6.2.1 *Differentiating by Level of Development*

Table 6.2 reports the results for the specification that differentiates by level of development. Concerning the law on the books indicators, there is no effect for any income group, with the exception of stocks value traded in the case of the indices of strength of creditor rights and investor protection that carry a significantly positive coefficient for less developed countries, and for developed countries in the case of the strength of investor protection index. Stronger creditor rights also reduce income inequality in less developed countries. In addition, greater credit information disclosure appears to raise stocks value traded in both less developed and developed countries, as well as to reduce the unemployment rate in less developed countries. However, it does not raise access to credit, which is the outcome it primarily aims to affect.

Concerning the law in action variables associated with the efficiency of debt and contract enforcement, there is evidence that a higher recovery rate is associated with more stocks value traded in developed countries. In addition, a more efficient contract enforcement by courts increases the access to credit as measured by our three proxies for financial intermediary development in developed countries, thereby reducing private gross fixed capital formation in less developed countries. As far as regulatory outcomes are concerned, there is evidence that greater time required to start a business, obtain construction permits, pay taxes and trade across borders reduces stocks value traded only in less developed countries. In addition, labor market outcomes (as measured by the unemployment rate) appear to worsen when the time required to obtain construction permits and trade across borders increases in less developed countries. There is also evidence that the greater the time required to obtain construction permits, the higher the income inequality in less developed countries. Finally, the time required to import significantly reduces domestic credit to the private sector at the 10% level for the group of developed countries.

[3]Government effectiveness reflects perceptions about the quality of public administration. Year 2000. The scale ranges from −2.5 to 2.5, where a higher value indicates better institutions. It comes from the Worldwide Governance Indicators (WGI) project [see Kaufmann et al. (2009), from Teorell et al. (2011)].

Table 6.2 The effect of legal rules on financial and economic outcomes: differentiation by level of development

		Creditor rights		Investor protection		Credit information		Recovery rate		Contract enforc.		Starting a business	
		Coeff/SE	Obs	Coeff/SE	Obs	Coeff/SE	Obs	Coeff/SE	Obs	Coeff/SE	Obs	Coeff/SE	Obs
		(1)		(2)		(3)		(4)		(5)		(6)	
Stock market capitalization	Below the median	3.13	263	−0.015	263	−0.591	263	0.429	263	6.302	263	−7.043	263
		(2.606)		(5.381)		(2.805)		(1.121)		(15.504)		(7.162)	
	Above the median	−4.217		−1.48		−0.483		0.653		76.585		−6.081	
		(4.346)		(7.34)		(2.028)		(0.434)		(87.042)		(6.148)	
Stocks traded	Below the median	7.723**	240	13.449**	240	5.03*	240	1.632	240	5.939	240	−16.875**	240
		(3.131)		(5.583)		(2.591)		(1.073)		(20.552)		(8.311)	
	Above the median	6.147		10.129*		6.267**		1.387**		−95.786		−1.085	
		(6.447)		(5.645)		(2.495)		(0.543)		(78.803)		(7.429)	
Domestic credit to private sector by banks	Below the median	0.718	321	0.684	321	0.912	321	−0.199	321	15.695	321	−1.525	321
		(0.881)		(0.753)		(1.105)		(0.288)		(11.954)		(2.057)	
	Above the median	1.248		−3.721		0.632		0.17		−38.548**		−2.703	
		(1.422)		(5.705)		(1.163)		(0.145)		(16.081)		(1.769)	
Domestic credit provided by financial sector	Below the median	−0.005	321	−0.014	321	1.614	321	−0.378	321	11.853	321	−0.788	321
		(1.111)		(1.153)		(1.173)		(0.268)		(14.615)		(2.298)	
	Above the median	3.486		−1.177		1.933		0.126		−49.056**		−3.864	
		(2.352)		(7.788)		(1.307)		(0.271)		(19.616)		(2.566)	
Domestic credit to private sector	Below the median	0.803	321	0.344	321	0.942	321	−0.182	321	17.225	321	−1.779	321
		(0.813)		(0.9)		(1.116)		(0.298)		(11.72)		(2.11)	
	Above the median	1.421		−2.264		0.501		0.168		−38.773**		−2.77	
		(1.544)		(6.32)		(1.159)		(0.149)		(16.532)		(1.835)	

Foreign direct investment	Below the median	0.151	513	−0.038	513	0.038	513	0.153	513	0.127	513	0.71	513
		(0.315)		(0.693)		(0.336)		(0.147)		(2.386)		(1.24)	
	Above the median	0.164		−0.656		−0.435		0.055		2.174		1.744	
		(0.612)		(0.688)		(0.332)		(0.064)		(4.576)		(1.589)	
Trade	Below the median	−0.539	494	0.084	494	−0.868	494	−0.108	494	−1.665	494	5.995	494
		(1.254)		(1.351)		(0.915)		(0.517)		(10.586)		(5.515)	
	Above the median	−1.797		0.568		0.827		0.207		18.838		−0.583	
		(2.315)		(2.553)		(1.052)		(0.278)		(20.856)		(2.566)	
Private gross fixed capital formation	Below the median	0.085	255	−0.573	255	−0.422	255	0.076	255	−8.881*	255	−0.254	255
		(0.296)		(0.69)		(0.415)		(0.159)		(5.341)		(1.022)	
	Above the median	−0.913		−0.516		0.009		0.005		−0.621		−1.369	
		(0.602)		(1.16)		(0.386)		(0.207)		(6.71)		(0.832)	
New business density	Below the median	0.069	349	0.177	349	0.054	349	0.035	349	−1.407	349	−0.321	349
		(0.102)		(0.15)		(0.093)		(0.03)		(0.923)		(0.274)	
	Above the median	0.853		0.161		−0.252		0.009		1.031		0.249	
		(0.661)		(0.588)		(0.206)		(0.028)		(3.458)		(0.625)	
Unemployment rate	Below the median	−0.087	476	−0.228	476	−0.288*	476	−0.034	476	−2.277	476	0.424	476
		(0.072)		(0.196)		(0.172)		(0.043)		(2.788)		(0.257)	
	Above the median	−0.271		0.505		−0.02		−0.065		4.309		−0.47	
		(0.303)		(0.969)		(0.222)		(0.069)		(3.77)		(0.496)	
Income GINI index	Below the median	−0.588**	272	−0.19	272	−0.131	272	0.144	272	−3.338	272	0.534	272
		(0.226)		(0.451)		(0.277)		(0.154)		(3.304)		(0.938)	
	Above the median	−0.25		−0.097		−0.075		−0.002		−0.432		−0.485	
		(0.644)		(0.61)		(0.239)		(0.043)		(2.353)		(0.617)	

(continued)

Table 6.2 (continued)

		Registering a property		Construction permits		Paying taxes		Time to export		Time to import	
		Coeff/SE	Obs	Coeff/SE	Obs	Coeff/SE	Obs	Coeff/SE	Obs	Coeff/SE	Obs
		(7)		(8)		(9)		(10)		(11)	
Stock market capitalization	Below the median	3.971	263	−2.494	263	8.425	263	−14.901	263	−20.716	263
		(7.202)		(9.7)		(10.942)		(19.706)		(15.954)	
	Above the median	1.963		−22.061		−5.065		−46.074		−47.376	
		(3.866)		(27.395)		(14.694)		(37.969)		(31.486)	
Stocks traded	Below the median	−10.751	240	−19.636**	240	−19.421**	240	−42.446*	240	−37.342**	240
		(6.933)		(8.478)		(9.416)		(21.776)		(16.591)	
	Above the median	−4.847		23.407		−3.454		−29.18		−25.517	
		(4.896)		(26.244)		(23.499)		(47.577)		(27.616)	
Domestic credit to private sector by banks	Below the median	0.586	321	−5.024	321	−1.62	319	−12.335	321	−6.744	321
		(2.101)		(4.71)		(4.145)		(12.031)		(8.553)	
	Above the median	0.121		−0.473		0.787		−20.836		−10.779	
		(2.653)		(8.01)		(5.919)		(17.927)		(6.891)	
Domestic credit provided by financial sector	Below the median	1.019	321	−7.635	321	−9.209	319	−7.427	321	−1.905	321
		(2.637)		(4.664)		(5.725)		(13.172)		(9.536)	
	Above the median	−0.465		−3.018		−7.467		−17.342		−6.448	
		(1.94)		(8.075)		(7.012)		(18.762)		(8.302)	
Domestic credit to private sector	Below the median	−0.258	321	−5.189	321	−4.008	319	−11.636	321	−6.025	321
		(2.169)		(4.562)		(3.937)		(12.185)		(8.646)	
	Above the median	0.362		−0.836		0.192		−23.182		−13.047*	
		(2.626)		(7.995)		(6.033)		(18.193)		(7.33)	

Foreign direct investment	Below the median	1.009	513	−0.421	513	−0.034	511	−1.373	513	−0.792	513
		(0.971)		(2.761)		(1.872)		(2.905)		(2.36)	
	Above the median	1.185		−1.563		2.017		3.304		3.919	
		(1.459)		(2.249)		(2.867)		(3.356)		(3.11)	
Trade	Below the median	0.225	494	9.303	494	5.229	492	7.765	494	1.373	494
		(2.69)		(11.197)		(6.29)		(8.331)		(5.642)	
	Above the median	−1.2		0.898		−7.498		3.625		−0.476	
		(2.079)		(9.899)		(8.4)		(9.577)		(9.339)	
Private gross fixed capital formation	Below the median	−1.127	255	0.008	255	6.205***	255	3.036	255	3.172	255
		(1.176)		(2.57)		(1.76)		(2.907)		(2.234)	
	Above the median	−0.294		−1.097		0.981		−0.81		−0.168	
		(1.312)		(2.23)		(2.429)		(4.037)		(3.805)	
New business density	Below the median	−0.34	349	−0.818	349	−0.132	347	−1.301	349	−1.021	349
		(0.297)		(0.517)		(0.529)		(0.988)		(0.676)	
	Above the median	0.031		−1.04		1.731		0.324		0.409	
		(0.275)		(1.252)		(1.16)		(2.932)		(2.528)	
Unemployment rate	Below the median	0.337	476	1.562**	476	0.85	474	3.163**	476	2.182**	476
		(0.324)		(0.695)		(0.603)		(1.495)		(0.993)	
	Above the median	−0.756		0.131		−1.902		1.124		0.111	
		(0.509)		(1.313)		(1.526)		(1.389)		(1.139)	
Income GINI index	Below the median	0.987	272	2.439*	272	−0.137	271	2.141	272	3.396	272
		(1.106)		(1.422)		(2.052)		(2.418)		(2.19)	
	Above the median	−0.218		−0.114		−1.159		0.745		1.219	
		(0.37)		(1.18)		(1.242)		(2.162)		(2.004)	

Notes: Panel specification with averaged annual data over 3-year periods (2006–2014). Clustered standard errors in parentheses. The regressions include the lag of GDP growth, country and period dummies, and a constant term. All these variables are omitted for space considerations

*, ** and *** denote statistical significance at the 10, 5 and 1% levels, respectively

6.2.2 Differentiating by Institutional Quality

Tables 6.3 presents the estimates for the specification that differentiates according to the rule of law score. It is worth noting that greater strength of creditor rights and investor protection, credit information disclosure and efficiency of debt enforcement (as measured by the recovery rate) are associated with higher stocks value traded generally in countries with weak rule of law. This may stem from the fact that law on the books, information disclosure and debt enforcement efficiency levels are initially small in countries with weak rule of law. Hence, these legal rights had more room for improvement in weakly institutionalized countries, which may be the reason for their positive impact on stock market development. There is also evidence that the higher the time required to enforce a contract in court, the lower the development of the financial intermediary sector, as measured by the three credit variables.

In addition, there is evidence that a higher regulatory burden associated with starting a business, registering a property, obtaining construction permits, paying taxes and trading across borders leads to a lower stocks value traded also in countries with weak rule of law. This may imply that regulation is likely to be more associated with corruption in weakly institutionalized environments. In addition, the regulatory burden linked to starting a business, obtaining construction permits, paying taxes and trading across borders increases the unemployment rate in weakly institutionalized countries, whereas a higher time required to start a business, register a property and pay taxes reduces the unemployment rate in countries with rule of law above the median. This reflects a potentially different role of regulation depending on the institutional context. Finally, income inequality appears to be reduced when creditor rights are strong in weakly institutionalized countries and when the regulatory burden associated with obtaining construction permits and importing goods is lowered in countries with weak rule of law.

Overall, there is not a clear-cut pattern of results concerning the effect of legal rules and regulatory indicators on economic and financial development depending on the countries' level of rule of law. Fairly similar findings are obtained when we use government effectiveness as a differentiating factor.[4]

6.2.3 Differentiating by Legal Tradition

Table 6.5 presents the results for the specification that distinguishes between common law and civil law countries regarding the possible impact of legal rules and regulations on financial and economic development. The first noticeable difference between legal traditions is the strength of creditor rights, which both raises stocks value traded and reduces income inequality only in civil law countries. In

[4]See Table 6.4 for the detailed results.

Table 6.3 The effect of legal rules on financial and economic outcomes: differentiation by rule of law

		Creditor rights		Investor protection		Credit information		Recovery rate		Contract enforc.		Starting a business	
		Coeff/SE	Obs	Coeff/SE	Obs	Coeff/SE	Obs	Coeff/SE	Obs	Coeff/SE	Obs	Coeff/SE	Obs
		(1)		(2)		(3)		(4)		(5)		(6)	
Stock market capitalization	Below the median	3.932*	263	4.889	263	1.215	263	0.885	263	0.264	263	−8.618	263
		(2.145)		(4.852)		(2.098)		(0.586)		(13.716)		(6.112)	
	Above the median	−1.355		−4.978		−0.232		0.462		−5.474		−1.263	
		(4.141)		(10.523)		(2.26)		(0.59)		(27.04)		(3.73)	
Stocks traded	Below the median	7.787**	240	12.361***	240	5.577***	240	1.796**	240	11.273	240	−17.933**	240
		(2.97)		(4.484)		(1.866)		(0.771)		(15.124)		(7.287)	
	Above the median	2.707		5.831		3.177		0.81		−24.17		−3.449	
		(6.137)		(6.639)		(2.779)		(0.568)		(25.325)		(4.346)	
Domestic credit to private sector by banks	Below the median	0.622	319	0.145	319	1.121	319	0.104	319	14.207	319	−1.917	319
		(0.826)		(0.953)		(0.947)		(0.265)		(12.067)		(1.967)	
	Above the median	1.858		−2.595		0.296		0.052		−32.335*		−2.069	
		(2.783)		(8.379)		(1.368)		(0.221)		(18.686)		(2.1)	
Domestic credit provided by financial sector	Below the median	0.049	319	−0.52	319	1.838	319	−0.11	319	13.704	319	−1.373	319
		(1.077)		(1.158)		(1.205)		(0.282)		(13.735)		(2.27)	
	Above the median	2.894		1.375		1.584		0.052		−46.788**		−3.29	
		(2.628)		(10.817)		(1.317)		(0.359)		(22.484)		(2.876)	
Domestic credit to private sector	Below the median	0.675	319	−0.095	319	1.139	319	0.13	319	15.095	319	−1.996	319
		(0.767)		(1.032)		(0.947)		(0.276)		(11.989)		(1.991)	
	Above the median	2.27		−0.936		0.181		0.041		−31.566*		−2.413	
		(2.654)		(8.964)		(1.364)		(0.22)		(18.938)		(2.182)	
Foreign direct investment	Below the median	0.175	511	−0.128	511	0	511	0.126	511	−0.046	511	0.692	511
		(0.323)		(0.671)		(0.338)		(0.115)		(2.66)		(1.237)	
	Above the median	0.068		−0.348		−0.345		0.058		1.102		1.9	
		(0.4)		(0.708)		(0.332)		(0.071)		(4.991)		(1.648)	

(continued)

Table 6.3 (continued)

		Creditor rights		Investor protection		Credit information		Recovery rate		Contract enforc.		Starting a business	
		Coeff/SE	Obs	Coeff/SE	Obs	Coeff/SE	Obs	Coeff/SE	Obs	Coeff/SE	Obs	Coeff/SE	Obs
		(1)		(2)		(3)		(4)		(5)		(6)	
Trade	Below the median	−0.876	489	−0.01	489	−0.433	489	0.03	489	−6.079	489	5.027	489
		(1.317)		(1.404)		(0.812)		(0.436)		(10.734)		(5.405)	
	Above the median	1.173		1.263		0.325		0.236		10.883		1.528	
		(1.67)		(2.1)		(1.326)		(0.304)		(19.329)		(2.465)	
Private gross fixed capital formation	Below the median	−0.006	253	−0.637	253	−0.398	253	0.125	253	−5.954	253	−0.698	253
		(0.283)		(0.649)		(0.433)		(0.16)		(4.643)		(1.052)	
	Above the median	0.356		0.081		0.001		−0.115		−7.112		−0.621	
		(1.019)		(1.122)		(0.453)		(0.171)		(8.333)		(0.91)	
New business density	Below the median	0.127	351	0.154	351	−0.014	351	0.032	351	−1.132	351	−0.23	351
		(0.093)		(0.149)		(0.122)		(0.027)		(0.966)		(0.325)	
	Above the median	0.192		0.415		−0.085		0.008		−1.219		0.304	
		(0.418)		(0.688)		(0.179)		(0.033)		(2.803)		(0.617)	
Unemployment rate	Below the median	−0.107	472	−0.316	472	−0.427**	472	−0.07**	472	−3.035	472	0.578*	472
		(0.074)		(0.233)		(0.174)		(0.034)		(2.538)		(0.328)	
	Above the median	−0.063		1.115		0.15		−0.049		6.313		−0.765*	
		(0.333)		(1.08)		(0.182)		(0.072)		(4.137)		(0.439)	
Income GINI index	Below the median	−0.619***	274	−0.321	274	−0.246	274	−0.022	274	−2.445	274	0.722	274
		(0.218)		(0.443)		(0.288)		(0.11)		(3.349)		(0.831)	
	Above the median	0.158		0.997		0.171		0.041		−1.018		−0.808	
		(0.483)		(0.882)		(0.241)		(0.038)		(2.234)		(0.675)	

		Registering a property		Construction permits		Paying taxes		Time to export		Time to import	
		Coeff/SE	Obs	Coeff/SE	Obs	Coeff/SE	Obs	Coeff/SE	Obs	Coeff/SE	Obs
		(7)		(8)		(9)		(10)		(11)	
Stock market capitalization	Below the median	−1.793	263	−9.216	263	−1.429	263	−30.213**	263	−29.422**	263
		(4.329)		(8.203)		(12.849)		(15.107)		(12.158)	
	Above the median	1.264		14.796		−2.105		−12.535		−7.417	
		(3.375)		(18.915)		(13.47)		(37.134)		(25.173)	
Stocks traded	Below the median	−13.016**	240	−17.522***	240	−19.211**	240	−50.206**	240	−40.044***	240
		(5.324)		(6.54)		(9.114)		(19.91)		(14.66)	
	Above the median	−1.493		26.395		4.79		−39.02		−20.299	
		(4.013)		(22.593)		(24.807)		(51.923)		(28.98)	
Domestic credit to private sector by banks	Below the median	0.327	319	−4.36	319	−1.452	317	−14.513	319	−8.656	319
		(1.815)		(3.971)		(4.364)		(10.267)		(7.209)	
	Above the median	0.386		1.923		1.952		−21.666		−9.74	
		(3.1)		(16.944)		(6.341)		(22.114)		(8.797)	
Domestic credit provided by financial sector	Below the median	1.203	319	−6.768	319	−8.205	317	−8.446	319	−2.568	319
		(2.427)		(4.33)		(5.606)		(11.881)		(8.739)	
	Above the median	−0.877		−1.791		−9.228		−19.852		−7.037	
		(2.113)		(16.188)		(8.41)		(22.729)		(9.694)	
Domestic credit to private sector	Below the median	0.229	319	−4.768	319	−3.71	317	−14.659	319	−9.005	319
		(1.803)		(3.897)		(4.378)		(10.212)		(7.199)	
	Above the median	0.084		2.596		2.022		−23.77		−11.137	
		(3.157)		(17.01)		(6.283)		(22.613)		(9.409)	
Foreign direct investment	Below the median	0.898	511	−0.353	511	0.848	509	−0.931	511	−0.52	511
		(0.945)		(2.077)		(1.416)		(2.699)		(2.23)	
	Above the median	1.25		−1.573		0.907		3.569		4.277	
		(1.589)		(4.157)		(3.459)		(3.607)		(3.021)	

(continued)

Table 6.3 (continued)

		Registering a property		Construction permits		Paying taxes		Time to export		Time to import	
		Coeff/SE	Obs	Coeff/SE	Obs	Coeff/SE	Obs	Coeff/SE	Obs	Coeff/SE	Obs
		(7)		(8)		(9)		(10)		(11)	
Trade	Below the median	0.307	489	6.855	489	6.532	487	5.326	489	−0.699	489
		(2.213)		(8.252)		(4.787)		(7.828)		(5.028)	
	Above the median	−1.528		10.997		−9.954		10.468		5.013	
		(2.345)		(15.006)		(10.195)		(9.648)		(9.413)	
Private gross fixed capital formation	Below the median	−1.241	253	−0.5	253	4.204**	253	2.417	253	2.983	253
		(0.949)		(2.086)		(2.11)		(3.163)		(2.298)	
	Above the median	0.59		−0.132		4.812*		1.996		1.779	
		(1.185)		(2.559)		(2.55)		(3.751)		(3.57)	
New business density	Below the median	−0.209	351	−0.395	351	0.079	349	−0.913	351	−0.782	351
		(0.279)		(0.529)		(0.527)		(0.998)		(0.652)	
	Above the median	−0.095		−0.693		1.702		0.586		0.775	
		(0.291)		(1.007)		(1.366)		(3.073)		(2.457)	
Unemployment rate	Below the median	0.469	472	1.347*	472	1.341**	470	3.357**	472	2.149**	472
		(0.287)		(0.772)		(0.67)		(1.437)		(0.949)	
	Above the median	−1.135**		−0.848		−3.561**		0.282		−0.519	
		(0.509)		(2.049)		(1.72)		(1.448)		(1.174)	
Income GINI index	Below the median	0.943	274	2.035*	274	0.009	273	2.755	274	3.128*	274
		(0.867)		(1.209)		(1.508)		(2.004)		(1.784)	
	Above the median	−0.67		−1.553		−2.165		−1.956		−1.935	
		(0.411)		(1.485)		(1.419)		(2.103)		(1.869)	

Notes: Panel specification with averaged annual data over 3-year periods (2006–2014). Clustered standard errors in parentheses. The regressions include the lag of GDP growth, country and period dummies, and a constant term. All these variables are omitted for space considerations

*, ** and *** denote statistical significance at the 10, 5 and 1% levels, respectively

Table 6.4 The effect of legal rules on financial and economic outcomes: differentiation by government effectiveness

		Creditor rights		Investor protection		Credit information		Recovery rate		Contract enforc.		Starting a business	
		Coeff/SE	Obs	Coeff/SE	Obs	Coeff/SE	Obs	Coeff/SE	Obs	Coeff/SE	Obs	Coeff/SE	Obs
		(1)		(2)		(3)		(4)		(5)		(6)	
Stock market capitalization	Below the median	4.36**	263	3.484	263	1.275	263	0.885	263	−8.779	263	−8.194	263
		(2.151)		(4.911)		(1.98)		(0.763)		(21.418)		(5.912)	
	Above the median	−1.933		−0.691		−0.202		0.582		0.074		−2.256	
		(3.699)		(7.824)		(2.188)		(0.495)		(22.096)		(3.758)	
Stocks traded	Below the median	6.994***	240	11.166**	240	5.303***	240	2.363**	240	10.756	240	−19.305**	240
		(2.441)		(4.566)		(1.658)		(0.991)		(23.64)		(7.923)	
	Above the median	4.372		7.759		3.669		0.974*		−12.326		−4.835	
		(6.086)		(5.28)		(2.935)		(0.509)		(21.191)		(4.424)	
Domestic credit to private sector by banks	Below the median	0.675	319	−0.153	319	0.806	319	−0.087	319	6.371	319	−0.885	319
		(0.857)		(0.971)		(0.932)		(0.269)		(13.929)		(1.806)	
	Above the median	2.902		−0.547		0.764		0.122		−12.424		−3.413	
		(2.274)		(5.962)		(1.317)		(0.173)		(22.075)		(2.069)	
Domestic credit provided by financial sector	Below the median	0.104	319	−1.014	319	1.582	319	−0.328	319	7.677	319	−0.23	319
		(1.073)		(1.072)		(1.234)		(0.283)		(16.774)		(2.1)	
	Above the median	6.925**		3.123		1.881		0.096		−23.198		−4.441	
		(3.1)		(7.702)		(1.264)		(0.287)		(27.267)		(2.738)	
Domestic credit to private sector	Below the median	0.711	319	−0.49	319	0.844	319	−0.07	319	8.233	319	−0.875	319
		(0.806)		(1.03)		(0.924)		(0.282)		(14.254)		(1.806)	
	Above the median	4.392*		1.064		0.656		0.12		−12.152		−3.825*	
		(2.424)		(6.379)		(1.324)		(0.175)		(22.129)		(2.138)	
Foreign direct investment	Below the median	0.172	511	−0.117	511	0.1	511	0.187	511	1.301	511	0.669	511
		(0.312)		(0.686)		(0.345)		(0.152)		(3.084)		(1.318)	
	Above the median	0		−0.361		−0.445		0.038		0.097		1.825	
		(0.556)		(0.707)		(0.319)		(0.061)		(4.026)		(1.521)	

(continued)

Table 6.4 (continued)

		Creditor rights		Investor protection		Credit information		Recovery rate		Contract enforc.		Starting a business	
		Coeff/SE	Obs	Coeff/SE	Obs	Coeff/SE	Obs	Coeff/SE	Obs	Coeff/SE	Obs	Coeff/SE	Obs
		(1)		(2)		(3)		(4)		(5)		(6)	
Trade	Below the median	−0.744	489	−0.499	489	−0.721	489	0.136	489	−4.183	489	6.086	489
		(1.258)		(1.525)		(0.856)		(0.56)		(13.151)		(5.796)	
	Above the median	0.904		2.767		0.606		0.159		6.395		0.862	
		(2.4)		(1.81)		(1.205)		(0.295)		(16.078)		(2.249)	
Private gross fixed capital formation	Below the median	0.009	253	−0.609	253	−0.3	253	0.143	253	−1.798	253	−0.866	253
		(0.284)		(0.662)		(0.408)		(0.162)		(4.336)		(1.187)	
	Above the median	0.039		−0.254		−0.181		−0.102		−9.529**		−0.402	
		(1.017)		(1.193)		(0.493)		(0.163)		(4.558)		(0.823)	
New business density	Below the median	0.086	351	0.19	351	0.057	351	0.044	351	−1.692	351	−0.384	351
		(0.104)		(0.145)		(0.104)		(0.029)		(1.251)		(0.262)	
	Above the median	0.522		0.248		−0.158		0.007		−0.967		0.342	
		(0.461)		(0.616)		(0.174)		(0.029)		(2.267)		(0.572)	
Unemployment rate	Below the median	−0.101	472	−0.228	472	−0.292**	472	−0.064*	472	0.544	472	0.357	472
		(0.075)		(0.192)		(0.114)		(0.039)		(1.332)		(0.231)	
	Above the median	−0.142		0.617		−0.025		−0.055		1.94		−0.434	
		(0.356)		(1.021)		(0.251)		(0.066)		(4.537)		(0.478)	
Income GINI index	Below the median	−0.6***	274	−0.228	274	−0.178	274	0.083	274	−4.435	274	0.487	274
		(0.222)		(0.414)		(0.248)		(0.135)		(4.92)		(0.83)	
	Above the median	−0.059		0.273		0.107		0.011		−0.701		−0.622	
		(0.591)		(0.906)		(0.296)		(0.043)		(2.184)		(0.663)	

		Registering a property		Construction permits		Paying taxes		Time to export		Time to import	
		Coeff/SE	Obs	Coeff/SE	Obs	Coeff/SE	Obs	Coeff/SE	Obs	Coeff/SE	Obs
		(7)		(8)		(9)		(10)		(11)	
Stock market capitalization	Below the median	−3.487	263	−7.159	263	3.889	263	−29.488	263	−27.725*	263
		(4.977)		(10.008)		(10.659)		(18.388)		(14.25)	
	Above the median	1.325		6.433		−6.309		−20.004		−18.187	
		(3.258)		(13.568)		(13.405)		(26.923)		(18.74)	
Stocks traded	Below the median	−12.875**	240	−15.607**	240	−15.853*	240	−62.937**	240	−44.652***	240
		(5.458)		(6.355)		(8.551)		(25.572)		(16.764)	
	Above the median	−2.227		11.827		−2.892		−39.366		−25.972	
		(4.088)		(17.297)		(20.782)		(34.846)		(20.966)	
Domestic credit to private sector by banks	Below the median	0.041	319	−3.027	319	−0.158	317	−10.776	319	−5.528	319
		(1.768)		(3.668)		(4.36)		(10.32)		(7.302)	
	Above the median	0.614		−3.964		−1.436		−21.537		−11.883	
		(2.9)		(10.507)		(6.247)		(17.65)		(8.272)	
Domestic credit provided by financial sector	Below the median	1.202	319	−5.384	319	−7.273	317	−1.653	319	2.163	319
		(2.443)		(3.95)		(5.715)		(12.634)		(9.126)	
	Above the median	−0.67		−7.284		−11.022		−20.171		−9.461	
		(2.129)		(9.914)		(7.916)		(18.034)		(8.86)	
Domestic credit to private sector	Below the median	−0.105	319	−3.053	319	−2.143	317	−9.74	319	−4.941	319
		(1.746)		(3.506)		(4.432)		(10.33)		(7.316)	
	Above the median	0.371		−4.689		−2.38		−23.706		−13.712	
		(2.956)		(10.495)		(6.366)		(17.85)		(8.578)	
Foreign direct investment	Below the median	0.769	511	−0.725	511	−0.002	509	−1.602	511	−0.78	511
		(0.999)		(2.236)		(1.834)		(3.133)		(2.383)	
	Above the median	1.312		−0.502		1.921		2.959		3.658	
		(1.507)		(3.51)		(2.909)		(3.14)		(2.814)	

(continued)

Table 6.4 (continued)

		Registering a property		Construction permits		Paying taxes		Time to export		Time to import	
		Coeff/SE	Obs	Coeff/SE	Obs	Coeff/SE	Obs	Coeff/SE	Obs	Coeff/SE	Obs
		(7)		(8)		(9)		(10)		(11)	
Trade	Below the median	−0.014	489	9.022	489	5.38	487	8.426	489	0.656	489
		(2.323)		(8.609)		(5.987)		(9.346)		(5.768)	
	Above the median	−1.199		5.772		−6.825		6.299		2.011	
		(2.255)		(12.79)		(9.322)		(8.037)		(7.923)	
Private gross fixed capital formation	Below the median	−1.464*	253	−0.722	253	4.631**	253	1.384	253	2.667	253
		(0.863)		(2.157)		(1.991)		(2.738)		(2.14)	
	Above the median	0.556		0.618		3.342		3.822		2.855	
		(1.144)		(2.955)		(3.359)		(4.374)		(3.92)	
New business density	Below the median	−0.362	351	−0.705	351	−0.046	349	−1.848*	351	−1.198*	351
		(0.259)		(0.465)		(0.467)		(0.951)		(0.677)	
	Above the median	−0.001		−0.107		1.779		0.595		0.695	
		(0.286)		(0.941)		(1.319)		(2.248)		(1.83)	
Unemployment rate	Below the median	0.513**	472	0.93*	472	0.959*	470	2.54***	472	1.798**	472
		(0.237)		(0.526)		(0.568)		(0.958)		(0.757)	
	Above the median	−1.05**		0.454		−2.513		2.088		0.736	
		(0.502)		(2.166)		(1.539)		(1.956)		(1.408)	
Income GINI index	Below the median	0.539	274	2.136	274	−0.053	273	2.466	274	3.564	274
		(0.674)		(1.323)		(1.667)		(2.78)		(2.357)	
	Above the median	−0.372		−0.684		−1.557		0.776		0.511	
		(0.445)		(1.346)		(1.353)		(1.899)		(1.92)	

Notes: Panel specification with averaged annual data over 3-year periods (2006–2014). Clustered standard errors in parentheses. The regressions include the lag of GDP growth, country and period dummies, and a constant term. All these variables are omitted for space considerations

*, ** and *** denote statistical significance at the 10, 5 and 1% levels, respectively

Table 6.5 The effect of legal rules on financial and economic outcomes: differentiation by legal tradition

		Creditor rights		Investor protection		Credit information		Recovery rate		Contract enforc.		Starting a business	
		Coeff/SE	Obs	Coeff/SE	Obs	Coeff/SE	Obs	Coeff/SE	Obs	Coeff/SE	Obs	Coeff/SE	Obs
		(1)		(2)		(3)		(4)		(5)		(6)	
Stock market capitalization	Common law	0.189	266	9.65	266	0.756	266	1.466	266	137.97	266	−19.261	266
		(7.219)		(10.505)		(2.924)		(1.531)		(110.84)		(17.205)	
	Civil law	1.379		−2.874		−0.93		0.47		−13.829		−0.272	
		(2.62)		(5.22)		(2.239)		(0.501)		(20.714)		(4.345)	
Stocks traded	Common law	1.718	243	17.265**	243	4.945*	243	−0.266	243	−144.681	243	8.683	243
		(11.942)		(6.749)		(2.692)		(1.735)		(100.289)		(19.433)	
	Civil law	7.794**		9.082*		5.456**		1.512**		15.347		−7.74	
		(3.325)		(4.86)		(2.491)		(0.591)		(18.286)		(5.145)	
Domestic credit to private sector by banks	Common law	−0.315	322	0.198	322	−1.133	322	0.281	322	−9.618	322	−1.584	322
		(2.523)		(2.61)		(1.641)		(0.604)		(13.565)		(3.937)	
	Civil law	1.018		−0.254		1.194		0.06		−3.579		−2.057	
		(0.748)		(1.353)		(0.997)		(0.16)		(19.004)		(1.685)	
Domestic credit provided by financial sector	Common law	−1.446	322	5.142	322	1.263	322	0.754	322	−27.027	322	−2.594	322
		(3.125)		(4.281)		(1.322)		(0.633)		(16.541)		(5.569)	
	Civil law	0.786		−1.033		1.836		−0.056		−3.82		−2.004	
		(0.876)		(1.717)		(1.149)		(0.28)		(20.407)		(1.981)	
Domestic credit to private sector	Common law	0.421	322	1.981	322	−1.034	322	0.313	322	−7.943	322	−3.677	322
		(2.16)		(4.555)		(1.649)		(0.583)		(13.818)		(3.579)	
	Civil law	0.971		−0.493		1.133		0.061		−3.223		−2.032	
		(0.758)		(1.386)		(1.006)		(0.16)		(18.965)		(1.721)	
Foreign direct investment	Common law	−0.297	517	0.661	517	0.16	517	0.024	517	6.182*	517	0.016	517
		(0.845)		(1.079)		(0.288)		(0.186)		(3.417)		(1.023)	
	Civil law	0.239		−0.311		−0.264		0.09		−1.349		1.436	
		(0.263)		(0.635)		(0.294)		(0.066)		(3.702)		(1.195)	

(continued)

Table 6.5 (continued)

		Creditor rights		Investor protection		Credit information		Recovery rate		Contract enforc.		Starting a business	
		Coeff/SE	Obs	Coeff/SE	Obs	Coeff/SE	Obs	Coeff/SE	Obs	Coeff/SE	Obs	Coeff/SE	Obs
		(1)		(2)		(3)		(4)		(5)		(6)	
Trade	Common law	−3.006	498	−1.078	498	−0.211	498	−0.168	498	25.891	498	11.915	498
		(6.471)		(3.4)		(2.134)		(1.336)		(30.358)		(12.012)	
	Civil law	−0.241		0.356		−0.075		0.127		0.479		0.116	
		(1.166)		(1.284)		(0.783)		(0.282)		(10.167)		(1.757)	
Private gross fixed capital formation	Common law	1.239	256	1.426	256	0.483	256	0.142	256	−13.877	256	−1.851	256
		(1.915)		(1.435)		(0.495)		(0.25)		(8.413)		(1.738)	
	Civil law	−0.05		−0.726		−0.465		0.033		−3.732		−0.426	
		(0.269)		(0.62)		(0.381)		(0.15)		(4.821)		(0.89)	
New business density	Common law	−0.245	354	0.511	354	−0.039	354	0.127	354	0.325	354	0.427	354
		(0.326)		(1.348)		(0.112)		(0.153)		(4.739)		(1.222)	
	Civil law	0.166		0.141		−0.077		0.009		−0.25		−0.091	
		(0.111)		(0.152)		(0.135)		(0.022)		(1.448)		(0.269)	
Unemployment rate	Common law	−0.182	481	−0.196	481	−0.254**	481	−0.112	481	1.842	481	0.187	481
		(0.142)		(0.712)		(0.119)		(0.085)		(2.143)		(0.38)	
	Civil law	−0.093		−0.026		−0.142		−0.047		0.755		−0.078	
		(0.081)		(0.278)		(0.168)		(0.049)		(3.735)		(0.323)	
Income GINI index	Common law	0.059	275	0.604	275	0.114	275	0.425*	275	1.231	275	−2.491***	275
		(0.338)		(1.013)		(0.384)		(0.245)		(5.678)		(0.929)	
	Civil law	−0.549**		−0.203		−0.137		0.017		−2.043		−0.12	
		(0.221)		(0.404)		(0.228)		(0.045)		(2.39)		(0.556)	

		Registering a property		Construction permits		Paying taxes		Time to export		Time to import	
		Coeff/SE	Obs	Coeff/SE	Obs	Coeff/SE	Obs	Coeff/SE	Obs	Coeff/SE	Obs
		(7)		(8)		(9)		(10)		(11)	
Stock market capitalization	Common law	−2.887	266	−72.223	266	−8.811	266	−104.428	266	−86.31	266
		(7.004)		(55.211)		(15.706)		(71.1)		(53.912)	
	Civil law	3.183		3.351		6.736		−19.626		−15.86	
		(3.988)		(10.954)		(12.825)		(23.677)		(14.555)	
Stocks traded	Common law	−0.472	243	69.786	243	−7.344	243	−5.031	243	−10.704	243
		(11.847)		(48.747)		(29.794)		(81.444)		(45.096)	
	Civil law	−6.305		−7.938		−13.624		−41.002		−33.187*	
		(5.094)		(9.07)		(14.602)		(30.224)		(16.879)	
Domestic credit to private sector by banks	Common law	2.63	322	−9.421*	322	2.57	320	−7.716	322	−3.491	322
		(3.246)		(5.506)		(7.289)		(12.778)		(7.674)	
	Civil law	−0.685		−2.423		−1.239		−19.428		−11.099	
		(1.949)		(4.054)		(4.303)		(15.08)		(7.434)	
Domestic credit provided by financial sector	Common law	0.169	322	−10.571	322	−7.329	320	−7.617	322	−1.333	322
		(2.923)		(7.62)		(11.511)		(15.954)		(9.681)	
	Civil law	0.135		−5.236		−8.719		−14.033		−5.381	
		(1.961)		(3.972)		(5.423)		(15.682)		(8.347)	
Domestic credit to private sector	Common law	1.481	322	−8.05	322	2.38	320	−10.809	322	−4.712	322
		(3.685)		(5.622)		(7.086)		(14.081)		(8.38)	
	Civil law	−0.483		−2.912		−3.172		−19.642		−11.596	
		(1.965)		(3.987)		(4.346)		(15.109)		(7.452)	
Foreign direct investment	Common law	−0.588	517	−2.957	517	−5.791**	515	0.706	517	0.978	517
		(1.141)		(2.801)		(2.613)		(4.595)		(3.384)	
	Civil law	1.605		−0.339		2.563		0.562		0.852	
		(1.253)		(2.097)		(1.845)		(2.57)		(2.205)	

(continued)

Table 6.5 (continued)

		Registering a property		Construction permits		Paying taxes		Time to export		Time to import	
		Coeff/SE	Obs	Coeff/SE	Obs	Coeff/SE	Obs	Coeff/SE	Obs	Coeff/SE	Obs
		(7)		(8)		(9)		(10)		(11)	
Trade	Common law	1.897	498	29.525	498	−14.245	496	17.863	498	7.196	498
		(5.479)		(28.304)		(16.749)		(18.804)		(9.688)	
	Civil law	−1.435		−3.299		2.366		3.045		−1.778	
		(1.588)		(3.432)		(4.936)		(6.527)		(6.095)	
Private gross fixed capital formation	Common law	−2.973*	256	1.362	256	3.27	256	−1.041	256	−0.423	256
		(1.676)		(3.656)		(3.132)		(4.725)		(3.577)	
	Civil law	−0.21		−0.877		4.67**		2.825		3.407	
		(1.079)		(1.973)		(2.032)		(2.854)		(2.243)	
New business density	Common law	−0.036	354	−3.306**	354	0.984	352	−3.773	354	−3.093*	354
		(0.338)		(1.629)		(1.272)		(2.509)		(1.792)	
	Civil law	−0.106		−0.175		0.86		−0.075		−0.074	
		(0.247)		(0.528)		(0.811)		(1.838)		(1.217)	
Unemployment rate	Common law	−0.177	481	1.088*	481	−0.714	479	3.933**	481	2.395**	481
		(0.707)		(0.568)		(0.904)		(1.532)		(1.052)	
	Civil law	−0.442		0.737		−0.362		2.125		1.251	
		(0.442)		(1.006)		(0.869)		(1.292)		(0.854)	
Income GINI index	Common law	−2.51	275	1.642	275	−1.609	274	3.009	275	3.291*	275
		(2.175)		(1.445)		(1.155)		(2.346)		(1.915)	
	Civil law	−0.031		1.072		−0.692		1.524		2.24	
		(0.403)		(1.184)		(1.392)		(1.761)		(1.626)	

Notes: Panel specification with averaged annual data over 3-year periods (2006–2014). Clustered standard errors in parentheses. The regressions include the lag of GDP growth, country and period dummies, and a constant term. All these variables are omitted for space considerations

*, ** and *** denote statistical significance at the 10, 5 and 1% levels, respectively

this group, a higher recovery rate and a lower regulatory burden associated with importing goods raises stocks value traded. Concerning the differential effect in common law countries, greater credit information disclosure reduces the unemployment rate. As regards the regulatory indicators, a higher regulatory burden in terms of time required to obtain construction permits reduces domestic credit to the private sector by banks and new business registration, as well as increases the unemployment rate in common law countries. Likewise, greater time required to pay taxes reduces foreign direct investment, and greater time required to import goods lowers new business registrations as well as raises the unemployment rate and economic inequality in common law countries.

6.2.4 *Interacting Legal and Regulatory Indicators with the Level of Development*

Table 6.6 presents the results from a specification that interacts each legal and regulatory indicator with log GDP per capita in 2004. As in the baseline specification, most of the coefficients on both the legal indicator and interacted term are insignificant. The exceptions are associated with the positive impact of the strength of creditor rights on stock market capitalization, which appears to decrease as the income level rises. Something similar occurs with some regulatory indicators. As a matter of fact, the negative impact of higher time required to start a business, register a property and obtain construction permits on stocks value traded diminishes as the income level rises. The same occurs with the negative effect of the regulatory burden associated with trading across borders on foreign direct investment, and with paying taxes on new business registration. Likewise, the positive effect of higher time required to start a business, register a property and pay taxes on the unemployment rate appears to decrease as the income level rises. The same happens to the positive impact of a greater regulatory burden associated with starting a business, registering a property and obtaining construction permits on income inequality. Hence, this indicates that in the few instances in which we find evidence of a statistically significant impact of laws and regulations on development outcomes, the effect appears to be stronger the lower the level of income.

6.3 Graphical Analysis of the Relationship Between Legal Change and Financial and Economic Development

In this section we try to show intuitively the lack of relationship between the variation in legal rules and regulatory indicators between 2006 and 2014 and the variation that has taken place during that period in financial and economic development outcomes. For that purpose, we present Figs. 6.1 and 6.2 that plot the

Table 6.6 The effect of legal rules on financial and economic outcomes: interaction legal rules × Income in 2004

		Creditor rights		Investor protection		Credit information		Recovery rate		Contract enforc.		Starting a business	
		Coeff/SE	Obs	Coeff/SE	Obs	Coeff/SE	Obs	Coeff/SE	Obs	Coeff/SE	Obs	Coeff/SE	Obs
		(1)		(2)		(3)		(4)		(5)		(6)	
Stock market capitalization	Legal rule/reg.	31.529**	263	81.929	263	−2.995	263	−0.602	263	−464.488	263	10.899	263
		(15.583)		(58.82)		(11.133)		(5.792)		(391.354)		(65.334)	
	Interaction legal rule/reg × Ln income in 2004	−3.517*		−9.125		0.266		0.128		55.191		−1.747	
		(1.866)		(6.626)		(1.127)		(0.602)		(46.421)		(6.962)	
Stocks traded	Legal rule/reg.	15.463	240	95.135	240	11.932	240	10.659*	240	585.684	240	−155.597*	240
		(33.414)		(82.514)		(12.309)		(6.256)		(386.893)		(82.287)	
	Interaction legal rule/reg × Ln income in 2004	−0.937		−9.223		−0.721		−0.982		−69.237		15.697*	
		(3.94)		(9.176)		(1.423)		(0.642)		(45.976)		(8.858)	
Domestic credit to private sector by banks	Legal rule/reg.	−1.277	321	16.133	321	5.834	321	0.026	321	150.588	321	1.599	321
		(4.762)		(22.683)		(4.741)		(1.648)		(98.476)		(8.964)	
	Interaction legal rule/reg × Ln income in 2004	0.261		−1.952		−0.561		0.005		−18.024		−0.415	
		(0.589)		(2.775)		(0.512)		(0.174)		(11.011)		(0.943)	
Domestic credit provided by financial sector	Legal rule/reg.	−8.575	321	7.805	321	2.456	321	−0.075	321	141.131	321	11.355	321
		(6.614)		(28.008)		(5.621)		(2.676)		(117.773)		(14.243)	
	Interaction legal rule/reg × Ln income in 2004	1.138		−0.962		−0.08		0.007		−17.681		−1.541	
		(0.827)		(3.452)		(0.625)		(0.296)		(13.33)		(1.605)	
Domestic credit to private sector	Legal rule/reg.	−1.207	321	11.563	321	6.132	321	0.151	321	153.679	321	1.165	321
		(4.694)		(22.981)		(4.642)		(1.736)		(101.733)		(8.988)	
	Interaction legal rule/reg × Ln income in 2004	0.264		−1.403		−0.598		−0.008		−18.284		−0.385	
		(0.595)		(2.821)		(0.501)		(0.183)		(11.373)		(0.946)	

Foreign direct investment	Legal rule/reg.	−0.677	513	3.474	513	2.795	513	0.794	513	−13.605	513	−3.931	513
		(1.722)		(4.495)		(1.817)		(0.906)		(17.73)		(7.381)	
	Interaction legal rule/reg × Ln income in 2004	0.107		−0.44		−0.328		−0.077		1.645		0.587	
		(0.219)		(0.522)		(0.2)		(0.096)		(2.084)		(0.845)	
Trade	Legal rule/reg.	−4.653	494	1.863	494	−7.843	494	−0.319	494	−60.386	494	37.394	494
		(12.346)		(7.879)		(7.016)		(2.602)		(88.125)		(33.525)	
	Interaction legal rule/reg × Ln income in 2004	0.518		−0.2		0.856		0.046		7.698		−3.947	
		(1.519)		(0.963)		(0.781)		(0.274)		(10.595)		(3.55)	
Private gross fixed capital formation	Legal rule/reg.	2.82	255	5.275	255	0.201	255	0.937	255	−1.973	255	−2.091	255
		(1.714)		(3.186)		(1.974)		(0.984)		(25.178)		(5.058)	
	Interaction legal rule/reg × Ln income in 2004	−0.365*		−0.725*		−0.05		−0.105		−0.521		0.169	
		(0.219)		(0.409)		(0.215)		(0.114)		(2.94)		(0.59)	
New business density	Legal rule/reg.	−1.338	349	1.223	349	0.651	349	0.14	349	−13.081	349	−1.989	349
		(1.298)		(2.015)		(0.441)		(0.141)		(11.46)		(2.367)	
	Interaction legal rule/reg × Ln income in 2004	0.19		−0.125		−0.08		−0.013		1.417		0.219	
		(0.175)		(0.254)		(0.051)		(0.016)		(1.383)		(0.295)	
Unemployment rate	Legal rule/reg.	0.382	476	−3.322	476	−1.484*	476	−0.048	476	−15.287	476	3.384**	476
		(0.581)		(2.894)		(0.837)		(0.269)		(14.569)		(1.665)	
	Interaction legal rule/reg × Ln income in 2004	−0.063		0.393		0.145		−0.001		1.827		−0.386**	
		(0.081)		(0.367)		(0.092)		(0.033)		(1.71)		(0.194)	
Income GINI index	Legal rule/reg.	−3.266*	272	−3.558	272	−1.846	272	−0.091	272	−19.677	272	10.501**	272
		(1.686)		(4.052)		(2.977)		(0.927)		(17.389)		(5.15)	
	Interaction legal rule/reg × Ln income in 2004	0.34		0.387		0.196		0.011		1.93		−1.141**	
		(0.216)		(0.451)		(0.324)		(0.093)		(1.801)		(0.522)	

(continued)

Table 6.6 (continued)

		Registering a property		Construction permits		Paying taxes		Time to export		Time to import	
		Coeff/SE	Obs	Coeff/SE	Obs	Coeff/SE	Obs	Coeff/SE	Obs	Coeff/SE	Obs
		(7)		(8)		(9)		(10)		(11)	
Stock market capitalization	Legal rule/reg.	−2.798	263	68.585	263	−17.326	263	279.858	263	147.159	263
		(30.308)		(174.743)		(52.669)		(293.636)		(226.954)	
	Interaction legal rule/reg × Ln income in 2004	0.541		−8.908		2.169		−34.364		−20.18	
		(2.944)		(20.069)		(5.64)		(34.034)		(26.491)	
Stocks traded	Legal rule/reg.	−89.635**	240	−288.337*	240	−163.213	240	−201.537	240	−219.541	240
		(43.295)		(154.423)		(116.471)		(363.097)		(195.025)	
	Interaction legal rule/reg × Ln income in 2004	8.629*		31.387*		16.612		18.333		20.887	
		(4.379)		(17.252)		(13.504)		(42.479)		(22.279)	
Domestic credit to private sector by banks	Legal rule/reg.	2.985	321	−39.777	321	−13.539	319	32.327	321	−16.108	321
		(13.311)		(71.448)		(27.144)		(78.819)		(29.736)	
	Interaction legal rule/reg × Ln income in 2004	−0.295		4.203		1.45		−5.537		0.845	
		(1.472)		(8.36)		(3.136)		(10.165)		(3.228)	
Domestic credit provided by financial sector	Legal rule/reg.	13.191	321	−24.494	321	−8.105	319	46.262	321	0.743	321
		(17.444)		(68.962)		(30.524)		(79.131)		(35.689)	
	Interaction legal rule/reg × Ln income in 2004	−1.439		2.14		−0.045		−6.638		−0.552	
		(1.87)		(8.014)		(3.613)		(10.153)		(3.887)	
Domestic credit to private sector	Legal rule/reg.	−3.348	321	−35.266	321	−15.353	319	40.096	321	−7.565	321
		(12.648)		(71.604)		(26.775)		(80.258)		(31.246)	
	Interaction legal rule/reg × Ln income in 2004	0.381		3.655		1.468		−6.512		−0.212	
		(1.39)		(8.373)		(3.1)		(10.327)		(3.438)	
Foreign direct investment	Legal rule/reg.	−5.204	513	3.853	513	−17.027	511	−25.048*	513	−24.43*	513
		(8.315)		(19.531)		(15.321)		(14.45)		(13.392)	
	Interaction legal rule/reg × Ln income in 2004	0.688		−0.542		1.99		2.966*		2.967*	
		(0.962)		(2.171)		(1.785)		(1.695)		(1.588)	

Trade	Legal rule/reg.	−6.811	494	67.98	494	31.351	492	64.184	494	16.249	494
		(15.776)		(85.767)		(52.858)		(76.478)		(42.82)	
	Interaction legal rule/reg × Ln income in 2004	0.664		−7.02		−3.555		−6.722		−1.82	
		(1.694)		(9.391)		(5.92)		(8.641)		(5.137)	
Private gross fixed capital formation	Legal rule/reg.	−8.251	255	−3.991	255	19.95**	255	5.099	255	4.064	255
		(9.703)		(9.942)		(9.994)		(16.384)		(13.029)	
	Interaction legal rule/reg × Ln income in 2004	0.861		0.412		−1.832		−0.339		−0.164	
		(1.076)		(1.082)		(1.198)		(1.986)		(1.578)	
New business density	Legal rule/reg.	−1.225	349	2.065	349	−5.242**	347	0.916	349	−1.579	349
		(1.228)		(4.136)		(2.494)		(8.802)		(6.638)	
	Interaction legal rule/reg × Ln income in 2004	0.121		−0.332		0.664**		−0.164		0.123	
		(0.131)		(0.506)		(0.276)		(1.135)		(0.87)	
Unemployment rate	Legal rule/reg.	6.682***	476	4.915	476	11.24*	474	7.694*	476	7.024	476
		(2.346)		(3.884)		(6.522)		(4.594)		(4.332)	
	Interaction legal rule/reg × Ln income in 2004	−0.766***		−0.455		−1.289*		−0.618		−0.647	
		(0.253)		(0.478)		(0.761)		(0.518)		(0.496)	
Income GINI index	Legal rule/reg.	8.127*	272	19.518**	272	1.483	271	19.233	272	21.184	272
		(4.535)		(8.712)		(11.052)		(22.612)		(19.149)	
	Interaction legal rule/reg × Ln income in 2004	−0.847*		−2.005**		−0.236		−2.01		−2.123	
		(0.457)		(0.943)		(1.096)		(2.492)		(2.117)	

Notes: Panel specification with averaged annual data over 3-year periods (2006–2014). Clustered standard errors in parentheses. The regressions include the lag of GDP growth, country and period dummies, and a constant term. All these variables are omitted for space considerations

*, ** and *** denote statistical significance at the 10, 5 and 1% levels, respectively

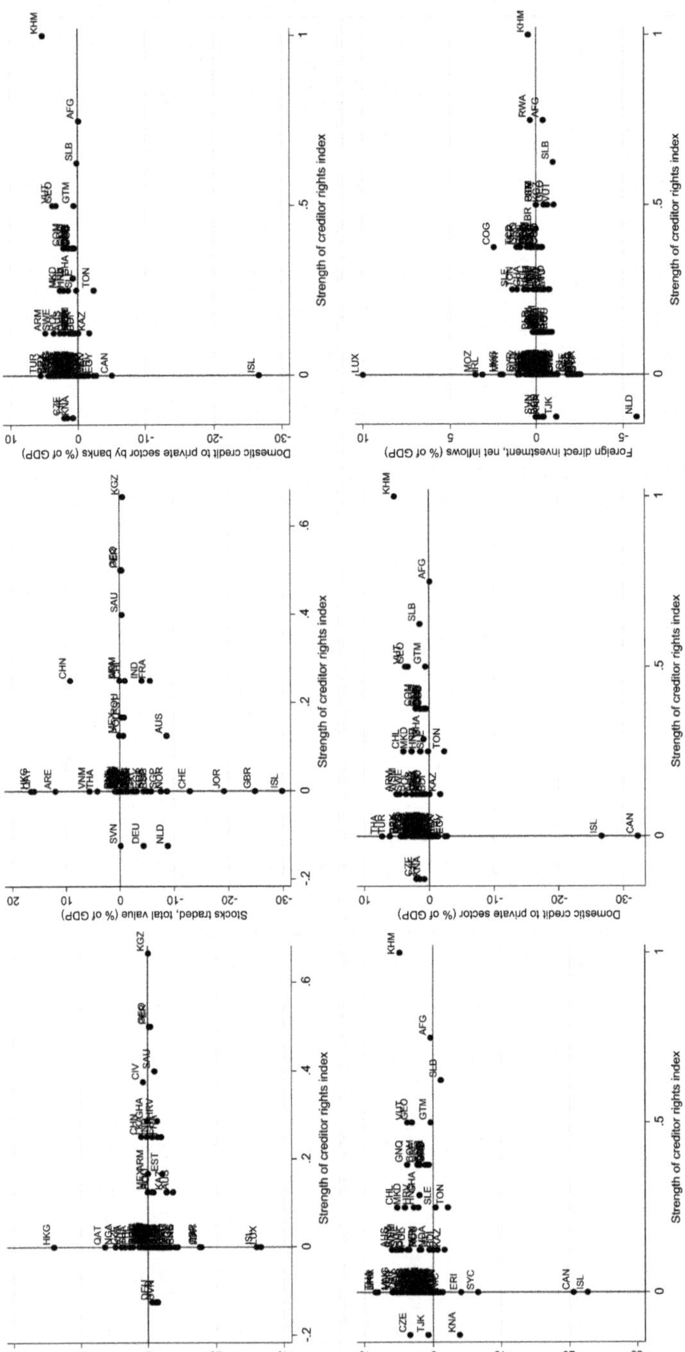

Fig. 6.1 Change in creditor rights against change in financial and economic outcomes

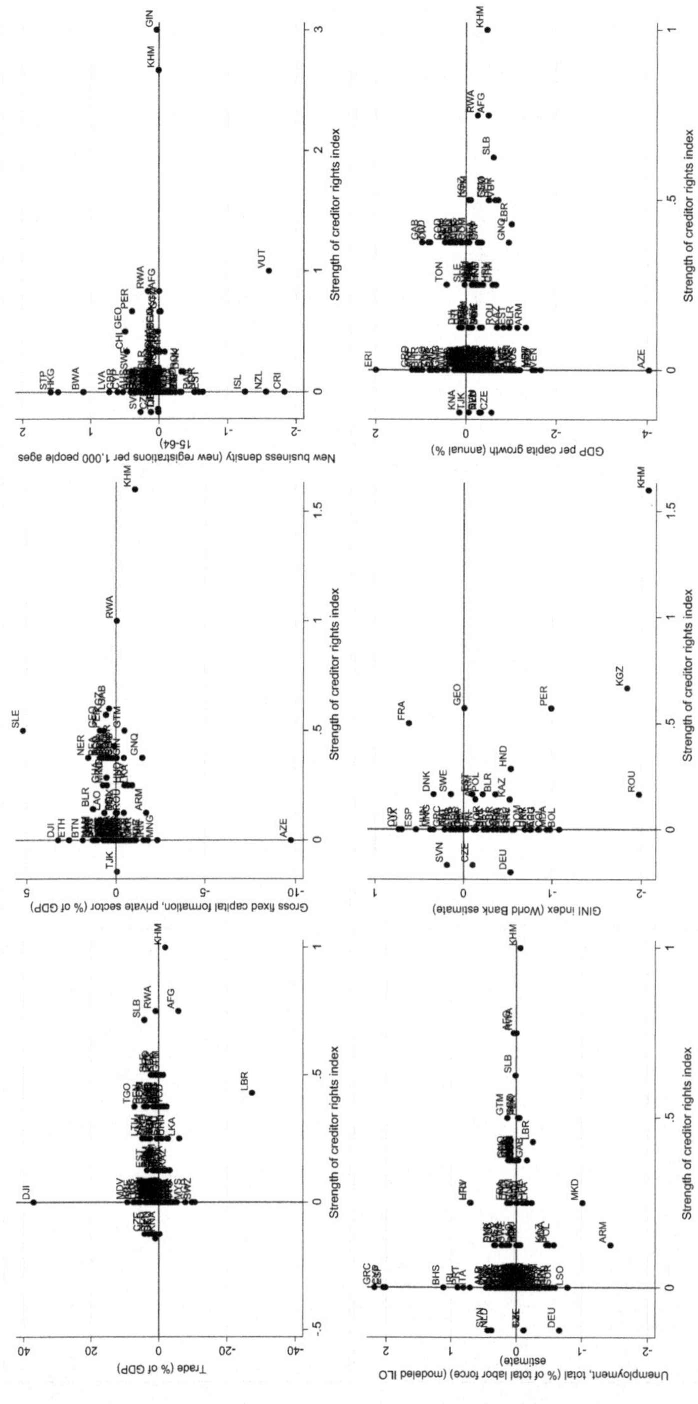

Fig. 6.1 (continued)

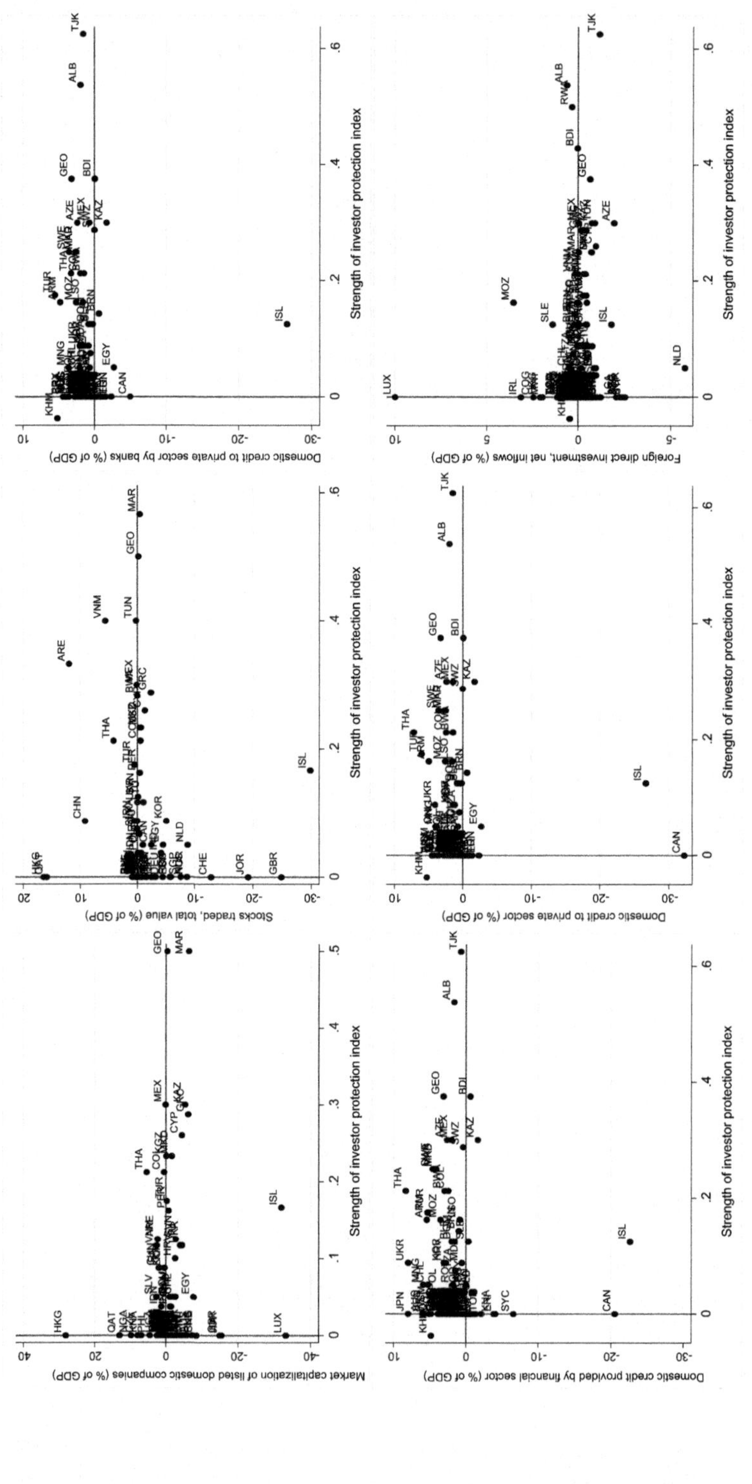

Fig. 6.2 Change in investor rights against change in financial and economic outcomes

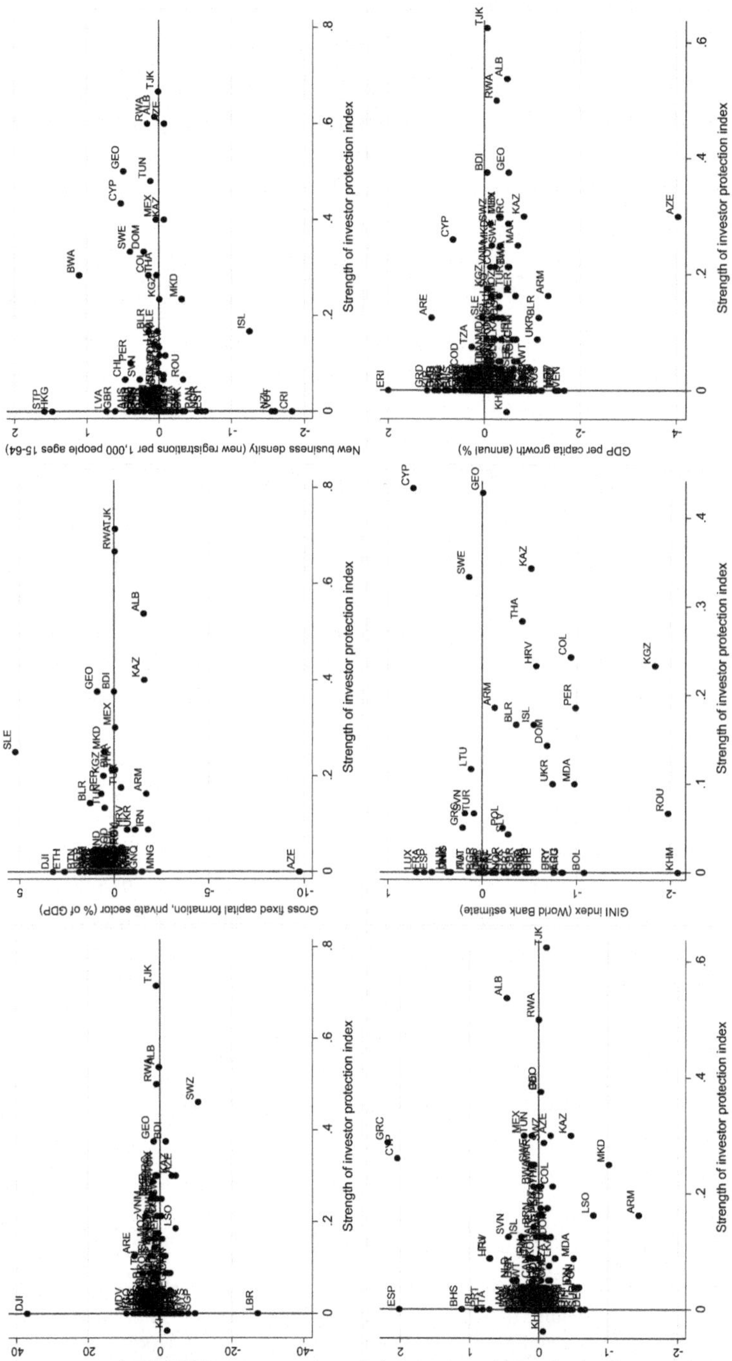

Fig. 6.2 (continued)

average annual variation in each of the development outcomes over the period 2006–2014 against the average annual variation in the indicators of law on the books, i.e., strength of creditor rights and investor protection indices, respectively.[5] The vertical and horizontal lines serve to see whether the change in the respective variable for each country in the sample is above, below or equal to zero. These plots enable us to identify the specific countries in which an improvement in legal rules is associated with an improvement in developmental outcomes.

As can be observed in most cases, there is generally a lack of clear relationship between changes in legal rules and regulations and changes in developmental outcomes. This is reflected in the fact that the wide variation in the extent of legal change across countries is not accompanied with such a high degree of variation in development outcomes. In the case of the investor protection index, this observation is more apparent than for the creditor rights index.

In order to have a clear idea of the statistical significance of the relationship between changes in law on the books and variations in financial and economic development outcomes, Table 6.7 presents the coefficient estimates that back up the lack of a statistically significant relationship between both sets of variables found in most cases. Only in the cases of economic inequality at the 1% level, and foreign direct investment, stocks value traded and domestic credit to private sector at the 10% level does a rise in creditor rights strength bring a statistically significant improvement in development outcomes. It is also worth noting that average variations in investor rights protection are not associated with average changes in most of the economic and financial development outcomes considered, being new business density the exception.

Taken as a whole, these results broadly confirm the panel data evidence provided above, which failed to render clear-cut support for a statistically significant impact of legal and regulatory changes on financial and economic development. As mentioned above, this lack of a consistent pattern of effects casts doubts on the intended positive impacts of reforms on creating market-friendly investor environments. Although such reforms may be desirable, our results suggest that, at the very least, are not sufficient to achieve their goals.

[5]Figures A.1–A.4 plot the average annual variation in each of the development outcomes over the period 2006–2014 against the average annual variation in the indicators of debt recovery rate, contract enforcement, starting a business and registering a property, respectively. It is remarkable that the results appear in line with those for the law on the books indicators.

Table 6.7 Average annual change in legal rules against average annual change in financial and economic outcomes (2006–2014)

Dependent variable →	Stock market capitalization	Stocks traded	Domestic credit to private sector by banks	Domestic credit provided by financial sector	Domestic credit to private sector	Foreign direct investment	Trade	Private gross fixed capital formation	New business density	Unemployment rate	Income GINI index	GDP per capita growth
	(1)	(2)	(3)	(4)	(5)	(6)	(7)	(8)	(8)	(10)	(11)	(12)
Panel A: Creditor rights												
Creditor rights	2.914	3.187	1.761	1.786	2.579*	0.72*	−1.424	0.502	−0.043	−0.125	−0.971***	0.129
	(2.297)	(2.613)	(1.213)	(1.374)	(1.413)	(0.389)	(1.963)	(0.648)	(0.081)	(0.105)	(0.272)	(0.199)
Constant	−2.151**	−1.579**	0.72**	1.197**	0.551	−0.212*	0.319	−0.053	0.011	0.034	−0.234***	−0.264***
	(0.828)	(0.723)	(0.362)	(0.455)	(0.525)	(0.118)	(0.378)	(0.191)	(0.038)	(0.04)	(0.07)	(0.056)
R^2	0	0	0.01	0.01	0.01	0.01	0	0.01	0	0	0.19	0
Obs.	94	87	110	110	110	174	170	90	123	161	55	174
Panel B: Investor protection												
Investor rights	−4.22	6.293	0.892	1.692	2.423	−0.723	−0.73	−0.077	0.343*	0.233	−0.236	−0.825
	(5.548)	(4.368)	(1.702)	(2.189)	(2.252)	(0.599)	(2.558)	(0.88)	(0.182)	(0.382)	(0.787)	(0.537)
Constant	−1.775**	−1.862**	0.826***	1.256***	0.638	−0.1	0.215	0.026	−0.018	0.008	−0.304***	−0.206***
	(0.817)	(0.71)	(0.249)	(0.389)	(0.457)	(0.105)	(0.415)	(0.168)	(0.042)	(0.03)	(0.093)	(0.049)
R^2	0.00	0.02	0.00	0.00	0.00	0.00	0.00	0.00	0.02	0.00	0.00	0.02
Obs.	94	87	110	110	110	174	170	90	123	161	55	174

Notes: Robust standard errors are in parentheses
*, ** and *** denote statistical significance at the 10, 5 and 1% levels, respectively

Chapter 7
Sensitivity Analyses on the Effect of Legal Rules Variation on Economic and Financial Performance

Abstract This chapter presents several robustness checks so as to determine whether the lack of a clear-cut impact of legal rules and regulatory indicators on economic and financial performance holds for alternative legal indicators, some of which extend over lengthier periods than the Doing Business indicators. Other sensitivity analyses entail the use of alternative estimators such as the difference GMM estimator of Arellano and Bond (Rev Econ Stud 58(2):277–297) and the system GMM estimator of Arellano and Bover (J Econ 68(1):29–51). The lack of effect of legal rules and regulatory indicators on financial and economic performance may indicate the existence of a gap between intended legal and regulatory reforms and the reality on the ground.

This chapter presents several robustness checks so as to determine whether the lack of a clear-cut impact of legal rules and regulatory indicators on economic and financial performance holds for alternative legal indicators, some of which extend over lengthier periods than the Doing Business indicators. Other sensitivity analyses entail the use of alternative estimators such as the difference GMM estimator of Arellano and Bond (1991) and the system GMM estimator of Arellano and Bover (1995).

7.1 Using Alternative Legal Indicators

In this section we use the Global Financial Development Database of the World Bank as an alternative to the World Development Indicators as far as the measures of financial development are concerned. The reason for this is that the former source has lengthier series than the latter, which is a requirement for the specifications estimated with alternative legal indicators. More specifically, the financial development outcomes used are the ratio of private credit by deposit money banks and other financial institutions to GDP, stock market capitalization to GDP, stock market total value traded to GDP, and number of listed companies per million people.[1]

[1]We have checked that our baseline results obtained for the specifications using the Doing Business indicators generally hold when the World Development Indicators measures of financial development are replaced by those of the Global Financial Development Database. As with the

D. Oto-Peralías, D. Romero-Ávila, *Legal Traditions, Legal Reforms and Economic Performance*, Contributions to Economics, DOI 10.1007/978-3-319-67041-6_7

We first employ the updated shareholder protection index developed by Siems (2008) and further used by Armour et al. (2009b), which covers 25 countries over the period 1995–2005. This index covers a much wider range of types of legal rules of company law and securities law than La Porta et al. (1997).[2] It is based on ten variables that include the following dimensions: powers of the general meeting for de facto changes, agenda setting power, anticipation of shareholder decision facilitated, prohibition of multiple voting rights, independent board members, feasibility of director's dismissal, private enforcement of director duties, shareholder action against resolutions of the general meeting, mandatory bid, and disclosure of major share ownership.

Table 7.1 presents the results of the LSDV specification using annual data and averaging the annual data over 3-year periods. Neither the specification with no additional control nor the one including lagged GDP growth renders any statistically significant impact of the shareholder protection index on economic and financial performance. The estimates of the respective panel specification with annual data support the existence of a statistically significant negative effect on stocks value traded over GDP.[3]

Table 7.1 also presents the results of the LSDV specification using annual and 3-year averaged data for an alternative creditor rights index provided by the CBR at Cambridge University. This index covers 25 countries over the period 1995–2005. Unlike the La Porta et al. (1997)'s creditor rights index that only focused on bankruptcy law, this creditor index considers other dimensions such as legal protection made available to creditors through secured credit and other contract-based mechanisms, and through company laws (Armour et al. 2009a). More specifically, this creditor index is based on the following ten dimensions: minimum share capital, dividend restriction, directors' duties towards creditors, non-possessory security interests and its registration, out-of-court enforcement of security interests, power to commence bankruptcy proceedings, stay of secured creditors in insolvency proceedings, outcome of bankruptcy proceedings, and rank order of secured creditors (Armour et al. 2009c).

It is worth noting that there is no statistically significant effect of this creditor rights index on economic development outcomes. In the case of the financial development outcomes, the evidence is highly disappointing since it indicates that greater creditor rights are associated with both lower private credit by deposit money banks and other financial institutions as well as with lower stock market total value traded to GDP.

---

former source, there is no statistically significant effect of law on the books on any of the financial development measures.

[2]This dataset is available online on the website of the Center for Business Research (CBR) at the University of Cambridge: http://www.cbr.cam.ac.uk/research/research-projects/completed-projects/law-finance-development/

[3]In this case we did not use the Gini index due to the low number of observations.

Table 7.1 The effect of legal rules on financial and economic outcomes: Creditor and investor rights over the period 1995–2005

	Creditor rights index		Shareholder protection index		Creditor rights index		Shareholder protection index	
	Lag GDP growth included				Lag GDP growth not included			
	(1)		(2)		(3)		(4)	
Panel A: Panel of 3-year averages								
Private credit by deposit money banks and other financial inst.	−105.124**	98	−42.341	98	−99.296**	100	−39.998	100
	(46.092)		(46.069)		(43.238)		(45.711)	
Stock market capitalization to GDP (%)	−70.695	98	−14.296	98	−80.494	100	−16.421	100
	(86.396)		(51.304)		(84.598)		(58.235)	
Stock market total value traded to GDP (%)	−168.366*	98	−119.059	98	−179.809*	99	−128.993	99
	(96.413)		(77.777)		(101.959)		(78.912)	
Number of listed companies per 1,000,000 people	−89.097	98	−89.687	98	−74.471	100	−77.404	100
	(124.877)		(73.387)		(115.371)		(63.029)	
Foreign direct investment, net inflows (% of GDP)	1.272	98	−1.737	98	−0.171	100	−1.741	100
	(4.027)		(2.926)		(4.423)		(2.67)	
Trade (% of GDP)	21.395	98	13.933	98	19.808	100	14.316	100
	(22.785)		(14.778)		(20.567)		(14.093)	
Gross fixed capital formation, private sector (% of GDP)	3.195	40	5.559	40	−1.075	40	10.063	40
	(20.833)		(14.393)		(25.787)		(16.447)	
Unemployment, total (% of total labor force) (modeled ILO)	1.371	98	7.799	98	2.283	100	7.455	100
	(6.729)		(6.849)		(5.865)		(6.822)	
Panel B: Panel of annual data								
Private credit by deposit money banks and other financial inst.	−92.349**	267	−24.496	267	−82.611**	271	−25.81	271
	(36.324)		(30.575)		(35.43)		(29.676)	
Stock market capitalization to GDP (%)	−38.164	271	−14.876	271	−45.991	274	−6.373	274
	(57.878)		(28.302)		(57.586)		(28.999)	

(continued)

Table 7.1 (continued)

	Creditor rights index		Shareholder protection index		Creditor rights index		Shareholder protection index	
	Lag GDP growth included				Lag GDP growth not included			
	(1)		(2)		(3)		(4)	
Stock market total value traded to GDP (%)	−153.321**	271	−80.144**	271	−160.27**	272	−70.722*	272
	(71.584)		(34.701)		(76.805)		(38.777)	
Number of listed companies per 1,000,000 people	−68.059	271	−62.956	271	−59.773	275	−54.347	275
	(91.771)		(42.833)		(87.756)		(40.15)	
Foreign direct investment, net inflows (% of GDP)	0.238	271	5.87	271	−0.835	275	6.048	275
	(4.179)		(8.665)		(4.128)		(8.054)	
Trade (% of GDP)	9.211	271	13.95	271	9.201	275	12.612	275
	(17.922)		(9.067)		(16.971)		(9.431)	
Gross fixed capital formation, private sector (% of GDP)	1.618	110	2.348	110	−2.839	110	6.776	110
	(20.97)		(9.822)		(23.309)		(10.523)	
Unemployment, total (% of total labor force) (modeled ILO)	−0.636	271	6.436	271	0.857	275	4.798	275
	(4.584)		(3.904)		(4.157)		(3.711)	

Notes: Regressions include a constant term, which is omitted for space considerations. Standard errors clustered by country are in parentheses. Creditor and investor rights stem from Siems (2008) and Armour et al. (2009a)

*, ** and *** denote statistical significance at the 10, 5 and 1% levels, respectively

Table 7.2 presents the results using the creditor rights index proposed by Djankov et al. (2007). This creditor rights index follows very closely the one constructed by La Porta et al. (1997). It expands the sample from 49 to 133 countries and covers every year between 1978 and 2003. This index measures four powers of secured lenders in bankruptcy proceedings: (1) whether there are restrictions in the event of a debtor's filing for reorganization, (2) whether there is no automatic stay or asset freeze imposed by the court once the petition for reorganization is approved, (3) whether secured creditors are paid first in the liquidation proceedings, and (4) whether an administrator, instead of management, is in charge of running the business during reorganization (Djankov et al. 2007).

The LSDV specification using 3-year averages does not provide clear evidence of a statistically significant impact of creditor rights on economic or financial development outcomes. The LSDV specification with annual data and lagged GDP growth as a control only renders a statistically significant effect of creditor rights on economic inequality, which carries a wrong sign. The specification with 3-year averaged data renders a marginally significant negative effect on the number of listed companies. Overall, this again supports the lack of a consistent relationship between law on the books and finance, which stands against the law and finance view.

Table 7.3 reports the estimates obtained using a measure of the quality of contract enforcement given by the formalism of civil procedure for the case of eviction of a tenant and collection of a check. These measures are developed by Balas et al. (2009) for 40 countries over the period 1950–2000. The LSDV specification with both 3-year averaged data and annual data only renders evidence that higher formalism for the case of eviction is associated with higher unemployment. In the specification that includes lagged GDP growth as additional control with both 3-year averaged and annual data, higher formalism both in eviction and collecting a check appears to have a statistically significant impact (though with the wrong sign) on foreign direct investment.

Taken as a whole, this sensitivity analysis appears to show that the lack of a consistent effect of legal rules and regulatory indicators on economic and financial development outcomes are not only a feature found for the Doing Business database, but it is also obtained for alternative law on the books indicators regarding the protection of shareholders and creditor rights as well as for other indicators concerning legal formalism of civil procedure.

7.2 Using Alternative Panel Estimations: Difference and System GMM Estimators

The results from the application of the difference GMM estimator proposed by Arellano and Bond (1991) and the system GMM estimator by Arellano and Bover (1995) and Blundell and Bond (1998) are presented in Tables 7.4 and 7.5,

Table 7.2 The effect of legal rules on financial and economic outcomes: Creditor rights over the period 1978–2002 (Djankov et al. 2007)

	Creditor rights index			
	Lag GDP growth included		Lag GDP growth not included	
	(1)		(2)	
Panel A: Panel of 3-year averages				
Private credit by deposit money banks and other financial inst.	0.372	783	0.005	806
	(3.856)		(3.748)	
Stock market capitalization to GDP (%)	−7.899	349	−6.985	355
	(11.796)		(10.956)	
Stock market total value traded to GDP (%)	−7.089	342	−7.137	347
	(9.21)		(8.322)	
Number of listed companies per 1,000,000 people	−6.312*	386	−8.145*	392
	(3.642)		(4.603)	
Foreign direct investment, net inflows (% of GDP)	−0.144	854	0.039	882
	(0.611)		(0.576)	
Trade (% of GDP)	−3.624	868	−3.779	903
	(3.685)		(3.491)	
Gross fixed capital formation, private sector (% of GDP)	1.708	485	1.624	498
	(1.34)		(1.639)	
Unemployment, total (% of total labor force) (modeled ILO)	−0.075	495	−0.019	515
	(0.394)		(0.343)	
GINI index (World Bank estimate)	1.384	326	0.949	340
	(1.202)		(1.015)	
Panel B: Panel of annual data				
Private credit by deposit money banks and other financial inst.	0.863	2355	0.517	2417
	(3.064)		(3.011)	
Stock market capitalization to GDP (%)	−2.897	948	−3.498	955
	(8.444)		(8.684)	
Stock market total value traded to GDP (%)	−3.143	931	−3.916	936
	(6.868)		(6.968)	
Number of listed companies per 1,000,000 people	−6.103	1115	−5.938	1128
	(3.992)		(3.596)	
Foreign direct investment, net inflows (% of GDP)	−0.035	2630	0.039	2675
	(0.498)		(0.5)	
Trade (% of GDP)	−4.184	2700	−3.715	2758
	(3.095)		(3.025)	
Gross fixed capital formation, private sector (% of GDP)	1.073	1420	1.239	1434
	(1.298)		(1.299)	
Unemployment, total (% of total labor force) (modeled ILO)	−0.179	1493	−0.125	1534
	(0.364)		(0.318)	
GINI index (World Bank estimate)	1.664**	454	0.948	460
	(0.764)		(0.813)	

Notes: Regressions include a constant term, which is omitted for space considerations. Standard errors clustered by country are in parentheses

*, ** and *** denote statistical significance at the 10, 5 and 1% levels, respectively

Table 7.3 The effect of legal rules on financial and economic outcomes: Formalism index 1960–2000 (Balas et al. 2009)

	Formalism index—Eviction		Formalism index—Check collection		Formalism index—Eviction		Formalism index—Check collection	
	Lag GDP growth included				Lag GDP growth not included			
	(1)		(2)		(3)		(4)	
Panel A: Panel of 3-year averages								
Private credit by deposit money banks and other financial inst.	−5.403	441	−5.435	441	−5.989	485	−6.421*	485
	(6.258)		(3.65)		(6.048)		(3.656)	
Stock market capitalization to GDP (%)	3.927	176	9.279	176	4.606	176	9.16	176
	(21.717)		(17.718)		(20.055)		(17.776)	
Stock market total value traded to GDP (%)	−3.079	175	−5.069	175	−2.908	175	−5.53	175
	(10.965)		(14.374)		(10.477)		(14.826)	
Number of listed companies per 1,000,000 people	2.275	178	−3.784	178	2.223	178	−3.622	178
	(4.928)		(4.089)		(5.005)		(3.898)	
Foreign direct investment, net inflows (% of GDP)	0.642**	387	0.334*	387	0.502	398	0.322	398
	(0.291)		(0.167)		(0.332)		(0.201)	
Trade (% of GDP)	2.633	482	0.957	482	3.525	534	−0.495	534
	(2.748)		(3.793)		(2.707)		(5.015)	
Gross fixed capital formation, private sector (% of GDP)	2.844	178	2.843	178	2.848	180	2.865	180
	(2.429)		(2.207)		(2.843)		(2.469)	
Unemployment, total (% of total labor force) (modeled ILO)	3.823***	160	0.982	160	3.861***	160	0.882	160
	(1.029)		(2.411)		(1.229)		(2.511)	
GINI index (World Bank estimate)	−20.484	111	−8.271	111	−19.838	111	−7.914	111
	(16.142)		(6.471)		(15.696)		(6.638)	

(continued)

Table 7.3 (continued)

	Formalism index—Eviction		Formalism index—Check collection		Formalism index—Eviction		Formalism index—Check collection	
	Lag GDP growth included				Lag GDP growth not included			
	(1)		(2)		(3)		(4)	
Panel B: Panel of annual data								
Private credit by deposit money banks and other financial inst.	−5.385	1287	−5.079	1287	−5.45	1361	−5.574*	1361
	(5.646)		(3.324)		(5.492)		(3.265)	
Stock market capitalization to GDP (%)	2.021	421	13.07	421	3.492	421	14.862	421
	(18.672)		(12.676)		(18.035)		(12.643)	
Stock market total value traded to GDP (%)	−3.686	419	−0.569	419	−0.996	419	1.981	419
	(11.978)		(11.12)		(10.241)		(10.34)	
Number of listed companies per 1,000,000 people	1.828	459	−0.957	459	1.557	459	−1.293	459
	(3.964)		(1.967)		(3.923)		(1.968)	
Foreign direct investment, net inflows (% of GDP)	0.543*	1085	0.289**	1085	0.485	1108	0.274	1108
	(0.271)		(0.142)		(0.304)		(0.168)	
Trade (% of GDP)	2.549	1438	0.674	1438	3.42	1554	−0.393	1554
	(2.341)		(3.603)		(2.406)		(4.601)	
Gross fixed capital formation, private sector (% of GDP)	2.463	489	2.631	489	2.564	493	2.578	493
	(2.113)		(2.071)		(2.443)		(2.242)	
Unemployment, total (% of total labor force) (modeled ILO)	2.814***	400	0.658	400	2.863***	400	0.311	400
	(0.738)		(1.799)		(0.872)		(1.718)	
GINI index (World Bank estimate)	−13.2	145	−5.568	145	−13.164	145	−5.565	145
	(11.353)		(4.37)		(11.214)		(4.299)	

Notes: Regressions include a constant term, which is omitted for space considerations. Standard errors clustered by country are in parentheses
*, ** and *** denote statistical significance at the 10, 5 and 1% levels, respectively

Table 7.4 The effect of legal rules on financial and economic outcomes: Difference GMM estimator

	Stock market capitalization	Stocks traded	Domestic credit to private sector by banks	Domestic credit provided by financial sector	Domestic credit to private sector	Foreign direct investment	Trade	Private gross fixed capital formation	New business density	Unemployment rate	Income GINI index
	(1)	(2)	(3)	(4)	(5)	(6)	(7)	(8)	(8)	(10)	(11)
Panel A: Creditor rights and GDP growth											
Creditor rights	−3.903	75.757	0.935	1.657	0.472	−0.093	−0.834	−0.024	−0.106	−0.264	−0.352
	(14.2)	(48.48)	(2.12)	(3.02)	(2.16)	(0.77)	(1.68)	(0.87)	(0.29)	(0.26)	(0.68)
GDP growth	−0.077	1.528	−0.465**	−1.122**	−0.444*	−0.001	0.826**	0.071	0.084	−0.026	0.112**
	(0.92)	(1.44)	(0.23)	(0.48)	(0.24)	(0.1)	(0.32)	(0.24)	(0.06)	(0.03)	(0.05)
Arellano-Bond test for AR(2)	0.234	0.138	0.378	0.965	0.446	0.908	0.225	0.005	0.501	0.117	0.35
Hansen test of overid. restr.	0.021	0.779	0.231	0.17	0.37	0.118	0.342	0.075	0.429	0.001	0.142
Number of obs.	623	545	849	849	849	1357	1292	632	638	1258	328
Panel B: Creditor rights											
Creditor rights	−4.371	95.401	0.118	0.659	0.096	−1.088	0.437	0.188	−0.037	−0.133	−0.009
	(23.5)	(79.73)	(1.79)	(2.3)	(1.75)	(0.99)	(1.59)	(0.68)	(0.38)	(0.25)	(0.68)
Arellano-Bond test for AR(2)	0.211	0.173	0.264	0.493	0.341	0.93	0.298	0.003	0.854	0.087	0.634
Hansen test of overid. restr.	0.508	0.958	0.098	0.018	0.162	0.133	0.752	0.053	0.124	0.003	0.352
Number of obs.	623	545	857	857	857	1365	1300	633	642	1281	328
Panel C: Investor protection and GDP growth											
Investor protection	13.642	24.466	−1.762	−3.527	−3.807	1.439	−5.782	−1.95	0.145	−0.769	2.602
	(21.31)	(15.89)	(3.36)	(5.43)	(4.11)	(2.75)	(6.97)	(2.66)	(1.13)	(0.82)	(2.18)

(continued)

Table 7.4 (continued)

	Stock market capitalization	Stocks traded	Domestic credit to private sector by banks	Domestic credit provided by financial sector	Domestic credit to private sector	Foreign direct investment	Trade	Private gross fixed capital formation	New business density	Unemployment rate	Income GINI index
	(1)	(2)	(3)	(4)	(5)	(6)	(7)	(8)	(8)	(10)	(11)
GDP growth	0.586	−0.104	−0.291	−0.479	−0.244	0.013	0.775*	0.046	0.106	−0.031	0.112
	(0.61)	(0.57)	(0.21)	(0.42)	(0.27)	(0.13)	(0.4)	(0.21)	(0.12)	(0.04)	(0.1)
Arellano-Bond test for AR(2)	0.196	0.115	0.316	0.526	0.336	0.921	0.406	0.006	0.425	0.157	0.832
Hansen test of overid. restr.	0.05	0.43	0.383	0.562	0.302	0.348	0.433	0.292	0.297	0.001	0.19
Number of obs.	623	545	849	849	849	1357	1292	632	638	1258	328
Panel D: Investor protection											
Investor protection	−3.285	23.372	−2.833	−4.706	−5.524	−2.437	−10.052	−0.323	0.047	0.353	0.227
	(29.69)	(26.45)	(4.14)	(4.37)	(4.97)	(2.96)	(9.37)	(2.55)	(0.77)	(0.96)	(1.75)
Arellano-Bond test for AR(2)	0.195	0.118	0.258	0.401	0.276	0.872	0.466	0.003	0.844	0.078	0.707
Hansen test of overid. restr.	0.116	0.658	0.583	0.667	0.627	0.317	0.821	0.28	0.176	0	0.29
Number of obs.	623	545	857	857	857	1365	1300	633	642	1281	328

Note: Regressions estimated with the two-step difference GMM estimator using the STATA program xtabond2 (Roodman 2006). For the first-differenced equation, the second lags of the explanatory variables (all treated as endogenous) are used as instruments. The exogenous variables are the period dummies. Robust standard errors are in parentheses

*, ** and *** denote statistical significance at the 10, 5 and 1% levels, respectively

Table 7.5 The effect of legal rules on financial and economic outcomes: System GMM estimator

	Stock market capitalization	Stocks traded	Domestic credit to private sector by banks	Domestic credit provided by financial sector	Domestic credit to private sector	Foreign direct investment	Trade	Private gross fixed capital formation	New business density	Unemployment rate	Income GINI index
	(1)	(2)	(3)	(4)	(5)	(6)	(7)	(8)	(8)	(10)	(11)
Panel A: Creditor rights and GDP growth											
Creditor rights	−4.402	1.042	4.801	−1.333	3.967	0.371*	3.96	0.918*	0.404	−0.838	−1.682***
	(8.07)	(4.95)	(3.52)	(3.47)	(3.75)	(0.21)	(2.94)	(0.52)	(0.3)	(0.51)	(0.62)
GDP growth	0.777	−0.024	0.044	−0.057	0.058	0.066	−0.804	−0.339	−0.038	−0.117	0.4**
	(0.87)	(0.76)	(0.59)	(0.38)	(0.62)	(0.06)	(0.93)	(0.33)	(0.13)	(0.08)	(0.19)
Arellano-Bond test for AR(2)	0.24	0.157	0.321	0.449	0.426	0.87	0.258	0.004	0.888	0.102	0.132
Hansen test of overid. restr.	0.116	0.128	0.112	0.13	0.129	0.205	0.159	0.184	0.398	0.004	0.273
Number of obs.	727	641	958	958	958	1533	1464	728	849	1421	506
Panel B: Creditor rights											
Creditor rights	−7.251*	−1.212	−1.971	−5.678	−2.789	0.173	0.951	0.29	0.009	−1.186**	−0.829
	(4.07)	(3.87)	(3.04)	(3.52)	(2.8)	(0.58)	(1.95)	(0.58)	(0.49)	(0.48)	(0.67)
Arellano-Bond test for AR(2)	0.224	0.155	0.256	0.376	0.299	0.91	0.308	0.002	0.849	0.051	0.533
Hansen test of overid. restr.	0.802	0.272	0.032	0.054	0.093	0.169	0.59	0.154	0.467	0.016	0.213
Number of obs.	727	641	967	967	967	1542	1473	729	854	1445	507
Panel C: Investor protection and GDP growth											
Investor protection	18.659**	16.707**	5.723	4.22	6.881	0.45	3.917	1.974**	0.363	−0.462	−2.08
	(8.82)	(7.8)	(4.36)	(6)	(4.45)	(0.39)	(5.25)	(0.83)	(0.52)	(0.92)	(1.84)

(continued)

Table 7.5 (continued)

	Stock market capitalization	Stocks traded	Domestic credit to private sector by banks	Domestic credit provided by financial sector	Domestic credit to private sector	Foreign direct investment	Trade	Private gross fixed capital formation	New business density	Unemployment rate	Income GINI index
	(1)	(2)	(3)	(4)	(5)	(6)	(7)	(8)	(8)	(10)	(11)
GDP growth	0.628	−0.912	−0.387	−0.945	−0.389	0.082	−0.743	−0.281	−0.11	−0.097	0.366*
	(0.82)	(1)	(0.43)	(0.73)	(0.51)	(0.07)	(0.76)	(0.31)	(0.11)	(0.1)	(0.2)
Arellano-Bond test for AR(2)	0.205	0.138	0.379	0.8	0.549	0.875	0.15	0.005	0.501	0.161	0.126
Hansen test of overid. restr.	0.197	0.11	0.07	0.353	0.072	0.187	0.175	0.112	0.508	0.006	0.109
Number of obs.	727	641	958	958	958	1533	1464	728	849	1421	506
Panel D: Investor protection											
Investor protection	10.628	10.915*	−2.773	−4.065	−2.009	−1.155	−9.607	0.539	−0.724	0.825	−2.594
	(11.12)	(6.61)	(4.01)	(6.18)	(4.78)	(0.88)	(8.92)	(1.36)	(0.58)	(1.36)	(2.14)
Arellano-Bond test for AR(2)	0.181	0.139	0.255	0.409	0.31	0.89	0.46	0.002	0.837	0.082	0.195
Hansen test of overid. restr.	0.431	0.278	0.794	0.797	0.812	0.462	0.531	0.647	0.683	0.003	0.192
Number of obs.	727	641	967	967	967	1542	1473	729	854	1445	507

Note: Regressions estimated with the two-step system GMM estimator using the STATA program xtabond2 (Roodman 2006). For the first-differenced equation, the second lags of the explanatory variables (all treated as endogenous) are used as instruments. For the level equation, the lagged first-differences of the explanatory variables are used as instruments. The exogenous variables are the period dummies. Robust standard errors are in parentheses

*, ** and *** denote statistical significance at the 10, 5 and 1% levels, respectively

respectively. The difference GMM estimator addresses endogeneity problems by using previous realizations of the regressors to instrument for their current values in the first-differenced specification. However, Arellano and Bover (1995) and Blundell and Bond (1998) show that in the case of highly persistent regressors, lagged levels of the variables are weak instruments for the first-differenced regressors. This leads to a fall in precision as well as to biased coefficients. In order to overcome these shortcomings, they recommend the use of the system GMM estimator that utilizes instruments in levels and first-differences to improve efficiency. The system GMM estimator thus employs previous realizations of the regressors to instrument for their current values in the first-differenced specification and the lagged differences for the regression in levels. In order to avoid using an excessive number of instruments in a context with a relatively short cross-country dimension, we follow the suggestion of Roodman (2009) and limit the set of instruments to the minimum, i.e. to the first available: x_{it-2} for the specification in first-differences and Δx_{it-1} for the specification in levels. We use the two-step estimator and all our regressors are treated as endogenous variables (except for the time-period dummies). The consistency of the difference and system estimator depends on the validity of the instruments and the absence of serial correlation of second-order in the error term. Therefore, we test these assumptions using the Hansen test for over-identifying restrictions and the test for second-order autocorrelation proposed by Arellano and Bond (1991). Failure to reject the null hypotheses of overall validity of the instruments and absence of second-order serial correlation in the error for the respective tests would give support to the model.

Since the use of 3-year averaged data would make infeasible the use of this estimator, we have no choice but to use annual data over the period 2006–2014. In addition, in this robustness check the focus is on the impact of law on the books variables (i.e., creditor rights and investor protection) on economic and financial developmental outcomes.

It is worth noting that endogeneity concerns do not appear to have driven the lack of an effect of legal rules on outcomes found when we applied the LSDV estimator. Again, there is consistent evidence of the absence of a statistically significant impact of law on the books on economic and financial performance, irrespective of the inclusion of lagged GDP growth as a control variable. Indeed, when we apply the system GMM estimator for the specification that includes lagged GDP growth as a control variable, a higher score in creditor rights only has a statistically significant positive effect on foreign direct investment and private gross fixed capital formation at the 10% level, while it reduces income inequality at the 1% significance level. As far as the specification for investor protection is concerned, a stronger investor protection is only associated with a rise in the ratios of stocks value listed and traded to GDP and private fixed capital formation at the 5% significance level. We should be confident with these results since the Hansen test for overidentifying restrictions indicates that the instruments are valid and the Arellano and Bond (1991) test for AR(2) autocorrelation rules out the existence of second-order autocorrelation in most of the cases.

In all, the evidence gathered in these extensive sensitivity analyses appears to back the baseline finding of the lack of an effect of legal rules and regulatory indicators on economic and financial performance obtained with the application of the LSDV estimator.

7.3 General Discussion

The lack of a statistically significant impact of legal rules and regulatory indicators on economic and financial performance may indicate the existence of a gap between intended legal and regulatory reforms and the reality on the ground. This is consistent with the evidence provided by Hallward-Driemeier and Prichett (2011), who found only weak correlations between changes over time in Doing Business indicators and firm-level Enterprise Surveys.[4] This indicates that outcome-based legal indicators derived from the direct experience of firms, which can better measure the consequences arising from the actual implementation and enforcement of laws in practice, are far from the intended legal and regulatory changes measured in the Doing Business reports.

As pointed out by Belsley (2015), the fact that Doing Business indicators are used in policy dialogue or as a form of conditionality at the time of qualifying for aid grants may lead many developing nations to try to improve their Doing Business ranking by making pro forma changes in laws without much substantive value or visible improvements in results or behavior. Rwanda is a case in point. This nation ranked 47 in the 2015 Doing Business report, despite having a level of GDP per capita below $1000 and almost half of its population in poverty (Belsley 2015).

In addition, legal and regulatory reforms in developing nations that mechanically adopt organizational forms from prosperous nations, without a thorough analysis of their specific policy priorities to improve their framework for governance and institutional reform as a way to foster their state capacity to deliver growth and social advancement, are likely to render governance reforms mostly ineffective. According to Belsley (2015, p. 112), "certain policy reforms are likely to have complementarities across several policy dimensions—economic and noneconomic—like steps to speed up court decisions and to train more competent

[4]Whereas the former (obtained from local experts on a specific legal/regulation area) measures what a standardized firm should expect if it complies with all official regulations and legal requirements in place, the latter (obtained from face-to-face interviews with managers) measures the actual experiences of a firm regarding a particular legal or regulatory aspect in the normal course of business, which does not necessarily entail the full compliance or enforcement of the laws and regulations in place. According to Hallward-Driemeier and Pritchett (2015, p. 123), "the estimate of legally required time for firms to complete certain legal and regulatory processes provided by the Doing Business survey does not summarize even modestly well the experience of firms as reported by the Enterprise Surveys". They warn against "thinking about regulations as creating 'rules' to be followed", particularly in environments in which stringent regulations affecting investment meet weak governmental implementation and enforcement capabilities.

lawyers". Hence, the reduction of legal formalism may not yield the intended positive fruits, if the country lacks the judicial human capital and infrastructure required for effectively implementing that reform and benefiting from it. In a similar spirit, Dixit (2009, p. 21) recommends that, before replacing existing institutions with new ones, countries' policy makers "should determine whether existing institutions and organizations are there for a good reason, and how [their] reforms would interact with them in the short and the long run. ... [I]t is better to start with a presumption in favor of what has existed for a while than the presumption that everything should be changed to match the successful formal institutions in advanced countries". He further argues that countries' decision makers should listen to all sectors (including supranational agencies, academic experts, journalists and practitioners), "but should not slavishly follow any one, not even their own prior dogmatic belief. Instead, they should study their situation in light of theories and other cases, and then make their own choice". With all these caveats in mind, "the Doing Business report is destined to be most effective as a tool for inspiring debate over policy change in countries that already have an interest in making policy reforms" (Belsley 2015, p. 118).

Chapter 8
The Effectiveness of Legal Reforms and the Gap Between Law on the Books and the Reality on the Ground

Abstract This chapter conducts an exploratory analysis of the determinants of the effectiveness of legal reforms and the gap between legal rules and the reality on the ground. The empirical approach employed to measure whether legal reforms have been effective or not is by comparing the magnitude of the change in legal reforms versus the change in financial and economic outcomes. Concerning the determinants of the effectiveness of legal reforms, although the importance of each factor depends on the specific rule and outcome variable, institutional quality and mineral abundance have a positive impact on legal reform effectiveness. Concerning the gap between legal rules and economic performance, we construct an indicator of the gap as the difference between distance to the frontier in legal rules and distance to the frontier in economic outcomes, where distance to the frontier measures the distance of each economy to the best performance observed for each indicator. As regards the determinants of the gap between law on the books and the reality on the ground, the evidence supports the fact that common law countries are systematically associated with a larger gap in both creditor rights and investor protection with respect to financial depth and entrepreneurship. In addition, institutional quality is found to reduce the gap between creditor rights and investor protection relative to performance in terms of financial depth and entrepreneurship.

The previous chapter shows that legal reforms are not systematically related to better economic and financial outcomes. This finding means that, on average, there is not a common trend, but it is possible to identify countries in which legal reforms have been overall successful. Therefore, the comparison between successful and unsuccessful countries that have implemented legal reforms can provide clues about what makes legal reforms work well. The first part of this chapter aims to conduct a preliminary analysis to investigate the factors that contribute to the effectiveness of legal reforms, that is, whether changes in legal rules materialize into improvements in economic and financial outcomes. In the second part, we study a related phenomenon, i.e., the gap between law on the books and the reality on the ground.

D. Oto-Peralías, D. Romero-Ávila, *Legal Traditions, Legal Reforms and Economic Performance*, Contributions to Economics, DOI 10.1007/978-3-319-67041-6_8

8.1 Explanatory Factors for the Effectiveness of Legal Reforms: A Preliminary Analysis

Overall, there are 59 and 57 economies that have improved their creditor rights and investor rights over the period 2006–2014, respectively. The rationale behind these legal reforms is that by strengthening the protection of creditor and investor rights, financial markets will prosper, promoting in turn economic activity. Figures 8.1 and 8.2 depict those countries that have improved the score in the creditor right index and the investor protection index between 2006 and 2014.

The empirical approach employed to measure whether legal reforms have been effective or not is by comparing the magnitude of the change in legal reforms vs. the change in financial and economic outcomes. Figure 8.3 shows the relationship of average annual change in financial depth and new business density with either average annual change in the creditor rights index (Panel A) or average annual change in the investor protection index (Panel B). We can observe that, although on average there is no relationship between legal changes and economic changes, there are countries that have been more successful than others. Countries in the first quadrant (+, +) have experienced an increase in both dimensions, while economies in the fourth quadrant (+, −) have experienced an improvement in legal rules but a decline in economic/financial outcomes. Countries close to the horizontal line (value 0 on the y-axis) have conducted legal reforms, but without any impact on economic/financial outcomes. Finally, economies depicted in gray have not carried out legal reforms conducive to improving the protection of creditor and investor rights. It is remarkable that most of the countries that have implemented reforms are relatively close to the horizontal line, which implies that their effect on the ratio of private credit by deposit money banks and other financial institutions to GDP and new business density is close to zero or small.

Fig. 8.1 Creditor rights reforms around the world (2006–2014). Notes: Average annual change in creditor rights during the period 2006–2014 (a *darker* color means a higher value). Countries in white have not improved their creditor rights, and countries with missing data on legal rules do not appear in the map

Fig. 8.2 Investor protection reforms around the world (2006–2014). Notes: Average annual change in investor protection during the period 2006–2014 (a *darker* color means a higher value). Countries in *white* have not improved their creditor rights, and countries with missing data on legal rules do not appear in the map

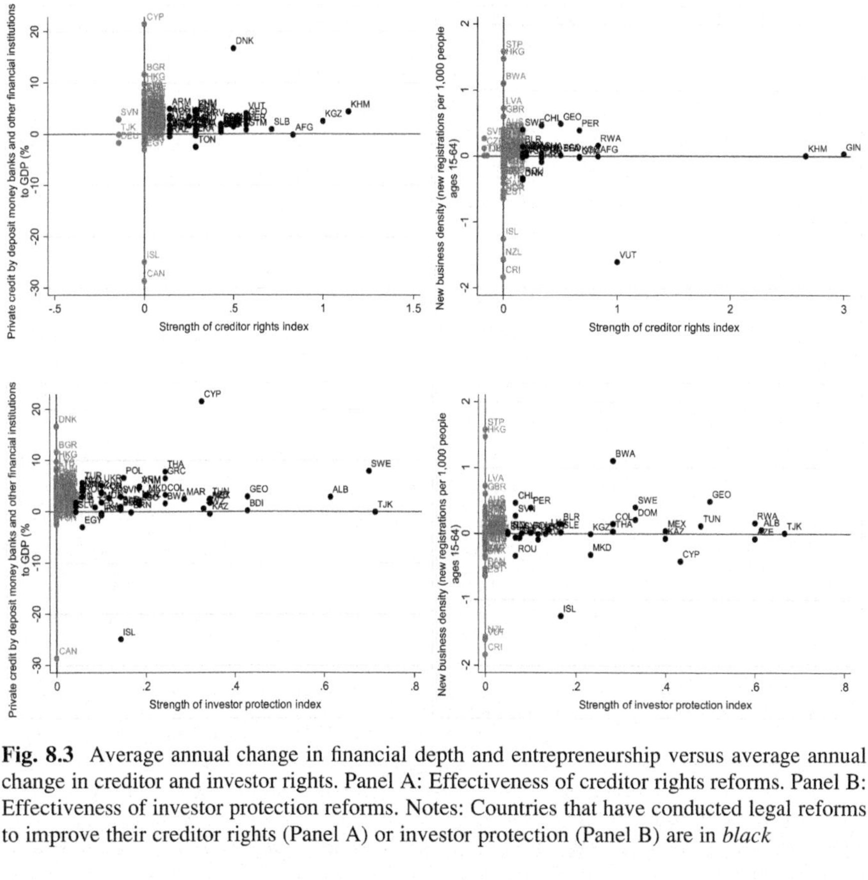

Fig. 8.3 Average annual change in financial depth and entrepreneurship versus average annual change in creditor and investor rights. Panel A: Effectiveness of creditor rights reforms. Panel B: Effectiveness of investor protection reforms. Notes: Countries that have conducted legal reforms to improve their creditor rights (Panel A) or investor protection (Panel B) are in *black*

Given this cross-country heterogeneity in terms of relative changes in legal rules and economic/financial indicators, it is possible to analyze what factors are correlated with the effectiveness of legal reforms. This is an important question because it may give clues about the specific contexts in which a legal reform is likely to be effective. To conduct such an analysis it is necessary to create an indicator of legal reforms effectiveness. We measure the effectiveness of legal reforms as follows:

$$\textit{Effectiveness} = \frac{\textit{Average annual change in economic or financial outcomes}\ (2006-2014)}{\textit{Average annual change in legal rules}\ (2006-2014)}$$

In this section we focus on two outcome variables to measure the effectiveness of legal reforms: (1) financial depth [i.e., private credit over GDP (%)] as a proxy for financial development, and (2) new business density as a proxy for economic dynamism and entrepreneurship.[1] For illustrative purposes, Figure 8.4 shows the values for the indicators of legal reform effectiveness in creditor rights. It is worth noting that the effectiveness of legal reforms—according to our definition—has been much higher in some countries than in others. For example, according to Panel A, a one point increase in creditor rights is associated with more than a 30% points increase in private credit to GDP in Denmark and Armenia, whereas with only a 10% points increase in France and with very small increases or even negative changes in Chad and Sri Lanka. Panel B also shows substantial heterogeneity in the effectiveness of creditor rights reforms in promoting entrepreneurship.[2] In addition, a one point increase in creditor rights is related to around a two-and-a-half percentage points increase in new registrations per 1000 people aged between 15 and 64 in Sweden, whereas the effect is close to zero in countries like Togo, Senegal, Syria, Burkina Faso and Haiti, and highly negative in Vanuatu, Romania and Denmark.

Table 8.1 analyzes the determinants of the effectiveness of creditor rights reforms in financial depth and entrepreneurship. The sample of countries is restricted to those that have improved their creditor rights over the period of study. As possible determinants of legal reform effectiveness, we employ several institutional, historical and geographic factors, conditional on the fact that the country has implemented a legal reform. We always control for log GDP per capita in 2006 to take into account that the level of economic development may affect the effectiveness of legal reforms in a number of ways. For example, more developed countries are closer to the frontier in economic performance and perhaps it is more difficult to further improve their economic and financial performance. On the

[1]Financial depth comes from the Global Financial Development Database and covers the period 2006–2013. We prefer to use this source rather than the World Development Indicators due to its higher geographic coverage. New business density comes from the World Development Indicators and is available for the period 2006–2014, although for many countries there are some years with missing data. We use all available data.

[2]The number of observations in Panel B is lower due to the fact that data on new business density are missing in some years for many countries.

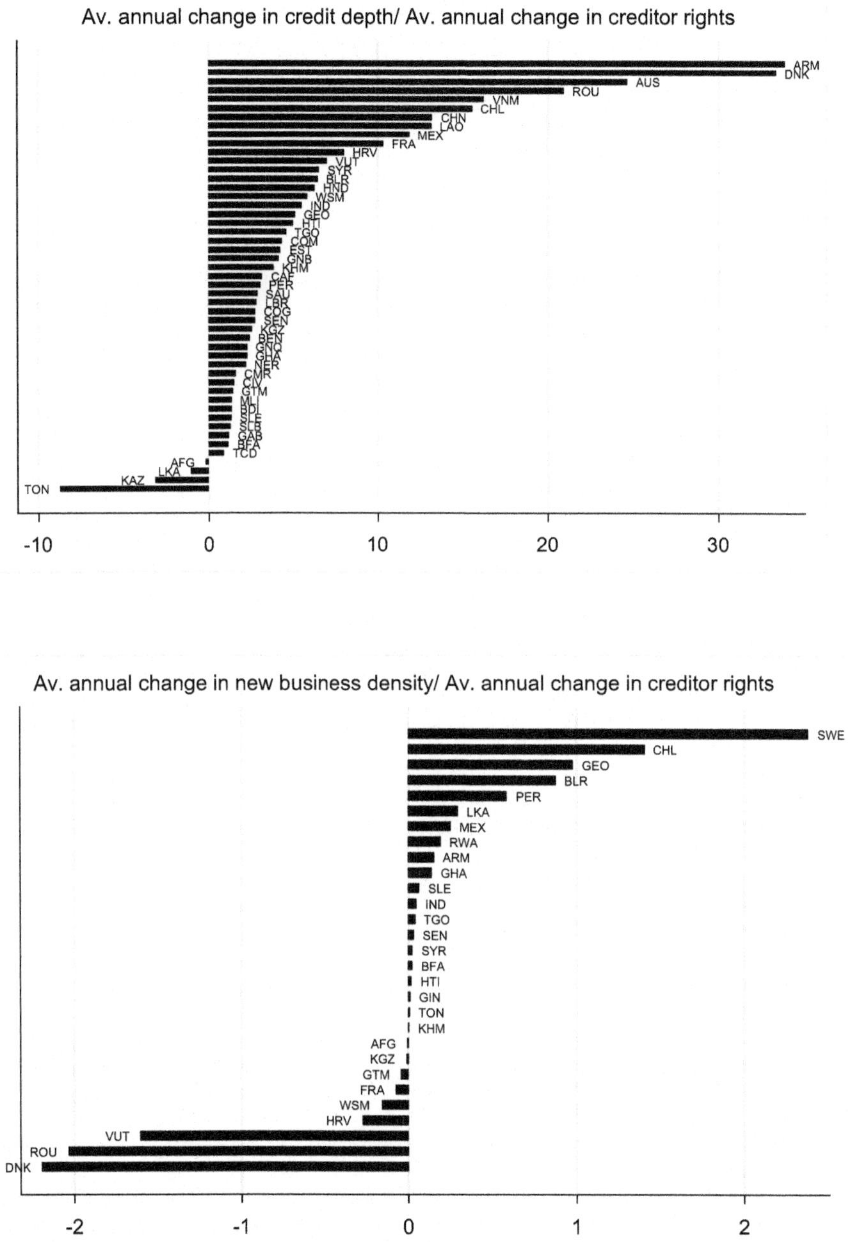

Fig. 8.4 Effectiveness of creditor rights reforms. Panel A: Effectiveness of creditor rights reforms in financial depth. Panel B: Effectiveness of creditor rights reforms in new business density

Table 8.1 Determinants of the effectiveness of creditor rights reforms

	Financial depth (private credit over GDP)							Entrepreneurship (new business density)						
	(1)	(2)	(3)	(4)	(5)	(6)	(7)	(8)	(9)	(10)	(11)	(12)	(13)	(14)
Ln GDP pc	2.53***	1.467**	0.64	2.118**	1.914**	1.435	1.406*	−0.003	0.044	−0.043	0.089	0.059	−0.041	−0.3
	(0.867)	(0.723)	(0.637)	(0.874)	(0.84)	(0.883)	(0.8)	(0.174)	(0.151)	(0.127)	(0.183)	(0.161)	(0.16)	(0.252)
Rule of law		2.608*					3.508*		−0.09					0.394
		(1.451)					(1.844)		(0.236)					(0.387)
Control of corruption			4.7***							0.075				
			(1.422)							(0.365)				
Political stability				1.292			−1.217				−0.225			−0.08
				(0.942)			(1.366)				(0.182)			(0.321)
Catholics					−0.102**		−0.115**					0.001		0.006
					(0.039)		(0.044)					(0.008)		(0.009)
Muslims					−0.084***		−0.088**					−0.002		−0.004
					(0.03)		(0.032)					(0.006)		(0.008)
Protestants					−0.029		−0.045					−0.008		−0.008
					(0.074)		(0.069)					(0.013)		(0.015)
Ethnic fractionalization					−9.163**		−9.801**					0.214		0.523
					(3.438)		(4.16)					(0.769)		(0.857)
Common law					−6.114*		−9.7***					−0.047		0.02
					(3.134)		(3.401)					(0.512)		(0.609)
Latitude						16.221*	−4.008						0.6	1.951
						(8.712)	(7.705)						(1.211)	(1.483)
Mineral resources						0.371*	0.735***						0.089	0.065
						(0.199)	(0.258)						(0.071)	(0.05)
R^2	0.20	0.25	0.34	0.21	0.45	0.28	0.54	0.00	0.00	0.00	0.03	0.08	0.05	0.15
Number of obs.	49	49	49	49	49	48	48	29	29	29	29	29	28	28

Notes: In columns 1–7 the sample is restricted to available data during the period 2006–2013, while columns 8–14 refer to the period 2006–2014. Only countries that improved their creditor rights during the respective period are considered. Regressions include a constant term, which is omitted for space considerations. Robust standard errors are in parentheses

*, ** and *** denote statistical significance at the 10, 5 and 1% levels, respectively

contrary, developed countries may have a particular general business environment that makes legal reform more successful. Column 1 of Table 8.1 indicates that the effectiveness of legal reforms is positively associated with economic development. The coefficient on log GDP per capita is highly statistically significant and only this variable explains 20% of the variability in legal reform effectiveness.

Institutional factors such as rule of law and control of corruption are positively related to legal reform effectiveness as well (note that this is conditional on controlling for income). The explanatory power of control of corruption is particularly high. This variable along with log GDP per capita explains a third of the variability in our indicator of reform effectiveness.[3] Religious affiliation is also a relevant factor. The percentage of Muslims and Catholics appears to be negatively related to the effectiveness of reforms in creditor rights. In the case of the percentage of Muslims, this result is probably driven by the particularities of Islamic finance. Religious affiliations other than Catholicism, Islam and Protestantism, which are captured by the constant term, are positively related to reform effectiveness, reflecting perhaps successful experiences in some Asian countries.

Ethnolinguistic fractionalization appears to reduce the effectiveness of legal reforms. Interestingly, common law countries have been less successful with legal reforms, particularly if we look at column 7. In addition, geography matters: countries rich in mineral resources have been more successful than countries lacking these resources, and higher distance from the equator as measured by latitude is associated with higher legal reform effectiveness. Columns 8–14 of Table 8.1 show the results regarding the effectiveness of creditor rights reforms in new business density. The picture is much less clear since all coefficients are statistically insignificant, which is probably due to the low number of observations in this sample.[4]

In unreported robustness checks, we replicate Table 8.1 adding average GDP growth as an additional control, and the results are qualitatively the same. Therefore, we can be confident that our results are not driven by other variables affecting the overall performance of the economy or by the fact that some countries suffered the 2007–2008 financial crisis more severely than others.

Now we turn to the effectiveness of legal reforms in investor rights. Figure 8.5 shows the values of the indicators of legal reform effectiveness for financial depth and new business density. There is also significant heterogeneity in the effectiveness of legal reforms, which calls for an analysis of its determinants. According to the figures, it is apparent that Iceland is an outlier since it was one of the countries most severely hit by the crisis. Consequently, when analyzing the determinants of legal reform effectiveness for investor protection, we remove Iceland from the sample. Table 8.2 reports the results. Broadly speaking, the results are similar to those obtained for creditor rights reforms. The findings suggest that institutions

[3] Rule of law, control of corruption and political stability correspond to the year 2006.

[4] In columns 7 and 14 we do not include "control of corruption" because it is highly correlated with "rule of law" ($\rho = 94\%$).

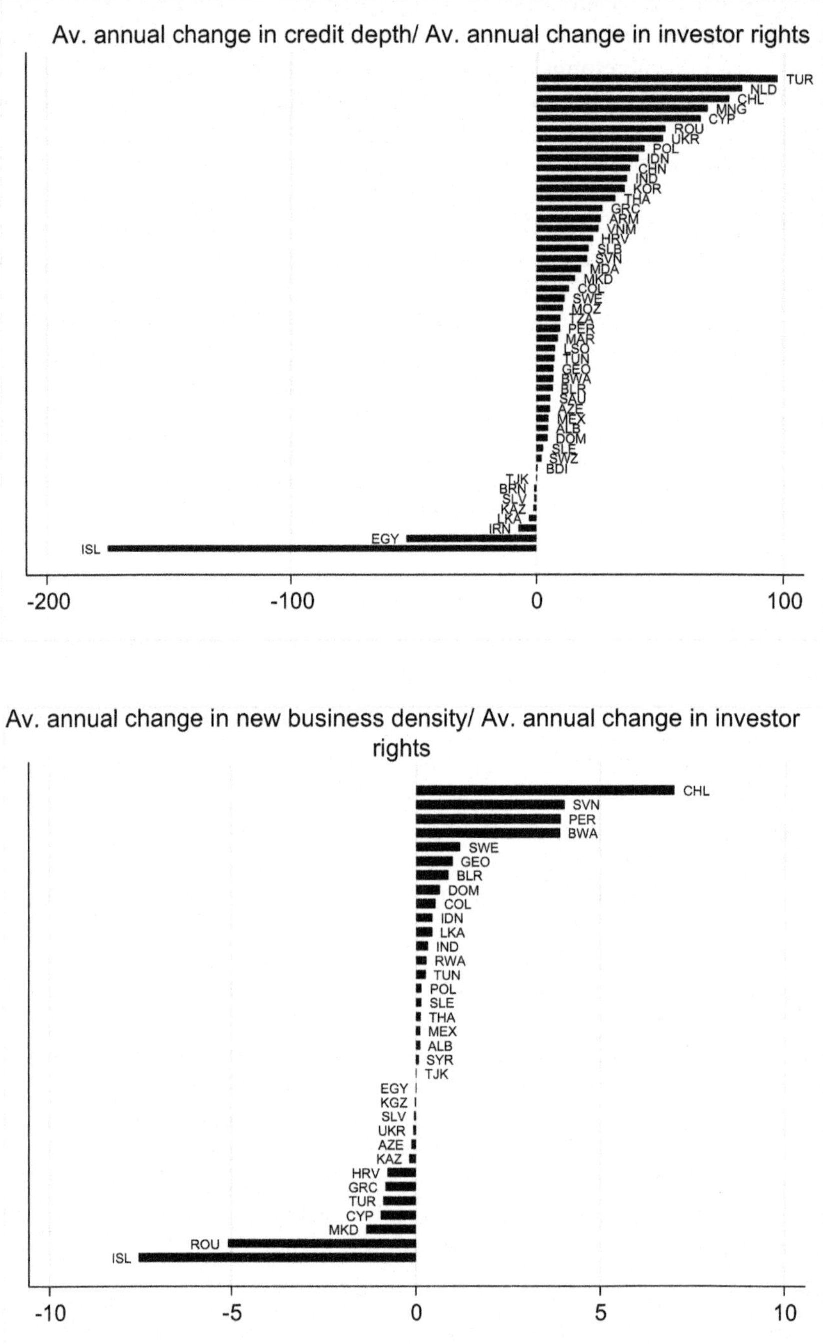

Fig. 8.5 Effectiveness of investor protection reforms. Panel A: Effectiveness of investor protection reforms in financial depth. Panel B: Effectiveness of investor protection reforms in new business density

Table 8.2 Determinants of the effectiveness of investor protection reforms

	Financial depth (private credit over GDP)							Entrepreneurship (new business density)						
	(1)	(2)	(3)	(4)	(5)	(6)	(7)	(8)	(9)	(10)	(11)	(12)	(13)	(14)
Ln GDP pc	6.534**	0.633	1.282	4.785	6.383**	4.773*	0.878	0.179	−0.333	−0.675*	−0.126	0.002	0.188	−0.388
	(2.736)	(3.111)	(2.938)	(3.09)	(2.838)	(2.644)	(2.898)	(0.235)	(0.292)	(0.335)	(0.215)	(0.245)	(0.225)	(0.401)
Rule of law		15.16**					15.879**		1.126					0.858
		(6.959)					(7.777)		(0.729)					(1.156)
Control of corruption			13.205							1.836**				
			(8.219)							(0.747)				
Political stability				5.591			−3.462				0.654			0.107
				(5.666)			(4.498)				(0.514)			(0.649)
Catholics					−0.15		−0.127					0.026*		0.018
					(0.101)		(0.098)					(0.014)		(0.013)
Muslims					−0.246		−0.203					0.007		0.006
					(0.159)		(0.157)					(0.011)		(0.013)
Protestants					−0.212		−0.319					0.036*		0.018
					(0.342)		(0.378)					(0.019)		(0.029)
Ethnic fractionalization					−7.114		4.03					0.063		1.288
					(16.848)		(17.41)					(1.496)		(2.372)
Common law					−5.454		−2.499					1.05		0.294
					(8.239)		(10.109)					(0.885)		(1.123)
Latitude						32.19*	27.096						−1.066	1.192
						(18.281)	(25.334)						(1.171)	(1.519)
Mineral resources						5.999***	5.163***						0.923***	0.753***
						(1.688)	(1.369)						(0.088)	(0.245)
R^2	0.10	0.19	0.16	0.12	0.20	0.24	0.36	0.01	0.11	0.25	0.05	0.22	0.47	0.55
Number of obs.	47	47	47	47	47	47	47	33	33	33	33	33	33	33

Notes: In columns 1–7 the sample is restricted to available data during the period 2006–2013, while columns 8–14 refer to the period 2006–2014. Only countries that improved their investor protection index during the respective period are considered. Regressions include a constant term, which is omitted for space considerations. Robust standard errors are in parentheses

*, ** and *** denote statistical significance at the 10, 5 and 1% levels, respectively

matter for the effectiveness of investor protection reforms in increasing financial depth and new business density—since rule of law is statistically significant at the 5% level for explaining financial depth and control of corruption is statistically significant at the 5% level for explaining entrepreneurship. Moreover, it seems that countries rich in natural resources have done better concerning the effectiveness of reforms in investor protection in terms of reaching a higher level of financial depth and entrepreneurship, since the coefficient is always positive and statistically significant at the 1% level.

To sum up, this exploratory analysis about the determinants of the effectiveness of legal reforms suggests that: (1) there is heterogeneity in the impact of legal reforms on economic and financial outcomes, and (2) there are factors correlated with the effectiveness of legal reforms. Although the importance of each factor depends on the specific legal rule and outcome variable, it seems that institutional quality and mineral resource abundance have a positive impact on legal reform effectiveness. However, one needs to be cautious when interpreting these results due to the low number of observations and the potential bias from omitted variables.

8.2 Gap Between Law on the Books and the Reality on the Ground

A related issue to the (in)effectiveness of legal reforms is the existence of a gap between legal rules and the reality on the ground. Governments may officially pursue certain policies, but if they lack the capacity to deliver public goods, then these intended policies do not materialize into real economic and social changes. Consequently, if legal reforms do not translate into better economic performance, a gap between what is written on the book of law and economic reality will arise. The existence of a gap would suggest that there are factors interfering in the link between legal rules and economic incentives; that is, something prevents legal changes from creating incentives in economic agents. This section constitutes a first attempt to the study of this issue.

Firstly, it is necessary to create a measure of the gap between legal rules and economic performance. We construct an indicator of the gap as follows:

$$Gap = DTF\,in\,legal\,rules - DTF\,in\,economic\,outcomes$$

where DFT means *distance to the frontier* and measures the distance of each economy to the best performance observed for each indicator. A value of 100 in DTF reflects that the country is on the "frontier", that is, has the best performance, while a value of 0 means that it has the worst performance. The indicators of DTF in creditor rights and investor protection are taken from the Doing Business Project (2015). DTF in economic and financial outcomes are calculated following the Doing Business' methodology. Thus, DTF is computed as:

$$DTF = \frac{Country's\ score\ for\ the\ indicator - Score\ of\ the\ lowest\ performance\ country}{Score\ of\ the\ highest\ performance\ country - Score\ of\ the\ lowest\ performance\ country} \times 100$$

More synthetically:

$$DTF = \frac{Country's\ score - Minimum\ value}{Maximum\ value - Minimum\ value} \times 100$$

Given the fact that there are countries with very high values in some indicators (for example Iceland in 2006 had 269.5% of private credit over GDP), it is recommended to use the 90th percentile as the value corresponding to the "frontier". Then, the previous formula can be written as:

$$DFT = \min\left(100, \frac{Country's\ score - Minimum\ value}{90th\ percentile - Minimum\ value} \times 100\right)$$

For illustrative purposes, Figure 8.6 shows the values of the gap between creditor rights and financial depth (year 2006). A positive value of the gap indicates that a country is closer to the frontier in legal rules (i.e., creditor rights) than in financial performance (i.e., private credit over GDP). A negative value means the opposite,

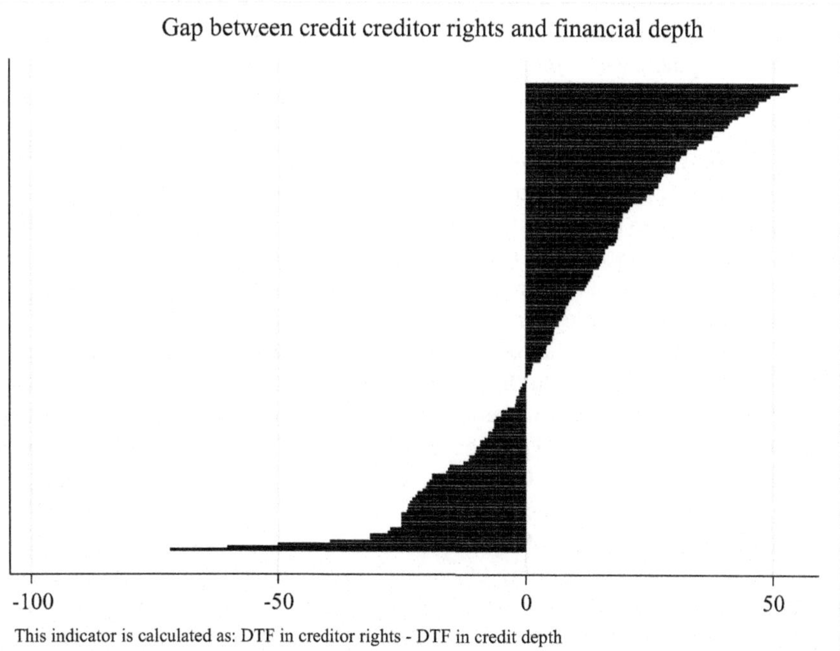

Fig. 8.6 Gap between creditor rights and financial depth

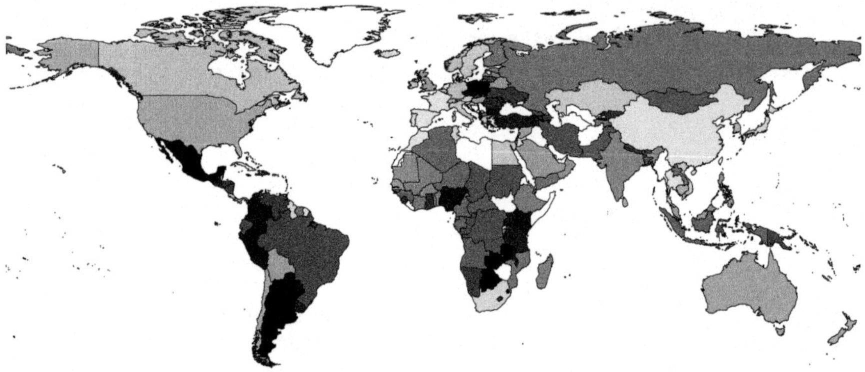

Fig. 8.7 Gap between creditor rights and financial depth (2006). Notes: DTF in creditor rights—DTF in financial depth 2006 (a *darker* color means a higher value). Countries with missing data on the gap are in *white*

that is, a better relative performance in financial outcomes. Figure 8.7 depicts the geographic distribution of values for this indicator. It is interesting to observe that industrialized countries along with others like China have negative and low gaps, whereas countries in Latin America, Africa, Eastern Europe and the Middle East have positive gaps. This is a confirmation of the well-known fact that for many countries legal rules do not go hand in hand with economic performance.

The aforementioned regional pattern in the gap between legal rules and financial performance suggests that there are factors that systematically affect the capacity of legal rules to generate incentives in economic agents. Columns 1–7 of Table 8.3 analyze the determinants of the gap between creditor rights and financial depth. Column 1 shows that the gap is lower in richer countries, which was already noticed when describing Fig. 8.7. Columns 2–4 suggest that institutional quality—measured through rule of law, control of corruption and political stability—systematically reduces the gap between creditor rights and financial depth. This may indicate that for creditor rights to have an effective influence on the financial system, the institutional environment must create certain conditions such as a transparent public administration, sufficient legal infrastructure, judicial independence, etc.

Regarding religious affiliation, the coefficients are not significantly different from the group that remains in the constant (i.e., "other religious affiliations"), but there are still differences across religious affiliations. For instance, the coefficient on Muslims is statistically and significantly lower than the coefficient on Catholics. Therefore, when compared to Catholics, the percentage of Muslim population in a country reduces the gap between legal rules and financial depth. This may be due to the fact that the protection of creditor rights is low in Muslim countries since according to Islamic law lending at interest is forbidden. Despite this fact, there is still a significant level of financial depth. As regards the rest of explanatory variables, ethnolinguistic fractionalization appears to increase the gap, although the coefficient is no longer significant when including all the controls in the same specification. Finally, common law countries have a larger gap than civil law

Table 8.3 Determinants of the gap between creditor rights and financial depth and entrepreneurship

	Financial depth (private credit over GDP)							Entrepreneurship (new business density)						
	(1)	(2)	(3)	(4)	(5)	(6)	(7)	(8)	(9)	(10)	(11)	(12)	(13)	(14)
Ln GDP pc	−5.236***	0.623	−0.629	−3.749***	−4.919***	−4.62***	0.59	−1.792	−1.676	−2.236	1.742	−0.548	−2.156	−1.162
	(0.881)	(1.615)	(1.578)	(1.217)	(1.199)	(1.119)	(1.534)	(1.498)	(2.614)	(2.536)	(2.278)	(2.007)	(1.897)	(2.752)
Rule of law		−11.993***					−18.556***		0.061					6.868
		(2.545)					(3.894)		(4.829)					(5.986)
Control of corruption			−9.043***							1.081				
			(2.455)							(4.358)				
Political stability				−3.919*			2.945				−7.818**			−11.058***
				(2.167)			(2.67)				(3.81)			(3.545)
Catholics					0.084		0.101					0.077		0.091
					(0.072)		(0.075)					(0.11)		(0.115)
Muslims					−0.071		−0.053					−0.022		−0.045
					(0.075)		(0.071)					(0.078)		(0.081)
Protestants					−0.013		0.088					−0.162		−0.198
					(0.08)		(0.08)					(0.148)		(0.16)
Ethnic fractionalization					13.79*		10.886					6.217		3.037
					(7.865)		(7.614)					(14.396)		(14.69)
Common law					6.672*		15.797***					11.088*		12.561*
					(3.521)		(3.836)					(6.205)		(7.164)
Latitude						−7.332	24.585**						0.565	15.965
						(10.004)	(12.144)						(20.361)	(22.996)
Mineral resources						0.43	−0.216						2.064*	2.661**
						(0.667)	(0.622)						(1.075)	(1.163)
R^2	0.12	0.21	0.17	0.13	0.19	0.12	0.32	0.01	0.01	0.01	0.04	0.06	0.03	0.15
Number of obs.	156	154	154	154	151	153	149	110	109	109	109	107	107	105

Notes: Data correspond to the year 2006. Regressions include a constant term, which is omitted for space considerations. Robust standard errors are in parentheses

*, ** and *** denote statistical significance at the 10, 5 and 1% levels, respectively

countries, reflecting that the higher level of creditor rights in such countries are not systematically accompanied by better performance.

Columns 8–14 analyze the determinants of the gap between creditor rights and entrepreneurship. Fairly similar conclusions can be drawn. Institutional quality matters, although the only relevant institutional dimension in this case is political stability. In addition, common law countries and economies rich in mineral resources exhibit a larger gap.

Table 8.4 analyzes the determinants of the gap between investor protection and financial depth and entrepreneurship. The findings are also similar. The gap is generally lower for richer countries. Institutional quality also matters. In the case of financial depth, rule of law and control of corruption are the relevant dimensions, while for entrepreneurship political stability appears to be the most relevant institutional factor.[5] Common law countries are systematically associated with a larger gap, both with respect to financial depth and entrepreneurship. Therefore, the gap between legal rules and economic-financial performance is consistently higher in common law than in civil law countries. This reflects that protection to creditors and investors is stronger in the book of law than on the ground, thus suggesting that there are factors that interfere in the creation of right incentives from legal rules. This result is consistent with one of the criticism to the common law presented in Chap. 2, that is, that the common law was superficially implanted in many former colonies, which led to ineffective legal systems. More specifically, the explanation for this is that in large parts of its empire, Britain conducted a colonial policy known as "indirect rule" which did not intend to effectively introduce its legal system, especially in territories politically organized or extensively occupied by native population, like Sub-Saharan Africa. Instead, local rules were left almost intact and traditional chiefs concentrated all political and judicial powers in their hands, which resulted in the control of economic resources by elites. They had little incentive to protect property rights and enforce contracts, which inhibited the development of legal systems.

These results reported about the gap between legal rules and the reality on the ground are referred to the year 2006, the first year for which data are available for the legal rules indicators used. Given the evidence provided in Chap. 5 on the intensity of legal reforms conducted during the last decade, particularly in civil law countries, it is interesting to analyze using more recent data whether these results have changed over time. Tables 8.5 and 8.6 conduct the analysis for the year 2012. The most noticeable difference is that now the common law is not associated with a larger gap, except in one case in column 7 in Table 8.6. This result may reflect that civil law countries implementing legal reforms have managed to increase their protection to creditors and investors but, however, this legal change is not conducive to substantive changes which translate into actual improvements on the

[5]In column 7 of Table 8.4 political stability carries a positive and significant coefficient. This is probably due to collinearity between institutional indicators (the correlation between rule of law and political stability is 78.3%).

Table 8.4 Determinants of the gap between investor protection and financial depth and entrepreneurship

	Financial depth (private credit over GDP)							Entrepreneurship (new business density)						
	(1)	(2)	(3)	(4)	(5)	(6)	(7)	(8)	(9)	(10)	(11)	(12)	(13)	(14)
Ln GDP pc	−10.274***	−4.276***	−4.707***	−9.78***	−9.33***	−8.319***	−2.499*	−6.935***	−5.828***	−5.389**	−4.022*	−4.683**	−6.513***	−4.07*
	(1.128)	(1.544)	(1.563)	(1.381)	(1.391)	(1.343)	(1.491)	(1.482)	(2.179)	(2.23)	(2.055)	(1.897)	(1.875)	(2.308)
Rule of law		−12.327***					−20.502***		−1.913					2.579
		(2.486)					(3.264)		(3.947)					(4.744)
Control of corruption			−10.987***							−2.594				
			(2.596)							(3.826)				
Political stability				−1.313			7.293***				−6.436*			−6.471*
				(2.108)			(2.551)				(3.244)			(3.388)
Catholics					0.044		0.011					0.043		0.035
					(0.068)		(0.074)					(0.098)		(0.104)
Muslims					−0.023		−0.003					0.091		0.088
					(0.078)		(0.073)					(0.073)		(0.076)
Protestants					−0.086		0.006					−0.268**		−0.283**
					(0.09)		(0.091)					(0.131)		(0.141)
Ethnic fractionalization					10.555		5.355					−3.013		−6.984
					(7.757)		(7.527)					(12.91)		(14.521)
Common law					8.901**		15.159***					15.163**		15.148**
					(3.426)		(3.817)					(6.191)		(6.971)
Latitude						−24.047**	−0.948						−10.983	1.54
						(10.338)	(11.7)						(18.77)	(23.119)
Mineral resources						0.25	−0.253						1.067	2.145**
						(0.537)	(0.495)						(0.925)	(0.935)
R^2	0.36	0.43	0.42	0.36	0.40	0.37	0.51	0.14	0.14	0.14	0.16	0.23	0.17	0.29
Number of obs.	156	154	154	154	151	153	149	110	109	109	109	107	107	105

Notes: Data correspond to the year 2006. Regressions include a constant term, which is omitted for space considerations. Robust standard errors are in parentheses

*, ** and *** denote statistical significance at the 10, 5 and 1% levels, respectively

Table 8.5 Determinants of the gap between creditor rights and financial depth and entrepreneurship (Year 2012)

	Financial depth (private credit over GDP)							Entrepreneurship (new business density)						
	(1)	(2)	(3)	(4)	(5)	(6)	(7)	(8)	(9)	(10)	(11)	(12)	(13)	(14)
Ln GDP pc	−8.186***	−0.953	−2.217	−6.93***	−6.972***	−7.291***	0.688	−5.489***	0.454	−0.374	−1.232	−4.75**	−6.765***	1.149
	(1.271)	(1.779)	(1.805)	(1.582)	(1.48)	(1.428)	(1.969)	(1.93)	(2.832)	(2.549)	(2.319)	(2.232)	(2.391)	(3.752)
Rule of law		−15.019***					−21.97***		−9.908**					−10.245
		(2.911)					(4.175)		(4.805)					(6.675)
Control of corruption			−12.425***							−8.491**				
			(2.843)							(3.958)				
Political stability				−3.235			4.958				−9.195**			−4.906
				(2.48)			(3.666)				(3.57)			(4.351)
Catholics					−0.058		−0.08					−0.071		−0.055
					(0.089)		(0.091)					(0.12)		(0.132)
Muslims					−0.06		−0.064					−0.026		−0.091
					(0.084)		(0.09)					(0.098)		(0.11)
Protestants					0.028		0.108					−0.146		−0.06
					(0.095)		(0.096)					(0.151)		(0.175)
Ethnic fractionalization					16.064*		10.113					2.298		2.857
					(8.901)		(8.417)					(14.654)		(16.361)
Common law					−1.182		5.055					1.915		7.833
					(4.23)		(4.635)					(6.572)		(7.475)
Latitude						−14.455	5.385						2.945	11.065
						(12.57)	(12.477)						(18.482)	(22.766)
Mineral resources						−0.027	−0.583						−0.795	−0.629
						(0.616)	(0.602)						(0.917)	(0.953)
R^2	0.18	0.28	0.26	0.19	0.20	0.18	0.34	0.07	0.10	0.09	0.11	0.09	0.09	0.16
Number of obs.	151	150	150	150	148	148	146	103	102	102	102	100	99	98

Notes: Data correspond to the year 2012. Regressions include a constant term, which is omitted for space considerations. Robust standard errors are in parentheses

*, ** and *** denote statistical significance at the 10, 5 and 1% levels, respectively

Table 8.6 Determinants of the gap between investor protection and financial depth and entrepreneurship (Year 2012)

	Financial depth (private credit over GDP)							Entrepreneurship (new business density)						
	(1)	(2)	(3)	(4)	(5)	(6)	(7)	(8)	(9)	(10)	(11)	(12)	(13)	(14)
Ln GDP pc	−11.024***	−5.016***	−5.488***	−9.92***	−9.679***	−9.161***	−3.07	−8.463***	−4.51*	−4.823*	−4.002*	−6.966***	−8.652***	−3.373
	(1.265)	(1.751)	(1.803)	(1.622)	(1.442)	(1.422)	(1.865)	(1.692)	(2.672)	(2.719)	(2.182)	(1.935)	(2.082)	(3.291)
Rule of law		−12.518***					−17.799***		−6.559					−3.372
		(2.692)					(3.883)		(4.243)					(5.391)
Control of corruption			−11.569***							−6.026				
			(2.765)							(4.003)				
Political stability				−2.896			5.05				−9.746***			−7.233*
				(2.402)			(3.533)				(3.476)			(4.055)
Catholics					0.027		−0.016					0.03		0.038
					(0.078)		(0.085)					(0.109)		(0.123)
Muslims					0.066		0.076					0.162*		0.13
					(0.081)		(0.086)					(0.097)		(0.099)
Protestants					0.033		0.097					−0.1		−0.004
					(0.101)		(0.1)					(0.138)		(0.155)
Ethnic fractionalization					14.137*		6.848					−0.118		1.52
					(7.488)		(7.754)					(13.174)		(15.751)
Common law					5.976		8.211*					10.238		11.783
					(4.008)		(4.56)					(6.692)		(7.766)
Latitude						−29.918**	−9.173						−14.437	−0.327
						(11.828)	(13.881)						(19.13)	(24.448)
Mineral resources						0.296	−0.047						−1.502*	−1.003
						(0.513)	(0.477)						(0.902)	(1.02)
R^2	0.33	0.40	0.40	0.34	0.36	0.36	0.46	0.17	0.18	0.18	0.22	0.23	0.21	0.30
Number of obs.	151	150	150	150	148	148	146	103	102	102	102	100	99	98

Notes: Data correspond to the year 2012. Regressions include a constant term, which is omitted for space considerations. Robust standard errors are in parentheses

*, ** and *** denote statistical significance at the 10, 5 and 1% levels, respectively

ground. This interpretation is consistent with the evidence shown in Chap. 6 on the lack of a consistent effect of legal reforms on economic and financial outcomes.

8.3 Gap Between Law on the Books and Law in Action

The potential disparity between legal rules and the reality on the ground can also be analyzed within the realm of the legal system. Thus, even within the legal system, it is possible that *law on the books* is not reflected in *law in action*. This gap within the legal system can in turn be responsible for the previously analyzed gap between legal rules and economic performance. Arguably, changes in *law on the books* do not lead to real economic improvements if *law in action* remains unchanged and with a poor performance. For example, if a country increases its level of investor protection but, judicial procedures and contract enforcement remain very slow, then that reform is not likely to foster investment in the economy. This problem has become recurrent over the past decade. According to the Doing Business dataset, from 2006 to 2014 the strength of investor protection index improved 8% on average around the world. However, in 2014 the time required to enforce contracts (a clear indicator of *law in action*) is on average 7 days *more* than in 2006. Indeed, policymakers may officially pursue certain policies, but if they lack the capacity to deliver public goods, then the intended policies do not materialize into real economic and social changes. Therefore, the existence of a gap between law on the books and law in action can have important implications, and, for this reason, it is relevant to analyze its determinants. By adopting a policy-oriented perspective, we attempt to identify examples of countries implementing reforms successfully and, in the same way, to learn from cases in which legal reforms were not followed by real improvements on the ground. Drawing on both types of experiences may be of help to determine how societies should better design and implement legal changes.

As a first step, it is necessary to create a measure of the gap between law on the books and law in action. Similarly to the previous section, we construct an indicator of the gap as follows[6]:

$$Gap = DTF\,in\,legal\,rules - DTF\,in\,law\,in\,action$$

We employ the same measures of legal rules previously used in this chapter, that is, creditor rights and investor protection, and regarding law in action, we employ contract enforcement and debt recovery rate (i.e., resolving insolvency) as a measure of debt enforcement efficiency. Figure 8.8 shows the values of the gap between creditor rights and contract enforcement. The economy with the highest gap is Trinidad and Tobago (42.73) and the one with the lowest is Belarus (−68.6). Figure 8.9 shows the geographic distribution of values for this indicator.

[6]Data for DTF in legal rules and law in action come from the Doing Business Project (2015).

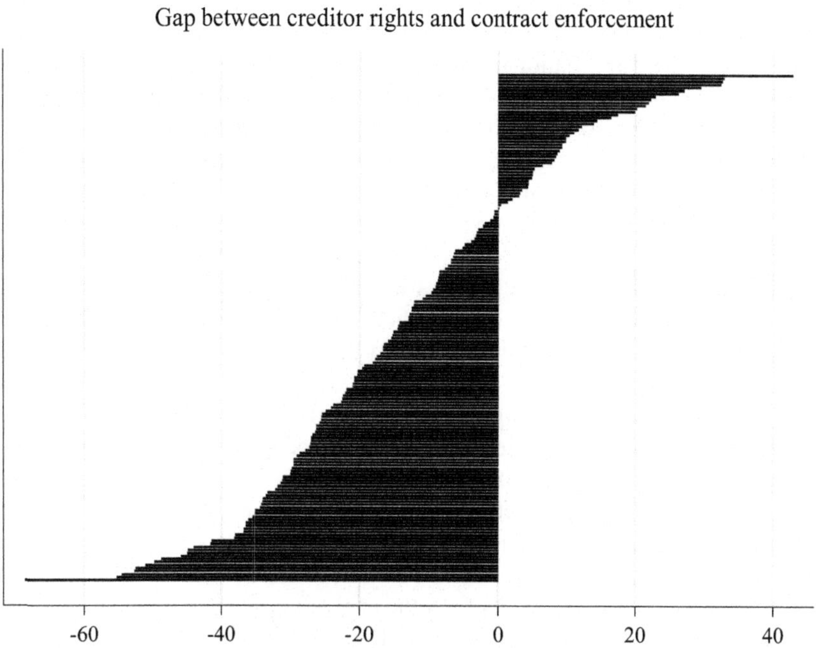

Fig. 8.8 Gap between creditor rights and contract enforcement

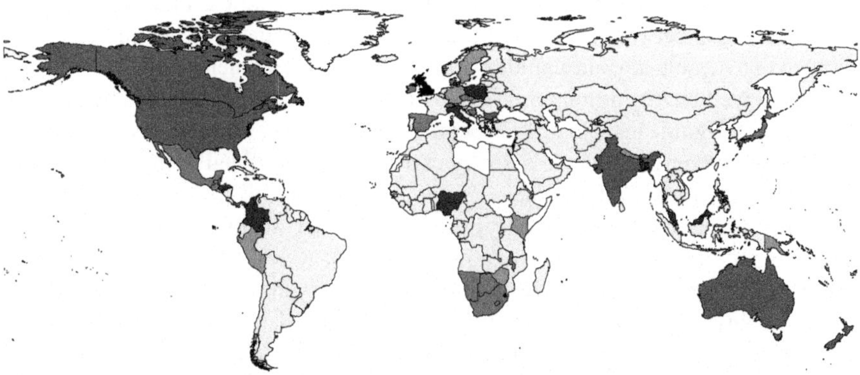

Fig. 8.9 Gap between creditor rights and contract enforcement (2006). Notes: DTF in creditor rights—DTF in financial depth 2006 (a *darker* color means a higher value). Countries with missing data on the gap are in *white*, while countries with gaps equal to or lower than zero are in *light gray*

Interestingly, the gap is higher for common law countries (the British islands, North America, etc.) and Central Europe, and lower (and even negative) in many countries of Asia.

Tables 8.7 and 8.8 report the results from the analysis of the determinants of the gap between law on the books and law in action. We use as dependent variables four gaps: (1) gap between creditor rights and contract enforcement, (2) gap between creditor rights and recovery rate, (3) gap between investor protection and contract enforcement, and (4) gap between investor protection and recovery rate.

Regarding the determinants of the gap between creditor rights and contract enforcement (columns 1–7 of Table 8.7), income appears positively correlated with it. This reflects the fact that rich countries provide good protection to creditors in the book of law but, however, they are not so diligent in the efficient application of legal rules. Institutional quality does not play a very clear-cut role since the coefficients are sometimes positive and others negative. However, if we look at the most complete specification, political stability reduces the gap in a significant way. Religion also matters. The joint significance test of the three religious affiliation variables is highly statistically significant, with Catholicism increasing the gap and Islam decreasing it. Ethnic fractionalization also appears to increase the gap, which is consistent with the prediction that it may reduce the efficacy of the government in proving public goods (Alesina et al. 1999, 2003). Moreover, it is clear again that common law countries have a much larger gap than civil law countries (19 points higher, after controlling for a wide array of variables).

Columns 8–14 report the results from the analysis of the determinants of the gap between creditor rights and debt recovery efficiency. Income does not play a clear role now. With respect to institutional quality, column 14 shows that rule of law is important in reducing the gap. Religious affiliation also matters (the coefficient on Catholics is significantly different from the coefficient on Muslims). Again, common law countries have a larger gap than civil law countries. Finally, Table 8.8 analyzes the gap between protection to investors and financial depth and entrepreneurship. The results are similar although a number of comments have to be made. The role played by institutions and religion is more limited, as indicated by the lack of statistical significance in the respective coefficients. Common law countries again have a larger gap, which is a very consistent result. Finally, the gap is larger in the tropics than in cold latitudes.

At this point it is important to note that a large positive gap is something negative, but similarly, a large negative gap is not necessarily desirable, since it may reflect bad performance in law in action and an even worse score in law on the books. To investigate this issue, we replace negative values with zeros in the indicators of the gap between law on the books and law in action. In this way, the gap can be either positive or zero, but not negative. Unreported regressions show that the results are qualitatively similar when we focus on non-negative gaps.

Finally, Tables 8.9 and 8.10 analyze the determinants of the gap for the year 2012. Results are fairly consistent with the previous findings. Remarkably, the gap for common law countries is still larger than for civil law countries, with the difference being usually statistically significant, although its magnitude is somewhat smaller than in 2006. Concerning the institutional variables, there is some evidence that better institutions in the form of higher political stability reduce the gap between creditor rights and contract enforcement in 2012 for the more

Table 8.7 Determinants of the gap between creditor rights and contract enforcement and debt recovery

	Contract enforcement							Debt recovery						
	(1)	(2)	(3)	(4)	(5)	(6)	(7)	(8)	(9)	(10)	(11)	(12)	(13)	(14)
Ln GDP pc	4.966***	2.501	2.502	5.239***	4.711***	5.988***	3.714**	−1.82*	−0.4	−0.223	−2.548**	−2.229*	−0.347	0.534
	(0.881)	(1.654)	(1.632)	(1.171)	(1.1)	(1.303)	(1.665)	(0.957)	(1.52)	(1.541)	(1.231)	(1.232)	(1.253)	(1.7)
Rule of law		4.657*					4.707		−3.272					−9.417**
		(2.647)					(3.846)		(2.58)					(3.93)
Control of corruption			4.564*							−3.568				
			(2.444)							(2.486)				
Political stability				−1.315			−5.752**				1.52			4.386
				(2.022)			(2.425)				(1.997)			(2.662)
Catholics					0.079		0.103*					0.085		0.073
					(0.053)		(0.054)					(0.06)		(0.067)
Muslims					−0.068		−0.084					−0.099		−0.086
					(0.051)		(0.052)					(0.069)		(0.069)
Protestants					0.001		0.003					−0.035		−0.006
					(0.067)		(0.063)					(0.084)		(0.09)
Ethnic fractionalization					10.998		12.229*					6.591		4.327
					(6.696)		(6.803)					(6.865)		(7.594)
Common law					18.14***		19.119***					9.1**		12.001***
					(3.031)		(3.373)					(3.706)		(4.008)
Latitude						−17.267	10.776						−20.78*	−0.992
						(11.166)	(11.376)						(11.284)	(13.874)
Mineral resources						0.408	0.016						0.55	0.109
						(0.52)	(0.496)						(0.557)	(0.606)
R^2	0.14	0.15	0.15	0.13	0.34	0.14	0.38	0.02	0.03	0.03	0.02	0.12	0.05	0.16
Number of obs.	168	165	165	165	161	163	158	168	165	165	165	161	163	158

Notes: Data correspond to the year 2006. Regressions include a constant term, which is omitted for space considerations. Robust standard errors are in parentheses

*, ** and *** denote statistical significance at the 10, 5 and 1% levels, respectively

Table 8.8 Determinants of the gap between investor protection and contract enforcement and debt recovery

	Contract enforcement							Debt recovery						
	(1)	(2)	(3)	(4)	(5)	(6)	(7)	(8)	(9)	(10)	(11)	(12)	(13)	(14)
Ln GDP pc	0.121	−1.951	−1.238	−0.045	0.566	2.405**	1.122	−6.665***	−4.852***	−3.963**	−7.832***	−6.375***	−3.93***	−2.059
	(0.954)	(1.525)	(1.485)	(1.216)	(1.061)	(1.21)	(1.642)	(1.077)	(1.714)	(1.689)	(1.361)	(1.188)	(1.294)	(1.775)
Rule of law		3.939*					3.243		−3.99					−10.88***
		(2.327)					(3.163)		(2.846)					(3.652)
Control of corruption			2.413							−5.72**				
			(2.349)							(2.788)				
Political stability				−0.019			−2.906				2.817			7.232***
				(1.938)			(2.202)				(2.212)			(2.56)
Catholics					0.048		0.014					0.054		−0.016
					(0.048)		(0.056)					(0.058)		(0.066)
Muslims					−0.001		−0.013					−0.031		−0.015
					(0.054)		(0.057)					(0.069)		(0.069)
Protestants					−0.075		−0.075					−0.111		−0.084
					(0.064)		(0.065)					(0.082)		(0.09)
Ethnic fractionalization					5.962		4.112					1.555		−3.791
					(6.51)		(6.889)					(7.193)		(7.376)
Common law					20.473***		17.725***					11.433***		10.606**
					(2.998)		(3.7)					(4.065)		(4.238)
Latitude						−33.917***	−16.363						−37.43***	−28.131**
						(8.476)	(9.898)						(10.135)	(11.31)
Mineral resources						0.136	−0.038						0.279	0.056
						(0.568)	(0.535)						(0.584)	(0.638)
R^2	0.00	0.02	0.01	0.00	0.26	0.09	0.28	0.19	0.21	0.22	0.20	0.24	0.25	0.32
Number of obs.	168	165	165	165	161	163	158	168	165	165	165	161	163	158

Notes: Data correspond to the year 2006. Regressions include a constant term, which is omitted for space considerations. Robust standard errors are in parentheses

*, ** and *** denote statistical significance at the 10, 5 and 1% levels, respectively

Table 8.9 Determinants of the gap between creditor rights and contract enforcement and debt recovery (Year 2012)

	Contract enforcement							Debt recovery						
	(1)	(2)	(3)	(4)	(5)	(6)	(7)	(8)	(9)	(10)	(11)	(12)	(13)	(14)
Ln GDP pc	2.078**	1.727	2.086	2.31*	1.699	1.997	3.155*	−4.492***	−0.318	−0.426	−4.852***	−4.891***	−3.896**	0.21
	(1.041)	(1.698)	(1.439)	(1.222)	(1.225)	(1.375)	(1.827)	(1.123)	(1.656)	(1.672)	(1.449)	(1.29)	(1.493)	(1.866)
Rule of law		0.318					−0.708		−8.164***					−14.154***
		(2.656)					(3.616)		(2.585)					(3.76)
Control of corruption			−0.388							−8.031***				
			(2.122)							(2.504)				
Political stability				−1.089			−5.364**				0.947			4.502
				(1.997)			(2.518)				(2.26)			(3.128)
Catholics					−0.09		−0.078					−0.042		−0.068
					(0.059)		(0.062)					(0.07)		(0.07)
Muslims					−0.164***		−0.207***					−0.162**		−0.161**
					(0.056)		(0.061)					(0.078)		(0.078)
Protestants					−0.13**		−0.083					−0.189**		−0.133
					(0.065)		(0.066)					(0.089)		(0.093)
Ethnic fractionalization					−0.396		−1.341					−2.449		−6.156
					(6.677)		(6.958)					(7.495)		(7.829)
Common law					9.174***		11.498***					2.84		5.171
					(2.951)		(3.108)					(3.98)		(4.22)
Latitude						−1.865	6.115						−9.298	−0.07
						(9.813)	(11.959)						(12.094)	(14.345)
Mineral resources						−0.143	−0.465						0.009	−0.115
						(0.539)	(0.545)						(0.489)	(0.584)
R^2	0.02	0.02	0.02	0.02	0.12	0.02	0.17	0.08	0.12	0.12	0.08	0.13	0.08	0.20
Number of obs.	175	173	173	173	169	170	167	175	173	173	173	169	170	167

Notes: Data correspond to the year 2012. Regressions include a constant term, which is omitted for space considerations. Robust standard errors are in parentheses

*, ** and *** denote statistical significance at the 10, 5 and 1% levels, respectively

Table 8.10 Determinants of the gap between investor protection and contract enforcement and debt recovery (Year 2012)

	Contract enforcement							Debt recovery						
	(1)	(2)	(3)	(4)	(5)	(6)	(7)	(8)	(9)	(10)	(11)	(12)	(13)	(14)
Ln GDP pc	−0.792	−2.287	−1.497	−0.517	−0.958	0.609	−0.23	−7.362***	−4.332**	−4.009**	−7.679***	−7.548***	−5.284***	−3.175*
	(0.972)	(1.622)	(1.468)	(1.243)	(1.064)	(1.202)	(1.761)	(1.073)	(1.724)	(1.729)	(1.395)	(1.081)	(1.205)	(1.731)
Rule of law		2.6					4.341		−5.883**					−9.104***
		(2.359)					(3.124)		(2.754)					(3.451)
Control of corruption			1.063							−6.579**				
			(2.071)							(2.691)				
Political stability				−1.146			−6.456**				0.89			3.41
				(1.902)			(2.51)				(2.27)			(2.7)
Catholics					0.005		−0.011					0.054		0
					(0.049)		(0.053)					(0.055)		(0.06)
Muslims					−0.023		−0.06					−0.021		−0.015
					(0.049)		(0.052)					(0.065)		(0.064)
Protestants					−0.094		−0.059					−0.153*		−0.11
					(0.059)		(0.056)					(0.078)		(0.08)
Ethnic fractionalization					−3.468		−6.013					−5.522		−10.829
					(5.943)		(6.247)					(6.552)		(6.858)
Common law					16.435***		14.393***					10.1***		8.066**
					(2.799)		(3.424)					(3.826)		(3.957)
Latitude						−21.241***	−13.179						−28.674***	−19.365*
						(7.884)	(9.818)						(8.98)	(11.205)
Mineral resources						0.074	−0.077						0.225	0.273
						(0.493)	(0.419)						(0.484)	(0.531)
R^2	0.00	0.01	0.01	0.01	0.19	0.04	0.23	0.22	0.24	0.25	0.21	0.26	0.26	0.32
Number of obs.	175	173	173	173	169	170	167	175	173	173	173	169	170	167

Notes: Data correspond to the year 2012. Regressions include a constant term, which is omitted for space considerations. Robust standard errors are in parentheses

*, ** and *** denote statistical significance at the 10, 5 and 1% levels, respectively

complete specification. Columns 9 and 14 in Table 8.9 show that stronger rule of law reduces the gap between creditor rights and debt enforcement efficiency in 2012, while column 10 indicates that higher control of corruption reduces the gap between creditor rights and debt recovery rate. Along similar lines, column 7 in Table 8.10 backs up the existence of a statistically significant negative impact of political stability on the gap between investor protection and contract enforcement. Likewise, columns 9 and 14 in Table 8.10 show that a higher score of rule of law reduces the gap between investor protection and debt enforcement efficiency in 2012. The same occurs with control of corruption in column 10.

8.4 Summary of Results

To sum up, in this chapter we have conducted a preliminary exploratory analysis of the determinants of the effectiveness of legal reforms as well as of the gap between legal rules and the reality on the ground. Concerning legal reform effectiveness, there are differences among countries in the extent to which changes in creditor and investor rights are associated with changes in financial and economic outcomes. These differences allow us to analyze the potential determinants of legal reform effectiveness. When focusing on the effectiveness of creditor rights reforms in promoting financial development (measured by private credit over GDP), results are very intuitive. The income level, rule of law, and mineral resource abundance are factors positively related to legal reform effectiveness, while the percentage of Catholics and Muslims, ethnolinguistic fractionalization, and the common law have a negative impact. When looking at the results for other indicators of reform effectiveness, the evidence is less clear but suggests that institutional quality and mineral resource abundance are relevant explanatory factors. Nonetheless, these findings have to be interpreted with caution due to the limited number of observations and potential biases due to omitted variables.

We have also analyzed the related question of the gap between legal rules and the reality on the ground, which is a consequence of the lack of effectiveness of legal rules. Two types of gaps have been studied: the gap between legal rules and financial depth and entrepreneurship, and the gap between law on the books and law in action. The evidence appears to support the fact that institutional quality is a factor that usually reduces the gap. A robust result in this regard is that common law countries have a larger gap than civil law countries, which reflects that the protection afforded to creditors and investors is higher in this legal family but it is not fully translated into substantive changes in the real economy. Interestingly, from 2006 to 2012 the larger gap in common law relative to civil law countries has diminished. This is probably a consequence of the reform agenda in civil law countries aimed to increase the protection to creditors and investors, which however has not materialized into improvements on the ground.

Chapter 9
Conclusions

Abstract The purpose of this chapter is to provide some concluding remarks on the implications of having no effect from changes in legal rules and regulatory indicators on changes in economic and financial performance across countries. In sum, all the evidence gathered indicates that legal and regulatory reforms in developing nations that mechanically adopt organizational forms from prosperous nations, without a thorough analysis of their specific policy priorities to improve their framework for governance as a way to foster their state capacity to deliver growth and social progress, are likely to render governance reforms mostly ineffective. In addition, the enactment of reforms introducing new legal rules and regulations may not yield the intended positive benefits, if the country lacks the judicial human capital and legal infrastructure required for effectively implementing the targeted reforms and properly enforcing the new laws.

Nowadays it is widely accepted that legal reforms aimed at creating market-friendly regulatory environments are crucial for the economic success of countries. We review this question both from the point of view of the literature and from the perspective of the empirical evidence. Thus, the purpose of this monograph has been twofold. First, we have conducted a critical review of the legal origins literature, which is arguably the main theoretical basis behind this renewed interest in legal rules and reforms. Second, we have investigated whether legal reforms intended to create market-friendly regulatory business environments have a positive impact on economic and financial outcomes. In addition, we have conducted an exploratory and preliminary analysis of the determinants of the effectiveness of legal reforms and the gap between law on the books and the reality on the ground.

We have divided our review of the Legal Origins literature into three parts. A first set of criticisms builds on colonialism and the associated distribution of legal traditions, a second set of criticisms is based on political economy arguments, and a third set is based on the quality and reliability of early indicators of legal rules and outcomes. It is pertinent to be aware that, despite these criticisms, the Legal Origins Theory has deeply influenced our understanding of how to improve legal systems in order to foster financial development and promote economic activity. The bottom line of our review is that the imitation of other legal systems should be made very carefully, and it is generally more desirable to improve existing regulations and the enforcement of current laws instead of importing poorly-enforced foreign rules.

D. Oto-Peralías, D. Romero-Ávila, *Legal Traditions, Legal Reforms and Economic Performance*, Contributions to Economics, DOI 10.1007/978-3-319-67041-6_9

In the second part of this monograph, we have first analyzed the evolution of legal rules and regulations during the last decade (2006–2014). For that purpose, we use legal/regulatory indicators from the Doing Business Project (2015). Our findings indicate that countries have actively reformed their legal systems during this period, particularly French civil law countries. A process of convergence in the evolution of legal rules and regulations is observed: countries starting in 2006 in a lower position have improved more than countries with better initial scores. In addition, French civil law countries have reformed their legal systems to a larger extent than common law countries and, consequently, have improved more in the majority of the Doing Business indicators considered. Therefore, for those indicators that exhibit convergence between the civil law tradition and the British common law, the legacy of legal origins did not prevent cross-legal tradition differences from narrowing down over the past decade. This would contradict the Legal Origins Theory that predicts the persistence over time of the differences in legal and regulatory standards across legal traditions.

Second, we have estimated fixed-effects panel regressions to analyze the relationship between changes in legal rules and regulations and changes in the real economy. Our findings point to a lack of systematic effects of legal rules and regulations on economic and financial outcomes. This result stands in stark contrast to the widespread belief that reforms aiming to strengthen investor and creditor rights (or other market-friendly policies aimed at reducing the regulatory burden) lead to better economic and financial outcomes. It seems that improvements in these legal rules are not sufficient conditions for that. This is consistent with the evidence provided by Hallward-Driemeier and Prichett (2011), who found almost no correlations between changes over time in Doing Business indicators and firm-level Enterprise Surveys. This indicates that outcome-based legal indicators derived from the direct experience of firms, which can better measure the consequences arising from the actual implementation and enforcement of laws in practice, are far from the intended legal and regulatory changes measured in the Doing Business reports.

Finally, we have conducted an exploratory analysis of the determinants of the effectiveness of legal reforms and of the gap between legal rules and the reality on the ground. Measuring legal reform effectiveness as the ratio between variation in economic outcomes and variation in legal rules, we find considerable differences among countries. These differences allow us to analyze the potential determinants of legal reform effectiveness. The evidence is not conclusive but suggests that institutional quality and mineral resource abundance are factors positively related to the effectiveness of legal reforms. These findings have to be interpreted with caution due to the limited number of observations and potential biases caused by omitted variables. In addition, we have also analyzed the related question of the gap between legal rules and the reality on the ground, both in terms of financial and economic outcomes and in terms of law in action. The evidence appears to support the fact that institutional quality is a factor that reduces the gap most of the times. A notable result in this regard is that common law countries have a larger gap than civil law countries, although the difference has diminished from 2006 to 2012 and in some cases disappeared. This is likely a consequence of the reform agenda in civil law countries aimed at increasing the protection to creditors and investors, which however has not materialized into improvements on the ground. This accords with the assessment provided in the World Development Report 2017 (World Bank 2017), which warns reforming nations against mechanically adopting organizational forms from prosperous countries without generating an actual improvement in final outcomes or behavioral patterns. The result of this is that the content of the laws and regulations concerning the ease of doing business ends up differing a lot from the actual experience of firms, bureaucrats and citizens.

Taken as a whole, all the evidence gathered in this book indicates that legal and regulatory reforms in developing nations that mechanically adopt organizational forms from prosperous nations, without a thorough analysis of their specific policy priorities to improve their framework for governance and institutional reform as a way to foster their state capacity to deliver growth and social progress, are likely to render governance reforms mostly ineffective. In addition, the enactment of reforms introducing new legal rules and regulations may not yield the intended positive benefits, if the country lacks the judicial human capital and legal infrastructure required for effectively implementing the targeted reforms and properly enforcing the new laws.

Appendix

Table A.1 Data description and sources

Variable	Description	Source
Legal rules/regulations		
Doing business		
Strength of creditor rights index	The strength of legal rights index. According to the Doing Business' methodology, this index *"measures the degree to which collateral and bankruptcy laws protect the rights of borrowers and lenders. It includes eight aspects related to legal rights in collateral law and two aspects in bankruptcy law. A score of 1 is assigned for each of such aspects of the laws considered."* The indicator ranges from 0 to 10, with higher scores implying higher creditor rights.	Doing Business Project
Strength of investor protection index	The strength of investor protection index. According to the Doing Business' methodology, this indicator *"measures the strength of minority shareholder protections against directors' misuse of corporate assets for personal gain. It distinguishes three dimensions of investor protections: transparency of related-party transactions (extent of disclosure index), extent of liability for self-dealing (extent of director liability index) and shareholders' ability to sue officers and directors for misconduct (the ease of shareholder suits index). The strength of investor protection index averages the three indices and ranges from 0 to 10, with higher values indicating more investor protection."*	Doing Business Project

(continued)

D. Oto-Peralías, D. Romero-Ávila, *Legal Traditions, Legal Reforms and Economic Performance*, Contributions to Economics, DOI 10.1007/978-3-319-67041-6

Table A.1 (continued)

Variable	Description	Source
Depth of credit information index	The depth of credit information index. According to the Doing Business' methodology, this indicator *"measures rules and practices affecting the coverage, scope and accessibility of credit information available through either a public credit registry or a private credit bureau. A score of 1 is assigned for each of the six features of the public credit registry or private credit bureau (or both)."* The indicator ranges from 0 to 6, with higher values reflecting more information available.	Doing Business Project
Recovery rate (%)	*"The recovery rate measures the outcome of insolvency proceedings involving domestic entities. This measure is recorded as cents on the dollar recouped by creditors through reorganization, liquidation or debt enforcement (foreclosure) proceedings. The calculation takes into account the outcome: whether the business emerges from the proceedings as a going concern or the assets are sold piecemeal. Then the costs of the proceedings are deducted (1 cent for each percentage point of the value of the debtor's estate). Finally, the value lost as a result of the time the money remains tied up in insolvency proceedings is taken into account, including the loss of value due to depreciation. The recovery rate is the present value of the remaining proceeds"* (Doing Business' methodology).	Doing Business Project
Time to enforce a contract (Ln)	Time (in days) to enforce contracts. We apply the logarithmic transformation. This is a measure of the efficiency of the judicial system in resolving a commercial dispute. According to the Doing Business' methodology, it *"represents the number of calendar days counted from the moment the plaintiff decides to file the lawsuit in court until payment. This includes both the days when actions take place and the waiting periods between. The average duration of different stages of dispute resolution is recorded: the completion of service of process (time to file and serve the case), the issuance of judgment (time for the trial and obtaining the judgment) and the moment of payment (time for enforcement of the judgment)."*	Doing Business Project

(continued)

Table A.1 (continued)

Variable	Description	Source
Time to start a business (Ln)	Number of days required to register a firm. We apply the logarithmic transformation. According to the Doing Business' methodology, this variable "*captures the median duration (in calendar days) that incorporation lawyers indicate is necessary in practice to complete a procedure with minimum follow-up with government agencies and no extra payments. It is assumed that the minimum time required for each procedure is one day. Although procedures may take place simultaneously, they cannot start on the same day (that is, simultaneous procedures start on consecutive days). A procedure is considered completed once the company has received the final document, such as the company registration certificate or tax number. If a procedure can be accelerated for an additional cost, the fastest procedure is chosen if that option is more beneficial to the economy's ranking.*"	Doing Business Project
Time to register a property (Ln)	Number of days required to register a property. We apply the logarithmic transformation. According to the Doing Business' methodology, this variable "*captures the median duration (in calendar days) that property lawyers, notaries or registry officials indicate is necessary to complete a procedure. It is assumed that the minimum time required for each procedure is one day. Although procedures may take place simultaneously, they cannot start on the same day. It is assumed that the buyer does not waste time and commits to completing each remaining procedure without delay. If a procedure can be accelerated for an additional cost, the fastest legal procedure available and used by the majority of property owners is chosen. If procedures can be undertaken simultaneously, it is assumed that they are.*"	Doing Business Project
Time to obtain construction permits	This indicator measures the median duration (in days) that takes in practice to complete all procedures required for a firm in the construction industry to build a warehouse. We apply the logarithmic transformation. According to the Doing Business' methodology, "*it is assumed that the minimum time required for each procedure is one day, except for procedures that can be fully completed online, for which the time required is recorded as half a day. Although procedures may take*	Doing Business Project

(continued)

Table A.1 (continued)

Variable	Description	Source
	place simultaneously, they cannot start on the same day [...] with the exception of procedures that can be fully completed online. If a procedure can be accelerated legally for an additional cost and the accelerated procedure is used by the majority of companies, the fastest time to complete a procedure is chosen. It is assumed that [the construction company] does not waste time and commits to completing each remaining procedure without delay. The time that [the construction company] spends on gathering information is not taken into account."	
Time required to pay taxes (Ln)	This indicator measures "*the time to prepare, file and pay (or withhold) three major types of taxes: the corporate income tax, value added or sales tax, and labor taxes, including payroll taxes and social security contributions.*" Time is expressed in hours per year.	Doing Business Project
Time to export (Ln)	This indicator measures the "*time for border compliance that includes time for obtaining, preparing and submitting documents during port or border handling, customs clearance and inspection procedures*". Time is expressed in hours.	Doing Business Project
Time to import (Ln)	This indicator measures the "*time for border compliance that includes time for obtaining, preparing and submitting documents during port or border handling, customs clearance and inspection procedures*". Time is expressed in hours.	Doing Business Project
Others		
Creditor rights 1995–2005	Unlike the La Porta et al. (1997)'s creditor rights index that only focused on bankruptcy law, this creditor index considers other dimensions such as legal protection made available to creditors through secured credit and other contract-based mechanisms, and through company laws (Armour et al. 2009a). More specifically, this creditor index is based on the following ten dimensions: minimum share capital, dividend restriction, directors' duties towards creditors, non-possessory security interests and its registration, out-of-court enforcement of security interests, power to commence bankruptcy proceedings, stay of secured creditors in insolvency proceedings, outcome of bankruptcy proceedings, and rank order of secured creditors (Armour et al. 2009c).	Armour et al. (2009a, c)

(continued)

Table A.1 (continued)

Variable	Description	Source
Shareholder protection index 1995–2005	This index covers a much wider range of types of legal rules of company law and securities law than La Porta et al. (1997). It is based on ten variables that include the following dimensions: powers of the general meeting for *de facto* changes, agenda setting power, anticipation of shareholder decision facilitated, prohibition of multiple voting rights, independent board members, feasibility of director's dismissal, private enforcement of director duties, shareholder action against resolutions of the general meeting, mandatory bid, and disclosure of major share ownership.	Armour et al. (2009a), Siems (2008)
Creditor rights 1978–2002	*An index aggregating creditor rights, following* La Porta et al. (1998). *A score of one is assigned when each of the following rights of secured lenders are defined in laws and regulations: First, there are restrictions, such as creditor consent or minimum dividends, for a debtor to file for reorganization. Second, secured creditors are able to seize their collateral after the reorganization petition is approved, i.e. there is no "automatic stay" or "asset freeze." Third, secured creditors are paid first out of the proceeds of liquidating a bankrupt firm, as opposed to other creditors such as government or workers. Finally, if management does not retain administration of its property pending the resolution of the reorganization. The index ranges from 0 (weak creditor rights) to 4 (strong creditor rights) and is constructed as at January for every year from 1978 to 2003.*	Djankov et al. (2007)
Formalism index—Eviction 1960–2000	*Index of substantive and procedural statutory intervention in judicial cases of eviction of a tenant for nonpayment at lower-level civil trial courts for each year between 1950 and 2000. The index is formed, as in* Djankov et al. (2003), *by adding up the following indices: (i) professionals vs. laymen; (ii) written vs. oral elements; (iii) legal justification; (iv) statutory regulation of evidence; (v) control of superior review; (vi) engagement formalities; and (vii) independent procedural actions. The index ranges from 0 to 7, where 7 means a higher level of control or intervention in the judicial process. Some of the components of the index are defined differently than in* Djankov et al. (2003).	Balas et al. (2009)

(continued)

Table A.1 (continued)

Variable	Description	Source
Form. index—Check collection 1960–2000	*Index of substantive and procedural statutory intervention in judicial cases of collection of a bounced check at lower-level civil trial courts for each year between 1950 and 2000. The index is formed, as in* Djankov et al. (2003), *by adding up the following indices: (i) professionals vs. laymen; (ii) written vs. oral elements; (iii) legal justification; (iv) statutory regulation of evidence; (v) control of superior review; (vi) engagement formalities; and (vii) independent procedural actions. The index ranges from 0 to 7, where 7 means a higher level of control or intervention in the judicial process. Some of the components of the index are defined differently than in* Djankov et al. (2003).	Balas et al. (2009)
Dependent variables		
Market capitalization of listed domestic companies (% of GDP)	*Market capitalization (also known as market value) is the share price times the number of shares outstanding (including their several classes) for listed domestic companies. Investment funds, unit trusts, and companies whose only business goal is to hold shares of other listed companies are excluded. Data are end of year values.*	World Bank Open Databases
Stocks traded, total value (% of GDP)	*The value of shares traded is the total number of shares traded, both domestic and foreign, multiplied by their respective matching prices. Figures are single counted (only one side of the transaction is considered). Companies admitted to listing and admitted to trading are included in the data. Data are end of year values.*	World Bank Open Databases
Domestic credit to private sector by banks (% of GDP)	*Domestic credit to private sector by banks refers to financial resources provided to the private sector by other depository corporations (deposit taking corporations except central banks), such as through loans, purchases of nonequity securities, and trade credits and other accounts receivable, that establish a claim for repayment. For some countries these claims include credit to public enterprises.*	World Bank Open Databases

(continued)

Table A.1 (continued)

Variable	Description	Source
Domestic credit provided by financial sector (% of GDP)	*Domestic credit provided by the financial sector includes all credit to various sectors on a gross basis, with the exception of credit to the central government, which is net. The financial sector includes monetary authorities and deposit money banks, as well as other financial corporations where data are available (including corporations that do not accept transferable deposits but do incur such liabilities as time and savings deposits). Examples of other financial corporations are finance and leasing companies, money lenders, insurance corporations, pension funds, and foreign exchange companies.*	World Bank Open Databases
Domestic credit to private sector (% of GDP)	*Domestic credit to private sector refers to financial resources provided to the private sector by financial corporations, such as through loans, purchases of nonequity securities, and trade credits and other accounts receivable, that establish a claim for repayment. For some countries these claims include credit to public enterprises. The financial corporations include monetary authorities and deposit money banks, as well as other financial corporations where data are available (including corporations that do not accept transferable deposits but do incur such liabilities as time and savings deposits). Examples of other financial corporations are finance and leasing companies, money lenders, insurance corporations, pension funds, and foreign exchange companies.*	World Bank Open Databases
Foreign direct investment, net inflows (% of GDP)	*Foreign direct investment are the net inflows of investment to acquire a lasting management interest (10 percent or more of voting stock) in an enterprise operating in an economy other than that of the investor. It is the sum of equity capital, reinvestment of earnings, other long-term capital, and short-term capital as shown in the balance of payments. This series shows net inflows (new investment inflows less disinvestment) in the reporting economy from foreign investors, and is divided by GDP.*	World Bank Open Databases
Trade (% of GDP)	*Trade is the sum of exports and imports of goods and services measured as a share of gross domestic product.*	World Bank Open Databases

(continued)

Table A.1 (continued)

Variable	Description	Source
Gross fixed capital formation, private sector (% of GDP)	*Private investment covers gross outlays by the private sector (including private nonprofit agencies) on additions to its fixed domestic assets.*	World Bank Open Databases
New business density (new registrations per 1000 people ages 15–64)	*New businesses registered are the number of new limited liability corporations registered in the calendar year.*	World Bank Open Databases
Unemployment, total (% of total labor force) (modeled ILO estimate)	*Unemployment refers to the share of the labor force that is without work but available for and seeking employment.*	World Bank Open Databases
GINI index (World Bank estimate)	*Gini index measures the extent to which the distribution of income (or, in some cases, consumption expenditure) among individuals or households within an economy deviates from a perfectly equal distribution. A Lorenz curve plots the cumulative percentages of total income received against the cumulative number of recipients, starting with the poorest individual or household. The Gini index measures the area between the Lorenz curve and a hypothetical line of absolute equality, expressed as a percentage of the maximum area under the line. Thus a Gini index of 0 represents perfect equality, while an index of 100 implies perfect inequality.*	World Bank Open Databases
GDP per capita growth (annual %)	*Annual percentage growth rate of GDP per capita based on constant local currency. Aggregates are based on constant 2010 U.S. dollars. GDP per capita is gross domestic product divided by midyear population. GDP at purchaser's prices is the sum of gross value added by all resident producers in the economy plus any product taxes and minus any subsidies not included in the value of the products. It is calculated without making deductions for depreciation of fabricated assets or for depletion and degradation of natural resources.*	World Bank Open Databases
Private credit by deposit money banks and other financial institutions to GDP (%)	*Private credit by deposit money banks and other financial institutions to GDP, calculated using the following deflation method: {(0.5)* [Ft/P_et + Ft−1/P_et−1]}/[GDPt/P_at] where F is credit to the private sector, P_e is end-of period CPI, and P_a is average annual CPI. Raw data are from the electronic version of the IMF's International Financial*	The Global Financial Development Database

(continued)

Table A.1 (continued)

Variable	Description	Source
	Statistics. Private credit by deposit money banks and other financial institutions (IFS lines 22d, 42d, FOSAOP and FFSAP); GDP in local currency (IFS line NGDP); end-of period CPI (IFS line PCPI); and average annual CPI is calculated using the monthly CPI values (IFS line PCPI)	
Stock market capitalization to GDP (%)	*Value of listed shares to GDP, calculated using the following deflation method: {(0.5)* [Ft/P_et + Ft−1/P_et−1]}/[GDPt/P_at] where F is stock market capitalization, P_e is end-of period CPI, and P_a is average annual CPI. End-of period CPI (IFS line PCPI) and average annual CPI is calculated using the monthly CPI values (IFS line PCPI).*	The Global Financial Development Database
Stock market total value traded to GDP (%)	*Total value of all traded shares in a stock market exchange as a percentage of GDP. The following deflation method is used: {(0.5)* [Ft/P_et + Ft−1/P_et−1]}/[GDPt/P_at] where F is stock market capitalization, P_e is end-of period CPI, and P_a is average annual CPI. End-of period CPI (IFS line PCPI) and average annual CPI is calculated using the monthly CPI values (IFS line PCPI).*	The Global Financial Development Database
Number of listed companies per 1,000,000 people	*Number of publicly listed companies per 1,000,000 people. Number of listed domestic companies is the domestically incorporated companies listed on the country's stock exchanges at the end of the year. This indicator does not include investment companies, mutual funds, or other collective investment vehicles.*	The Global Financial Development Database
Others		
GDP per capita, PPP (constant 2011 international $)	*GDP per capita based on purchasing power parity (PPP). PPP GDP is gross domestic product converted to international dollars using purchasing power parity rates. An international dollar has the same purchasing power over GDP as the U.S. dollar has in the United States. GDP at purchaser's prices is the sum of gross value added by all resident producers in the economy plus any product taxes and minus any subsidies not included in the value of the products. It is calculated without making deductions for depreciation of fabricated assets or for depletion and degradation of natural resources. Data are in constant 2011 international dollars.*	World Bank Open Databases

(continued)

Table A.1 (continued)

Variable	Description	Source
Rule of law (Worldwide Governance Indicators)	Confidence in and compliance with the rules of society. It comes from the Worldwide Governance Indicators (WGI) project. Year 2000. The scale ranges from −2.5 to 2.5, where a higher value indicates better institutions.	Kaufmann et al. (2009), from Teorell et al. (2011)
Government effectiveness (Worldwide Governance Indicators)	Indicator reflecting perceptions about the quality of public administration. Year 2000. The scale ranges from −2.5 to 2.5, where a higher value indicates better institutions.	Kaufmann et al. (2009), from Teorell et al. (2011)
Legal origins	A dummy variable that identifies the legal origin of the Company law or Commercial Code of each country. The four origins are English, French, German, and Nordic.	La Porta et al. (2008)
Variables used in Chapter 8 (and not described above)		
Dependent variables		
Effectiveness of creditor rights reforms in financial depth (private credit over GDP) 2006–2013	Average annual change in financial depth (defined as private credit over GDP) divided by average annual change in the strength of creditor rights index. Averages are calculated for the period 2006–2013.	Doing Business Project, The Global Financial Development Database, and World Bank Open Databases
Effectiveness of creditor rights reforms in entrepreneurship (new business density)	Average annual change in entrepreneurship (defined as new business density) divided by average annual change in the strength of creditor rights index. Averages are calculated for the period 2006–2014.	Doing Business Project, The Global Financial Development Database, and World Bank Open Databases
Effectiveness of investor protection reforms in financial depth (private credit over GDP) 2006–2013	Average annual change in financial depth (defined as private credit over GDP) divided by average annual change in the strength of investor protection index. Averages are calculated for the period 2006–2013.	Doing Business Project, The Global Financial Development Database, and World Bank Open Databases
Effectiveness of investor protection reforms in entrepreneurship (new business density)	Average annual change in entrepreneurship (defined as new business density) divided by average annual change in the strength of investor protection index. Averages are calculated for the period 2006–2014.	Doing Business Project, The Global Financial Development Database, and World Bank Open Databases
Gap between creditor rights and financial depth (private credit over GDP) 2006	Distance to the frontier (DTF) in the strength of creditor rights index minus DTF in financial depth (private credit over GDP), measured in 2006. DTF measures the distance of each economy to the best performance observed for each indicator. A value of 100 in DTF reflects that the country is on the "frontier", that is, has the best performance, while a value of 0 means that it has the worst performance. The	Doing Business Project, The Global Financial Development Database, and World Bank Open Databases

(continued)

Table A.1 (continued)

Variable	Description	Source
	indicators of DTF in legal rules are taken from the Doing Business Project, while DTF in economic and financial outcomes are calculated following the Doing Business' methodology. See more details in the main text.	
Gap between creditor rights and entrepreneurship (new business density) 2006	DTF in the strength of creditor rights index minus DTF in entrepreneurship (new business density), measured in 2006.	Doing Business Project, The Global Financial Development Database, and World Bank Open Databases
Gap between investor protection and financial depth (private credit over GDP) 2006	DTF in the strength of investor protection index minus DTF in financial depth (private credit over GDP), measured in 2006.	Doing Business Project, The Global Financial Development Database, and World Bank Open Databases
Gap between investor protection and entrepreneurship (new business density) 2006	DTF in the strength of investor protection index minus DTF in entrepreneurship (new business density), measured in 2006.	Doing Business Project, The Global Financial Development Database, and World Bank Open Databases
Gap between creditor rights and contract enforcement 2006	DTF in the strength of creditor rights index minus DTF in time to enforce a contract, measured in 2006.	Doing Business Project.
Gap between creditor rights and debt recovery 2006	DTF in the strength of creditor rights index minus DTF in recovery rate, measured in 2006.	Doing Business Project.
Gap between investor protection and contract enforcement 2006	DTF in the strength of investor protection minus DTF in time to enforce a contract, measured in 2006.	Doing Business Project.
Gap between investor protection and debt recovery 2006	DTF in the strength of investor protection minus DTF in recovery rate, measured in 2006.	Doing Business Project.
Independent variables		
Control of corruption (Worldwide Governance Indicators) 2006	Indicator that reflects perceptions about the abuse of public power for private gain and the capture of the state by elites and private interests. Year 2000. The scale ranges from −2.5 to 2.5, where a higher value indicates better institutions.	Kaufmann et al. (2009), from Teorell et al. (2011).
Rule of law (Worldwide Governance Indicators) 2006	Confidence in and compliance with the rules of society. It comes from the Worldwide Governance Indicators (WGI) project. Year 2000. The scale ranges from −2.5 to 2.5, where a higher value indicates better institutions.	Kaufmann et al. (2009), from Teorell et al. (2011).

(continued)

Table A.1 (continued)

Variable	Description	Source
Political stability	Indicator measuring perceptions about the likelihood of destabilization or subversion of government. Year 2006. The scale ranges from −2.5 to 2.5, where a higher value indicates better institutions.	Kaufmann et al. (2009), from Teorell et al. (2011).
Catholics	Catholics as a percentage of population in 1985–1995.	La Porta et al. (1999), from Teorell et al. (2011)
Muslims	Muslims as a percentage of population in 1985–1995.	La Porta et al. (1999), from Teorell et al. (2011)
Protestants	Protestants as a percentage of population in 1985–1995.	La Porta et al. (1999), from Teorell et al. (2011)
Other religion	Population professing other religions as a percentage of population in 1985–1995.	La Porta et al. (1999), from Teorell et al. (2011)
Ethnic fractionalization (not corresponding to a specific year)	Probability that two randomly selected individuals from a given country do not belong to the same ethnolinguistic group.	Alesina et al. (2003), from Teorell et al. (2011).
Latitude	The absolute value of the latitude of the capital city divided by 90.	La Porta et al. (1999), from Teorell et al. (2011).
Mineral resources	Average of mineral rents over GDP during the period 1960–2000.	World Development Indicators

Table A.2 List of countries with their codes

Country code	Country name	Country code	Country name	Country code	Country name
ABW	Aruba	COD	Congo, Dem. Rep.	HKG	Hong Kong SAR, China
AFG	Afghanistan	COG	Congo, Rep.	HND	Honduras
AGO	Angola	COL	Colombia	HRV	Croatia
ALB	Albania	COM	Comoros	HTI	Haiti
AND	Andorra	CPV	Cabo Verde	HUN	Hungary
ARE	United Arab Emirates	CRI	Costa Rica	IDN	Indonesia
ARG	Argentina	CYM	Cayman Islands	IND	India
ARM	Armenia	CYP	Cyprus	IRL	Ireland
ATG	Antigua and Barbuda	CZE	Czech Republic	IRN	Iran, Islamic Rep.
AUS	Australia	DEU	Germany	IRQ	Iraq
AUT	Austria	DJI	Djibouti	ISL	Iceland
AZE	Azerbaijan	DMA	Dominica	ISR	Israel
BDI	Burundi	DNK	Denmark	ITA	Italy
BEL	Belgium	DOM	Dominican Republic	JAM	Jamaica
BEN	Benin	DZA	Algeria	JOR	Jordan
BFA	Burkina Faso	ECU	Ecuador	JPN	Japan
BGD	Bangladesh	EGY	Egypt, Arab Rep.	KAZ	Kazakhstan
BGR	Bulgaria	ERI	Eritrea	KEN	Kenya
BHR	Bahrain	ESP	Spain	KGZ	Kyrgyz Republic
BHS	Bahamas, The	EST	Estonia	KHM	Cambodia
BIH	Bosnia and Herzegovina	ETH	Ethiopia	KIR	Kiribati
BLR	Belarus	FIN	Finland	KNA	St. Kitts and Nevis
BLZ	Belize	FJI	Fiji	KOR	Korea, Rep.
BMU	Bermuda	FRA	France	KWT	Kuwait
BOL	Bolivia	FSM	Micronesia, Fed. Sts.	LAO	Lao PDR

(continued)

Table A.2 (continued)

Country code	Country name	Country code	Country name	Country code	Country name
BRA	Brazil	GAB	Gabon	LBN	Lebanon
BRB	Barbados	GBR	United Kingdom	LBR	Liberia
BRN	Brunei Darussalam	GEO	Georgia	LBY	Libya
BTN	Bhutan	GHA	Ghana	LCA	St. Lucia
BWA	Botswana	GIN	Guinea	LIE	Liechtenstein
CAF	Central African Republic	GMB	Gambia, The	LKA	Sri Lanka
CAN	Canada	GNB	Guinea-Bissau	LSO	Lesotho
CHE	Switzerland	GNQ	Equatorial Guinea	LTU	Lithuania
CHL	Chile	GRC	Greece	LUX	Luxembourg
CHN	China	GRD	Grenada	LVA	Latvia
CIV	Cote d'Ivoire	GTM	Guatemala	MAC	Macao SAR, China
CMR	Cameroon	GUY	Guyana	MAR	Morocco

Country code	Country name	Country code	Country name	Country code	Country name
MCO	Monaco	SDN	Sudan	YEM	Yemen, Rep.
MDA	Moldova	SEN	Senegal	ZAF	South Africa
MDG	Madagascar	SGP	Singapore	ZMB	Zambia
MDV	Maldives	SLB	Solomon Islands	ZWE	Zimbabwe
MEX	Mexico	SLE	Sierra Leone		
MKD	Macedonia, FYR	SLV	El Salvador		
MLI	Mali	SMR	San Marino		
MLT	Malta	SOM	Somalia		
MNG	Mongolia	STP	Sao Tome and Principe		
MOZ	Mozambique	SUR	Suriname		
MRT	Mauritania	SVK	Slovak Republic		

MUS	Mauritius	SVN	Slovenia		
MWI	Malawi	SWE	Sweden		
MYS	Malaysia	SWZ	Swaziland		
NAM	Namibia	SYC	Seychelles		
NER	Niger	SYR	Syrian Arab Republic		
NGA	Nigeria	TCD	Chad		
NIC	Nicaragua	TGO	Togo		
NLD	Netherlands	THA	Thailand		
NOR	Norway	TJK	Tajikistan		
NPL	Nepal	TKM	Turkmenistan		
NZL	New Zealand	TON	Tonga		
OMN	Oman	TTO	Trinidad and Tobago		
PAK	Pakistan	TUN	Tunisia		
PAN	Panama	TUR	Turkey		
PER	Peru	TUV	Tuvalu		
PHL	Philippines	TZA	Tanzania		
PNG	Papua New Guinea	UGA	Uganda		
POL	Poland	UKR	Ukraine		
PRI	Puerto Rico	URY	Uruguay		
PRT	Portugal	USA	United States		
PRY	Paraguay	UZB	Uzbekistan		
QAT	Qatar	VCT	St. Vincent and the Grenadines		
ROU	Romania	VEN	Venezuela, RB		
RUS	Russian Federation	VNM	Vietnam		
RWA	Rwanda	VUT	Vanuatu		
SAU	Saudi Arabia	WSM	Samoa		

Table A.3 The effect of legal rules on financial and economic outcomes: LSDV model. Without additional control

	Creditor rights		Investor protection		Credit information		Recovery rate		Contract enforc.		Starting a business	
	Coeff/SE	Obs	Coeff/SE	Obs	Coeff/SE	Obs	Coeff/SE	Obs	Coeff/SE	Obs	Coeff/SE	Obs
	(1)		(2)		(3)		(4)		(5)		(6)	
Stock market capitalization	1.224	266	−0.736	266	−0.522	266	0.567	266	38.419	266	−6.175	266
	(2.717)		(5.456)		(2.021)		(0.473)		(48.734)		(5.694)	
Stocks traded	7.059**	243	10.905**	243	5.367**	243	1.316**	243	−43.088	243	−2.845	243
	(3.336)		(4.75)		(2.252)		(0.557)		(52.294)		(6.857)	
Domestic credit to private sector by banks	0.812	325	−0.205	325	0.763	325	0.076	325	−5.841	325	−2.077	325
	(0.823)		(1.161)		(0.92)		(0.148)		(13.249)		(1.81)	
Domestic credit provided by financial sector	0.395	325	−0.26	325	1.699	325	−0.005	325	−11.188	325	−2.086	325
	(1.053)		(1.638)		(1.071)		(0.244)		(16.074)		(2.165)	
Domestic credit to private sector	0.908	325	−0.182	325	0.73	325	0.08	325	−5.111	325	−2.255	325
	(0.774)		(1.278)		(0.927)		(0.148)		(13.196)		(1.854)	
Foreign direct investment	0.213	520	−0.191	520	−0.201	520	0.096	520	−0.017	520	1.072	520
	(0.293)		(0.596)		(0.269)		(0.066)		(2.831)		(1.041)	
Trade	−0.958	501	0.352	501	0.03	501	0.069	501	13.746	501	3.143	501
	(1.328)		(1.294)		(0.84)		(0.313)		(12.18)		(4.037)	
Private gross fixed capital formation	0.043	256	−0.598	256	−0.293	256	0.088	256	−7.451	256	−0.82	256
	(0.298)		(0.635)		(0.337)		(0.143)		(4.56)		(0.786)	
New business density	0.103	354	0.18	354	−0.058	354	0.016	354	0.304	354	0.028	354
	(0.11)		(0.194)		(0.113)		(0.022)		(1.945)		(0.469)	
Unemployment rate	−0.139*	485	−0.029	485	−0.136	485	−0.057	485	1.793	485	0.02	485
	(0.084)		(0.275)		(0.145)		(0.051)		(2.709)		(0.268)	
Income GINI index	−0.538**	276	−0.053	276	−0.025	276	0.023	276	0.302	276	−0.211	276
	(0.222)		(0.376)		(0.203)		(0.047)		(2.009)		(0.576)	
GDP pc growth	0.03	521	−0.69	521	−0.618***	521	0.028	521	−0.821	521	0.971**	521
	(0.207)		(0.493)		(0.235)		(0.052)		(1.378)		(0.486)	

	Registering a property		Construction permits		Paying taxes		Time to export		Time to import	
	Coeff/SE	Obs	Coeff/SE	Obs	Coeff/SE	Obs	Coeff/SE	Obs	Coeff/SE	Obs
	(7)		(8)		(9)		(10)		(11)	
Stock market capitalization	2.344	266	−16.563	266	2.209	266	−31.636	266	−30.739*	266
	(3.914)		(21.027)		(11.335)		(25.715)		(18.218)	
Stocks traded	−5.845	243	10.731	243	−12.058	243	−35.9	243	−29.007*	243
	(4.878)		(19.042)		(13.454)		(30.815)		(17.059)	
Domestic credit to private sector by banks	0.428	325	−3.373	325	−0.085	323	−16.512	325	−8.77	325
	(1.959)		(3.517)		(3.593)		(13.852)		(6.929)	
Domestic credit provided by financial sector	0.178	325	−5.97	325	−8.162*	323	−12.14	325	−3.902	325
	(1.815)		(3.664)		(4.673)		(14.838)		(8.109)	
Domestic credit to private sector	0.224	325	−3.597	325	−1.738	323	−17.358	325	−9.482	325
	(1.99)		(3.439)		(3.62)		(13.962)		(7.03)	
Foreign direct investment	1.212	520	−0.9	520	1.136	518	0.838	520	0.976	520
	(1.039)		(1.814)		(1.661)		(2.673)		(2.218)	
Trade	−1.218	501	4.968	501	−2.387	499	6.167	501	0.714	501
	(1.876)		(8.032)		(5.773)		(6.687)		(5.251)	
Private gross fixed capital formation	−0.518	256	−0.321	256	4.784***	256	2.565	256	2.708	256
	(0.921)		(2.029)		(1.79)		(3.148)		(2.444)	
New business density	−0.112	354	−0.955	354	0.756	352	−0.588	354	−0.536	354
	(0.234)		(0.676)		(0.657)		(1.719)		(1.127)	
Unemployment rate	−0.468	485	0.843	485	−0.648	483	2.34**	485	1.452*	485
	(0.387)		(0.758)		(0.754)		(1.152)		(0.769)	
Income GINI index	−0.099	276	0.9	276	−1.043	275	1.453	276	2.247	276
	(0.398)		(1.192)		(1.223)		(1.759)		(1.62)	
GDP pc growth	1.149**	521	0.695	521	3.713**	519	1.636	521	1.179	521
	(0.503)		(1.247)		(1.6)		(1.344)		(1.181)	

Notes: Panel specification with averaged annual data over 3-year periods (2006–2014). Clustered standard errors in parentheses. The regressions include country and period dummies, and a constant term. All these variables are omitted for space considerations

*, ** and *** denote statistical significance at the 10, 5 and 1% levels, respectively

Table A.4 The effect of legal rules on financial and economic outcomes: LSDV model. Annual data

	Creditor rights		Investor protection		Credit information		Recovery rate		Contract enforc.		Starting a business	
	Coeff/SE	Obs	Coeff/SE	Obs	Coeff/SE	Obs	Coeff/SE	Obs	Coeff/SE	Obs	Coeff/SE	Obs
	(1)		(2)		(3)		(4)		(5)		(6)	
Stock market capitalization	0.737	727	−0.23	727	0.736	727	0.438	727	41.824	727	−4.671	727
	(1.77)		(3.826)		(1.435)		(0.288)		(45.672)		(4.485)	
Stocks traded	4.382*	641	9.881***	641	3.456**	641	0.706**	641	−59.279	641	−1.525	641
	(2.368)		(3.375)		(1.515)		(0.331)		(49.551)		(6.051)	
Domestic credit to private sector by banks	0.731	959	−0.07	959	0.607	959	0.102	959	−5.618	959	−2.176	959
	(0.686)		(0.922)		(0.556)		(0.086)		(8.692)		(1.477)	
Domestic credit provided by financial sector	0.316	959	0.1	959	1.145*	959	0.072	959	−10.488	959	−2.234	959
	(0.893)		(1.218)		(0.629)		(0.153)		(10.631)		(1.685)	
Domestic credit to private sector	0.802	959	−0.115	959	0.581	959	0.111	959	−4.935	959	−2.387	959
	(0.651)		(1.016)		(0.557)		(0.089)		(8.674)		(1.512)	
Foreign direct investment	0.145	1534	−0.257	1534	−0.024	1534	0.048	1534	0.738	1534	0.792	1534
	(0.247)		(0.449)		(0.16)		(0.036)		(1.997)		(0.744)	
Trade	−0.841	1465	−0.15	1465	−0.002	1465	0.021	1465	14.18	1465	2.128	1465
	(0.976)		(0.965)		(0.511)		(0.199)		(9.08)		(2.63)	
Private gross fixed capital formation	0.095	729	−0.485	729	−0.114	729	0.073	729	−7**	729	−0.916	729
	(0.235)		(0.513)		(0.199)		(0.055)		(3.41)		(0.572)	
New business density	0.109	851	0.188	851	0.016	851	0.014	851	0.203	851	−0.002	851
	(0.077)		(0.159)		(0.09)		(0.013)		(1.593)		(0.379)	
Unemployment rate	−0.115*	1428	−0.027	1428	−0.141	1428	−0.032	1428	1.322	1428	0.076	1428
	(0.063)		(0.206)		(0.096)		(0.025)		(1.799)		(0.192)	
Income GINI index	−0.438**	506	−0.144	506	0.022	506	−0.001	506	0.845	506	−0.284	506
	(0.212)		(0.361)		(0.144)		(0.041)		(1.534)		(0.364)	

	Registering a property		Construction permits		Paying taxes		Time to export		Time to import	
	Coeff/SE	Obs	Coeff/SE	Obs	Coeff/SE	Obs	Coeff/SE	Obs	Coeff/SE	Obs
	(7)		(8)		(9)		(10)		(11)	
Stock market capitalization	0.917	727	−13.35	727	2.512	727	−26.839*	727	−26.861**	727
	(2.402)		(15.307)		(8.62)		(15.103)		(12.472)	
Stocks traded	−5.683	641	12.491	641	−8.577	641	−44.786**	641	−47.046*	641
	(3.601)		(16.312)		(11.852)		(21.739)		(26.544)	
Domestic credit to private sector by banks	0.379	959	−3.248	959	−0.438	952	−12.45	959	−7.076	959
	(1.485)		(2.648)		(2.841)		(8.298)		(4.515)	
Domestic credit provided by financial sector	0.062	959	−7.045***	959	−7.441*	952	−10.67	959	−4.541	959
	(1.37)		(2.604)		(3.816)		(9.151)		(4.917)	
Domestic credit to private sector	0.2	959	−3.223	959	−1.884	952	−13.365	959	−7.792*	959
	(1.496)		(2.587)		(2.844)		(8.373)		(4.594)	
Foreign direct investment	0.856	1534	−0.451	1534	1.168	1527	0.266	1534	0.604	1534
	(0.703)		(1.316)		(1.472)		(1.71)		(1.394)	
Trade	−1.256	1465	2.144	1465	−1.237	1458	3.87	1465	1.026	1465
	(1.423)		(5.192)		(4.308)		(4.163)		(3.139)	
Private gross fixed capital formation	−0.281	729	0.002	729	4.043***	729	1.235	729	1.548	729
	(0.675)		(1.306)		(1.357)		(1.64)		(1.361)	
New business density	−0.159	851	−1.046	851	0.782	847	−0.729	851	−0.584	851
	(0.219)		(0.635)		(0.604)		(1.026)		(0.717)	
Unemployment rate	−0.35	1428	0.559	1428	−0.41	1421	1.509**	1428	1.086**	1428
	(0.272)		(0.556)		(0.607)		(0.729)		(0.547)	
Income GINI index	−0.023	506	0.641	506	−0.798	505	0.571	506	1.275	506
	(0.331)		(1.152)		(1.225)		(1.176)		(1.082)	

Notes: Panel of annual data over the period 2006–2014. Clustered standard errors in parentheses. The regressions include the lag of GDP growth, country and period dummies, and a constant term. All these variables are omitted for space considerations

*, ** and *** denote statistical significance at the 10, 5 and 1% levels, respectively

Table A.5 The effect of legal rules on financial and economic outcomes: LSDV model. Annual data, without additional control

	Creditor rights		Investor protection		Credit information		Recovery rate		Contract enforc.		Starting a business	
	Coeff/SE	Obs	Coeff/SE	Obs	Coeff/SE	Obs	Coeff/SE	Obs	Coeff/SE	Obs	Coeff/SE	Obs
	(1)		(2)		(3)		(4)		(5)		(6)	
Stock market capitalization	0.788	727	−0.272	727	0.704	727	0.444	727	41.024	727	−4.668	727
	(1.796)		(3.839)		(1.403)		(0.296)		(46.1)		(4.49)	
Stocks traded	4.442*	641	9.818***	641	3.405**	641	0.718**	641	−59.502	641	−1.477	641
	(2.369)		(3.41)		(1.503)		(0.341)		(49.114)		(6.003)	
Domestic credit to private sector by banks	0.719	967	−0.096	967	0.582	967	0.1	967	−4.923	967	−2.131	967
	(0.683)		(0.936)		(0.536)		(0.086)		(8.406)		(1.431)	
Domestic credit provided by financial sector	0.305	967	0.135	967	1.181*	967	0.067	967	−9.568	967	−2.328	967
	(0.908)		(1.236)		(0.608)		(0.156)		(10.322)		(1.638)	
Domestic credit to private sector	0.791	967	−0.142	967	0.555	967	0.109	967	−4.304	967	−2.338	967
	(0.647)		(1.025)		(0.538)		(0.089)		(8.392)		(1.468)	
Foreign direct investment	0.155	1542	−0.257	1542	−0.03	1542	0.05	1542	0.564	1542	0.795	1542
	(0.249)		(0.446)		(0.155)		(0.037)		(1.979)		(0.742)	
Trade	−0.803	1473	−0.142	1473	−0.012	1473	0.029	1473	13.46	1473	2.118	1473
	(0.981)		(0.981)		(0.507)		(0.197)		(9.005)		(2.61)	
Private gross fixed capital formation	0.083	729	−0.514	729	−0.182	729	0.076	729	−7.123**	729	−0.894	729
	(0.247)		(0.511)		(0.197)		(0.056)		(3.441)		(0.564)	
New business density	0.118	854	0.184	854	0	854	0.015	854	0.179	854	0.007	854
	(0.077)		(0.158)		(0.088)		(0.014)		(1.598)		(0.371)	
Unemployment rate	−0.126*	1445	0.005	1445	−0.113	1445	−0.037	1445	1.337	1445	0.024	1445
	(0.064)		(0.206)		(0.096)		(0.027)		(1.805)		(0.193)	
Income GINI index	−0.439**	507	−0.146	507	0.027	507	−0.001	507	0.876	507	−0.291	507
	(0.212)		(0.363)		(0.142)		(0.041)		(1.518)		(0.363)	
GDP pc growth	−0.01	1546	−0.59*	1546	−0.414***	1546	0.032	1546	−0.774	1546	0.907**	1546
	(0.173)		(0.345)		(0.148)		(0.029)		(1.094)		(0.381)	

	Registering a property		Construction permits		Paying taxes		Time to export		Time to import	
	Coeff/SE	Obs	Coeff/SE	Obs	Coeff/SE	Obs	Coeff/SE	Obs	Coeff/SE	Obs
	(7)		(8)		(9)		(10)		(11)	
Stock market capitalization	0.951	727	−13.341	727	2.576	727	−26.527*	727	−26.757**	727
	(2.371)		(15.311)		(8.576)		(15.202)		(12.532)	
Stocks traded	−5.633	641	12.459	641	−8.419	641	−44.541**	641	−46.916*	641
	(3.595)		(16.3)		(11.824)		(21.743)		(26.479)	
Domestic credit to private sector by banks	0.376	967	−3.308	967	−0.379	960	−12.312	967	−6.943	967
	(1.457)		(2.61)		(2.721)		(8.184)		(4.414)	
Domestic credit provided by financial sector	−0.056	967	−6.898***	967	−7.813**	960	−10.59	967	−4.539	967
	(1.342)		(2.59)		(3.628)		(9.021)		(4.846)	
Domestic credit to private sector	0.204	967	−3.279	967	−1.789	960	−13.205	967	−7.642*	967
	(1.471)		(2.549)		(2.718)		(8.259)		(4.489)	
Foreign direct investment	0.883	1542	−0.42	1542	1.195	1535	0.379	1542	0.672	1542
	(0.7)		(1.31)		(1.448)		(1.683)		(1.375)	
Trade	−1.144	1473	2.32	1473	−1.311	1466	4.449	1473	1.403	1473
	(1.41)		(5.178)		(4.328)		(4.175)		(3.166)	
Private gross fixed capital formation	−0.162	729	0.082	729	4.227***	729	1.648	729	1.792	729
	(0.684)		(1.39)		(1.375)		(1.769)		(1.445)	
New business density	−0.142	854	−1.057*	854	0.848	850	−0.687	854	−0.564	854
	(0.217)		(0.629)		(0.595)		(1.027)		(0.717)	
Unemployment rate	−0.395	1445	0.559	1445	−0.611	1438	1.402**	1445	1.037*	1445
	(0.266)		(0.503)		(0.578)		(0.699)		(0.534)	
Income GINI index	−0.028	507	0.647	507	−0.806	506	0.564	507	1.281	507
	(0.332)		(1.161)		(1.222)		(1.186)		(1.083)	
GDP pc growth	0.593*	1546	0.299	1546	3.256***	1539	0.921	1546	0.819	1546
	(0.339)		(0.801)		(1.152)		(0.822)		(0.762)	

Notes: Panel of annual data over the period 2006–2014. Clustered standard errors in parentheses. The regressions include country and period dummies, and a constant term. All these variables are omitted for space considerations
*, ** and *** denote statistical significance at the 10, 5 and 1% levels, respectively

Table A.6 The effect of legal rules on financial and economic outcomes: differentiation by level of development. Without additional control

		Creditor rights		Investor protection		Credit information		Recovery rate		Contract enforc.		Starting a business	
		Coeff/SE	Obs	Coeff/SE	Obs	Coeff/SE	Obs	Coeff/SE	Obs	Coeff/SE	Obs	Coeff/SE	Obs
		(1)		(2)		(3)		(4)		(5)		(6)	
Stock market capitalization	Below the median	3.062	263	0.11	263	−0.585	263	0.415	263	0.916	263	−7.051	263
		(2.509)		(5.393)		(2.772)		(1.103)		(9.049)		(7.157)	
	Above the median	−4.116		−1.268		−0.443		0.656		70.793		−6.09	
		(4.345)		(7.47)		(1.953)		(0.44)		(83.219)		(6.224)	
Stocks traded	Below the median	7.677**	240	13.432**	240	5.023*	240	1.562	240	18.326*	240	−16.927**	240
		(3.088)		(5.439)		(2.552)		(1.065)		(10.484)		(8.186)	
	Above the median	6.175		10.114*		6.239***		1.385**		−85.449		−1.117	
		(6.48)		(5.8)		(2.366)		(0.542)		(76.203)		(7.376)	
Domestic credit to private sector by banks	Below the median	0.8	321	0.708	321	0.909	321	−0.152	321	13.704	321	−1.61	321
		(0.868)		(0.733)		(1.082)		(0.303)		(11.002)		(2.094)	
	Above the median	1.067		−3.706		0.562		0.164		−39.108**		−2.82	
		(1.264)		(5.726)		(1.15)		(0.15)		(16.587)		(1.864)	
Domestic credit provided by financial sector	Below the median	0.044	321	−0.004	321	1.613	321	−0.354	321	11.008	321	−0.82	321
		(1.117)		(1.152)		(1.159)		(0.278)		(13.983)		(2.353)	
	Above the median	3.379		−1.17		1.896		0.123		−49.293**		−3.907	
		(2.098)		(7.773)		(1.261)		(0.277)		(19.86)		(2.621)	
Domestic credit to private sector	Below the median	0.884	321	0.367	321	0.939	321	−0.136	321	15.228	321	−1.862	321
		(0.806)		(0.89)		(1.091)		(0.313)		(10.747)		(2.149)	
	Above the median	1.244		−2.249		0.433		0.162		−39.335**		−2.884	
		(1.421)		(6.327)		(1.143)		(0.154)		(17.019)		(1.928)	
Foreign direct investment	Below the median	0.225	513	−0.015	513	0.043	513	0.19	513	−1.022	513	0.577	513
		(0.301)		(0.708)		(0.344)		(0.146)		(2.482)		(1.266)	
	Above the median	0.028		−0.778		−0.502		0.046		1.241		1.783	
		(0.6)		(0.662)		(0.329)		(0.062)		(4.739)		(1.605)	

Trade	Below the median	−1.016	494	−0.051	494	−0.907	494	−0.356	494	4.102	494	6.951	494
		(1.442)		(1.322)		(0.931)		(0.452)		(9.828)		(6.521)	
	Above the median	−0.982		1.279		1.239		0.26		23.915		−0.703	
		(1.668)		(2.805)		(1.149)		(0.298)		(20.802)		(2.557)	
Private gross fixed capital formation	Below the median	0.141	255	−0.589	255	−0.441	255	0.143	255	−10.349*	255	−0.472	255
		(0.311)		(0.707)		(0.44)		(0.165)		(5.73)		(1.019)	
	Above the median	−1.225		−0.638		−0.079		0.002		−0.655		−1.402*	
		(0.764)		(1.193)		(0.395)		(0.204)		(6.79)		(0.823)	
New business density	Below the median	0.048	349	0.177	349	0.054	349	0.026	349	−0.965	349	−0.312	349
		(0.103)		(0.149)		(0.092)		(0.03)		(0.761)		(0.274)	
	Above the median	0.88		0.188		−0.222		0.012		1.317		0.241	
		(0.67)		(0.573)		(0.214)		(0.03)		(3.445)		(0.62)	
Unemployment rate	Below the median	−0.141*	476	−0.24	476	−0.284*	476	−0.065	476	−1.541	476	0.524**	476
		(0.079)		(0.193)		(0.162)		(0.047)		(2.458)		(0.248)	
	Above the median	−0.147		0.611		0.044		−0.056		5.081		−0.496	
		(0.301)		(1.028)		(0.237)		(0.067)		(4.063)		(0.52)	
Income GINI index	Below the median	−0.587**	272	−0.149	272	−0.094	272	0.128	272	−1.223	272	0.544	272
		(0.23)		(0.446)		(0.278)		(0.155)		(3.684)		(0.96)	
	Above the median	−0.225		0.058		0.036		0.001		1.551		−0.499	
		(0.646)		(0.681)		(0.239)		(0.047)		(2.199)		(0.662)	
GDP pc growth	Below the median	0.048	517	−0.692	517	−0.58*	517	0.142**	517	−0.367	517	1.017	517
		(0.22)		(0.63)		(0.308)		(0.07)		(1.971)		(0.654)	
	Above the median	−0.241		−0.725*		−0.686**		−0.035		−1.269		0.942*	
		(0.595)		(0.392)		(0.332)		(0.053)		(1.819)		(0.558)	

(continued)

Table A.6 (continued)

		Registering a property		Construction permits		Paying taxes		Time to export		Time to import	
		Coeff/SE	Obs	Coeff/SE	Obs	Coeff/SE	Obs	Coeff/SE	Obs	Coeff/SE	Obs
		(7)		(8)		(9)		(10)		(11)	
Stock market capitalization	Below the median	4.025	263	−2.445	263	8.317	263	−14.828	263	−20.716	263
		(7.225)		(9.638)		(10.769)		(19.306)		(15.921)	
	Above the median	1.858		−22.048		−5.29		−46.019		−47.4	
		(3.829)		(27.514)		(14.528)		(37.894)		(31.597)	
Stocks traded	Below the median	−10.67	240	−19.787**	240	−19.568**	240	−42.549**	240	−37.316**	240
		(7.043)		(7.666)		(9.061)		(21.243)		(16.599)	
	Above the median	−4.942		23.387		−3.559		−29.286		−25.838	
		(4.837)		(26.143)		(23.341)		(47.028)		(27.191)	
Domestic credit to private sector by banks	Below the median	0.63	321	−4.899	321	−0.937	319	−12.191	321	−6.95	321
		(2.015)		(4.605)		(3.729)		(11.597)		(8.47)	
	Above the median	0.319		−0.419		0.946		−20.773		−10.907	
		(2.588)		(8.053)		(5.791)		(17.907)		(7.065)	
Domestic credit provided by financial sector	Below the median	1.039	321	−7.578*	321	−8.834*	319	−7.363	321	−1.994	321
		(2.567)		(4.49)		(5.151)		(12.885)		(9.583)	
	Above the median	−0.375		−2.993		−7.38		−17.314		−6.504	
		(1.768)		(8.116)		(6.883)		(18.677)		(8.425)	
Domestic credit to private sector	Below the median	−0.215	321	−5.066	321	−3.292	319	−11.495	321	−6.227	321
		(2.09)		(4.405)		(3.363)		(11.747)		(8.565)	
	Above the median	0.555		−0.782		0.358		−23.12		−13.173*	
		(2.557)		(8.049)		(5.926)		(18.172)		(7.511)	
Foreign direct investment	Below the median	1.016	513	−0.521	513	0.229	511	−1.416	513	−0.875	513
		(0.993)		(2.9)		(1.94)		(2.966)		(2.397)	
	Above the median	1.316		−1.407		2.259		3.633		4.168	
		(1.488)		(2.228)		(2.845)		(3.414)		(3.122)	

Trade	Below the median	0.318	494	9.89	494	3.713	492	8.21	494	2.164	494
		(2.576)		(12.812)		(6.08)		(9.085)		(5.333)	
	Above the median	−2.033		0.08		−8.755		1.724		−1.844	
		(2.284)		(10.044)		(8.395)		(9.613)		(9.248)	
Private gross fixed capital formation	Below the median	−1.206	255	−0.007	255	6.634***	255	3.175	255	3.094	255
		(1.184)		(2.855)		(1.803)		(3.321)		(2.455)	
	Above the median	−0.103		−0.773		1.455		−0.107		0.189	
		(1.321)		(2.138)		(2.338)		(4.145)		(3.94)	
New business density	Below the median	−0.33	349	−0.84*	349	−0.273	347	−1.361	349	−1.003	349
		(0.292)		(0.498)		(0.43)		(0.92)		(0.675)	
	Above the median	−0.001		−1.085		1.627		0.265		0.361	
		(0.284)		(1.239)		(1.129)		(2.912)		(2.52)	
Unemployment rate	Below the median	0.332	476	1.619**	476	0.627	474	3.2**	476	2.239**	476
		(0.307)		(0.623)		(0.592)		(1.364)		(0.949)	
	Above the median	−0.864*		−0.009		−2.159		0.925		−0.094	
		(0.486)		(1.315)		(1.565)		(1.403)		(1.155)	
Income GINI index	Below the median	0.984	272	2.058	272	−0.514	271	1.982	272	3.411	272
		(1.16)		(1.664)		(1.798)		(2.5)		(2.2)	
	Above the median	−0.282		−0.15		−1.381		0.682		1.195	
		(0.376)		(1.227)		(1.247)		(2.225)		(2.127)	
GDP pc growth	Below the median	1.401	517	0.502	517	4.456*	515	1.332	517	0.962	517
		(1.04)		(1.766)		(2.629)		(1.566)		(1.344)	
	Above the median	1.028**		0.97		2.862***		2.08		2.246	
		(0.433)		(1.352)		(1.059)		(1.931)		(1.763)	

Notes: Panel specification with averaged annual data over 3-year periods (2006–2014). Clustered standard errors in parentheses. The regressions include country and period dummies, and a constant term. All these variables are omitted for space considerations

*, ** and *** denote statistical significance at the 10, 5 and 1% levels, respectively

Table A.7 The effect of legal rules on financial and economic outcomes: differentiation by level of development. Annual data

		Creditor rights		Investor protection		Credit information		Recovery rate		Contract enforc.		Starting a business	
		Coeff/SE	Obs	Coeff/SE	Obs	Coeff/SE	Obs	Coeff/SE	Obs	Coeff/SE	Obs	Coeff/SE	Obs
		(1)		(2)		(3)		(4)		(5)		(6)	
Stock market capitalization	Below the median	2.663	718	0.257	718	1.577	718	0.323	718	−15.395	718	−7.709	718
		(1.621)		(4.835)		(2.172)		(0.559)		(13.887)		(5.147)	
	Above the median	−3.446		−0.421		−0.201		0.523*		72.932		−4.277	
		(2.647)		(4.925)		(1.346)		(0.312)		(63.411)		(4.917)	
Stocks traded	Below the median	4.814**	632	12.873***	632	3.19	632	0.76*	632	18.722	632	−14.517**	632
		(2.371)		(4.722)		(1.921)		(0.422)		(11.866)		(5.783)	
	Above the median	3.921		9.179**		4.13***		0.793**		−87.162		0.024	
		(4.71)		(4.063)		(1.51)		(0.396)		(62.006)		(6.508)	
Domestic credit to private sector by banks	Below the median	0.667	957	0.744	957	0.626	957	−0.072	957	8.791	957	−1.66	957
		(0.729)		(0.635)		(0.648)		(0.175)		(7.69)		(1.699)	
	Above the median	1.225		−2.841		0.574		0.171**		−31.04**		−2.894*	
		(1.016)		(4.333)		(0.713)		(0.086)		(12.266)		(1.473)	
Domestic credit provided by financial sector	Below the median	−0.077	957	0.118	957	1.007	957	−0.183	957	7.652	957	−0.963	957
		(0.935)		(0.958)		(0.679)		(0.168)		(9.405)		(1.844)	
	Above the median	3.339**		0.036		1.385*		0.172		−42.508***		−4.005**	
		(1.599)		(5.261)		(0.751)		(0.183)		(15.793)		(1.938)	
Domestic credit to private sector	Below the median	0.729	957	0.343	957	0.631	957	−0.065	957	9.947	957	−2.008	957
		(0.682)		(0.777)		(0.647)		(0.179)		(7.597)		(1.756)	
	Above the median	1.363		−1.677		0.493		0.18*		−31.19**		−2.914*	
		(1.125)		(4.678)		(0.711)		(0.093)		(12.552)		(1.514)	

Foreign direct investment	Below the median	0.163	1523	−0.079	1523	0.06	1523	0.077	1523	−0.501	1523	0.431	1523
		(0.252)		(0.559)		(0.19)		(0.063)		(1.865)		(0.981)	
	Above the median	−0.002		−0.729		−0.154		0.03		2.067		1.253	
		(0.576)		(0.464)		(0.19)		(0.043)		(3.421)		(1.061)	
Trade	Below the median	−0.887	1454	−0.622	1454	−0.73	1454	−0.343	1454	3.643	1454	5.295	1454
		(1.07)		(1.08)		(0.554)		(0.227)		(5.511)		(4.276)	
	Above the median	−0.582		0.973		1.059		0.26		24.803		−1.094	
		(1.384)		(1.875)		(0.815)		(0.194)		(16.595)		(1.924)	
Private gross fixed capital formation	Below the median	0.163	727	−0.529	727	−0.237	727	0.09	727	−10.044**	727	−0.63	727
		(0.245)		(0.571)		(0.256)		(0.061)		(4.2)		(0.729)	
	Above the median	−0.748*		−0.262		0.106		0.045		−0.859		−1.404**	
		(0.43)		(0.879)		(0.261)		(0.09)		(5.4)		(0.662)	
New business density	Below the median	0.074	840	0.19	840	0.085	840	0.023	840	−0.974	840	−0.354	840
		(0.075)		(0.123)		(0.072)		(0.02)		(0.603)		(0.216)	
	Above the median	0.419		0.185		−0.066		0.01		1.06		0.177	
		(0.371)		(0.436)		(0.165)		(0.017)		(2.735)		(0.492)	
Unemployment rate	Below the median	−0.109*	1416	−0.231	1416	−0.234*	1416	−0.021	1416	−1.165	1416	0.487**	1416
		(0.059)		(0.156)		(0.123)		(0.021)		(1.635)		(0.187)	
	Above the median	−0.193		0.523		−0.005		−0.043		3.951		−0.343	
		(0.192)		(0.697)		(0.141)		(0.038)		(2.909)		(0.364)	
Income GINI index	Below the median	−0.494**	498	−0.171	498	−0.005	498	0.036	498	0.824	498	0.284	498
		(0.206)		(0.568)		(0.209)		(0.121)		(2.542)		(0.819)	
	Above the median	−0.106		−0.184		0.023		−0.012		0.803		−0.42	
		(0.92)		(0.405)		(0.197)		(0.045)		(1.808)		(0.378)	

(continued)

Table A.7 (continued)

		Registering a property		Construction permits		Paying taxes		Time to export		Time to import	
		Coeff/SE	Obs	Coeff/SE	Obs	Coeff/SE	Obs	Coeff/SE	Obs	Coeff/SE	Obs
		(7)		(8)		(9)		(10)		(11)	
Stock market capitalization	Below the median	−0.165	718	−1.649	718	10.031	718	−11.202	718	−17.195	718
		(5.243)		(7.882)		(8.839)		(10.461)		(10.568)	
	Above the median	1.19		−15.821		−4.596		−43.063*		−40.194**	
		(2.334)		(18.079)		(11.428)		(22.844)		(18.185)	
Stocks traded	Below the median	−9.976*	632	−18.391**	632	−15.992**	632	−26.056*	632	−29.799**	632
		(5.823)		(7.019)		(7.809)		(14.227)		(14.395)	
	Above the median	−5.338		18.756		−1.883		−62.991**		−71.188*	
		(3.573)		(19.834)		(19.203)		(29.153)		(39.036)	
Domestic credit to private sector by banks	Below the median	0.614	957	−4.442	957	−0.97	950	−8.821	957	−5.293	957
		(1.526)		(3.246)		(2.989)		(6.801)		(5.468)	
	Above the median	0.221		−0.874		0.301		−16.747		−9.205*	
		(1.969)		(6.761)		(4.333)		(11.309)		(4.688)	
Domestic credit provided by financial sector	Below the median	1.1	957	−8.489***	957	−7.439	950	−6.233	957	−2.657	957
		(1.968)		(3.168)		(4.555)		(7.365)		(5.783)	
	Above the median	−0.64		−4.178		−7.444		−15.908		−6.79	
		(1.325)		(5.921)		(5.03)		(12.648)		(5.339)	
Domestic credit to private sector	Below the median	−0.09	957	−4.382	957	−3.041	950	−8.568	957	−4.843	957
		(1.582)		(3.07)		(2.721)		(6.894)		(5.551)	
	Above the median	0.397		−0.917		−0.28		−19.041*		−11.313**	
		(1.929)		(6.777)		(4.419)		(11.454)		(4.989)	
Foreign direct investment	Below the median	0.66	1523	0.34	1523	0.011	1516	−1.446	1523	−0.961	1523
		(0.726)		(1.765)		(1.468)		(1.894)		(1.571)	
	Above the median	0.967		−1.342		2.501		2.749		3.005	
		(1.013)		(1.901)		(2.632)		(2.515)		(2.156)	

Trade	Below the median	0.653	1454	5.679	1454	3.656	1447	6.426	1454	3.254	1454
		(1.593)		(7.171)		(4.458)		(5.532)		(3.408)	
	Above the median	−2.287		−1.312		−6.709		0.24		−1.762	
		(1.908)		(7.74)		(6.658)		(6.676)		(5.724)	
Private gross fixed capital formation	Below the median	−0.403	727	0.343	727	5.483***	727	2.036	727	2.131	727
		(0.759)		(1.729)		(1.261)		(1.744)		(1.402)	
	Above the median	−0.19		−0.53		0.782		−1.933		−1.033	
		(0.977)		(1.659)		(1.921)		(2.272)		(2.103)	
New business density	Below the median	−0.471*	840	−0.872*	840	−0.472	836	−1.059**	840	−0.88**	840
		(0.254)		(0.454)		(0.379)		(0.467)		(0.402)	
	Above the median	−0.016		−1.206		1.594*		−0.311		−0.129	
		(0.254)		(1.075)		(0.924)		(2.002)		(1.63)	
Unemployment rate	Below the median	0.25	1416	1.067**	1416	0.82	1409	2.135**	1416	1.827**	1416
		(0.226)		(0.464)		(0.558)		(0.979)		(0.772)	
	Above the median	−0.653*		0.057		−1.872		0.483		−0.065	
		(0.342)		(0.96)		(1.2)		(0.812)		(0.666)	
Income GINI index	Below the median	0.803	498	1.017	498	0.004	497	0.477	498	1.584	498
		(0.752)		(1.819)		(1.239)		(1.524)		(1.589)	
	Above the median	−0.29		0.416		−1.529		0.691		1.19	
		(0.304)		(1.022)		(1.695)		(1.764)		(1.622)	

Notes: Panel of annual data over the period 2006–2014. Clustered standard errors in parentheses. The regressions include lag GDP growth, country and period dummies, and a constant term. All these variables are omitted for space considerations

*, ** and *** denote statistical significance at the 10, 5 and 1% levels, respectively

Table A.8 The effect of legal rules on financial and economic outcomes: differentiation by level of development. Annual data, without additional control

		Creditor rights		Investor protection		Credit information		Recovery rate		Contract enforc.		Starting a business	
		Coeff/SE	Obs	Coeff/SE	Obs	Coeff/SE	Obs	Coeff/SE	Obs	Coeff/SE	Obs	Coeff/SE	Obs
		(1)		(2)		(3)		(4)		(5)		(6)	
Stock market capitalization	Below the median	2.714	718	0.239	718	1.576	718	0.33	718	−16.006	718	−7.796	718
		(1.666)		(4.819)		(2.17)		(0.565)		(14.247)		(5.177)	
	Above the median	−3.413		−0.475		−0.248		0.527		71.902		−4.258	
		(2.655)		(4.956)		(1.271)		(0.32)		(64.096)		(4.942)	
Stocks traded	Below the median	4.845**	632	12.908***	632	3.195	632	0.772*	632	18.746	632	−14.567**	632
		(2.371)		(4.761)		(1.933)		(0.429)		(11.824)		(5.855)	
	Above the median	4.047		9.07**		3.971***		0.806*		−87.288		0.087	
		(4.674)		(4.132)		(1.469)		(0.407)		(61.304)		(6.443)	
Domestic credit to private sector by banks	Below the median	0.667	957	0.738	957	0.616	957	−0.07	957	8.793	957	−1.632	957
		(0.727)		(0.623)		(0.636)		(0.177)		(7.676)		(1.645)	
	Above the median	1.224		−2.843		0.556		0.171**		−31.045**		−2.884*	
		(1.014)		(4.335)		(0.694)		(0.086)		(12.306)		(1.46)	
Domestic credit provided by financial sector	Below the median	−0.082	957	0.187	957	1.042	957	−0.2	957	7.605	957	−1.122	957
		(0.959)		(0.974)		(0.665)		(0.169)		(9.421)		(1.804)	
	Above the median	3.35**		0.053		1.454*		0.176		−42.293***		−4.058**	
		(1.635)		(5.262)		(0.733)		(0.185)		(15.87)		(1.916)	
Domestic credit to private sector	Below the median	0.729	957	0.335	957	0.62	957	−0.062	957	9.95	957	−1.97	957
		(0.68)		(0.764)		(0.635)		(0.181)		(7.581)		(1.706)	
	Above the median	1.362		−1.679		0.472		0.179*		−31.204**		−2.901*	
		(1.124)		(4.68)		(0.692)		(0.093)		(12.594)		(1.503)	
Foreign direct investment	Below the median	0.167	1523	−0.087	1523	0.056	1523	0.08	1523	−0.491	1523	0.443	1523
		(0.254)		(0.56)		(0.191)		(0.064)		(1.853)		(0.978)	
	Above the median	0.003		−0.741		−0.17		0.03		1.994		1.267	
		(0.575)		(0.457)		(0.179)		(0.043)		(3.43)		(1.063)	

Trade	Below the median	−0.878	1454	−0.65	1454	−0.745	1454	−0.334	1454	3.693	1454	5.325	1454
		(1.072)		(1.108)		(0.557)		(0.226)		(5.496)		(4.258)	
	Above the median	−0.567		0.945		1.008		0.261		24.585		−1.057	
		(1.389)		(1.872)		(0.8)		(0.193)		(16.564)		(1.91)	
Private gross fixed capital formation	Below the median	0.16	727	−0.531	727	−0.291	727	0.102	727	−10.228**	727	−0.632	727
		(0.259)		(0.575)		(0.252)		(0.064)		(4.21)		(0.723)	
	Above the median	−0.877*		−0.43		0.01		0.031		−0.855		−1.342**	
		(0.526)		(0.888)		(0.267)		(0.091)		(5.474)		(0.637)	
New business density	Below the median	0.083	840	0.187	840	0.076	840	0.026	840	−0.958	840	−0.349	840
		(0.074)		(0.12)		(0.07)		(0.019)		(0.602)		(0.211)	
	Above the median	0.422		0.177		−0.086		0.011		1.005		0.193	
		(0.374)		(0.439)		(0.161)		(0.018)		(2.744)		(0.485)	
Unemployment rate	Below the median	−0.119**	1418	−0.206	1418	−0.219*	1418	−0.03	1418	−1.24	1418	0.437**	1418
		(0.06)		(0.141)		(0.119)		(0.022)		(1.602)		(0.174)	
	Above the median	−0.207		0.562		0.045		−0.043		4.172		−0.392	
		(0.206)		(0.71)		(0.15)		(0.04)		(3.003)		(0.376)	
Income GINI index	Below the median	−0.494**	498	−0.173	498	−0.004	498	0.035	498	0.796	498	0.28	498
		(0.206)		(0.572)		(0.21)		(0.12)		(2.558)		(0.82)	
	Above the median	−0.116		−0.185		0.031		−0.012		0.878		−0.427	
		(0.906)		(0.406)		(0.199)		(0.045)		(1.807)		(0.378)	
GDP pc growth	Below the median	−0.013	1535	−0.635	1535	−0.423**	1535	0.079**	1535	−1.288	1535	1.014*	1535
		(0.184)		(0.459)		(0.199)		(0.036)		(1.571)		(0.546)	
	Above the median	−0.045		−0.494*		−0.414**		−0.003		−0.243		0.802**	
		(0.426)		(0.276)		(0.205)		(0.033)		(1.486)		(0.4)	

(continued)

Table A.8 (continued)

		Registering a property		Construction permits		Paying taxes		Time to export		Time to import	
		Coeff/SE	Obs	Coeff/SE	Obs	Coeff/SE	Obs	Coeff/SE	Obs	Coeff/SE	Obs
		(7)		(8)		(9)		(10)		(11)	
Stock market capitalization	Below the median	−0.197	718	−1.681	718	10.011	718	−10.899	718	−17.078	718
		(5.272)		(7.91)		(8.937)		(10.353)		(10.559)	
	Above the median	1.242		−15.799		−4.434		−42.745*		−39.91**	
		(2.285)		(18.105)		(11.303)		(23.015)		(18.359)	
Stocks traded	Below the median	−10.088*	632	−18.611***	632	−15.963**	632	−25.744*	632	−29.678**	632
		(5.818)		(7.042)		(7.852)		(14.183)		(14.447)	
	Above the median	−5.259		18.778		−1.591		−62.836**		−70.702*	
		(3.566)		(19.807)		(19.138)		(29.138)		(38.833)	
Domestic credit to private sector by banks	Below the median	0.621	957	−4.447	957	−0.978	950	−8.758	957	−5.235	957
		(1.484)		(3.257)		(2.878)		(6.704)		(5.377)	
	Above the median	0.226		−0.873		0.298		−16.727		−9.174*	
		(1.956)		(6.77)		(4.283)		(11.279)		(4.631)	
Domestic credit provided by financial sector	Below the median	0.941	957	−8.275**	957	−8.012*	950	−6.552	957	−2.982	957
		(1.955)		(3.192)		(4.279)		(7.332)		(5.734)	
	Above the median	−0.75		−4.235		−7.694		−16.009		−6.962	
		(1.306)		(5.901)		(4.98)		(12.537)		(5.287)	
Domestic credit to private sector	Below the median	−0.074	957	−4.396	957	−2.987	950	−8.491	957	−4.771	957
		(1.54)		(3.083)		(2.589)		(6.798)		(5.46)	
	Above the median	0.408		−0.914		−0.257		−19.017*		−11.275**	
		(1.917)		(6.789)		(4.374)		(11.428)		(4.931)	
Foreign direct investment	Below the median	0.676	1523	0.312	1523	0.079	1516	−1.416	1523	−0.943	1523
		(0.724)		(1.774)		(1.498)		(1.882)		(1.562)	
	Above the median	0.98		−1.322		2.552		2.79		3.044	
		(1.012)		(1.915)		(2.614)		(2.503)		(2.141)	

Trade	Below the median	0.715	1454	5.584	1454	3.726	1447	6.504	1454	3.3	1454
		(1.625)		(7.177)		(4.522)		(5.508)		(3.418)	
	Above the median	−2.242		−1.267		−6.659		0.333		−1.664	
		(1.883)		(7.728)		(6.634)		(6.675)		(5.736)	
Private gross fixed capital formation	Below the median	−0.374	727	0.275	727	5.582***	727	2.417	727	2.317	727
		(0.781)		(1.864)		(1.311)		(1.899)		(1.502)	
	Above the median	−0.004		−0.218		1.17		−1.379		−0.514	
		(0.99)		(1.636)		(1.84)		(2.277)		(2.059)	
New business density	Below the median	−0.463*	840	−0.912**	840	−0.404	836	−1.01**	840	−0.858**	840
		(0.251)		(0.44)		(0.39)		(0.47)		(0.398)	
	Above the median	0.004		−1.196		1.659*		−0.273		−0.102	
		(0.251)		(1.076)		(0.924)		(2.013)		(1.632)	
Unemployment rate	Below the median	0.19	1418	1.131**	1418	0.589	1411	2.033**	1418	1.763**	1418
		(0.195)		(0.464)		(0.471)		(0.943)		(0.754)	
	Above the median	−0.702**		−0.006		−2.064*		0.361		−0.17	
		(0.342)		(0.967)		(1.216)		(0.817)		(0.674)	
Income GINI index	Below the median	0.801	498	1.028	498	0.003	497	0.449	498	1.579	498
		(0.753)		(1.831)		(1.224)		(1.522)		(1.597)	
	Above the median	−0.296		0.415		−1.542		0.709		1.203	
		(0.308)		(1.02)		(1.691)		(1.75)		(1.614)	
GDP pc growth	Below the median	0.66	1535	0.357	1535	3.854**	1528	0.89	1535	0.8	1535
		(0.768)		(0.997)		(1.916)		(0.768)		(0.845)	
	Above the median	0.569**		0.278		2.55***		0.98		1.263	
		(0.264)		(1.093)		(0.781)		(1.421)		(1.23)	

Notes: Panel of annual data over the period 2006–2014. Clustered standard errors in parentheses. The regressions include country and period dummies, and a constant term. All these variables are omitted for space considerations

*, ** and *** denote statistical significance at the 10, 5 and 1% levels, respectively

Table A.9 The effect of legal rules on financial and economic outcomes: differentiation by rule of law. Without additional control

		Creditor rights		Investor protection		Credit information		Recovery rate		Contract enforc.		Starting a business	
		Coeff/SE	Obs	Coeff/SE	Obs	Coeff/SE	Obs	Coeff/SE	Obs	Coeff/SE	Obs	Coeff/SE	Obs
		(1)		(2)		(3)		(4)		(5)		(6)	
Stock market capitalization	Below the median	3.935*	263	4.882	263	1.191	263	0.885	263	0.241	263	−8.608	263
		(2.121)		(4.977)		(1.894)		(0.562)		(9.923)		(6.119)	
	Above the median	−1.343		−4.994		−0.239		0.462		−5.505		−1.232	
		(4.085)		(10.766)		(2.242)		(0.59)		(23.546)		(3.788)	
Stocks traded	Below the median	7.786***	240	12.407***	240	5.587***	240	1.733**	240	15.319	240	−17.927**	240
		(2.91)		(4.422)		(1.811)		(0.764)		(9.79)		(7.246)	
	Above the median	2.642		5.884		3.189		0.808		−19.588		−3.515	
		(6.154)		(6.848)		(2.705)		(0.569)		(26.717)		(4.27)	
Domestic credit to private sector by banks	Below the median	0.636	322	0.118	322	1.019	322	0.125	322	13.318	322	−1.959	322
		(0.801)		(0.936)		(0.888)		(0.274)		(9.907)		(1.987)	
	Above the median	2.024		−2.481		0.338		0.044		−32.952*		−2.166	
		(2.73)		(8.264)		(1.404)		(0.22)		(19.305)		(2.199)	
Domestic credit provided by financial sector	Below the median	0.051	322	−0.542	322	1.757	322	−0.102	322	14.112	322	−1.398	322
		(1.071)		(1.146)		(1.128)		(0.29)		(11.907)		(2.298)	
	Above the median	2.942		1.405		1.597		0.049		−47.019**		−3.304	
		(2.666)		(10.594)		(1.346)		(0.363)		(22.863)		(2.94)	
Domestic credit to private sector	Below the median	0.689	322	−0.119	322	1.036	322	0.151	322	14.034	322	−2.038	322
		(0.745)		(1.021)		(0.884)		(0.285)		(9.876)		(2.014)	
	Above the median	2.431		−0.824		0.225		0.034		−32.195		−2.512	
		(2.614)		(8.818)		(1.4)		(0.219)		(19.542)		(2.272)	
Foreign direct investment	Below the median	0.238	514	−0.115	514	−0.04	514	0.158	514	−1.505	514	0.549	514
		(0.308)		(0.685)		(0.34)		(0.115)		(2.651)		(1.261)	
	Above the median	0.134		−0.419		−0.372		0.052		0.087		1.918	
		(0.411)		(0.697)		(0.331)		(0.069)		(5.136)		(1.663)	

Trade	Below the median	−1.201	492	−0.003	492	−0.311	492	−0.162	492	−1.213	492	5.882	492
		(1.472)		(1.377)		(0.805)		(0.399)		(10.581)		(6.381)	
	Above the median	0.891		1.941		0.51		0.296		16.934		1.339	
		(1.588)		(2.438)		(1.484)		(0.325)		(19.873)		(2.478)	
Private gross fixed capital formation	Below the median	0.021	253	−0.676	253	−0.466	253	0.174	253	−7.472	253	−0.859	253
		(0.3)		(0.662)		(0.451)		(0.159)		(5.334)		(1.024)	
	Above the median	0.433		0.058		−0.01		−0.097		−7.394		−0.717	
		(1.134)		(1.205)		(0.468)		(0.173)		(8.573)		(0.972)	
New business density	Below the median	0.107	351	0.159	351	−0.001	351	0.027	351	−0.646	351	−0.23	351
		(0.089)		(0.146)		(0.117)		(0.027)		(0.752)		(0.325)	
	Above the median	0.168		0.425		−0.083		0.011		−0.83		0.302	
		(0.416)		(0.677)		(0.183)		(0.034)		(2.932)		(0.612)	
Unemployment rate	Below the median	−0.144*	476	−0.309	476	−0.394**	476	−0.095**	476	−2.345	476	0.65**	476
		(0.079)		(0.226)		(0.167)		(0.036)		(2.124)		(0.313)	
	Above the median	−0.083		1.187		0.181		−0.042		7.135		−0.786*	
		(0.362)		(1.15)		(0.198)		(0.07)		(4.423)		(0.462)	
Income GINI index	Below the median	−0.612***	275	−0.287	275	−0.158	275	−0.031	275	−0.49	275	0.698	275
		(0.229)		(0.442)		(0.286)		(0.109)		(3.509)		(0.856)	
	Above the median	0.123		1.246		0.21		0.045		1.011		−0.802	
		(0.519)		(0.907)		(0.243)		(0.038)		(2.201)		(0.73)	
GDP pc growth	Below the median	0	512	−0.739	512	−0.766**	512	0.073	512	−0.36	512	1.15*	512
		(0.225)		(0.602)		(0.301)		(0.079)		(2.144)		(0.634)	
	Above the median	0.216		−0.492		−0.444		−0.014		−1.011		0.71	
		(0.391)		(0.374)		(0.306)		(0.053)		(1.973)		(0.565)	

(continued)

Table A.9 (continued)

		Registering a property		Construction permits		Paying taxes		Time to export		Time to import	
		Coeff/SE	Obs	Coeff/SE	Obs	Coeff/SE	Obs	Coeff/SE	Obs	Coeff/SE	Obs
		(7)		(8)		(9)		(10)		(11)	
Stock market capitalization	Below the median	−1.762	263	−8.93	263	−1.291	263	−29.701*	263	−29.384**	263
		(4.394)		(8.573)		(13.054)		(15.067)		(12.261)	
	Above the median	1.284		14.923		−2.067		−12.399		−7.398	
		(3.422)		(19.152)		(13.485)		(37.016)		(25.103)	
Stocks traded	Below the median	−13.112**	240	−17.637***	240	−19.386**	240	−50.322**	240	−40.092***	240
		(5.18)		(6.296)		(8.687)		(19.396)		(14.562)	
	Above the median	−1.542		26.386		4.827		−39.091		−20.725	
		(3.971)		(22.53)		(24.696)		(51.427)		(28.544)	
Domestic credit to private sector by banks	Below the median	0.397	322	−4.212	322	−0.569	320	−14.24	322	−8.761	322
		(1.678)		(3.83)		(3.875)		(9.775)		(7.103)	
	Above the median	0.556		1.349		1.653		−21.573		−9.744	
		(3.063)		(16.357)		(6.399)		(22.193)		(8.948)	
Domestic credit provided by financial sector	Below the median	1.196	322	−6.699	322	−7.718	320	−8	322	−2.344	322
		(2.272)		(4.12)		(4.863)		(11.484)		(8.751)	
	Above the median	−0.799		−2.079		−9.339		−19.628		−6.887	
		(1.989)		(15.397)		(8.584)		(22.783)		(9.823)	
Domestic credit to private sector	Below the median	0.303	322	−4.601	322	−2.782	320	−14.352	322	−9.086	322
		(1.668)		(3.727)		(3.807)		(9.734)		(7.11)	
	Above the median	0.25		2.012		1.686		−23.682		−11.147	
		(3.119)		(16.419)		(6.346)		(22.681)		(9.552)	
Foreign direct investment	Below the median	0.975	514	−0.295	514	1.215	512	−0.685	514	−0.473	514
		(0.957)		(2.143)		(1.353)		(2.725)		(2.256)	
	Above the median	1.353		−1.537		0.912		3.871		4.479	
		(1.618)		(4.154)		(3.491)		(3.651)		(3.015)	

Trade	Below the median	0.048	492	7.086	492	3.753	490	6.516	492	0.501	492
		(2.259)		(9.008)		(4.912)		(8.364)		(4.755)	
	Above the median	−2.258		10.59		−10.311		8.744		3.605	
		(2.58)		(15.467)		(10.095)		(9.829)		(9.34)	
Private gross fixed capital formation	Below the median	−1.087	253	−0.346	253	4.919**	253	2.725	253	2.96	253
		(0.948)		(2.285)		(2.137)		(3.621)		(2.544)	
	Above the median	0.585		−0.09		4.474*		2.116		1.824	
		(1.233)		(2.396)		(2.651)		(3.877)		(3.623)	
New business density	Below the median	−0.223	351	−0.442	351	−0.062	349	−0.985	351	−0.786	351
		(0.271)		(0.501)		(0.411)		(0.936)		(0.644)	
	Above the median	−0.111		−0.686		1.667		0.564		0.766	
		(0.304)		(1)		(1.358)		(3.06)		(2.454)	
Unemployment rate	Below the median	0.416	476	1.371*	476	0.986	474	3.312**	476	2.191**	476
		(0.264)		(0.696)		(0.645)		(1.294)		(0.895)	
	Above the median	−1.222**		−0.91		−3.672**		0.166		−0.667	
		(0.492)		(2.098)		(1.771)		(1.465)		(1.167)	
Income GINI index	Below the median	0.876	275	1.732	275	−0.298	274	2.658	275	3.143*	275
		(0.868)		(1.349)		(1.342)		(2.114)		(1.808)	
	Above the median	−0.719		−1.517		−2.403		−2.144		−2.16	
		(0.459)		(1.57)		(1.476)		(2.13)		(1.963)	
GDP pc growth	Below the median	1.647*	512	1.279	512	4.818**	510	1.764	512	0.843	512
		(0.894)		(1.438)		(2.298)		(1.638)		(1.404)	
	Above the median	0.776**		−1.182		2.072*		1.132		1.606	
		(0.382)		(1.856)		(1.051)		(1.78)		(1.652)	

Notes: Panel specification with averaged annual data over 3-year periods (2006–2014). Clustered standard errors in parentheses. The regressions include country and period dummies, and a constant term. All these variables are omitted for space considerations

*, ** and *** denote statistical significance at the 10, 5 and 1% levels, respectively

Table A.10 The effect of legal rules on financial and economic outcomes: differentiation by rule of law. Annual data

		Creditor rights		Investor protection		Credit information		Recovery rate		Contract enforc.		Starting a business	
		Coeff/SE	Obs	Coeff/SE	Obs	Coeff/SE	Obs	Coeff/SE	Obs	Coeff/SE	Obs	Coeff/SE	Obs
		(1)		(2)		(3)		(4)		(5)		(6)	
Stock market capitalization	Below the median	3.077**	718	4.77	718	3.092*	718	0.687**	718	−8.927	718	−8.156**	718
		(1.347)		(3.558)		(1.581)		(0.266)		(11.811)		(3.918)	
	Above the median	−1.776		−4.968		−0.065		0.371		−3.218		0.71	
		(2.812)		(8.115)		(1.552)		(0.395)		(21.054)		(2.746)	
Stocks traded	Below the median	5.227**	632	11.07***	632	4.669***	632	1.04***	632	14.711	632	−15.362***	632
		(2.142)		(3.067)		(1.48)		(0.302)		(10.639)		(4.828)	
	Above the median	1.801		6.251		1.703		0.646*		−22.405		−3.29	
		(4.133)		(5.363)		(1.896)		(0.37)		(19.811)		(3.402)	
Domestic credit to private sector by banks	Below the median	0.521	950	0.193	950	0.704	950	0.125	950	7.634	950	−2.022	950
		(0.675)		(0.755)		(0.535)		(0.165)		(7.67)		(1.61)	
	Above the median	2.197		−1.92		0.393		0.083		−24.461*		−2.331	
		(2.083)		(6.846)		(0.938)		(0.12)		(13.503)		(1.775)	
Domestic credit provided by financial sector	Below the median	−0.091	950	−0.355	950	1.117*	950	−0.038	950	7.736	950	−1.608	950
		(0.902)		(0.927)		(0.637)		(0.161)		(9.178)		(1.82)	
	Above the median	3.304		2.76		1.163		0.139		−36.452**		−3.327	
		(2.078)		(7.765)		(0.886)		(0.234)		(17.321)		(2.196)	
Domestic credit to private sector	Below the median	0.549	950	−0.088	950	0.702	950	0.139	950	8.309	950	−2.188	950
		(0.633)		(0.835)		(0.529)		(0.172)		(7.644)		(1.646)	
	Above the median	2.58		−0.524		0.317		0.088		−23.761*		−2.612	
		(2.006)		(7.212)		(0.938)		(0.121)		(13.655)		(1.817)	

Foreign direct investment	Below the median	0.179	1516	−0.148	1516	0.027	1516	0.075	1516	−0.259	1516	0.392	1516
		(0.26)		(0.523)		(0.189)		(0.054)		(1.996)		(0.967)	
	Above the median	0.036		−0.584		−0.061		0.027		0.255		1.44	
		(0.411)		(0.539)		(0.187)		(0.044)		(3.393)		(1.106)	
Trade	Below the median	−1.039	1439	−0.609	1439	−0.186	1439	−0.167	1439	1.808	1439	4.257	1439
		(1.085)		(1.084)		(0.476)		(0.245)		(6.133)		(4.188)	
	Above the median	0.652		1.799		0.308		0.232		15.159		1.018	
		(1.225)		(1.656)		(1.017)		(0.213)		(13.905)		(1.78)	
Private gross fixed capital formation	Below the median	0.079	720	−0.551	720	−0.198	720	0.125**	720	−6.229	720	−0.913	720
		(0.239)		(0.524)		(0.265)		(0.059)		(4.167)		(0.732)	
	Above the median	0.437		0.381		0.056		−0.055		−8.487		−0.949	
		(0.766)		(1.238)		(0.316)		(0.08)		(6.154)		(0.748)	
New business density	Below the median	0.104	843	0.168	843	0.036	843	0.022	843	−0.543	843	−0.253	843
		(0.071)		(0.121)		(0.081)		(0.018)		(0.566)		(0.261)	
	Above the median	0.231		0.451		0.038		0.012		−1.055		0.236	
		(0.261)		(0.563)		(0.18)		(0.02)		(2.052)		(0.505)	
Unemployment rate	Below the median	−0.122**	1401	−0.292*	1401	−0.321**	1401	−0.04**	1401	−1.874	1401	0.601**	1401
		(0.06)		(0.176)		(0.123)		(0.018)		(1.514)		(0.233)	
	Above the median	−0.047		1.06		0.12		−0.033		5.442*		−0.598*	
		(0.21)		(0.804)		(0.117)		(0.04)		(3.05)		(0.312)	
Income GINI index	Below the median	−0.552***	505	−0.298	505	−0.106	505	−0.077	505	1.668	505	0.35	505
		(0.208)		(0.429)		(0.204)		(0.08)		(2.341)		(0.618)	
	Above the median	0.646		0.635		0.336**		0.043		0.123		−0.669	
		(0.592)		(0.664)		(0.138)		(0.032)		(1.665)		(0.423)	

(continued)

Table A.10 (continued)

		Registering a property		Construction permits		Paying taxes		Time to export		Time to import	
		Coeff/SE	Obs	Coeff/SE	Obs	Coeff/SE	Obs	Coeff/SE	Obs	Coeff/SE	Obs
		(7)		(8)		(9)		(10)		(11)	
Stock market capitalization	Below the median	−3.351	718	−10.479*	718	−2.022	718	−21.667**	718	−23.062***	718
		(2.947)		(5.901)		(10.624)		(9.251)		(7.679)	
	Above the median	0.574		15.148		1.188		−13.244		−7.318	
		(2.123)		(12.889)		(9.906)		(19.37)		(15.437)	
Stocks traded	Below the median	−12.156***	632	−16.388***	632	−17.769**	632	−28.881**	632	−24.146***	632
		(3.755)		(5.136)		(7.284)		(11.854)		(8.546)	
	Above the median	−2.693		19.742		9.418		−35.97		−20.464	
		(2.976)		(14.76)		(20.612)		(27.266)		(15.981)	
Domestic credit to private sector by banks	Below the median	0.444	950	−3.939	950	−0.781	943	−11.358*	950	−7.007	950
		(1.364)		(2.91)		(3.157)		(5.838)		(4.575)	
	Above the median	0.408		0.139		0.829		−15.247		−8.036	
		(2.22)		(11.77)		(4.516)		(13.37)		(6.148)	
Domestic credit provided by financial sector	Below the median	1.227	950	−7.134**	950	−6.591	943	−8.255	950	−3.818	950
		(1.821)		(3.082)		(4.209)		(6.667)		(5.052)	
	Above the median	−0.922		−6.356		−9.55		−15.306		−6.481	
		(1.414)		(9.681)		(6.083)		(14.645)		(6.73)	
Domestic credit to private sector	Below the median	0.351	950	−4.086	950	−2.691	943	−11.516*	950	−7.297	950
		(1.355)		(2.809)		(3.085)		(5.861)		(4.617)	
	Above the median	0.158		0.948		0.658		−17.398		−9.562	
		(2.236)		(11.847)		(4.523)		(13.653)		(6.566)	
Foreign direct investment	Below the median	0.849	1516	0.138	1516	0.833	1509	−0.673	1516	−0.349	1516
		(0.699)		(1.355)		(1.016)		(1.712)		(1.417)	
	Above the median	0.812		−0.709		1.535		2.327		3.368	
		(1.053)		(3.357)		(3.2)		(2.697)		(2.163)	

Trade	Below the median	0.298	1439	3.777	1439	4.268	1432	4.579	1439	1.742	1439
		(1.451)		(5.178)		(3.56)		(5.158)		(2.928)	
	Above the median	−2.455		8.722		−8.419		4.921		1.717	
		(2.09)		(10.103)		(7.788)		(6.59)		(6.346)	
Private gross fixed capital formation	Below the median	−0.83	720	−0.085	720	3.751**	720	1.307	720	1.779	720
		(0.789)		(1.455)		(1.647)		(1.928)		(1.434)	
	Above the median	0.57		0.466		4.86**		1.005		0.759	
		(0.784)		(1.761)		(2.013)		(2.053)		(2.173)	
New business density	Below the median	−0.31	843	−0.475	843	−0.211	839	−0.895*	843	−0.686*	843
		(0.24)		(0.471)		(0.403)		(0.517)		(0.401)	
	Above the median	−0.136		−0.597		1.729		0.072		0.595	
		(0.283)		(0.659)		(1.156)		(2.008)		(1.658)	
Unemployment rate	Below the median	0.385*	1401	0.977*	1401	1.18**	1394	2.393**	1401	1.782**	1401
		(0.21)		(0.556)		(0.553)		(0.998)		(0.738)	
	Above the median	−0.931***		−0.798		−3.269**		−0.267		−0.663	
		(0.341)		(1.417)		(1.315)		(0.768)		(0.727)	
Income GINI index	Below the median	0.767	505	1.008	505	0.219	504	1.578	505	2.116	505
		(0.606)		(1.235)		(1.193)		(1.644)		(1.386)	
	Above the median	−0.738*		−1.379		−2.849**		−2.231		−2.122*	
		(0.414)		(1.687)		(1.367)		(1.378)		(1.228)	

Notes: Panel of annual data over the period 2006–2014. Clustered standard errors in parentheses. The regressions include lag GDP growth, country and period dummies, and a constant term. All these variables are omitted for space considerations

*, ** and *** denote statistical significance at the 10, 5 and 1% levels, respectively

Table A.11 The effect of legal rules on financial and economic outcomes: differentiation by rule of law. Annual data, without additional control

		Creditor rights		Investor protection		Credit information		Recovery rate		Contract enforc.		Starting a business	
		Coeff/SE	Obs	Coeff/SE	Obs	Coeff/SE	Obs	Coeff/SE	Obs	Coeff/SE	Obs	Coeff/SE	Obs
		(1)		(2)		(3)		(4)		(5)		(6)	
Stock market capitalization	Below the median	3.174**	718	4.729	718	3.056*	718	0.71***	718	−9.256	718	−8.349**	718
		(1.353)		(3.556)		(1.563)		(0.265)		(12.09)		(3.947)	
	Above the median	−1.561		−5.19		−0.166		0.387		−5.088		0.783	
		(2.862)		(8.249)		(1.539)		(0.403)		(21.462)		(2.738)	
Stocks traded	Below the median	5.245**	632	11.015***	632	4.665***	632	1.063***	632	14.987	632	−15.525***	632
		(2.112)		(3.05)		(1.48)		(0.306)		(10.67)		(4.935)	
	Above the median	2.015		6.131		1.586		0.664*		−23.623		−3.161	
		(4.125)		(5.431)		(1.852)		(0.378)		(19.844)		(3.338)	
Domestic credit to private sector by banks	Below the median	0.509	958	0.169	958	0.679	958	0.122	958	8.377	958	−1.985	958
		(0.671)		(0.744)		(0.513)		(0.166)		(7.3)		(1.551)	
	Above the median	2.175		−1.955		0.37		0.081		−24.404*		−2.274	
		(2.081)		(6.838)		(0.924)		(0.121)		(13.539)		(1.752)	
Domestic credit provided by financial sector	Below the median	−0.096	958	−0.295	958	1.159*	958	−0.057	958	8.578	958	−1.763	958
		(0.923)		(0.935)		(0.616)		(0.162)		(8.802)		(1.768)	
	Above the median	3.268		2.692		1.194		0.144		−36.199**		−3.333	
		(2.085)		(7.755)		(0.866)		(0.237)		(17.408)		(2.17)	
Domestic credit to private sector	Below the median	0.538	958	−0.112	958	0.677	958	0.137	958	8.955	958	−2.145	958
		(0.629)		(0.822)		(0.507)		(0.173)		(7.287)		(1.589)	
	Above the median	2.561		−0.555		0.293		0.086		−23.72*		−2.557	
		(2.004)		(7.203)		(0.925)		(0.121)		(13.691)		(1.795)	
Foreign direct investment	Below the median	0.187	1524	−0.151	1524	0.022	1524	0.078	1524	−0.535	1524	0.397	1524
		(0.261)		(0.522)		(0.188)		(0.055)		(1.971)		(0.962)	
	Above the median	0.049		−0.577		−0.068		0.028		0.19		1.441	
		(0.413)		(0.534)		(0.181)		(0.045)		(3.403)		(1.108)	

Trade	Below the median	−1.005	1447	−0.607	1447	−0.193	1447	−0.158	1447	0.749	1447	4.246	1447
		(1.089)		(1.103)		(0.48)		(0.244)		(6.264)		(4.166)	
	Above the median	0.703		1.846		0.299		0.238		15.01		0.996	
		(1.228)		(1.656)		(1.009)		(0.211)		(13.888)		(1.766)	
Private gross fixed capital formation	Below the median	0.059	720	−0.58	720	−0.274	720	0.134**	720	−6.495	720	−0.867	720
		(0.25)		(0.524)		(0.262)		(0.059)		(4.197)		(0.722)	
	Above the median	0.438		0.252		−0.013		−0.069		−8.326		−0.931	
		(0.848)		(1.284)		(0.309)		(0.084)		(6.139)		(0.724)	
New business density	Below the median	0.112	846	0.162	846	0.02	846	0.024	846	−0.51	846	−0.235	846
		(0.07)		(0.119)		(0.079)		(0.017)		(0.555)		(0.25)	
	Above the median	0.245		0.447		0.017		0.013		−1.122		0.246	
		(0.262)		(0.564)		(0.176)		(0.021)		(2.059)		(0.5)	
Unemployment rate	Below the median	−0.129**	1418	−0.253	1418	−0.289**	1418	−0.05***	1418	−1.912	1418	0.531**	1418
		(0.061)		(0.16)		(0.118)		(0.019)		(1.453)		(0.221)	
	Above the median	−0.096		1.076		0.151		−0.034		5.633*		−0.643*	
		(0.224)		(0.821)		(0.125)		(0.042)		(3.145)		(0.331)	
Income GINI index	Below the median	−0.553***	506	−0.3	506	−0.104	506	−0.077	506	1.63	506	0.348	506
		(0.209)		(0.432)		(0.203)		(0.08)		(2.368)		(0.619)	
	Above the median	0.621		0.634		0.34**		0.043		0.229		−0.674	
		(0.592)		(0.665)		(0.139)		(0.032)		(1.692)		(0.423)	
GDP pc growth	Below the median	−0.053	1520	−0.64	1520	−0.487**	1520	0.052	1520	−0.592	1520	1.112**	1520
		(0.189)		(0.423)		(0.197)		(0.04)		(1.493)		(0.524)	
	Above the median	0.213		−0.401		−0.318		0.007		−0.948		0.642	
		(0.311)		(0.32)		(0.201)		(0.033)		(1.774)		(0.419)	

(continued)

Table A.11 (continued)

		Registering a property		Construction permits		Paying taxes		Time to export		Time to import	
		Coeff/SE	Obs	Coeff/SE	Obs	Coeff/SE	Obs	Coeff/SE	Obs	Coeff/SE	Obs
		(7)		(8)		(9)		(10)		(11)	
Stock market capitalization	Below the median	−3.204	718	−10.464*	718	−2.045	718	−21.062**	718	−23.017***	718
		(2.971)		(5.839)		(10.839)		(9.234)		(7.704)	
	Above the median	0.66		15.155		1.592		−12.855		−6.937	
		(2.157)		(12.946)		(9.832)		(19.495)		(15.446)	
Stocks traded	Below the median	−11.972***	632	−16.467***	632	−17.716**	632	−28.552**	632	−24.251***	632
		(3.709)		(5.195)		(7.32)		(11.853)		(8.625)	
	Above the median	−2.64		19.7		9.805		−35.836		−19.929	
		(2.977)		(14.711)		(20.58)		(27.458)		(15.776)	
Domestic credit to private sector by banks	Below the median	0.409	958	−4.013	958	−0.74	951	−11.262*	958	−6.913	958
		(1.294)		(2.905)		(3.015)		(5.731)		(4.489)	
	Above the median	0.427		0.175		0.897		−15.103		−7.864	
		(2.213)		(11.654)		(4.493)		(13.314)		(6.039)	
Domestic credit provided by financial sector	Below the median	0.997	958	−7.068**	958	−7.13*	951	−8.189	958	−3.738	958
		(1.786)		(3.099)		(3.934)		(6.655)		(5.05)	
	Above the median	−0.972		−5.929		−9.558		−15.225		−6.597	
		(1.402)		(9.525)		(6.11)		(14.493)		(6.591)	
Domestic credit to private sector	Below the median	0.329	958	−4.148	958	−2.591	951	−11.396*	958	−7.185	958
		(1.287)		(2.805)		(2.933)		(5.752)		(4.529)	
	Above the median	0.178		0.962		0.73		−17.254		−9.381	
		(2.231)		(11.73)		(4.498)		(13.599)		(6.454)	
Foreign direct investment	Below the median	0.91	1524	0.193	1524	0.886	1517	−0.495	1524	−0.256	1524
		(0.691)		(1.351)		(1.013)		(1.681)		(1.41)	
	Above the median	0.815		−0.742		1.538		2.352		3.392	
		(1.052)		(3.343)		(3.196)		(2.686)		(2.138)	

Trade	Below the median	0.55	1447	4.081	1447	4.113	1440	5.453	1447	2.275	1447
		(1.49)		(5.167)		(3.605)		(5.229)		(3)	
	Above the median	−2.465		8.592		−8.543		5.009		1.784	
		(2.075)		(10.084)		(7.766)		(6.592)		(6.355)	
Private gross fixed capital formation	Below the median	−0.649	720	0.034	720	4.126**	720	1.739	720	1.952	720
		(0.807)		(1.549)		(1.644)		(2.117)		(1.549)	
	Above the median	0.631		0.476		4.61**		1.305		1.189	
		(0.846)		(1.729)		(2.15)		(2.084)		(2.147)	
New business density	Below the median	−0.274	846	−0.478	846	−0.094	842	−0.823	846	−0.658*	846
		(0.24)		(0.462)		(0.388)		(0.519)		(0.397)	
	Above the median	−0.131		−0.635		1.773		0.076		0.594	
		(0.281)		(0.663)		(1.165)		(2.03)		(1.668)	
Unemployment rate	Below the median	0.307*	1418	0.916*	1418	0.897*	1411	2.258**	1418	1.755**	1418
		(0.183)		(0.483)		(0.476)		(0.939)		(0.712)	
	Above the median	−0.961***		−0.777		−3.381**		−0.337		−0.743	
		(0.348)		(1.446)		(1.356)		(0.783)		(0.736)	
Income GINI index	Below the median	0.758	506	1.01	506	0.219	505	1.551	506	2.121	506
		(0.603)		(1.247)		(1.188)		(1.668)		(1.389)	
	Above the median	−0.743*		−1.342		−2.864**		−2.202		−2.112*	
		(0.417)		(1.68)		(1.371)		(1.367)		(1.226)	
GDP pc growth	Below the median	0.972	1520	0.931	1520	3.934**	1513	1.1	1520	0.654	1520
		(0.694)		(0.855)		(1.715)		(0.875)		(0.885)	
	Above the median	0.324		−1.365		2.238***		0.344		0.882	
		(0.218)		(1.472)		(0.852)		(1.386)		(1.309)	

Notes: Panel of annual data over the period 2006–2014. Clustered standard errors in parentheses. The regressions include country and period dummies, and a constant term. All these variables are omitted for space considerations

*, ** and *** denote statistical significance at the 10, 5 and 1% levels, respectively

Table A.12 The effect of legal rules on financial and economic outcomes: differentiation by government effectiveness. Without additional control

		Creditor rights		Investor protection		Credit information		Recovery rate		Contract enforc.		Starting a business	
		Coeff/SE	Obs	Coeff/SE	Obs	Coeff/SE	Obs	Coeff/SE	Obs	Coeff/SE	Obs	Coeff/SE	Obs
		(1)		(2)		(3)		(4)		(5)		(6)	
Stock market capitalization	Below the median	4.363**	263	3.466	263	1.275	263	0.886	263	−8.737	263	−8.21	263
		(2.069)		(5.016)		(1.985)		(0.741)		(21.232)		(5.805)	
	Above the median	−1.934		−0.766		−0.209		0.582		−0.598		−2.23	
		(3.7)		(8.044)		(2.122)		(0.491)		(15.169)		(3.818)	
Stocks traded	Below the median	6.929***	240	11.179**	240	5.287***	240	2.27**	240	11.01	240	−18.969**	240
		(2.362)		(4.552)		(1.675)		(0.966)		(22.271)		(7.789)	
	Above the median	4.412		7.846		3.743		0.961*		−6.074		−4.975	
		(6.092)		(5.525)		(2.703)		(0.508)		(19.888)		(4.313)	
Domestic credit to private sector by banks	Below the median	0.703	322	−0.15	322	0.748	322	−0.061	322	7.99	322	−0.963	322
		(0.843)		(0.963)		(0.897)		(0.277)		(13.116)		(1.868)	
	Above the median	3.027		−0.609		0.738		0.118		−13.863		−3.448	
		(2.268)		(5.992)		(1.298)		(0.174)		(22.326)		(2.089)	
Domestic credit provided by financial sector	Below the median	0.11	322	−1.022	322	1.521	322	−0.318	322	9.685	322	−0.275	322
		(1.074)		(1.068)		(1.184)		(0.288)		(15.924)		(2.165)	
	Above the median	6.957**		3.076		1.858		0.094		−23.321		−4.432	
		(3.147)		(7.716)		(1.245)		(0.287)		(28.105)		(2.762)	
Domestic credit to private sector	Below the median	0.739	322	−0.485	322	0.785	322	−0.044	322	9.485	322	−0.952	322
		(0.796)		(1.029)		(0.885)		(0.29)		(13.321)		(1.871)	
	Above the median	4.514*		1.007		0.632		0.116		−13.574		−3.863*	
		(2.404)		(6.389)		(1.304)		(0.176)		(22.407)		(2.155)	
Foreign direct investment	Below the median	0.238	514	−0.086	514	0.081	514	0.223	514	0.201	514	0.503	514
		(0.297)		(0.701)		(0.351)		(0.152)		(3.098)		(1.34)	
	Above the median	0.022		−0.483		−0.494		0.034		−1.25		1.859	
		(0.583)		(0.691)		(0.316)		(0.059)		(4.095)		(1.536)	

Trade	Below the median	−1.084	492	−0.586	492	−0.718	492	−0.103	492	−3.795	492	7.078	492
		(1.409)		(1.478)		(0.835)		(0.511)		(11.589)		(6.851)	
	Above the median	0.865		3.668		0.917		0.205		14.451		0.61	
		(2.454)		(2.228)		(1.364)		(0.32)		(15.323)		(2.237)	
Private gross fixed capital formation	Below the median	0.04	253	−0.617	253	−0.334	253	0.197	253	−2.355	253	−1.093	253
		(0.303)		(0.679)		(0.41)		(0.16)		(4.41)		(1.141)	
	Above the median	0.048		−0.506		−0.251		−0.09		−10.957**		−0.412	
		(1.111)		(1.424)		(0.533)		(0.169)		(4.965)		(0.917)	
New business density	Below the median	0.064	351	0.19	351	0.063	351	0.038	351	−1.487	351	−0.365	351
		(0.104)		(0.144)		(0.102)		(0.031)		(1.124)		(0.267)	
	Above the median	0.523		0.276		−0.145		0.009		−0.461		0.33	
		(0.466)		(0.601)		(0.179)		(0.03)		(2.265)		(0.567)	
Unemployment rate	Below the median	−0.139*	476	−0.234	476	−0.277**	476	−0.094**	476	0.673	476	0.45*	476
		(0.08)		(0.191)		(0.115)		(0.041)		(1.385)		(0.24)	
	Above the median	−0.145		0.727		0.023		−0.049		2.961		−0.466	
		(0.376)		(1.086)		(0.257)		(0.065)		(4.68)		(0.499)	
Income GINI index	Below the median	−0.599**	275	−0.219	275	−0.143	275	0.084	275	−3.954	275	0.533	275
		(0.23)		(0.422)		(0.253)		(0.131)		(5.08)		(0.854)	
	Above the median	−0.044		0.579		0.218		0.012		1.443		−0.659	
		(0.596)		(0.952)		(0.27)		(0.047)		(1.552)		(0.713)	
GDP pc growth	Below the median	0.025	512	−0.728	512	−0.59*	512	0.107	512	−1.352	512	1.121*	512
		(0.217)		(0.62)		(0.318)		(0.095)		(3.142)		(0.674)	
	Above the median	0.107		−0.563		−0.659**		−0.019		−0.321		0.78	
		(0.441)		(0.361)		(0.317)		(0.048)		(1.441)		(0.536)	

(continued)

Table A.12 (continued)

		Registering a property		Construction permits		Paying taxes		Time to export		Time to import	
		Coeff/SE	Obs	Coeff/SE	Obs	Coeff/SE	Obs	Coeff/SE	Obs	Coeff/SE	Obs
		(7)		(8)		(9)		(10)		(11)	
Stock market capitalization	Below the median	−3.481	263	−7.108	263	3.987	263	−29.468	263	−27.759**	263
		(5)		(10.26)		(10.923)		(18.406)		(13.934)	
	Above the median	1.339		6.499		−6.236		−19.682		−18.127	
		(3.305)		(13.962)		(13.408)		(26.376)		(18.759)	
Stocks traded	Below the median	−12.956**	240	−15.837**	240	−16.115**	240	−62.344**	240	−44.22***	240
		(5.323)		(6.208)		(8.077)		(25.574)		(16.67)	
	Above the median	−2.289		11.431		−2.99		−39.936		−26.661	
		(4.05)		(17.376)		(20.664)		(33.363)		(20.287)	
Domestic credit to private sector by banks	Below the median	0.073	322	−3.192	322	0.64	320	−11.047	322	−5.886	322
		(1.67)		(3.743)		(3.862)		(10.238)		(7.355)	
	Above the median	0.804		−3.502		−1.43		−21.094		−11.751	
		(2.829)		(10.613)		(6.085)		(17.277)		(8.206)	
Domestic credit provided by financial sector	Below the median	1.171	322	−5.473	322	−6.824	320	−1.544	322	2.247	322
		(2.321)		(3.909)		(5.037)		(12.549)		(9.262)	
	Above the median	−0.578		−7.075		−10.983		−19.774		−9.237	
		(1.968)		(10.207)		(7.9)		(17.63)		(8.829)	
Domestic credit to private sector	Below the median	−0.066	322	−3.197	322	−1.319	320	−9.989	322	−5.278	322
		(1.652)		(3.544)		(3.854)		(10.249)		(7.381)	
	Above the median	0.556		−4.243		−2.388		−23.268		−13.589	
		(2.886)		(10.609)		(6.211)		(17.485)		(8.527)	
Foreign direct investment	Below the median	0.829	514	−0.769	514	0.327	512	−1.488	514	−0.8	514
		(1.011)		(2.328)		(1.85)		(3.164)		(2.421)	
	Above the median	1.424		−0.228		2.024		3.363		3.917	
		(1.534)		(3.491)		(2.91)		(3.133)		(2.807)	

Trade	Below the median	−0.127	492	10.019	492	2.97	490	11.17	492	2.465	492
		(2.329)		(9.917)		(5.625)		(10.174)		(5.242)	
	Above the median	−1.992		3.896		−7.81		3.908		0.318	
		(2.472)		(13.158)		(9.498)		(8.482)		(8.098)	
Private gross fixed capital formation	Below the median	−1.361*	253	−0.767	253	5.107**	253	1.282	253	2.473	253
		(0.808)		(2.297)		(1.948)		(2.887)		(2.326)	
	Above the median	0.646		1.428		3.7		4.639		3.367	
		(1.214)		(3.586)		(3.744)		(4.95)		(4.288)	
New business density	Below the median	−0.372	351	−0.714	351	−0.174	349	−1.846*	351	−1.154*	351
		(0.253)		(0.454)		(0.37)		(0.956)		(0.691)	
	Above the median	−0.019		−0.179		1.705		0.496		0.633	
		(0.296)		(0.898)		(1.295)		(2.203)		(1.81)	
Unemployment rate	Below the median	0.478**	476	1.069**	476	0.665	474	2.685***	476	1.919**	476
		(0.226)		(0.523)		(0.531)		(1)		(0.769)	
	Above the median	−1.144**		0.209		−2.698*		1.817		0.515	
		(0.476)		(2.136)		(1.592)		(1.818)		(1.364)	
Income GINI index	Below the median	0.477	275	2.007	275	−0.381	274	2.655	275	3.707	275
		(0.695)		(1.455)		(1.469)		(2.75)		(2.352)	
	Above the median	−0.423		−0.971		−1.789		0.396		0.259	
		(0.458)		(1.383)		(1.381)		(2.013)		(2.095)	
GDP pc growth	Below the median	1.598*	512	1.106	512	5.073**	510	0.808	512	0.509	512
		(0.964)		(1.549)		(2.461)		(1.646)		(1.346)	
	Above the median	0.864**		−0.319		2.068**		2.159		1.902	
		(0.393)		(1.624)		(0.965)		(1.807)		(1.773)	

Notes: Panel specification with averaged annual data over 3-year periods (2006–2014). Clustered standard errors in parentheses. The regressions include country and period dummies, and a constant term. All these variables are omitted for space considerations

*, ** and *** denote statistical significance at the 10, 5 and 1% levels, respectively

Table A.13 The effect of legal rules on financial and economic outcomes: differentiation by government effectiveness. Annual data

		Creditor rights		Investor protection		Credit information		Recovery rate		Contract enforc.		Starting a business	
		Coeff/SE	Obs	Coeff/SE	Obs	Coeff/SE	Obs	Coeff/SE	Obs	Coeff/SE	Obs	Coeff/SE	Obs
		(1)		(2)		(3)		(4)		(5)		(6)	
Stock market capitalization	Below the median	3.119***	718	3.059	718	2.756	718	0.601	718	−25.542	718	−6.387*	718
		(1.171)		(4.115)		(1.668)		(0.381)		(15.769)		(3.704)	
	Above the median	−1.868		−0.076		0.445		0.496		0.914		−0.542	
		(2.768)		(5.355)		(1.574)		(0.303)		(15.691)		(2.787)	
Stocks traded	Below the median	4.573**	632	11.432***	632	3.782***	632	1.114***	632	4.946	632	−15.388***	632
		(1.806)		(3.349)		(1.03)		(0.388)		(19.995)		(4.834)	
	Above the median	2.737		7.512*		2.698		0.748**		−11.958		−4.52	
		(4.287)		(3.964)		(2.081)		(0.316)		(16.904)		(3.363)	
Domestic credit to private sector by banks	Below the median	0.58	950	−0.061	950	0.504	950	−0.013	950	2.308	950	−1.096	950
		(0.709)		(0.804)		(0.531)		(0.155)		(7.048)		(1.562)	
	Above the median	2.956**		−0.237		0.694		0.142		−12.087		−3.419**	
		(1.468)		(4.324)		(0.863)		(0.098)		(15.927)		(1.646)	
Domestic credit provided by financial sector	Below the median	−0.055	950	−0.871	950	0.955	950	−0.188	950	3.882	950	−0.465	950
		(0.909)		(0.891)		(0.654)		(0.151)		(8.666)		(1.716)	
	Above the median	6.205***		3.497		1.351*		0.166		−22.282		−4.365**	
		(1.984)		(4.942)		(0.807)		(0.188)		(20.779)		(2.045)	
Domestic credit to private sector	Below the median	0.586	950	−0.465	950	0.512	950	−0.007	950	3.537	950	−1.203	950
		(0.672)		(0.864)		(0.519)		(0.162)		(7.172)		(1.593)	
	Above the median	4.06**		0.995		0.621		0.151		−11.849		−3.749**	
		(1.558)		(4.55)		(0.867)		(0.103)		(15.997)		(1.679)	

Foreign direct investment	Below the median	0.162	1516	−0.141	1516	0.116	1516	0.098	1516	0.731	1516	0.329	1516
		(0.25)		(0.558)		(0.197)		(0.066)		(2.117)		(1.042)	
	Above the median	0.102		−0.512		−0.165		0.019		−0.518		1.412	
		(0.57)		(0.455)		(0.182)		(0.04)		(2.915)		(1.01)	
Trade	Below the median	−0.947	1439	−1.13	1439	−0.331	1439	−0.119	1439	−0.173	1439	5.283	1439
		(1.046)		(1.211)		(0.499)		(0.3)		(5.765)		(4.534)	
	Above the median	0.515		2.654*		0.433		0.147		14.255		0.397	
		(1.722)		(1.403)		(0.927)		(0.213)		(11.531)		(1.603)	
Private gross fixed capital formation	Below the median	0.089	720	−0.487	720	−0.175	720	0.128**	720	−2.369	720	−1.13	720
		(0.241)		(0.564)		(0.281)		(0.064)		(3.117)		(0.815)	
	Above the median	0.235		−0.461		−0.023		−0.02		−9.7**		−0.624	
		(0.666)		(1.097)		(0.289)		(0.067)		(4.04)		(0.676)	
New business density	Below the median	0.093	843	0.216*	843	0.084	843	0.031	843	−1.367*	843	−0.444**	843
		(0.075)		(0.121)		(0.074)		(0.019)		(0.763)		(0.214)	
	Above the median	0.299		0.235		−0.021		0.009		−0.619		0.253	
		(0.251)		(0.441)		(0.163)		(0.018)		(1.756)		(0.448)	
Unemployment rate	Below the median	−0.107*	1401	−0.239	1401	−0.204***	1401	−0.033*	1401	0.445	1401	0.438**	1401
		(0.061)		(0.16)		(0.067)		(0.019)		(0.892)		(0.19)	
	Above the median	−0.204		0.611		−0.064		−0.038		2.385		−0.322	
		(0.254)		(0.714)		(0.191)		(0.037)		(3.232)		(0.349)	
Income GINI index	Below the median	−0.486**	505	−0.257	505	−0.054	505	0.013	505	−1.455	505	0.319	505
		(0.206)		(0.487)		(0.176)		(0.073)		(5.046)		(0.691)	
	Above the median	−0.043		0.079		0.145		−0.004		1.343		−0.557	
		(0.945)		(0.568)		(0.249)		(0.049)		(1.404)		(0.403)	

(continued)

Table A.13 (continued)

		Registering a property		Construction permits		Paying taxes		Time to export		Time to import	
		Coeff/SE	Obs	Coeff/SE	Obs	Coeff/SE	Obs	Coeff/SE	Obs	Coeff/SE	Obs
		(7)		(8)		(9)		(10)		(11)	
Stock market capitalization	Below the median	−4.211	718	−7.098	718	5.239	718	−17.823*	718	−20.844**	718
		(3.255)		(7.5)		(8.511)		(9.338)		(8.301)	
	Above the median	0.515		7.881		−4.312		−18.042		−15.578	
		(2.093)		(10.5)		(10.484)		(14.893)		(11.675)	
Stocks traded	Below the median	−12.505***	632	−11.25**	632	−14.164**	632	−26.422*	632	−25.154**	632
		(3.835)		(4.849)		(6.748)		(15.167)		(10.417)	
	Above the median	−3.081		8.188		1.197		−34.244*		−21.671*	
		(3.004)		(12.444)		(17.715)		(18.654)		(11.289)	
Domestic credit to private sector by banks	Below the median	0.197	950	−3.068	950	0.351	943	−8.487	950	−4.441	950
		(1.352)		(2.702)		(3.128)		(5.81)		(4.678)	
	Above the median	0.591		−3.445		−1.749		−16.103		−10.066*	
		(2.067)		(8.763)		(4.385)		(10.692)		(5.591)	
Domestic credit provided by financial sector	Below the median	1.253	950	−6.599**	950	−5.643	943	−3.522	950	−0.355	950
		(1.862)		(2.955)		(4.414)		(6.954)		(5.327)	
	Above the median	−0.748		−8.081		−10.91*		−16.518		−8.843	
		(1.419)		(7.29)		(5.622)		(11.501)		(5.842)	
Domestic credit to private sector	Below the median	0.065	950	−2.901	950	−1.36	943	−7.872	950	−4.083	950
		(1.333)		(2.544)		(3.11)		(5.83)		(4.721)	
	Above the median	0.384		−3.786		−2.642		−18.189*		−11.814**	
		(2.085)		(8.796)		(4.475)		(10.815)		(5.807)	
Foreign direct investment	Below the median	0.592	1516	0.026	1516	0.003	1509	−1.763	1516	−0.94	1516
		(0.732)		(1.422)		(1.395)		(2.074)		(1.572)	
	Above the median	0.973		−0.346		2.509		2.6		3.308*	
		(1.023)		(2.961)		(2.725)		(2.252)		(1.916)	

Trade	Below the median	0.096	1439	5.938	1439	3.41	1432	7.487	1439	2.934	1439
		(1.46)		(5.564)		(3.957)		(6.258)		(3.373)	
	Above the median	−2.166		3.271		−6.186		2.162		0.242	
		(2)		(9.121)		(7.493)		(5.59)		(5.173)	
Private gross fixed capital formation	Below the median	−0.894	720	−0.346	720	4.022***	720	0.663	720	1.759	720
		(0.783)		(1.468)		(1.512)		(1.449)		(1.38)	
	Above the median	0.412		1.47		4.109		2.057		1.015	
		(0.766)		(2.555)		(2.791)		(2.783)		(2.283)	
New business density	Below the median	−0.476**	843	−0.744*	843	−0.398	839	−1.408***	843	−0.969**	843
		(0.226)		(0.41)		(0.359)		(0.452)		(0.417)	
	Above the median	−0.044		−0.175		1.653		0.091		0.43	
		(0.267)		(0.659)		(1.035)		(1.445)		(1.164)	
Unemployment rate	Below the median	0.409**	1401	0.612	1401	0.951*	1394	1.66**	1401	1.396**	1401
		(0.182)		(0.38)		(0.522)		(0.744)		(0.564)	
	Above the median	−0.863**		0.254		−2.529**		1.229		0.545	
		(0.334)		(1.595)		(1.206)		(1.182)		(1.049)	
Income GINI index	Below the median	0.434	505	1.158	505	0.089	504	1.02	505	1.89	505
		(0.544)		(1.351)		(1.134)		(1.838)		(1.782)	
	Above the median	−0.373		−0.666		−1.786		0.182		0.624	
		(0.387)		(1.519)		(1.736)		(1.614)		(1.514)	

Notes: Panel of annual data over the period 2006–2014. Clustered standard errors in parentheses. The regressions include lag GDP growth, country and period dummies, and a constant term. All these variables are omitted for space considerations

*, ** and *** denote statistical significance at the 10, 5 and 1% levels, respectively

Table A.14 The effect of legal rules on financial and economic outcomes: differentiation by government effectiveness. Annual data, without additional control

		Creditor rights		Investor protection		Credit information		Recovery rate		Contract enforc.		Starting a business	
		Coeff/SE	Obs	Coeff/SE	Obs	Coeff/SE	Obs	Coeff/SE	Obs	Coeff/SE	Obs	Coeff/SE	Obs
		(1)		(2)		(3)		(4)		(5)		(6)	
Stock market capitalization	Below the median	3.251***	718	2.976	718	2.804*	718	0.623	718	−26.008	718	−6.655*	718
		(1.176)		(4.068)		(1.655)		(0.381)		(16.404)		(3.67)	
	Above the median	−1.724		−0.215		0.315		0.515		−0.53		−0.481	
		(2.816)		(5.47)		(1.523)		(0.311)		(16.139)		(2.785)	
Stocks traded	Below the median	4.636**	632	11.301***	632	3.884***	632	1.137***	632	6.683	632	−15.65***	632
		(1.802)		(3.313)		(1.068)		(0.393)		(20.354)		(4.991)	
	Above the median	2.879		7.437*		2.525		0.767**		−13.185		−4.4	
		(4.273)		(4.003)		(1.986)		(0.324)		(16.926)		(3.305)	
Domestic credit to private sector by banks	Below the median	0.568	958	−0.084	958	0.483	958	−0.015	958	3.45	958	−1.068	958
		(0.705)		(0.79)		(0.51)		(0.157)		(6.849)		(1.487)	
	Above the median	2.93**		−0.271		0.667		0.14		−12.067		−3.365**	
		(1.466)		(4.325)		(0.845)		(0.099)		(15.911)		(1.622)	
Domestic credit provided by financial sector	Below the median	−0.06	958	−0.804	958	0.986	958	−0.207	958	5.147	958	−0.65	958
		(0.928)		(0.896)		(0.631)		(0.153)		(8.545)		(1.661)	
	Above the median	6.129***		3.455		1.395*		0.168		−22.187		−4.381**	
		(2.029)		(4.942)		(0.789)		(0.19)		(20.782)		(2.02)	
Domestic credit to private sector	Below the median	0.575	958	−0.488	958	0.49	958	−0.008	958	4.523	958	−1.168	958
		(0.668)		(0.849)		(0.498)		(0.163)		(6.942)		(1.521)	
	Above the median	4.038**		0.964		0.593		0.149		−11.835		−3.696**	
		(1.554)		(4.55)		(0.85)		(0.103)		(15.987)		(1.656)	
Foreign direct investment	Below the median	0.17	1524	−0.144	1524	0.114	1524	0.101	1524	0.352	1524	0.334	1524
		(0.251)		(0.558)		(0.197)		(0.067)		(2.122)		(1.038)	
	Above the median	0.118		−0.508		−0.175		0.02		−0.56		1.413	
		(0.573)		(0.45)		(0.173)		(0.04)		(2.914)		(1.012)	

Trade	Below the median	−0.913	1447	−1.128	1447	−0.333	1447	−0.11	1447	−1.484	1447	5.277	1447
		(1.049)		(1.228)		(0.504)		(0.299)		(5.744)		(4.51)	
	Above the median	0.57		2.693*		0.416		0.154		14.179		0.373	
		(1.731)		(1.404)		(0.916)		(0.211)		(11.523)		(1.592)	
Private gross fixed capital formation	Below the median	0.073	720	−0.509	720	−0.229	720	0.137**	720	−2.753	720	−1.108	720
		(0.254)		(0.566)		(0.272)		(0.063)		(3.361)		(0.805)	
	Above the median	0.181		−0.579		−0.127		−0.028		−9.669**		−0.563	
		(0.735)		(1.097)		(0.296)		(0.072)		(4.07)		(0.668)	
New business density	Below the median	0.103	846	0.21*	846	0.073	846	0.032*	846	−1.329	846	−0.424**	846
		(0.073)		(0.117)		(0.073)		(0.018)		(0.803)		(0.204)	
	Above the median	0.304		0.23		−0.046		0.01		−0.673		0.266	
		(0.253)		(0.444)		(0.159)		(0.019)		(1.761)		(0.442)	
Unemployment rate	Below the median	−0.116*	1418	−0.2	1418	−0.182***	1418	−0.044**	1418	0.286	1418	0.369**	1418
		(0.061)		(0.141)		(0.063)		(0.02)		(0.879)		(0.172)	
	Above the median	−0.237		0.634		−0.023		−0.04		2.548		−0.368	
		(0.26)		(0.727)		(0.194)		(0.039)		(3.328)		(0.363)	
Income GINI index	Below the median	−0.487**	506	−0.257	506	−0.053	506	0.013	506	−1.498	506	0.316	506
		(0.206)		(0.49)		(0.175)		(0.073)		(5.059)		(0.692)	
	Above the median	−0.053		0.072		0.15		−0.005		1.377		−0.563	
		(0.933)		(0.566)		(0.248)		(0.049)		(1.415)		(0.403)	
GDP pc growth	Below the median	−0.033	1520	−0.63	1520	−0.359*	1520	0.059	1520	−1.938	1520	1.149**	1520
		(0.181)		(0.452)		(0.207)		(0.047)		(2.056)		(0.563)	
	Above the median	0.228		−0.482*		−0.493**		0.009		0.066		0.644*	
		(0.359)		(0.269)		(0.202)		(0.03)		(1.295)		(0.383)	

(continued)

Table A.14 (continued)

		Registering a property		Construction permits		Paying taxes		Time to export		Time to import	
		Coeff/SE	Obs	Coeff/SE	Obs	Coeff/SE	Obs	Coeff/SE	Obs	Coeff/SE	Obs
		(7)		(8)		(9)		(10)		(11)	
Stock market capitalization	Below the median	−4.218	718	−7.112	718	5.153	718	−17.597*	718	−20.802**	718
		(3.323)		(7.358)		(8.781)		(9.547)		(8.426)	
	Above the median	0.63		7.913		−3.947		−17.399		−15.325	
		(2.121)		(10.57)		(10.481)		(14.885)		(11.668)	
Stocks traded	Below the median	−12.557***	632	−11.372**	632	−14.313**	632	−26.41*	632	−25.266**	632
		(3.91)		(4.842)		(6.81)		(15.577)		(10.705)	
	Above the median	−2.997		8.178		1.657		−33.84*		−21.44*	
		(2.985)		(12.418)		(17.583)		(18.62)		(11.137)	
Domestic credit to private sector by banks	Below the median	0.157	958	−3.165	958	0.355	951	−8.471	958	−4.388	958
		(1.294)		(2.718)		(2.977)		(5.737)		(4.589)	
	Above the median	0.612		−3.387		−1.676		−15.937		−9.894*	
		(2.054)		(8.773)		(4.366)		(10.581)		(5.484)	
Domestic credit provided by financial sector	Below the median	1.04	958	−6.433**	958	−6.278	951	−3.36	958	−0.28	958
		(1.835)		(2.965)		(4.11)		(6.928)		(5.322)	
	Above the median	−0.822		−8.053		−10.881*		−16.546		−8.915	
		(1.401)		(7.305)		(5.62)		(11.357)		(5.756)	
Domestic credit to private sector	Below the median	0.039	958	−2.991	958	−1.294	951	−7.839	958	−4.014	958
		(1.277)		(2.564)		(2.932)		(5.757)		(4.63)	
	Above the median	0.407		−3.733		−2.571		−18.015*		−11.633**	
		(2.075)		(8.806)		(4.457)		(10.705)		(5.696)	
Foreign direct investment	Below the median	0.657	1524	0.075	1524	0.06	1517	−1.56	1524	−0.831	1524
		(0.727)		(1.417)		(1.421)		(2.04)		(1.563)	
	Above the median	0.978		−0.353		2.518		2.643		3.33*	
		(1.023)		(2.973)		(2.712)		(2.225)		(1.893)	

Trade	Below the median	0.366	1447	6.226	1447	3.275	1440	8.477	1447	3.535	1447
		(1.509)		(5.554)		(4.002)		(6.346)		(3.456)	
	Above the median	−2.169		3.203		−6.313		2.315		0.325	
		(1.98)		(9.109)		(7.471)		(5.581)		(5.181)	
Private gross fixed capital formation	Below the median	−0.779	720	−0.302	720	4.292***	720	0.911	720	1.854	720
		(0.765)		(1.564)		(1.502)		(1.516)		(1.461)	
	Above the median	0.564		1.825		4.1		2.663		1.574	
		(0.826)		(2.643)		(2.928)		(3.043)		(2.422)	
New business density	Below the median	−0.445**	846	−0.775*	846	−0.274	842	−1.374***	846	−0.956**	846
		(0.224)		(0.396)		(0.351)		(0.45)		(0.411)	
	Above the median	−0.032		−0.166		1.701		0.142		0.454	
		(0.266)		(0.667)		(1.043)		(1.451)		(1.169)	
Unemployment rate	Below the median	0.342**	1418	0.619*	1418	0.675	1411	1.6**	1418	1.383**	1418
		(0.153)		(0.34)		(0.411)		(0.735)		(0.562)	
	Above the median	−0.902***		0.219		−2.659**		1.088		0.463	
		(0.338)		(1.6)		(1.236)		(1.134)		(1.018)	
Income GINI index	Below the median	0.431	506	1.162	506	0.076	505	1.012	506	1.898	506
		(0.544)		(1.363)		(1.125)		(1.842)		(1.786)	
	Above the median	−0.379		−0.653		−1.79		0.174		0.626	
		(0.391)		(1.527)		(1.74)		(1.63)		(1.52)	
GDP pc growth	Below the median	0.973	1520	0.82	1520	4.148**	1513	0.832	1520	0.431	1520
		(0.746)		(0.895)		(1.809)		(1.006)		(0.909)	
	Above the median	0.359		−0.839		2.121***		0.779		1.116	
		(0.218)		(1.359)		(0.785)		(1.148)		(1.21)	

Notes: Panel of annual data over the period 2006–2014. Clustered standard errors in parentheses. The regressions include country and period dummies, and a constant term. All these variables are omitted for space considerations

*, ** and *** denote statistical significance at the 10, 5 and 1% levels, respectively

Table A.15 The effect of legal rules on financial and economic outcomes: differentiation by legal tradition. Without additional control

		Creditor rights		Investor protection		Credit information		Recovery rate		Contract enforc.		Starting a business	
		Coeff/SE	Obs	Coeff/SE	Obs	Coeff/SE	Obs	Coeff/SE	Obs	Coeff/SE	Obs	Coeff/SE	Obs
		(1)		(2)		(3)		(4)		(5)		(6)	
Stock market capitalization	Common law	−0.02	266	9.769	266	0.709	266	1.431	266	137.701	266	−19.278	266
		(6.58)		(10.508)		(3.15)		(1.429)		(110.717)		(17.173)	
	Civil law	1.39		−2.643		−0.876		0.47		−8.285		−0.321	
		(2.62)		(5.371)		(2.152)		(0.497)		(13.228)		(4.404)	
Stocks traded	Common law	1.353	243	17.248**	243	4.964*	243	−0.336	243	−144.588	243	8.677	243
		(11.887)		(6.764)		(2.768)		(1.701)		(99.836)		(19.398)	
	Civil law	7.823**		9.144*		5.444**		1.504**		16.376		−7.78	
		(3.304)		(5.05)		(2.352)		(0.591)		(15.146)		(5.083)	
Domestic credit to private sector by banks	Common law	−0.169	325	0.38	325	−0.986	325	0.318	325	−9.733	325	−1.823	325
		(2.5)		(2.583)		(1.79)		(0.61)		(13.88)		(4.122)	
	Civil law	1.032		−0.29		1.11		0.06		−3.76		−2.105	
		(0.72)		(1.365)		(0.941)		(0.155)		(17.649)		(1.72)	
Domestic credit provided by financial sector	Common law	−1.38	325	5.182	325	1.333	325	0.77	325	−27.033	325	−2.647	325
		(3.124)		(4.264)		(1.438)		(0.647)		(16.68)		(5.728)	
	Civil law	0.793		−1.058		1.771		−0.057		−2.717		−2.026	
		(0.867)		(1.726)		(1.092)		(0.273)		(19.053)		(2.015)	
Domestic credit to private sector	Common law	0.559	325	2.155	325	−0.889	325	0.35	325	−8.07	325	−3.9	325
		(2.141)		(4.47)		(1.798)		(0.591)		(14.14)		(3.767)	
	Civil law	0.986		−0.525		1.051		0.062		−3.528		−2.077	
		(0.733)		(1.401)		(0.948)		(0.156)		(17.65)		(1.757)	
Foreign direct investment	Common law	−0.155	520	0.745	520	0.187	520	0.112	520	6.061*	520	−0.191	520
		(0.829)		(1.07)		(0.289)		(0.186)		(3.376)		(1.097)	
	Civil law	0.288		−0.324		−0.312		0.095		−2.87		1.393	
		(0.257)		(0.646)		(0.294)		(0.068)		(3.602)		(1.204)	

Trade	Common law	−3.798	501	−1.333	501	−0.267	501	−0.659	501	26.603	501	12.836	501
		(7.302)		(3.315)		(2.286)		(1.129)		(30.431)		(13.423)	
	Civil law	−0.463		0.518		0.112		0.116		7.503		0.315	
		(1.051)		(1.328)		(0.875)		(0.311)		(9.813)		(1.881)	
Private gross fixed capital formation	Common law	1.653	256	1.458	256	0.49	256	0.281	256	−14.57*	256	−2.422	256
		(1.839)		(1.5)		(0.542)		(0.198)		(8.652)		(1.547)	
	Civil law	−0.04		−0.766		−0.523		0.056		−5.025		−0.459	
		(0.284)		(0.636)		(0.393)		(0.154)		(5.672)		(0.909)	
New business density	Common law	−0.299	354	0.491	354	−0.055	354	0.113	354	0.387	354	0.436	354
		(0.317)		(1.324)		(0.109)		(0.15)		(4.72)		(1.2)	
	Civil law	0.15		0.15		−0.06		0.01		0.258		−0.096	
		(0.105)		(0.149)		(0.134)		(0.023)		(1.492)		(0.269)	
Unemployment rate	Common law	−0.304	485	−0.244	485	−0.266**	485	−0.173**	485	1.964	485	0.335	485
		(0.184)		(0.737)		(0.129)		(0.082)		(2.235)		(0.465)	
	Civil law	−0.119		0.001		−0.099		−0.05		1.717		−0.076	
		(0.082)		(0.292)		(0.172)		(0.05)		(3.782)		(0.331)	
Income GINI index	Common law	−0.295	276	0.638	276	0.036	276	0.382	276	2.454	276	−2.149**	276
		(0.267)		(0.949)		(0.347)		(0.245)		(4.57)		(0.931)	
	Civil law	−0.541**		−0.12		−0.037		0.018		0.082		−0.14	
		(0.224)		(0.402)		(0.224)		(0.048)		(2.157)		(0.581)	
GDP pc growth	Common law	0.096	521	0.468	521	−0.003	521	0.213	521	−1.069	521	−0.457	521
		(0.416)		(0.708)		(0.472)		(0.137)		(2.247)		(0.48)	
	Civil law	0.017		−0.855		−0.794***		0.015		−0.702		1.371***	
		(0.23)		(0.565)		(0.228)		(0.052)		(1.747)		(0.519)	

(continued)

Table A.15 (continued)

		Registering a property		Construction permits		Paying taxes		Time to export		Time to import	
		Coeff/SE	Obs	Coeff/SE	Obs	Coeff/SE	Obs	Coeff/SE	Obs	Coeff/SE	Obs
		(7)		(8)		(9)		(10)		(11)	
Stock market capitalization	Common law	−2.843	266	−72.292	266	−8.433	266	−104.446	266	−86.2	266
		(6.878)		(55.14)		(15.369)		(70.96)		(53.687)	
	Civil law	3.071		3.126		6.119		−19.738		−15.984	
		(3.919)		(11.186)		(12.259)		(23.178)		(14.578)	
Stocks traded	Common law	−0.343	243	69.798	243	−7.092	243	−5.011	243	−10.822	243
		(11.91)		(48.562)		(29.218)		(81.162)		(44.89)	
	Civil law	−6.36		−8.006		−13.869		−41.065		−33.293**	
		(5.021)		(9.291)		(13.942)		(29.539)		(16.669)	
Domestic credit to private sector by banks	Common law	2.746	325	−9.908*	325	1.521	323	−7.385	325	−3.29	325
		(3.245)		(5.643)		(7.646)		(12.608)		(7.719)	
	Civil law	−0.563		−2.358		−0.366		−19.178		−11.272	
		(1.83)		(4.082)		(3.754)		(14.775)		(7.437)	
Domestic credit provided by financial sector	Common law	0.219	325	−10.75	325	−7.802	323	−7.264	325	−1.077	325
		(2.836)		(7.833)		(11.708)		(15.778)		(9.643)	
	Civil law	0.161		−5.227		−8.225*		−13.564		−5.192	
		(1.806)		(4.006)		(4.632)		(15.411)		(8.478)	
Domestic credit to private sector	Common law	1.594	325	−8.547	325	1.255	323	−10.489	325	−4.523	325
		(3.689)		(5.767)		(7.463)		(13.931)		(8.43)	
	Civil law	−0.362		−2.828		−2.26		−19.364		−11.746	
		(1.845)		(3.999)		(3.724)		(14.804)		(7.464)	
Foreign direct investment	Common law	−0.519	520	−3.143	520	−6.136**	518	0.771	520	1.1	520
		(1.123)		(3.18)		(2.689)		(4.782)		(3.45)	
	Civil law	1.699		−0.211		2.838		0.855		0.937	
		(1.278)		(2.081)		(1.757)		(2.569)		(2.22)	

Trade	Common law	1.253	501	30.526	501	−11.43	499	17.614	501	6.46	501
		(5.578)		(30.694)		(16.509)		(19.36)		(8.746)	
	Civil law	−1.889		−3.543		−0.301		3.313		−1.091	
		(1.798)		(3.444)		(5.054)		(6.791)		(6.035)	
Private gross fixed capital formation	Common law	−2.844	256	0.932	256	2.805	256	−1.665	256	−0.607	256
		(1.734)		(4.224)		(3.31)		(4.964)		(3.774)	
	Civil law	−0.124		−0.618		5.361**		3.178		3.422	
		(1.067)		(2.104)		(2.044)		(3.205)		(2.448)	
New business density	Common law	−0.004	354	−3.287**	354	1.115	352	−3.779	354	−3.045*	354
		(0.338)		(1.65)		(1.205)		(2.505)		(1.816)	
	Civil law	−0.13		−0.234		0.685		−0.149		−0.093	
		(0.251)		(0.501)		(0.722)		(1.805)		(1.206)	
Unemployment rate	Common law	−0.231	485	1.232*	485	−0.46	483	4.205***	485	2.387**	485
		(0.687)		(0.655)		(1.035)		(1.571)		(1.004)	
	Civil law	−0.519		0.723		−0.684		2.021*		1.243	
		(0.417)		(0.938)		(0.894)		(1.193)		(0.813)	
Income GINI index	Common law	−2.351	276	1.625	276	−1.712	275	2.815	276	3.166	276
		(2.207)		(1.492)		(1.112)		(2.52)		(1.944)	
	Civil law	−0.088		0.867		−0.986		1.404		2.216	
		(0.399)		(1.249)		(1.287)		(1.801)		(1.657)	
GDP pc growth	Common law	0.253	521	−0.279	521	0.205	519	−2.434	521	−0.999	521
		(0.869)		(3.685)		(1.854)		(2.309)		(1.914)	
	Civil law	1.401**		0.995		4.516**		2.685*		1.879	
		(0.608)		(0.921)		(1.757)		(1.384)		(1.26)	

Notes: Panel specification with averaged annual data over 3-year periods (2006–2014). Clustered standard errors in parentheses. The regressions include country and period dummies, and a constant term. All these variables are omitted for space considerations

*, ** and *** denote statistical significance at the 10, 5 and 1% levels, respectively

Table A.16 The effect of legal rules on financial and economic outcomes: differentiation by legal traditions. Annual data

		Creditor rights		Investor protection		Credit information		Recovery rate		Contract enforc.		Starting a business	
		Coeff/SE	Obs	Coeff/SE	Obs	Coeff/SE	Obs	Coeff/SE	Obs	Coeff/SE	Obs	Coeff/SE	Obs
		(1)		(2)		(3)		(4)		(5)		(6)	
Stock market capitalization	Common law	0.073	727	8.65	727	3.368	727	0.547	727	111.363	727	−22.832	727
		(4.393)		(8.453)		(2.081)		(0.934)		(82.788)		(15.645)	
	Civil law	0.871		−1.77		−0.061		0.427		−11.439		0.044	
		(1.773)		(3.838)		(1.492)		(0.295)		(10.984)		(2.861)	
Stocks traded	Common law	1.985	641	17.641***	641	2.446	641	−1.871	641	−139.883*	641	14.815	641
		(6.324)		(5.698)		(2.705)		(2.249)		(81.543)		(20.489)	
	Civil law	4.877*		7.744**		3.609**		0.961***		12.512		−6.041	
		(2.456)		(3.393)		(1.621)		(0.303)		(15.802)		(3.705)	
Domestic credit to private sector by banks	Common law	−0.175	959	0.325	959	−0.657	959	0.273	959	−7.309	959	−1.823	959
		(1.79)		(1.874)		(0.911)		(0.392)		(8.285)		(2.876)	
	Civil law	0.97		−0.134		0.926		0.091		−4.464		−2.224	
		(0.626)		(1.098)		(0.602)		(0.088)		(12.656)		(1.419)	
Domestic credit provided by financial sector	Common law	−1.284	959	4.974	959	0.725	959	0.65	959	−20.175*	959	−2.805	959
		(2.366)		(3.089)		(0.767)		(0.433)		(10.68)		(3.816)	
	Civil law	0.737		−0.687		1.251*		0.032		−3.875		−2.156	
		(0.722)		(1.28)		(0.664)		(0.169)		(14.008)		(1.59)	
Domestic credit to private sector	Common law	0.366	959	1.755	959	−0.622	959	0.32	959	−6.351	959	−3.918	959
		(1.582)		(3.271)		(0.921)		(0.39)		(8.327)		(2.603)	
	Civil law	0.917		−0.418		0.883		0.097		−3.968		−2.18	
		(0.636)		(1.139)		(0.603)		(0.09)		(12.622)		(1.451)	

Foreign direct investment	Common law	−0.313	1534	0.774	1534	0.178	1534	0.011	1534	5.507**	1534	−0.218	1534
		(0.677)		(1.043)		(0.179)		(0.113)		(2.416)		(0.791)	
	Civil law	0.254		−0.411		−0.088		0.051		−1.92		1.033	
		(0.208)		(0.483)		(0.175)		(0.039)		(2.587)		(0.87)	
Trade	Common law	−2.777	1465	−3.275	1465	−0.414	1465	−0.602	1465	23.956	1465	10.469	1465
		(5.063)		(3.541)		(1.339)		(0.653)		(20.903)		(9.841)	
	Civil law	−0.494		0.186		0.118		0.065		8.749		0.016	
		(0.824)		(0.931)		(0.564)		(0.201)		(7.693)		(1.353)	
Private gross fixed capital formation	Common law	1.837	729	2.674	729	0.447	729	0.128	729	−15.328**	729	−2.365*	729
		(1.662)		(1.976)		(0.333)		(0.133)		(6.373)		(1.254)	
	Civil law	0		−0.709		−0.271		0.066		−4.021		−0.658	
		(0.217)		(0.493)		(0.236)		(0.058)		(4.456)		(0.637)	
New business density	Common law	−0.089	851	0.522	851	−0.005	851	0.078	851	0.407	851	0.442	851
		(0.287)		(1.051)		(0.067)		(0.082)		(3.574)		(1.044)	
	Civil law	0.126		0.155		0.022		0.01		0.075		−0.135	
		(0.076)		(0.125)		(0.111)		(0.014)		(1.295)		(0.206)	
Unemployment rate	Common law	−0.14	1428	−0.223	1428	−0.178**	1428	−0.089**	1428	0.937	1428	0.338	1428
		(0.103)		(0.517)		(0.076)		(0.043)		(1.402)		(0.368)	
	Civil law	−0.111*		0.001		−0.13		−0.028		1.524		0.005	
		(0.063)		(0.222)		(0.118)		(0.026)		(2.66)		(0.229)	
Income GINI index	Common law	−1.034**	506	0.314	506	0.133	506	0.24	506	5.19	506	−2.947**	506
		(0.434)		(0.656)		(0.287)		(0.177)		(3.627)		(1.163)	
	Civil law	−0.436**		−0.195		0.015		−0.003		0.596		−0.271	
		(0.214)		(0.398)		(0.153)		(0.042)		(1.607)		(0.365)	

(continued)

Table A.16 (continued)

		Registering a property		Construction permits		Paying taxes		Time to export		Time to import	
		Coeff/SE	Obs	Coeff/SE	Obs	Coeff/SE	Obs	Coeff/SE	Obs	Coeff/SE	Obs
		(7)		(8)		(9)		(10)		(11)	
Stock market capitalization	Common law	−3.542	727	−54.002	727	−4.084	727	−71.044*	727	−60.501**	727
		(3.812)		(37.269)		(12.093)		(39.234)		(28.37)	
	Civil law	1.62		3.42		4.938		−14.588		−14.162	
		(2.435)		(9.243)		(10.007)		(12.594)		(8.788)	
Stocks traded	Common law	−1.677	641	67.589*	641	−6.047	641	−89.958**	641	−92.643*	641
		(7.871)		(34.783)		(23.055)		(43.481)		(52.619)	
	Civil law	−6.204		−7.818		−9.58		−35.953**		−31.631**	
		(3.816)		(7.079)		(12.553)		(17.586)		(14.006)	
Domestic credit to private sector by banks	Common law	2.32	959	−7.982**	959	0.357	952	−4.769	959	−2.011	959
		(2.293)		(3.945)		(5.274)		(7.137)		(4.927)	
	Civil law	−0.567		−2.449		−0.593		−15.09		−9.588*	
		(1.458)		(3.12)		(3.062)		(9.136)		(4.944)	
Domestic credit provided by financial sector	Common law	0.229	959	−10.793**	959	−8.101	952	−7.658	959	−2.162	959
		(2.068)		(5.207)		(8.264)		(9.059)		(5.869)	
	Civil law	−0.019		−6.413**		−7.312*		−11.705		−5.72	
		(1.406)		(2.846)		(3.964)		(9.914)		(5.288)	
Domestic credit to private sector	Common law	1.448	959	−6.425	959	0.057	952	−7.766	959	−3.344	959
		(2.567)		(4.075)		(5.2)		(7.963)		(5.405)	
	Civil law	−0.409		−2.683		−2.263		−15.29*		−9.999**	
		(1.467)		(3.056)		(3.025)		(9.183)		(4.996)	
Foreign direct investment	Common law	−0.93	1534	−2.504	1534	−5.135**	1527	−1.583	1534	−0.196	1534
		(0.87)		(2.155)		(2.169)		(3.44)		(2.254)	
	Civil law	1.411		0.148		2.736*		0.841		0.943	
		(0.871)		(1.56)		(1.613)		(1.612)		(1.424)	

Trade	Common law	0.311	1465	21.455	1465	−7.919	1458	11.003	1465	4.242	1465
		(4.846)		(22.293)		(12.441)		(11.12)		(5.58)	
	Civil law	−1.716		−3.713		0.381		1.69		−0.32	
		(1.203)		(2.662)		(3.828)		(4.422)		(3.847)	
Private gross fixed capital formation	Common law	−0.884	729	1.548	729	3.413	729	−0.824	729	−0.824	729
		(0.96)		(2.669)		(2.671)		(2.173)		(1.884)	
	Civil law	−0.163		−0.317		4.243***		1.681		2.293	
		(0.767)		(1.399)		(1.534)		(1.788)		(1.442)	
New business density	Common law	0.018	851	−3.027**	851	1.482	847	−2.631*	851	−2.078**	851
		(0.362)		(1.393)		(1.119)		(1.496)		(1.032)	
	Civil law	−0.192		−0.228		0.631		−0.311		−0.117	
		(0.239)		(0.43)		(0.672)		(1.15)		(0.809)	
Unemployment rate	Common law	−0.115	1428	1.067**	1428	−0.358	1421	2.044***	1428	1.354***	1428
		(0.378)		(0.43)		(0.815)		(0.75)		(0.519)	
	Civil law	−0.408		0.408		−0.421		1.382*		0.997	
		(0.304)		(0.684)		(0.72)		(0.817)		(0.656)	
Income GINI index	Common law	−0.521	506	2.693*	506	−2.268***	505	1.396	506	1.625	506
		(1.955)		(1.586)		(0.797)		(1.194)		(1.134)	
	Civil law	−0.022		0.566		−0.725		0.54		1.263	
		(0.332)		(1.199)		(1.249)		(1.211)		(1.112)	

Notes: Panel of annual data over the period 2006–2014. Clustered standard errors in parentheses. The regressions include lag GDP growth, country and period dummies, and a constant term. All these variables are omitted for space considerations

*, ** and *** denote statistical significance at the 10, 5 and 1% levels, respectively

Table A.17 The effect of legal rules on financial and economic outcomes: differentiation by legal traditions. Annual data, without additional control

		Creditor rights		Investor protection		Credit information		Recovery rate		Contract enforc.		Starting a business	
		Coeff/SE	Obs	Coeff/SE	Obs	Coeff/SE	Obs	Coeff/SE	Obs	Coeff/SE	Obs	Coeff/SE	Obs
		(1)		(2)		(3)		(4)		(5)		(6)	
Stock market capitalization	Common law	0.172	727	8.644	727	3.377	727	0.568	727	111.058	727	−22.85	727
		(4.43)		(8.528)		(2.085)		(0.91)		(83.112)		(15.511)	
	Civil law	0.913		−1.815		−0.089		0.431		−12.207		0.05	
		(1.798)		(3.855)		(1.439)		(0.303)		(11.471)		(2.855)	
Stocks traded	Common law	2.047	641	17.594***	641	2.465	641	−1.801	641	−139.642*	641	14.794	641
		(6.338)		(5.793)		(2.736)		(2.249)		(81.715)		(20.479)	
	Civil law	4.938**		7.679**		3.546**		0.977***		11.036		−5.963	
		(2.451)		(3.442)		(1.604)		(0.309)		(16.156)		(3.663)	
Domestic credit to private sector by banks	Common law	−0.18	967	0.302	967	−0.673	967	0.27	967	−7.268	967	−1.784	967
		(1.783)		(1.878)		(0.904)		(0.393)		(8.38)		(2.9)	
	Civil law	0.955		−0.16		0.894		0.089		−3.368		−2.177	
		(0.618)		(1.119)		(0.579)		(0.088)		(11.904)		(1.368)	
Domestic credit provided by financial sector	Common law	−1.379	967	4.817	967	0.741	967	0.618	967	−19.39*	967	−2.619	967
		(2.382)		(3.086)		(0.766)		(0.431)		(10.84)		(3.812)	
	Civil law	0.748		−0.614		1.29**		0.029		−3.056		−2.29	
		(0.735)		(1.307)		(0.641)		(0.173)		(13.321)		(1.543)	
Domestic credit to private sector	Common law	0.365	967	1.736	967	−0.638	967	0.319	967	−6.346	967	−3.882	967
		(1.578)		(3.273)		(0.914)		(0.39)		(8.425)		(2.627)	
	Civil law	0.903		−0.443		0.851		0.095		−2.95		−2.134	
		(0.628)		(1.158)		(0.581)		(0.09)		(11.876)		(1.403)	
Foreign direct investment	Common law	−0.294	1542	0.798	1542	0.18	1542	0.022	1542	5.43**	1542	−0.241	1542
		(0.682)		(1.055)		(0.179)		(0.113)		(2.427)		(0.798)	
	Civil law	0.261		−0.415		−0.094		0.052		−2.104		1.04	
		(0.208)		(0.48)		(0.17)		(0.039)		(2.555)		(0.866)	

Trade	Common law	−2.71	1473	−3.213	1473	−0.413	1473	−0.564	1473	23.748	1473	10.366	1473
		(5.063)		(3.541)		(1.335)		(0.653)		(20.96)		(9.818)	
	Civil law	−0.46		0.188		0.103		0.071		7.84		0.044	
		(0.828)		(0.953)		(0.566)		(0.2)		(7.629)		(1.356)	
Private gross fixed capital formation	Common law	1.986	729	2.692	729	0.382	729	0.191	729	−15.498**	729	−2.563**	729
		(1.712)		(1.984)		(0.314)		(0.128)		(6.179)		(1.281)	
	Civil law	−0.02		−0.741		−0.34		0.062		−4.127		−0.598	
		(0.225)		(0.495)		(0.235)		(0.059)		(4.524)		(0.623)	
New business density	Common law	−0.063	854	0.516	854	−0.013	854	0.084	854	0.352	854	0.429	854
		(0.289)		(1.058)		(0.068)		(0.084)		(3.581)		(1.048)	
	Civil law	0.133*		0.151		0.004		0.01		0.07		−0.115	
		(0.076)		(0.123)		(0.108)		(0.014)		(1.297)		(0.199)	
Unemployment rate	Common law	−0.204*	1445	−0.258	1445	−0.173**	1445	−0.115***	1445	1.122	1445	0.375	1445
		(0.113)		(0.53)		(0.078)		(0.044)		(1.397)		(0.382)	
	Civil law	−0.115*		0.044		−0.095		−0.031		1.447		−0.069	
		(0.064)		(0.222)		(0.118)		(0.027)		(2.629)		(0.233)	
Income GINI index	Common law	−1.054**	507	0.312	507	0.13	507	0.231	507	5.035	507	−2.895**	507
		(0.414)		(0.664)		(0.289)		(0.174)		(3.496)		(1.122)	
	Civil law	−0.438**		−0.197		0.021		−0.004		0.645		−0.282	
		(0.214)		(0.401)		(0.15)		(0.042)		(1.584)		(0.364)	
GDP pc growth	Common law	0.244	1546	0.301	1546	−0.046	1546	0.151*	1546	−2.884	1546	−0.267	1546
		(0.264)		(0.467)		(0.271)		(0.085)		(1.943)		(0.425)	
	Civil law	−0.071		−0.72*		−0.526***		0.023		0.394		1.203***	
		(0.194)		(0.395)		(0.162)		(0.029)		(1.19)		(0.418)	

(continued)

Table A.17 (continued)

		Registering a property		Construction permits		Paying taxes		Time to export		Time to import	
		Coeff/SE	Obs	Coeff/SE	Obs	Coeff/SE	Obs	Coeff/SE	Obs	Coeff/SE	Obs
		(7)		(8)		(9)		(10)		(11)	
Stock market capitalization	Common law	−3.601	727	−54.021	727	−4.302	727	−71.138*	727	−60.557**	727
		(3.85)		(37.179)		(12.222)		(38.985)		(28.211)	
	Civil law	1.661		3.439		5.085		−14.374		−14.062	
		(2.379)		(9.257)		(9.814)		(12.391)		(8.779)	
Stocks traded	Common law	−1.854	641	67.532*	641	−6.494	641	−89.934**	641	−92.537*	641
		(7.916)		(34.855)		(23.078)		(43.285)		(52.41)	
	Civil law	−6.122		−7.843		−9.175		−35.689**		−31.497**	
		(3.797)		(7.057)		(12.513)		(17.57)		(13.96)	
Domestic credit to private sector by banks	Common law	2.319	967	−7.922*	967	0.447	960	−4.679	967	−1.861	967
		(2.294)		(4.048)		(5.31)		(7.164)		(4.872)	
	Civil law	−0.545		−2.53		−0.531		−14.887*		−9.438*	
		(1.389)		(3.085)		(2.896)		(8.96)		(4.822)	
Domestic credit provided by financial sector	Common law	0.343	967	−10.008*	967	−7.497	960	−7.305	967	−2.084	967
		(2.097)		(5.333)		(8.263)		(9.028)		(5.773)	
	Civil law	−0.246		−6.373**		−7.872**		−11.699		−5.744	
		(1.355)		(2.835)		(3.681)		(9.73)		(5.236)	
Domestic credit to private sector	Common law	1.445	967	−6.406	967	0.087	960	−7.688	967	−3.194	967
		(2.562)		(4.16)		(5.241)		(7.994)		(5.352)	
	Civil law	−0.384		−2.752		−2.136		−15.066*		−9.826**	
		(1.4)		(3.022)		(2.851)		(9.007)		(4.873)	
Foreign direct investment	Common law	−0.942	1542	−2.519	1542	−5.177**	1535	−1.6	1542	−0.186	1542
		(0.874)		(2.161)		(2.192)		(3.45)		(2.242)	
	Civil law	1.443*		0.191		2.743*		0.988		1.035	
		(0.867)		(1.55)		(1.565)		(1.578)		(1.409)	

Trade	Common law	0.258	1473	21.401	1473	−8.017	1466	11.034	1473	4.337	1473
		(4.844)		(22.266)		(12.43)		(11.1)		(5.569)	
	Civil law	−1.552		−3.443		0.273		2.455		0.179	
		(1.212)		(2.644)		(3.895)		(4.453)		(3.879)	
Private gross fixed capital formation	Common law	−0.94	729	1.76	729	2.832	729	−0.626	729	−0.435	729
		(1.05)		(3.1)		(2.849)		(2.329)		(1.968)	
	Civil law	−0.01		−0.265		4.665***		2.137		2.494	
		(0.77)		(1.436)		(1.507)		(1.926)		(1.534)	
New business density	Common law	−0.005	854	−3.061**	854	1.377	850	−2.67*	854	−2.098**	854
		(0.361)		(1.375)		(1.146)		(1.478)		(1.015)	
	Civil law	−0.168		−0.226		0.74		−0.261		−0.086	
		(0.234)		(0.425)		(0.655)		(1.144)		(0.81)	
Unemployment rate	Common law	−0.067	1445	1.06**	1445	−0.196	1438	2.14***	1445	1.367***	1445
		(0.371)		(0.446)		(0.859)		(0.759)		(0.518)	
	Civil law	−0.476		0.429		−0.693		1.232		0.928	
		(0.29)		(0.603)		(0.69)		(0.776)		(0.637)	
Income GINI index	Common law	−0.425	507	2.76*	507	−2.237***	506	1.43	507	1.659	507
		(1.882)		(1.545)		(0.785)		(1.182)		(1.116)	
	Civil law	−0.028		0.569		−0.735		0.531		1.267	
		(0.332)		(1.207)		(1.245)		(1.221)		(1.115)	
GDP pc growth	Common law	−0.338	1546	−0.946	1546	0.656	1539	−1.831	1546	−0.982	1546
		(0.552)		(2.469)		(1.401)		(1.583)		(1.182)	
	Civil law	0.874**		0.662		3.87***		1.768**		1.577*	
		(0.411)		(0.604)		(1.304)		(0.835)		(0.876)	

Notes: Panel of annual data over the period 2006–2014. Clustered standard errors in parentheses. The regressions include country and period dummies, and a constant term. All these variables are omitted for space considerations

*, ** and *** denote statistical significance at the 10, 5 and 1% levels, respectively

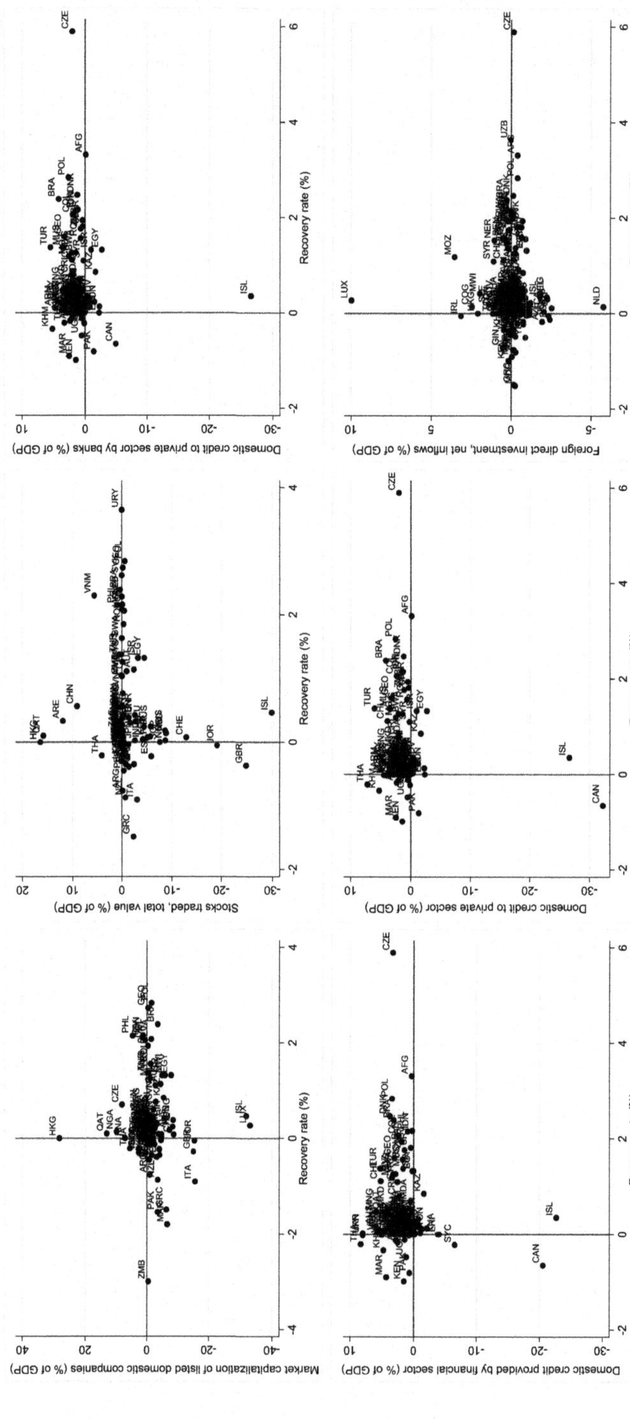

Fig. A.1 Change in recovery rate against change in financial and economic outcomes

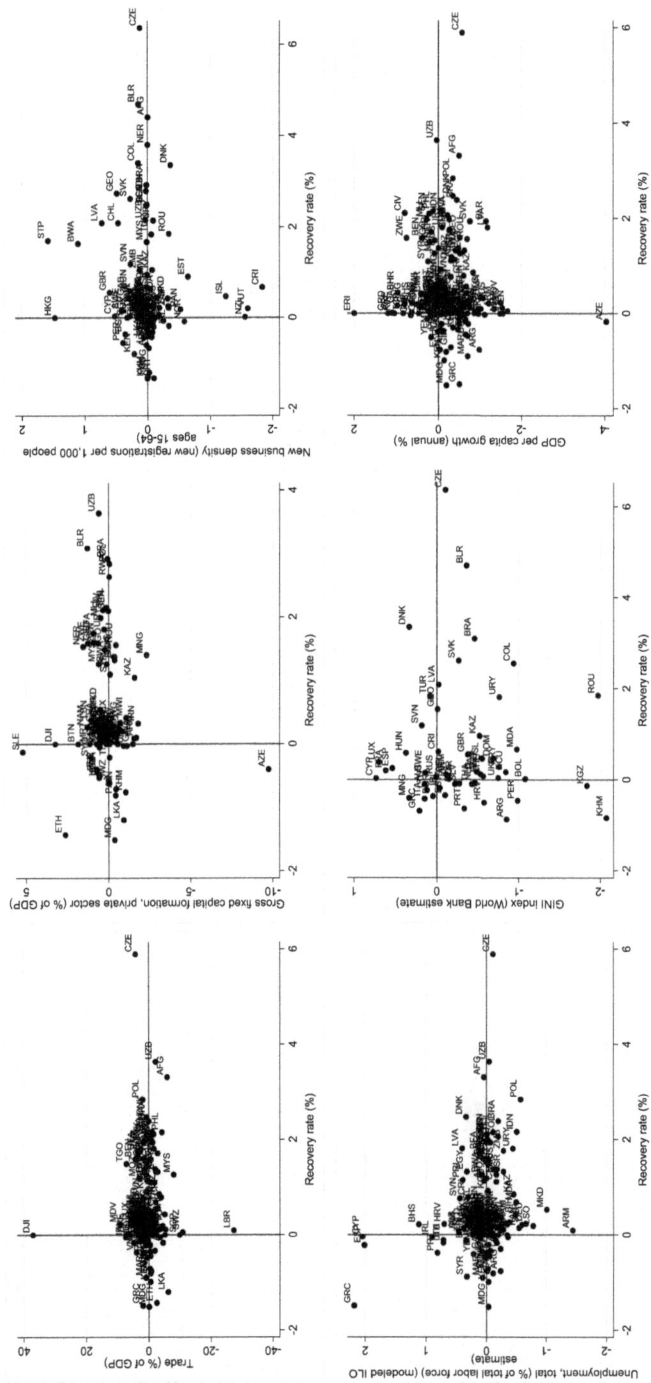

Fig. A.1 (continued)

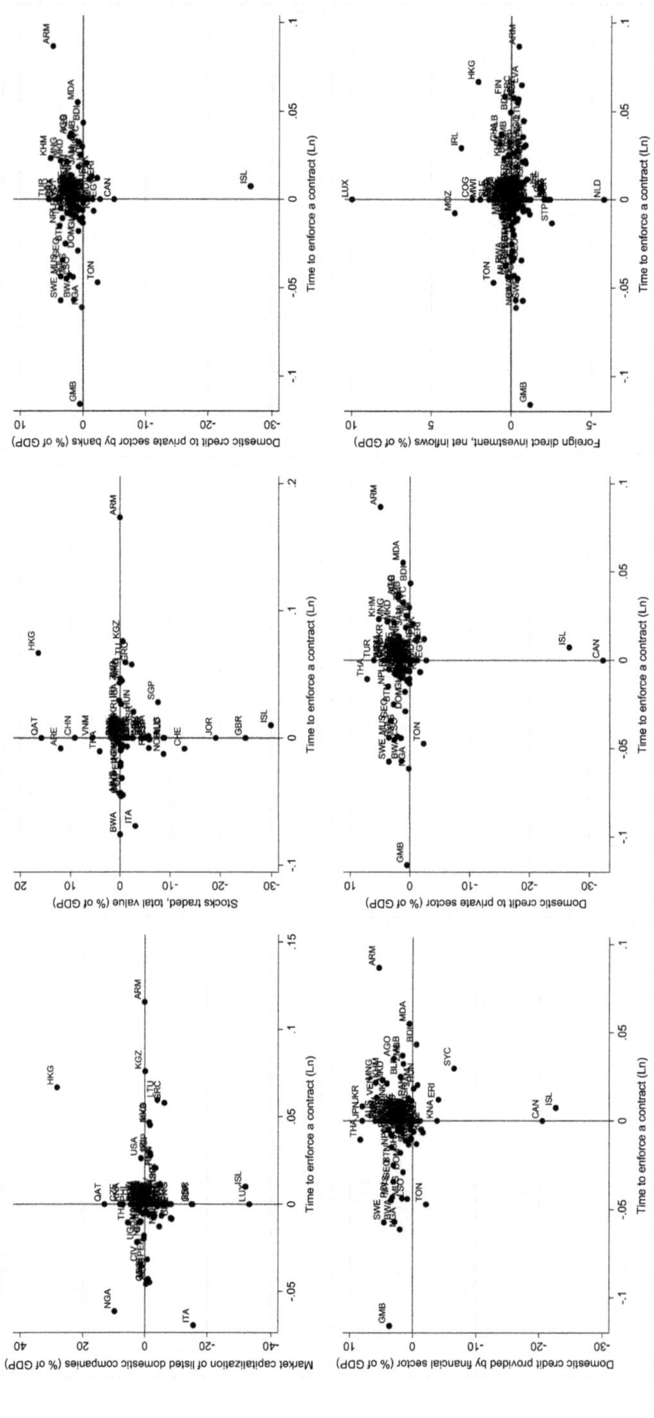

Fig. A.2 Change in contract enforcement against change in financial and economic outcomes

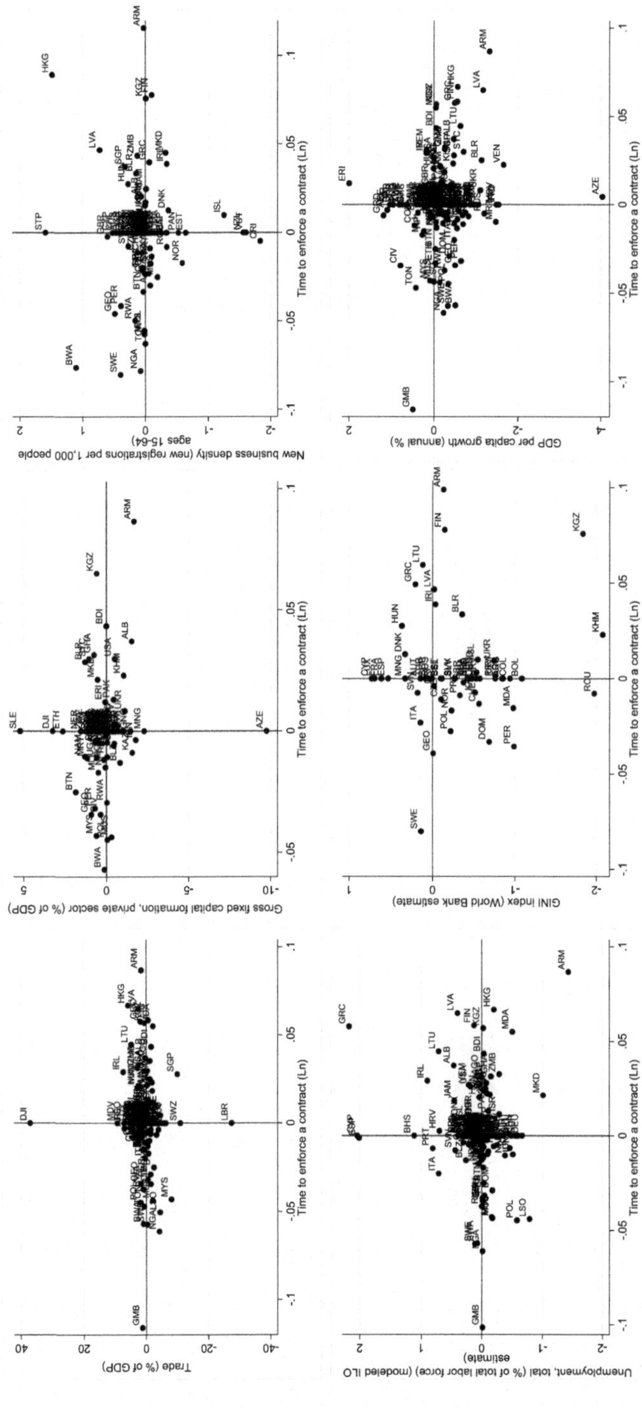

Fig. A.2 (continued)

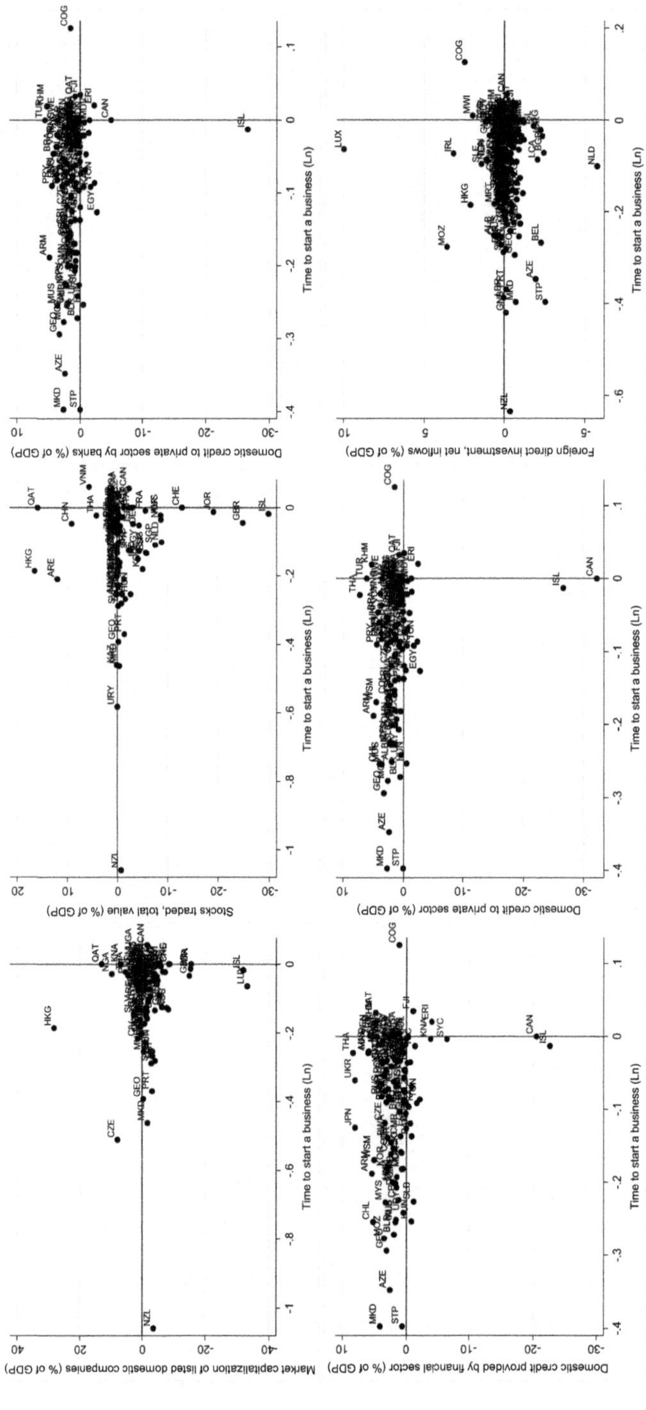

Fig. A.3 Change in starting a business against change in financial and economic outcomes

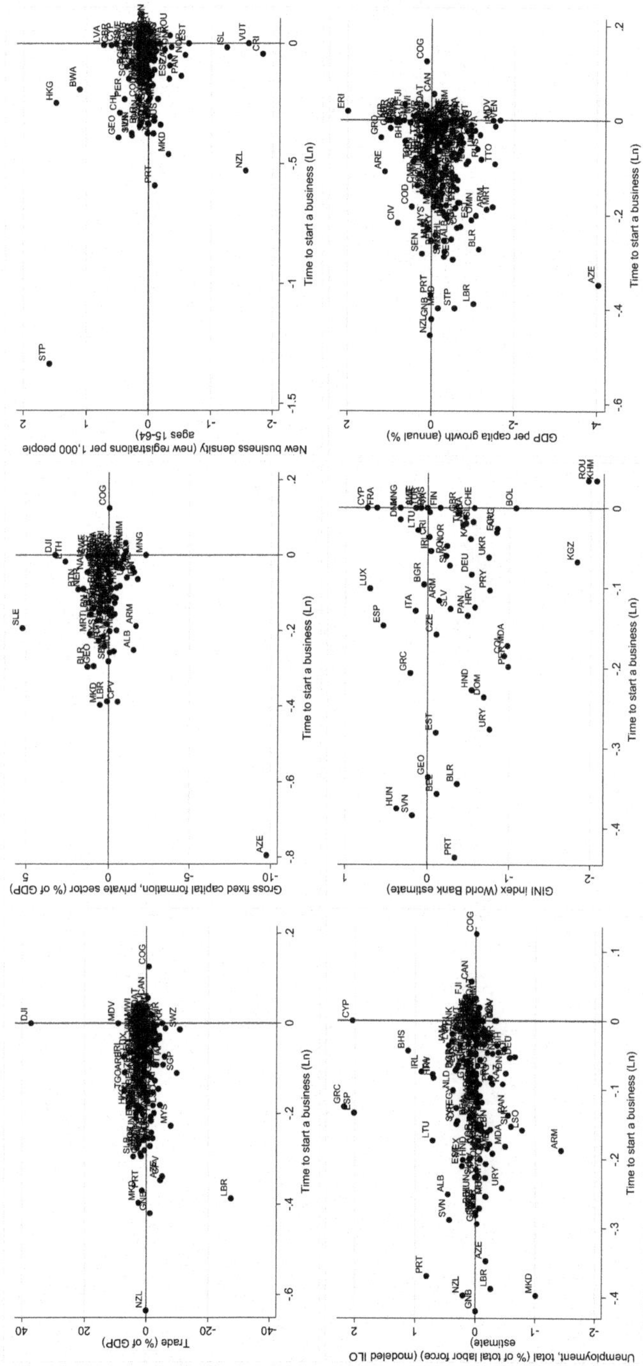

Fig. A.3 (continued)

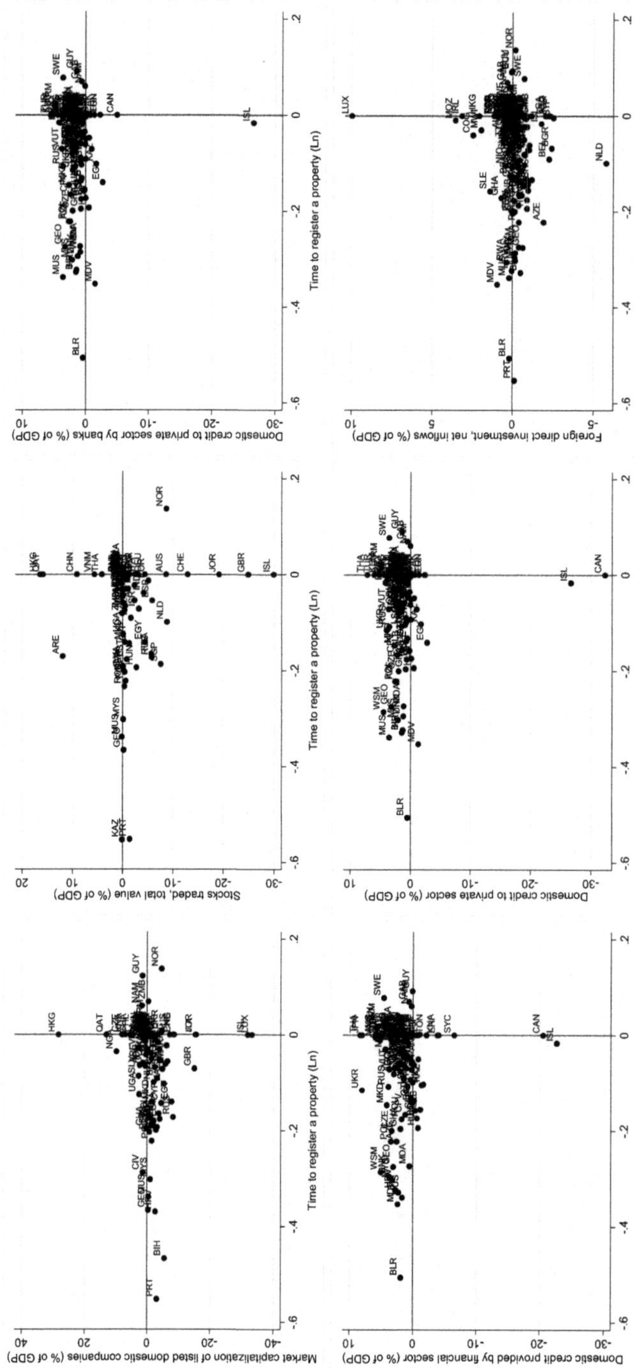

Fig. A.4 Change in registering a property against change in financial and economic outcomes

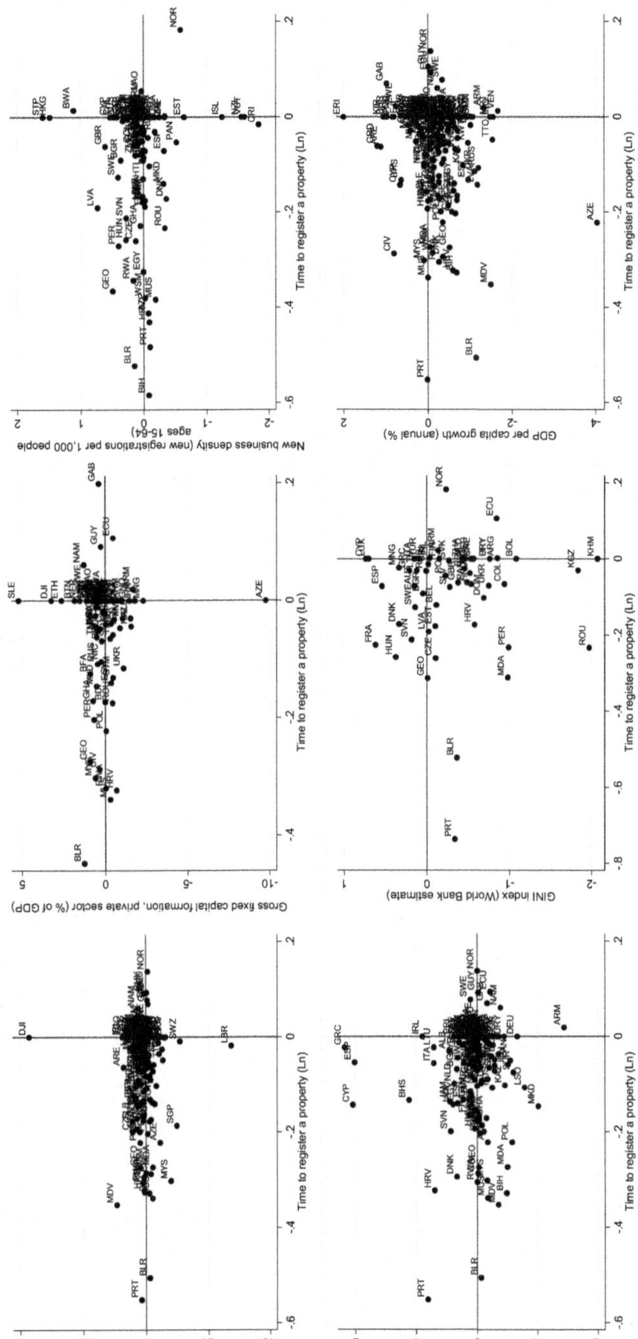

Fig. A.4 (continued)

References

Acemoglu D, Johnson S (2005) Unbundling institutions. J Polit Econ 113(5):949–995
Aghion P, Fally T, Scarpetta S (2007) Credit constraints as a barrier to the entry and post-entry growth of firms. Econ Policy 22(52):731–779
Alesina A, Baqir R, Easterly W (1999) Public goods and ethnic divisions. Q J Econ 114:1243–1284
Alesina A, Devleeschauwer A, Easterly W, Kurlat S, Wacziarg R (2003) Fractionalization. J Econ Growth 8:155–194
Araujo AP, Ferreira RV, Funchal B (2012) The Brazilian bankruptcy law experience. J Corp Finan 18(4):994–1004
Arellano M, Bond S (1991) Some tests of specification for panel data: Monte Carlo evidence and an application to employment equations. Rev Econ Stud 58(2):277–297
Arellano M, Bover O (1995) Another look at the instrumental variable estimation of error-components models. J Econ 68(1):29–51
Armour J, Deakin S, Lele P, Siems M (2009a) How legal norms evolve: evidence from a cross-country comparison of shareholder, creditor and worker protection. Am J Comparative Law 57:579–629
Armour J, Deakin S, Sarkar P, Siems M, Singh A (2009b) Shareholder protection and stock market development: an empirical test of the legal origins hypothesis. J Empir Leg Stud 6(2):343–380
Armour J, Deakin S, Mollica V, Siems M (2009c) Law and financial development: what we are learning from time-series evidence. Brigham Young Univ Law Rev 6:1435–1500
Axworthy CS (1976) Controlling the abuse of small claims courts. McGill Law J 22:480–495
Aytekin I, Miles M, Esen S (2013) Corporate governance: a comparative study of practices in Turkey and Canada. IUP J Corp Gov 12(2):7–27
Ayyagari M, Juarros PF, Martinez Peria MS, Singh S (2016) Access to finance and job growth: firm-level evidence across developing countries. Policy research working paper, no. WPS 7604. World Bank Group, Washington, DC
Azar ZR (2008) Bankruptcy policy: a review and critique of bankruptcy statutes and practices in fifty countries worldwide. Cardozo J Int Comp Law 16(2):279–378
Bae K-H, Goyal VK (2009) Creditor rights, enforcement, and bank loans. J Financ 64(2):823–860
Balas A, La Porta R, Lopez-de-Silanes F, Shleifer A (2009) The divergence of legal procedures. Am Econ J Econ Pol 1(2):138–162
Baliamoune-Lutz M, Garello P (2014) Tax structure and entrepreneurship. Small Bus Econ 42 (1):165–190
Ball GG, Kesan JP (2010) Judges, courts and economic development: the impact of judicial human capital on the efficiency and accuracy of the court system. Paper presented at the 15th Annual

D. Oto-Peralías, D. Romero-Ávila, *Legal Traditions, Legal Reforms and Economic Performance*, Contributions to Economics, DOI 10.1007/978-3-319-67041-6

Conference of the International Society for New Institutional Economics, Stanford University, Stanford, CA, June 16–18. http://papers.isnie.org/paper/716.html

Beck T, Levine R (2005) Legal institutions and financial development. In: Ménard C, Shirley MM (eds) Handbook of new institutional economics. Springer, Netherlands, pp 251–278

Beck T, Demirgüç-Kunt A, Levine R (2003) Law and finance: why does legal origin matter? J Comp Econ 31:653–675

Beck T, Lin C, Ma Y (2014) Why do firms evade taxes? The role of information sharing and financial sector outreach. J Financ 69(2):763–817

Becker J, Fuest C, Riedel N (2012) Corporate tax effects on the quality and quantity of FDI. Eur Econ Rev 56(8):1495–1511

Belitski M, Chowdhury F, Desai S (2016) Taxes, corruption, and entry. Small Bus Econ 47 (1):201–216

Belsley T (2015) Law, regulation, and the business climate: the nature and influence of the World Bank Doing Business Project. J Econ Perspect 29(3):99–120

Berglöf E, Pajuste A (2005) What do firms disclose and why? Enforcing corporate governance and transparency in Central and Eastern Europe. Oxf Rev Econ Policy 21(2):178–197

Berkowitz D, Pistor K, Richard J-F (2003a) The transplant effect. Am J Comp Law 51:163–203

Berkowitz D, Pistor K, Richard J-F (2003b) Economic development, legality, and the transplant effect. Eur Econ Rev 47:165–195

Berkowitz D, Lin C, Ma Y (2015) Do property rights matter? Evidence from a property law enactment. J Financ Econ 116(3):583–593

Bertolini L (2006) How to improve regulatory transparency: emerging lessons from an international assessment. Open Knowledge Note 11. World Bank Group, Washington, DC

Bertrand M, Duflo E, Mullainathan S (2004) How much should we trust differences-in-differences estimates? Q J Econ 119:249–275

Besley T, Burgess R (2000) Land reform, poverty reduction and growth: evidence from India. Q J Econ 115(2):389–430

Block J (2016) Corporate income taxes and entrepreneurship. IZA World of labor. ISSN 2054-9571. Iss. 257. doi:10.15185/izawol.257

Blundell RW, Bond SR (1998) Initial conditions and moment restrictions in dynamic panel data models. J Econ 87:115–143

Bose N, Murshid AP, Wurm MA (2012) The growth effects of property rights: the role of finance. World Dev 40(9):1784–1797

Braunerhjelm P, Eklund JE (2014) Taxes, tax administrative burdens and new firm formation. Kyklos 67(1):1–11

Brown M, Zehnder C (2007) Credit reporting, relationship banking, and loan repayment. J Money Credit Bank 39(8):1883–1918

Bruhn M, McKenzie D (2014) Entry regulation and the formalization of microenterprises in developing countries. World Bank Res Obs 29(2):186–201

Bueyuekkarabacak B, Valev N (2012) Credit information sharing and banking crises: an empirical investigation. J Macroecon 34(3):788–800

Cabral JE, Chavan A, Clarke TM, Greacen J, Hough BR, Rexer L, Ribadeneyra J, Zorza R (2012) Using technology to enhance access to justice. Harv J Law Technol 26(1):243–324

Calvino F, Criscuolo C, Menon C (2016) No country for young firms? Start-up dynamics and national policies. OECD Science, Technology, and industry policy paper no. 29. OECD, Paris

Carballo J, Schaur G, Volpe Martincus C (2016) The border labyrinth: information technologies and trade in the presence of multiple agencies. IDB working paper series N° IDB-WP-706. Inter-American Development Bank

Chakraborty P (2016) Judicial quality and regional firm performance: the case of Indian states. J Comp Econ 44(4):902–918

Chowdhury F, Terjesen S, Audretsch D (2015) Varieties of entrepreneurship: institutional drivers across entrepreneurial activity and country. Eur J Law Econ 40(1):121–148

Claessens S, Laeven L (2003) Financial development, property rights, and growth. J Financ 58 (6):2401–2436

Claessens S, Ueda K, Yafeh Y (2014) Institutions and financial frictions: estimating with structural restrictions on firm value and investment. J Dev Econ 110:107–122

Cuomo F, Zattoni A, Valentini G (2013) The effects of legal reforms on the ownership structure of listed companies. Ind Corp Chang 22(2):427–458

Dakolias M (1999) Court performance around the world: a comparative perspective. World Bank technical paper 430. World Bank, Washington, DC

Dam KW (2006a) The law-growth nexus: the rule of law and economic development. Brookings Institution Press, Chicago, IL

Dam KW (2006b) The judiciary and economic development. John M. Olin Law & economics working paper 287 (Second Series). University of Chicago Law School, Chicago

Daniels RJ, Trebilcock MJ, Carson LD (2011) The legacy of the Empire: the common law inheritance and commitments to legality in former British colonies. Am J Comp Law 59:111–178

de Andrade GH, Bruhn M, McKenzie D (2016) A helping hand or the long arm of the law? Experimental evidence on what governments can do to formalize firms. World Bank Econ Rev 30(1):24–54

Deakin S, Sarkar P, Singh A (2012) An end to consensus? The selective impact of corporate law reform on financial development. In: Aoki M, Binmore K, Deakin S, Gintis H (eds) Complexity and institutions: markets, norms and corporations. Palgrave Macmillan, Basingstoke

Deininger K, Feder G (2009) Land registration, governance, and development: evidence and implications for policy. World Bank Res Obs 24(2):233–266

Demirgüç-Kunt A, Horváth BL, Huizinga H (2016) How does long-term finance affect economic volatility? Policy research working paper WPS7535. World Bank, Washington, DC

Dennis A, Shepherd B (2011) Trade facilitation and export diversification. World Econ 34 (1):101–122

Dewaelheyns N, Van Hulle C (2008) Legal reform and aggregate small and micro business bankruptcy rates: evidence from the 1997 Belgian bankruptcy code. Small Bus Econ 31 (4):409–424

Dharmapala D, Hines JR Jr (2009) Which countries become tax havens? J Public Econ 93 (9–10):1058–1068

Divanbeigi R, Ramalho R (2015) Business regulations and growth. Policy research working paper 7299. World Bank, Washington, DC

Dixit A (2009) Governance institutions and economic activity. Am Econ Rev 99(1):5–24

Djankov S (2009) The regulation of entry: a survey. World Bank Res Obs 24(2):183–203

Djankov S, La Porta R, López-de-Silanes F, Shleifer A (2002) The regulation of entry. Q J Econ 117(1):1–37

Djankov S, La Porta R, López-de-Silanes F, Shleifer A (2003) Courts. Q J Econ 118(2):453–517

Djankov S, McLiesh C, Ramalho R (2006) Regulation and growth. Econ Lett 92(3):395–401

Djankov S, McLiesh C, Shleifer A (2007) Private credit in 129 countries. J Financ Econ 12 (2):77–99

Djankov S, La Porta R, López-de-Silanes F, Shleifer A (2008a) The law and economics of self-dealing. J Financ Econ 88(3):430–465

Djankov S, Hart O, McLiesh C, Shleifer A (2008b) Debt enforcement around the world. J Polit Econ 116(6):1105–1150

Djankov S, Ganser T, McLiesh C, Ramalho R, Shleifer A (2010a) The effect of corporate taxes on investment and entrepreneurship. Am Econ J Macroecon 2(3):31–64

Djankov S, Freund C, Pham C (2010b) Trading on time. Rev Econ Stat 92(1):166–173

Doblas-Madrid A, Minetti R (2013) Sharing information in the credit market: contract-level evidence from US firms. J Financ Econ 109(1):198–223

Doidge C, Karolyi GA, Stulz RM (2007) Why do countries matter so much for corporate governance? J Financ Econ 86(1):1–39

Doing Business Project (2015) International Finance Corporation. The World Bank, Washington, DC. http://www.doingbusiness.org. Last accessed 15 Mar 2015

Dougherty SM (2014) Legal reform, contract enforcement and firm size in Mexico. Rev Int Econ 22(4):825–844

Dreher A, Gassebner M (2013) Greasing the wheels? The impact of regulations and corruption on firm entry. Public Choice 155(3):413–432

Durand-Lasserve A, Selod H (2007) The formalization of urban land tenure in developing countries. Presented at the World Bank urban research symposium, May, Washington, DC

Elgin C, Oyvat C (2013) Lurking in the cities: urbanization and the informal economy. Struct Chang Econ Dyn 27:36–47

Enikolopov R, Petrova M, Stepanov S (2014) Firm value in crisis: effects of firm-level transparency and country-level institutions. J Bank Financ 46:72–84

Esposito G, Lanau S, Pompe S (2014) Judicial system reform in Italy: a key to growth. IMF working paper no. 14/32. International Monetary Fund, Washington, DC

Fang L, Rogerson R (2011) Product market regulation and market work: a benchmark analysis. Am Econ J Macroecon 3(2):163–188

Favara G, Schroth E, Valta P (2012) Strategic default and equity risk across countries. J Financ 67 (6):2051–2095

Fernandes AM, Hillberry RH, Mendoza Alcantara A (2015) Trade effects of customs reform: evidence from Albania. Policy research working paper no. WPS 7210. World Bank Group, Washington, DC

Field E (2007) Entitled to work: urban property rights and labor supply in Peru. Q J Econ 122 (4):1561–1602

Fieldhouse DK (1966) The colonial empires: a comparative survey from the eighteenth century. Weidenfeld and Nicolson, London

Fisman R, Svensson J (2007) Are corruption and taxation really harmful to growth? Firm level evidence. J Dev Econ 83(1):63–75

Foley CF, Greenwood R (2010) The evolution of corporate ownership after IPO: the impact of investor protection. Rev Financ Stud 23(3):1231–1260

Franks J, Loranth G (2014) A study of bankruptcy costs and the allocation of control. Rev Financ 18(3):961–997

Franks J, Volpin P, Wagner HF (2012) The life cycle of family ownership: International evidence. Rev Financ Stud 25(6):1675–1712

Freund C, Bolaky B (2008) Trade, regulations, and income. J Dev Econ 87(2):309–321

Freund C, Rocha N (2011) What constrains Africa's exports? World Bank Econ Rev 25 (3):361–386

Freund C, Hallward-Driemeier M, Rijkers B (2014) Deal and delays: firm-level evidence on corruption and policy implementation times. Policy research working paper no. 6949. World Bank, Washington, DC

Gahan PG, Ramsay I, Welsh MA (2014) Worker and shareholder protection in six countries: a longitudinal analysis. Available at Social Science Research Network (SSRN). doi:10.2139/ssrn.2536708

García-Posada M, Mora-Sanguinetti JS (2015) Does (average) size matter? Court enforcement, business demography and firm growth. Small Bus Econ 33:639–669

Gete P (2014) Dealing with construction permits, interest rate shocks and macroeconomic dynamics. Georgetown University Department of Economics working paper. Georgetown University, Washington, DC

Giacomelli S, Menon C (2013) Firm size and judicial efficiency in Italy: evidence from the neighbour's tribunal. Working paper no. 898. Bank of Italy, Rome

Giannetti C, Jentzsch N (2013) Credit reporting, financial intermediation and identification systems: International evidence. J Int Money Financ 33:60–80

Haidar JI, Hoshi T (2015) Implementing structural reforms in abenomics: how to reduce the cost of doing business in Japan. NBER Working Paper no. 21507. National Bureau of Economic Research, Massachusetts

Hallward-Driemeier M, Prichett L (2011) How business is done and the 'Doing Business' indicators: the investment climate when firms have climate control. Policy research working paper no. WPS 5563. World Bank, Washington, DC

Hallward-Driemeier M, Pritchett L (2015) How business is done in the developing world: deals versus rules. J Econ Perspect 29(3):121–140

Herrendorf B, Teixeira A (2011) Barriers to entry and development. Int Econ Rev 52(2):573–602

Herrero A, Henderson K (2001) The cost of resolving small business conflicts: the case of Peru. Sustainable Development Department Best Practices Series. Inter-American Development Bank, Washington, DC

Houston JF, Lin C, Lin P, Ma Y (2010) Creditor rights, information sharing, and bank risk taking. J Financ Econ 96(3):485–512

Husa J (2004) Classification of legal systems today – is it time for a memorial hymn? Revue Internationale de Droit Comparé 12:54

Ippoliti R, Melcarne A, Ramello GB (2014) Judicial efficiency and entrepreneurs' expectations on the reliability of European legal systems. Eur J Law Econ 40(1):75–94

Islam R (2003) Do more transparent governments govern better? Policy research working paper no. 3077. World Bank, Washington, DC

Iwanow T, Kirkpatrick C (2009) Trade facilitation and manufactured exports: is Africa different? World Dev 37(6):1039–1050

Jackson HE, Roe MJ (2009) Public and private enforcement of securities laws: resource-based evidence. J Financ Econ 93(2):207–238

Jacoby HG, Minten B (2007) Is land titling in Sub-Saharan Africa cost-effective? Evidence from Madagascar. World Bank Econ Rev 21(3):461–485

Jerbashian V, Kochanova A (2016) The impact of doing business regulations on investments in ICT. Empir Econ 50(3):991–1008

Johnson S, McMillan J, Woodruff C (2002) Property rights and finance. Am Econ Rev 92 (5):1335–1356

Katelouzou D, Siems MM (2015) Disappearing paradigms in shareholder protection: leximetric evidence for 30 countries, 1990–2013. Working paper no. 467. Centre for Business Research, University of Cambridge, Cambridge

Kaufmann D, Kraay A, Mastruzzi M (2009) Governance matters VIII: aggregate and individual governance indicators for 1996–2008. World Bank policy research paper no. 4978. World Bank, Washington, DC

Kenny C (2007) Construction, corruption, and developing countries. Policy research working paper no. 4271. World Bank, Washington, DC

Klapper L, Love I (2010) The impact of business environment reforms on new firm registration. World Bank Policy Research Working Paper no. 5493. World Bank, Washington DC

Klapper L, Love I (2011) The impact of the financial crisis on new firm registration. Econ Lett 113 (1):1–4

Klapper L, Laeven L, Rajan R (2006) Entry regulation as a barrier to entrepreneurship. J Financ Econ 82(3):591–629

Klerman DM, Mahoney PG, Spamann H, Weinstein MI (2011) Legal origin or colonial history? J Legal Anal 3:379–409

Klinger B, Schuendeln M (2011) Can entrepreneurial activity be taught? Quasi-experimental evidence from Central America. World Dev 39(9):1592–1610

Kose J, Litov L, Yeung B (2008) Corporate governance and risk-taking. J Financ 63(4):1679–1728

Kraay A, Tawara N (2013) Can specific policy indicators identify reform priorities? J Econ Growth 18:253–283

Kumar K (2006) English and French national identity: comparisons and contrasts. Nations Natl 12:413–432

La Porta R, Lopez-de-Silanes F, Shleifer A, Vishny RW (1997) Legal determinants of external finance. J Financ 52(3):1131–1150

La Porta R, Lopez-de-Silanes F, Shleifer A, Vishny RW (1998) Law and Finance. J Polit Econ 106:1113–1155

La Porta R, Lopez-de-Silanes F, Shleifer A, Vishny RW (1999) The quality of government. J Law Econ Org 15(1):222–279

La Porta R, Lopez-de-Silanes F, Shleifer A, Vishny RW (2002) Investor protection and corporate valuation. J Financ 57(3):1147–1170

La Porta R, Lopez-de-Silanes F, Shleifer A (2006) What works in securities laws? J Financ 61:1–33

La Porta R, Lopez-de-Silanes F, Shleifer A (2008) The economic consequences of legal origins. J Econ Lit 46:285–332

La Porta R, Lopez-de-Silanes F, Shleifer A (2013) Law and finance after a decade of research. In: Constantinides G, Harris M, Stulz RM (eds) Handbook of the economics of finance, vol 2A. Elsevier, Amsterdam, pp 425–491

Lange M (2004) British colonial legacies and political development. World Dev 32:905–922

Lawless M (2013) Do complicated tax systems prevent foreign direct investment? Economica 80 (317):1–22

Lele P, Siems M (2007) Shareholder protection: a leximetric approach. J Corp Law Stud 7:17–50

Levchenko AA (2007) Institutional quality and international trade. Rev Econ Stud 74:791–819

Li W-X, Chen C-S, French JJ (2012) The relationship between liquidity, corporate governance, and firm valuation: evidence from Russia. Emerg Mark Rev 13(4):465–477

LiPuma JA, Newbert SL, Doh JP (2013) The effect of institutional quality on firm export performance in emerging economies: a contingency model of firm age and size. Small Bus Econ 40(4):817–841

LoPucki L, Triantis GG (1994) A systems approach to comparing U.S. and Canadian reorganization of financially distressed companies. Harv Int Law Rev 35:267–343

Lyons M, Brown A, Msoka C (2014) Do micro enterprises benefit from the Doing Business reforms? The case of street-vending in Tanzania. Urban Stud 51(8):1593–1612

Malmendier U (2009) Law and finance 'at the origin'. J Econ Lit 47(4):1076–1108

Mamdani M (1996) Citizen and subject. Princeton University Press, Princeton, NJ

Martinez Peria MS, Singh S (2014) The impact of credit information sharing reforms on firm financing. World Bank policy research working paper no. WPS7013. World Bank, Washington, DC

Merryman JH (1969) The civil law tradition: an introduction to the legal systems of Western Europe and Latin America. Stanford University Press, Stanford

Merryman JH (1996) The French deviation. Am J Comp Law 44:109–119

Miceli TJ, Kieyah J (2003) The economics of land title reform. J Comp Econ 31(2):246–256

Michaels R (2009) Comparative law by numbers? Legal origins thesis, Doing Business reports, and the silence of traditional comparative law. Am J Comp Law 57:765–795

Miletkov M, Wintoki MB (2012) Financial development and the evolution of property rights and legal institutions. Emerg Mark Rev 13(4):650–673

Munemo J (2014) Business start-up regulations and the complementarity between foreign and domestic investment. Rev World Econ 150(4):745–761

Musacchio A (2007) Do legal origins have persistent effects over time? A look at law and finance around the world c. 1900. Harvard Business School working paper no. 08-030

Musacchio A (2008) Can civil law countries get good institutions? Lessons from the history of creditor rights and bond markets in Brazil. J Econ Hist 68(1):80–108

Nickell S (1981) Biases in dynamic models with fixed effects. Econometrica 49:1417–1426

Norbäck P-J, Persson L, Douhan R (2014) Entrepreneurship policy and globalization. J Dev Econ 110:22–38

Nunn N (2007) Relationship-specificity, incomplete contracts, and the pattern of trade. Q J Econ 122(2):569–600

Oto-Peralías D, Romero-Ávila D (2014a) The distribution of legal traditions around the world: a contribution to the Legal Origins Theory. J Law Econ 57(3):561–628

Oto-Peralías D, Romero-Ávila D (2014b) Legal traditions and initial endowments in shaping the path of financial development. J Money Credit Bank 46(1):43–77

Oto-Peralías D, Romero-Ávila D (2016) Colonial theories of institutional development: toward a model of styles of imperialism. Springer, Cham

Padilla JA, Pagano M (1997) Endogenous communication among lenders and entrepreneurial incentives. Rev Financ Stud 10:205–236

Padilla JA, Pagano M (2000) Sharing default information as a borrower discipline device. Eur Econ Rev 44:1951–1980

Pagano M, Jappelli T (1993) Information sharing in credit markets. J Financ 48:1693–1718

Paik Y (2013) The Bankruptcy Reform Act of 2005 and entrepreneurial activity. J Econ Manag Strateg 22(2):259–280

Pistor K, Raiser M, Gelfer S (2000) Law and finance in transition economies. Econ Transit 8 (2):325–368

Poel K, Marneffe W, Bielen S, van Aarle B, Vereeck L (2014) Administrative simplification and economic growth: a cross country empirical study. J Bus Admin Res 3(1):45–58

Qian J, Strahan PE (2007) How laws and institutions shape financial contracts: the case of bank loans. J Financ 62(6):2803–2834

Rajan RG, Zingales L (2003) The great reversals: the politics of financial development in the twentieth century. J Financ Econ 69:5–50

Reimann MW (2001) Beyond national systems: a comparative law for the international age. Tulane Law Review 75:1103–1119

Roe MJ (2006) Legal origins, politics, and modern stock markets. Harv Law Rev 120:460–527

Roe MJ (2007) Juries and the political economy of legal origin. J Comp Econ 35:294–308

Roe MJ, Siegel JI (2009) Finance and politics: a review essay based on Kenneth Dam's analysis of legal traditions in the law-growth nexus. J Econ Lit 47:781–800

Roodman D (2006) How to do xtabond2: an introduction to "difference" and "system" GMM in Stata. Center for Global Development working paper no. 103, Washington, DC

Roodman D (2009) A note on the theme of too many instruments. Oxf Bull Econ Stat 71:135–158

Rosales-López V (2008) Economics of court performance: an empirical analysis. Eur J Law Econ 25(3):231–251

Safavian M, Sharma S (2007) When do creditor rights work? J Comp Econ 35(3):484–508

Segal N (2007) The effect of reorganization proceedings on security interests: the position under English and U.S. law. Brooklyn J Int Law 32(3):927–982

Sereno L, Ma ED, Capuano JJ (2001) Justice and the social cost of doing business: the case of Philippines. World Bank, Manila

Sevcik P (2012) Financial contracts and the political economy of investor protection. Am Econ J Macroecon 4(4):163–197

Shepherd B, Wilson JS (2009) Trade facilitation in ASEAN member countries: measuring progress and assessing priorities. J Asian Econ 20:367–383

Sherwood RM, Shepherd G, de Souza CM (1994) Judicial systems and economic performance. Q Rev Econ Finance 34(suppl 1):101–116

Siems M (2008) Shareholder protection around the world ("Leximetric II"). Del J Corp Law 33:111–147

Spamann H (2010a) The 'Antidirector Rights Index' revisited. Rev Financ Stud 23:467–486

Spamann H (2010b) Legal origins, civil procedure, and the quality of contract enforcement. J Inst Theor Econ 166:149–165

Stel A, Storey D, Thurik A (2007) The effect of business regulations on nascent and young business entrepreneurship. Small Bus Econ 28(2):171–186

Teorell J, Samanni M, Holmberg S, Rothstein B (2011) The quality of government dataset. Version 6 Apr 11. The Quality of Government Institute, University of Gothenburg. http://www.qog.pol.gu.se

Visaria S (2009) Legal reform and loan repayment: the microeconomic impact of debt recovery tribunals in India. Am Econ J Appl Econ 1(3):59–81

Volpe Martincus C, Carballo J, Graziano A (2015) Customs. J Int Econ 96(1):119–137

von Lilienfeld-Toal U, Mookherjee D, Visaria S (2012) The distributive impact of reforms in credit enforcement: evidence from Indian debt recovery tribunals. Econometrica 80 (2):497–558

Williams CC (2014) Tackling enterprises operating in the informal sector in developing and transition economies: a critical evaluation of the neo-liberal policy approach. J Glob Entrep Res 2(9):1–17

World Bank (2004a) Doing business in 2004: understanding regulation. Oxford University Press on behalf of the World Bank, Washington, DC

World Bank (2004b) World development report 2005: a better investment climate for everyone. Oxford University Press, New York

World Bank (2015a) Doing Business Reforms since DB2006. Accessible at http://www.doingbusiness.org/reforms/reforms-count. Accessed 15 Nov 2015

World Bank (2015b) World development indicators. The World Bank, Washington, DC

World Bank (2016) Doing Business 2016: measuring regulatory quality and efficiency. World Bank Group, Washington, DC

World Bank (2017) World development report 2017: governance and the law. World Bank Group, Washington, DC

Yakovlev E, Zhuravskaya E (2013) The unequal enforcement of liberalization: evidence from Russia's reform of business regulation. J Eur Econ Assoc 11(4):808–838

Young C (1988) The African colonial state and its political legacy. In: Chazen N, Rothchild D (eds) The precarious balance: state and society in Africa. Westview Press, Boulder, CO, pp 25–66

Zweigert K, Kötz H (1998) An introduction to comparative law. Clarendon Press, Oxford

Printed by Printforce, the Netherlands